Government Finance
in Developing Countries

Studies of Government Finance: Second Series

TITLES PUBLISHED

Government Finance in Developing Countries

RICHARD GOODE

Studies of Government Finance

THE BROOKINGS INSTITUTION

WASHINGTON, D.C.

Copyright © 1984 by
THE BROOKINGS INSTITUTION
1775 Massachusetts Avenue, N.W., Washington, D.C. 20036

Library of Congress Cataloging in Publication data:

Goode, Richard.
  Government finance in developing countries.
  (Studies of Government Finance, 2d ser., no. 19)
  Includes bibliographical references and index.
  1. Finance, Public—Developing countries.   I. Title.
HJ1620.G66   1984   336′.09172′4   83-20989
ISBN 0-8157-3196-5
ISBN 0-8157-3195-7 (pbk.)

9 8 7 6 5 4 3 2 1

THE BROOKINGS INSTITUTION is an independent organization devoted to nonpartisan research, education, and publication in economics, government, foreign policy, and the social sciences generally. Its principal purposes are to aid in the development of sound public policies and to promote public understanding of issues of national importance.

The Institution was founded on December 8, 1927, to merge the activities of the Institute for Government Research, founded in 1916, the Institute of Economics, founded in 1922, and the Robert Brookings Graduate School of Economics and Government, founded in 1924.

The Board of Trustees is responsible for the general administration of the Institution, while the immediate direction of the policies, program, and staff is vested in the President, assisted by an advisory committee of the officers and staff. The by-laws of the Institution state: "It is the function of the Trustees to make possible the conduct of scientific research, and publication, under the most favorable conditions, and to safeguard the independence of the research staff in the pursuit of their studies and in the publication of the results of such studies. It is not a part of their function to determine, control, or influence the conduct of particular investigations or the conclusions reached."

The President bears final responsibility for the decision to publish a manuscript as a Brookings book. In reaching his judgment on the competence, accuracy, and objectivity of each study, the President is advised by the director of the appropriate research program and weighs the views of a panel of expert outside readers who report to him in confidence on the quality of the work. Publication of a work signifies that it is deemed a competent treatment worthy of public consideration but does not imply endorsement of conclusions or recommendations.

The Institution maintains its position of neutrality on issues of public policy in order to safeguard the intellectual freedom of the staff. Hence interpretations or conclusions in Brookings publications should be understood to be solely those of the authors and should not be attributed to the Institution, to its trustees, officers, or other staff members, or to the organizations that support its research.

Foreword

As GOVERNMENT BUDGETS have grown and economies have suffered inflation, stagnation, and external shocks, countries throughout the world have confronted intractable fiscal problems. Shortcomings in methods of budgeting, expenditure control, and taxation have become evident, despite many useful innovations. At the same time the standards by which performance is judged have—for good reasons—been raised. The fiscal problems of the developing countries are especially pressing because their governments have assumed large responsibilities and can ill afford to waste resources or frustrate popular aspirations.

This book is a comprehensive survey of current theories and practices in budgeting, expenditure analysis, taxation, borrowing, and financing government by money creation. In contrast to much of the literature on government finance, it examines these topics in relation to the institutions and problems in developing countries. The suitability of any fiscal measure, the author argues, depends on both the economic and political conditions and the administrative capabilities of the country seeking to implement it. He assesses a wide range of fiscal measures, from those that have evolved out of colonial traditions to the most innovative techniques. His evaluation is based not only on the feasibility or probable efficiency of the measure, but also on its contribution to the broad objectives of most developing countries: growth, economic stabilization, equitable distribution of income, and national self-reliance.

Richard Goode wrote this book after he became a guest scholar at Brookings in 1981. He was a staff member of the International Monetary Fund, 1951–59 and 1965–81, serving as the first director of the Fiscal Affairs Department in the later period. From 1959 to 1965 he was a senior staff member at Brookings.

The author wishes to acknowledge with thanks comments received from A. M. Abdel-Rahman, W. A. Beveridge, Richard M. Bird, Ralph C.

Bryant, Jesse Burkhead, Milka Casanegra de Jantscher, Luc De Wulf, Edward R. Fried, Leif Muten, Joseph A. Pechman, A. Premchand, Alan A. Tait, and Vito Tanzi. He has also benefited from access to the work of many former colleagues at the International Monetary Fund. Carol Cole Rosen edited the manuscript, and Penelope Harpold verified its factual content. Kirk Kimmell did most of the typing. The index was prepared by Ward and Silvan Indexing. This book is the nineteenth in the second series of Brookings Studies of Government Finance.

The views expressed here are those of the author and should not be ascribed to the trustees, officers, or staff members of the Brookings Institution.

BRUCE K. MACLAURY
President

Washington, D.C.
October 1983

Contents

Tables

CHAPTER ONE

Introduction

As GOVERNMENTS throughout the world have assumed more responsibility for the management of the economy, their financial transactions have increased in size and complexity. Particularly in developing countries, fiscal systems have been severely strained. This book examines fiscal problems, policies, and activities from the standpoint of the developing countries.

Government and Other Economic Sectors

The government sector of an economy may be distinguished from the enterprise sector and the household sector. In the government sector, activities are directed by political decisions, and outlays and receipts are controlled by a budgetary process. In the enterprise sector, market prices and costs usually guide the use of resources. The household sector, comprising individuals and families, receives income from, and makes payments to, both the other sectors.[1]

The distinction between the government sector and the enterprise sector is based not on ownership but on mode of operation. State-owned companies are prominent in many developing countries. They are part of the enterprise sector if they produce goods and services for sale and depend primarily on receipts from sales as their source of operating funds. State enterprises, to be sure, will have financial relations with the treasury in addition to those that are common to all enterprises; for example, the state enterprises will receive capital subscriptions or loans from the government and they may pay interest or dividends to it. So long as these organizations are responsive primarily to market forces, they are properly classified as

1. Other sectors that are often identified in national accounts are financial institutions, private nonprofit institutions, and the rest of the world.

enterprises and placed in a different category from government departments. This approach makes it possible to identify separate government and enterprise sectors in centrally planned socialist countries and to treat the government finances of those countries and of countries with mixed economies in the same framework.

In practice, public enterprises often are not allowed to operate according to market principles; they may, for example, be required to provide consumers with goods or services at prices below costs of production, or they may be assigned certain quasi-governmental functions. Because they lack the powers of taxation and money creation, the enterprises must look to government to cover any persistent shortfall of sales receipts below costs. Problems arise when the government fails to lay down clear guidelines for departures from normal enterprise operations and to make appropriate financial arrangements for them.

Government Finance and National Objectives

Adam Smith, a writer whose insights into economic development and public finance make his works more relevant to current issues than is often supposed, identified three duties of the sovereign: national defense, the administration of justice, and "erecting and maintaining those public institutions and those public works, which, though they may be in the highest degree advantageous to a great society, are, however, of such a nature, that the profit could never repay the expence to any individual or small number of individuals, and which it therefore cannot be expected that any individual or small number of individuals should erect or maintain."[2] Smith's characterization of the sovereign's duties resembles the modern technical concept of public goods (see chapter 3) but goes beyond that; it is broad enough to cover many, though not all, of the activities of governments in developing countries.

The economic objectives of the state are to provide the collective goods and services that correspond to the performance of its traditional functions and at the same time to promote growth and development, stability, equitable distribution of income and wealth, and national independence or self-reliance. This classification is based on deductive analysis and observation of behavior and political discussion. It is widely accepted by

2. *An Inquiry into the Nature and Causes of the Wealth of Nations*, ed. Edwin Cannan (Modern Library, 1937), p. 681.

writers on development and government finance, except that the objective of national economic independence is often overlooked.

The objectives are subject to interpretation and become meaningful only when given specific content and reflected in policies. Objectives and policies are determined by "policymakers," whose identity varies among countries depending on the political system and the influence of social, economic, and historical conditions. Policymakers include political leaders in the executive and legislative branches (where the two are separate), senior civil servants, and in many countries military leaders. They may be more or less responsive to the wishes of the population, but only rarely are they either guided solely by citizens' preferences or oblivious to popular desires. It may be presumed that political leaders are motivated not only by their publicly avowed objectives but also by their desire to remain in power and that most of the other policymakers are concerned also with maintaining and strengthening their agencies or services and their own positions.

The determination of national objectives is an aspect of the authoritative allocation of values, which Easton regards as the basic function of the political system.[3] A policy is necessary to help attain an objective. In Easton's words, it "consists of a web of decisions and actions that allocates values."[4] Decisions alone do not constitute a policy; they must be interpreted in a series of actions and narrower decisions.

Almost all policies require some government spending, but there are important differences of degree. Many policies rely primarily on government expenditures to influence the use of scarce resources, whereas others depend primarily on laws, regulations, and other direct controls. Government finance, clearly, is more concerned with the former than with the latter policies.

Fiscal Instruments

Fiscal instruments may be classified as government outlays or government receipts. Outlays include: (1) purchases of goods and services, sometimes called requited or exhaustive expenditures; (2) transfer payments, sometimes called nonrequited or nonexhaustive expenditures; and

3. David Easton, *The Political System: An Inquiry into the State of Political Science* (Knopf, 1959), pp. 129–41.
4. Ibid., p. 130.

(3) lending, including the acquisition of financial equities.[5] Purchases of goods and services are intended to carry out government activities by the direct utilization of economic resources. The employment of civil servants and construction of public works are major items in this category, which includes a range of purchases from paper clips to military aircraft. Transfer payments and lending, in contrast, are intended to provide enterprises and households with purchasing power to enable them to buy goods and services in the market. Transfer payments for social welfare have become a large element in the budgets of developed countries, but in most developing countries they are relatively small. In many developing countries, some of the functions of transfer payments are performed by subsidies to consumers in the form of below-cost sales by state enterprises.

Government receipts include: (1) taxes, (2) fees and income from state property and enterprises, (3) proceeds of the sale of land and other capital assets, (4) grants from other governments and international institutions, (5) borrowing, and (6) money creation.

Taxes are compulsory contributions for which no explicit, reciprocal benefit is provided to the taxpayer. They are intended to force the household or enterprise to surrender purchasing power (command over resources) to the government for its direct utilization or transfer to others. Taxes reduce the disposable income and wealth of those who bear them.

Government borrowing involves the transfer of purchasing power from resident households and enterprises, from nonresidents, or from other governments, in exchange for a promise to repay, usually with interest. Normally the transaction is voluntary on the part of lenders, though occasionally it has been compulsory. Borrowing from residents reduces their liquidity but does not reduce their wealth; lenders exchange one asset (cash) for another (a bond or other debt instrument). Borrowing from nonresidents does not release domestic resources to the government; it does, however, enable the borrowing country to import more and thus increase the quantity of goods and services available for the use of the government and others.

Money creation in the past took the form of the issue of fiat money by the state, that is, paper money or coins with nominal value in excess of

---

5. For a more elaborate classification of both outlays and receipts, see International Monetary Fund, *A Manual of Government Finance Statistics*, draft (Washington, D.C.: IMF, 1974). Government purchases of goods and services are often divided between consumption and investment; that usage is not followed here because neither the functions nor the means of financing the two categories differ as much as the distinction seems to imply. Debt repayments are here deducted from borrowing to produce a net figure and are not listed as outlays.

their commodity value. Its modern form is borrowing from the central bank. It enlarges claims on output and imports, with important consequences for the domestic economy and the balance of payments.

Taxes, borrowing, and money creation are treated in detail in later chapters. The heterogeneous nature of the other categories of receipts prevents simple but meaningful generalizations about their economic character. Fees and income from state property and enterprises are sizable in many countries and are especially important in oil countries that have nationalized petroleum deposits and in certain socialist countries. Proceeds of the sale of property generally are unimportant. Most developing countries receive some grants from abroad; in the majority of cases they are small, but in a few countries they make up a large fraction of total receipts.

It is illuminating to look at fiscal instruments and government transactions in the context of the national income and product accounts. A simple national income definitional equation is

$$Y = C + I + G + X - Z,$$

where Y is national income (gross national product), C is household consumption, I is enterprise investment, G is government expenditures for goods and services, X is exports of goods and services, and Z is imports. Among government transactions, only expenditures for goods and services enter directly into the equation; all other government outlays and receipts affect Y only as they influence C, I, X, or Z. The significance of this distinction will become clearer in later chapters.

Characteristics of Developing Countries

There are about 130 countries that are ordinarily classified as developing or less developed countries (the terms will be used interchangeably in this book). Included are all of Asia (except Japan), Africa, Latin America and the Caribbean, the Middle East, and some of the peripheral European countries. They are a diverse group, though some characteristics are widely shared. Broadly they may be classified into four subgroups: (1) the newly industrializing or semi-industrial countries such as Argentina, Brazil, Mexico, Korea, Singapore, and Turkey; (2) the least developed and very poor countries including much of Sub-Saharan Africa, Ethiopia, Haiti,

Afghanistan, Nepal, the two Yemens, and some others; (3) the major oil exporters; and (4) all the others, which make up the majority.[6]

Except for some of the Middle Eastern oil exporters, all the developing countries are poor compared with the more developed countries belonging to the Organization for Economic Cooperation and Development or with the USSR and a few other Eastern European countries. Population is growing rapidly in nearly all the developing countries. As death rates have been brought down by public health measures and improvements in nutrition, there has been no corresponding reduction in birth rates in most countries. The result is a young population, including a large proportion of children. Generally, the developing countries rely heavily on primary production of agricultural and mineral products. In many countries, a large proportion of the labor force is employed in agriculture; it is above 75 percent in most of the least developed countries.

The economies of the primary-producing countries are subject to instability in many ways. Crop yields vary with weather and other growing conditions. Prices of exports and imports fluctuate, often because of conditions in the industrial countries. Much of large-scale manufacturing and mining is controlled by foreign-based multinational corporations. Capital inflows, both private and official, are subject to external influences that can cause abrupt changes.

In addition to these economic characteristics, there are some widely shared cultural and political conditions that are significant for government

6. Country classifications are not universally accepted. The following are adopted in this book. The developing or less developed countries include all countries except 27 industrial countries, comprising 21 members of the Organization for Economic Cooperation and Development (all except Greece, Portugal, and Turkey) and 6 nonmarket industrial countries—Czechoslovakia, Bulgaria, the German Democratic Republic, Hungary, Poland, and the USSR. The approximately 130 developing countries, or less developed countries, are divided into the four subgroups: 16 semi-industrial—Argentina, Brazil, Colombia, Egypt, Greece, Israel, Mexico, the Philippines, Portugal, Romania, Singapore, South Africa, the Republic of Korea, Turkey, Uruguay, Yugoslavia; 23 least developed—Afghanistan, Benin, Bhutan, Burundi, the Central African Republic, Chad, Ethiopia, Guinea, Haiti, Laos, Lesotho, Malawi, Mali, Nepal, Niger, Rwanda, Somalia, Sudan, Tanzania, Uganda, Upper Volta, the Yemen Arab Republic, the People's Democratic Republic of Yemen; 12 major oil exporters—Algeria, Indonesia, Iran, Iraq, Kuwait, Libya, Nigeria, Oman, Qatar, Saudi Arabia, the United Arab Emirates, Venezuela; and about 80 others. This classification is based on the following publications: World Bank, *World Development Report 1981* (Oxford University Press, 1981), annex and p. 65; International Monetary Fund, *World Economic Outlook*, Occasional Paper 9 (Washington, D.C.: IMF, 1982), p. 140, and *International Financial Statistics*, monthly publication of the IMF. Spain is classified as an industrial country, in accordance with IMF practice; the World Bank classifies it as semi-industrial. The oil-exporting countries are those so identified by the IMF. An earlier United Nations list assigned seven additional countries to the least developed subgroup: Bangladesh, Botswana, Cape Verde, the Gambia, Maldives, Comoros, and Western Samoa; *Brandt Commission Papers: Selected Background Papers Prepared for the Independent Commission on International Development Issues, 1978–1979* (Geneva: Independent Commission on International Development Issues, 1981), p. 241.

finance. In many developing countries, illiteracy is widespread. Cultural and linguistic heterogeneity prevail in not a few countries. Institutions for the articulation and aggregation of the interests of various social and economic groups are often weak. Democratic, parliamentary systems of government are scarce. The military frequently plays an important role in decisionmaking. Government intervention in economic matters is common, classical liberalism is highly unusual, and socialist rhetoric is popular. Most of the countries of Africa, Asia, the Caribbean, and Oceania were colonies or protectorates of Great Britain, France, or other Western European countries until after World War II. The influence of the legal and administrative systems of the colonial powers is still strong. Centralization of governmental power and functions at the national level is common, and sharing with regions and localities exceptional. Some countries, however, especially several in Latin America, have established many decentralized agencies at the national level to carry out certain governmental functions. Within government ministries and departments, centralization of authority tends to be preferred to delegation of responsibility and power. Nationalistic views on both economics and politics are strongly held even in countries that lack common traditions, language, and religion that would distinguish them from their neighbors.

Although the developing countries share enough characteristics to permit a general treatment of their government finances, significant differences exist among subgroups and among individual countries. In the following chapters, such differences are occasionally noted. Inevitably, however, many of the generalizations will not apply to some developing countries.

The Approach of This Book

Economics is central to this book, but no attempt will be made to fit all points into a coherent exposition of formal theories or models. Political science, public administration, and law will be called on to help understand problems and appraise possible solutions. Although they will not be elaborated in the book, the subjects of accounting and statistics are needed by practitioners, and readers who are in command of them will see many opportunities for their application.

This book will give particular attention to the institutions and problems of the developing countries. A special effort will be made to avoid the kind of explicit or implicit assumptions about decisionmaking, legislation, administration, popular behavior, and efficient markets that make much of the literature on public finance seem only remotely related to conditions in developing countries.

The book is addressed to readers whose work or intellectual curiosity impels them to acquire a better basis for informed opinions on government finance in developing countries. They may include officials in those countries and also in aid-donor countries, staff members of international organizations, researchers, university teachers and students, and the small but highly prized class of general readers with wide interests and considerable patience.

CHAPTER TWO

Budgeting

A GOVERNMENT BUDGET is a financial plan covering outlays and receipts. Usually it is embodied in a document that may be called the budget, but the budget is much more than that. It is the outcome of a process that includes preparation of the financial plan, review of the plan by the legislature where there is one, execution of the plan, and (ideally) evaluation and public reporting of the results.

Most government policies involve outlays or receipts and should be reflected in the budget. Budgeting is technically and politically difficult for all countries, but particularly so for less developed countries. Above all, their governments tend to embrace objectives that are ambitious in relation to the means available for their attainment. The scarcity of means is indicated by low per capita national income and by conditions that result in low productivity and inefficient markets. Other forms of scarcity that complicate budgeting in the majority of less developed countries are a shortage of civil servants who are well trained and experienced in financial and economic matters and a lack of systems to provide needed information. The cyclical instability to which primary-producing countries are subject is a hazard to revenue forecasting; if the government attempts to use fiscal policy to mitigate such instability, heavy demands are placed on the budget process. Economic planning, which is widely considered essential to accelerate development, gives rise to problems of coordination between planning in the broad sense and budgeting.

The Multiple Purposes of Budgeting

Budgeting serves several purposes. First, it sets a framework for policy formation. This requires decisions about actions to be taken to reach objectives. Choices must be made about which of many competing proposals should be adopted to further particular national objectives and about the extent to which various objectives can be advanced simultaneously. Second, budgeting is a means of policy implementation. Here the standards of economy and efficiency—the use of the least costly means of carrying out policy decisions—apply. The budget is a guide for management, and at the same time budgetary procedures are instruments of administrative control. Third, the budget is a means of legal control. Typically, budget decisions are embodied in laws or decrees, and the process of budget formulation and execution is subject to a web of constitutional provisions, continuing laws, and procedural regulations. At each stage, the question can be raised whether actions have been taken or omitted in conformity with legal requirements. The emphasis in legal control is on the prevention of abuse of power and diversion or improper use of public funds. Fourth, the budget document may be a source of public information on past activities, current decisions, and future prospects. More broadly, the budget process can require the executive and legislative branches of a government to explain and justify their decisions and actions. This form of political accountability is most prominent in democratic, parliamentary systems but is not entirely absent in other regimes.

The multiplicity of purposes complicates budgeting, since the requirements of the different functions sometimes conflict and a variety of information is needed to serve them. Efforts to justify a major new program may divert attention from proposals for improving public administration. Legal controls may take the form of detailed specifications of amounts to be spent for various objects and of cumbersome procedures, both of which may hamper management flexibility and detract from efficiency. The kind of records that best serve the functions of legal and public accountability may not provide the information needed for policy formulation and appraisal of the effectiveness of policies. As all the purposes are valuable, conflicts usually should be resolved by compromise or the addition of information systems rather than by concentration on any one budgetary function.

Comprehensiveness

Comprehensiveness of the budget is a principle that specialists have strongly supported. It means that all governmental agencies should be covered by the budget and that all financial transactions should be included.

If the budget is not comprehensive there can be no assurance that scarce resources are allocated to the uses judged most urgent among relevant alternatives or that legal control and public accountability are properly enforced.

A suitably comprehensive budget will include only the agencies that are under the effective financial control of the budgeting government. A national government, for example, would not include in its budget the transactions of local governments if they have their own resources and responsibilities, but it would include grants in aid to the local governments. It would include any capital subscriptions, loans, and subsidies from the treasury to state enterprises and any dividends, interest, and loan repayments from them to the government but not their commercial transactions. Judgment must be exercised in classifying organizations as governmental agencies or as enterprises and in deciding when the degree of control over a governmental agency is sufficient to warrant its inclusion in the budget.[1]

The principle of budget comprehensiveness is often violated. First, certain kinds of transactions are omitted. Expenditures financed by foreign aid or loans may not be included; this is true in several francophone countries in Africa. In some countries part of military expenditures is not shown in the budget. Second, certain agencies that appear to perform governmental functions and that are financed by taxes or other compulsory contributions are not included in the budget in some countries. Social security systems are a leading example.[2] Practices vary with respect to postal systems and other organizations that sell services to users but that depend heavily on state financing and that are subject to detailed policy and administrative directives from the government. Third, the establishment of separate capital and current budgets may conflict with the principle of comprehensiveness if the two accounts are not well coordinated. The subject of coordination of separate capital and current budgets is discussed later in this chapter.

The preparation of a consolidated budget does not necessarily imply genuine comprehensiveness or unity of the budget. Some agencies may dispose of revenues obtained from independent sources and may be included in the budget only in a statistical or accounting sense. Portions of general revenues may be unavailable for allocation through the budget

1. See International Monetary Fund, *A Manual on Government Finance Statistics*, draft (Washington, D.C.: IMF, 1974), pp. 5–36.

2. In the United Nations system of national accounts, social security is a separate sector rather than a part of government. However, the International Monetary Fund's *Manual on Government Finance Statistics* and its *Government Finance Statistics Yearbook* include social security funds in government.

process because the proceeds of certain taxes are assigned to particular agencies or are earmarked for specific purposes. Occasionally a stated fraction of total revenue is dedicated to a specified purpose.

Often there is at least a loose connection between the base of an earmarked tax and the government expenditure that it finances. For example, gasoline tax revenue may be dedicated to road construction and maintenance or an export duty on coffee may be assigned to pay for coffee grading and marketing services. In such cases, the earmarked taxes resemble user charges and may be an application of the benefit principle of taxation (see chapter 4). Earmarking is nevertheless subject to criticism because the amount of tax borne by an individual may not relate closely to his use of the service and because the earmarked revenue may exceed or fall short of the amount that would be spent for the purpose if all revenues were devoted to purposes currently judged most urgent. These criticisms take on added force when there is no connection between the tax base and the object of expenditure. Earmarking can handicap orderly management of cash flow and debt, with some parts of the government running surpluses while others are forced to resort to short-term borrowing.

Earmarking is practiced in virtually all countries, and it is especially prevalent in Latin America. It has been carried to extreme lengths in Ecuador, Costa Rica, and Bolivia. In the 1960s, 65 percent of public revenue in Ecuador was administered by more than 700 public and semipublic agencies outside the budget, and in Costa Rica at least 60 percent of total current revenue was allocated in the form of fixed percentages to the university, the judiciary, and a series of specific purposes.[3] In Bolivia in 1974, 45 percent of total government revenues consisted of retained earnings of public enterprises and earmarked taxes and royalties. Taxes on beer were the largest source of earmarked tax revenues.[4]

The prevalence of earmarking indicates a lack of confidence in the governmental system and the budgetary process. Earmarking is prompted by a desire to protect particular programs, agencies, or regions from competition and to provide them larger or more stable shares of resources than they would otherwise obtain. The practice appears to be generally accepted for social security retirement systems. For other purposes, it is

---

3. Albert Waterston, *Development Planning: Lessons of Experience* (Johns Hopkins University Press for the World Bank, 1965), pp. 210, 212.

4. Richard A. Musgrave, *Fiscal Reform in Bolivia: Final Report of the Bolivian Mission on Tax Reform* (Harvard University Law School, 1981), pp. 152, 154.

opposed by most public finance specialists but has received support from sector experts who regard it as a way of ensuring resources for programs such as roads, agriculture, education, or public health. Earmarking has occasionally been introduced to provide for the service of external loans or for local matching funds for loans or grants.

A theoretical case for earmarking has been elaborated by economists who adopt an individualistic approach to public finance.[5] The argument is that each voter-taxpayer-beneficiary can more accurately compare the costs and benefits of specific services with earmarking than with general-fund budgeting. With earmarking, the results more closely approximate those of the market, which these economists take as the norm of economic efficiency. According to one proponent of this approach, general-fund budgeting will be favored by "the bureaucracy," who wish to expand the public sector, while taxpayer groups will favor earmarking.[6] Whatever may be the merits of the individualistic model as a political ideal—and they are debatable—it is not a useful description of actual behavior in democratic political systems, much less in those developing countries that lack provision for citizen participation.

The Budget Document

A good budget document includes text and tables designed to serve the multiple purposes of the budget. The text explains and justifies the decisions reflected in the budget. In many parliamentary systems, it usually takes the form of a wide-ranging speech by the minister of finance, which reviews economic conditions, expounds the government's policies, and summarizes the major proposals concerning revenues and expenditures. In other countries, the text, or budget message, is less important as an economic and political statement; it may deal mainly with the details of expenditure proposals.

Both expenditures and revenues should be covered and should be considered together. In some countries they are dealt with separately, with unfortunate consequences. The practice is especially noticeable in several

5. Knut Wicksell, "A New Principle of Just Taxation," in Richard A. Musgrave and Alan T. Peacock, eds., *Classics in the Theory of Public Finance* (London: Macmillan, 1958), pp. 72–118; James M. Buchanan, "The Economics of Earmarked Taxes," *Journal of Political Economy*, vol. 71 (October 1963), pp. 457–69, and Buchanan, *Public Finance in the Democratic Process: Fiscal Institutions and Individual Choice* (University of North Carolina Press, 1967), pp. 72–87.

6. Buchanan, "Economics of Earmarked Taxes," p. 467.

Commonwealth countries that follow the British tradition of having the cabinet and parliament make tax and expenditure decisions at different times.[7]

No one classification of outlays and receipts can serve equally well the different purposes of the budget. Historically, the purpose of political and legal control of spending dominated the budget process, and tabular classifications of transactions have been influenced by that priority. Classifying outlays by the spending agency facilitates legal control and accountability. These purposes are strengthened by adding an object classification, which shows purchases such as personal services, travel and transportation of goods, printing and publishing, equipment, and supplies. If desired, an object classification can be subdivided into finely detailed categories.

Agency and object classifications tell little about what the government is doing and are inadequate for appraising policies. For that purpose a functional classification of expenditures is more meaningful. It shows expenditures for purposes such as defense, education, health, and transportation.

A fourth classification, intended to facilitate economic analysis, shows the economic character of outlays. This classification distinguishes between current and capital items and between purchases of goods and services and transfer payments. The usual economic classification is of some value in assessing the macroeconomic impact of the budget, but it appears to be addressed more to the interests of national income statisticians than to the needs of budget officials. The object classification is also useful for some kinds of economic statistics and analysis.[8]

Illustrations of object, functional, and economic character classifications are given in table 2-1. Two classifications are often combined. For example, a cross-classification by function and economic character may be made. Object classifications are usually subitems in agency classifications and are seldom aggregated for the whole government. A few major functions, such as defense, are commonly assigned to separate departments, but generally the agency and functional classifications do not correspond closely.

Usually the budget tables show receipts from each tax and give some information on nontax revenues. An illustrative classification of revenues

---

7. Traditionally, what is called the budget in the United Kingdom is essentially a set of tax proposals. For critical comments, see *Budgetary Reform in the U.K.*, report of a committee chaired by Lord Armstrong of Sanderstead (Oxford University Press for the Institute for Fiscal Studies, 1980), pp. 7–12. Lord Armstrong was a former permanent secretary of the treasury and head of the civil service.

8. On classifications and their use, see Jesse Burkhead, *Government Budgeting* (Wiley, 1956), pp. 110–32.

Table 2-1. *Three Classifications of Government Expenditures*

Object classification[a]

Personnel compensation
  Full-time permanent positions
  Other positions
  Other personnel compensation
Personnel benefits
Travel and transportation of persons
Transportation of things
Communications, utilities, and rent
Printing and reproduction
Other services
Supplies and materials
Equipment
Grants, subsidies, and contributions
Insurance claims and indemnities
Reimbursable items
     Total expenditures

Functional classification[b]

General public services
Defense
Education
Health
Social security and welfare
Housing and community amenities
Other community and social services
Economic services
  Agriculture
  Mining
  Manufacturing
  Electricity
  Roads
  Water transport
  Railways
  Communications
  Other economic services
Unallocable and other purposes
  Interest on the public debt
  Other unallocable
    Total expenditures

Economic classification[b]

Current expenditures
  Expenditures on goods and services
    Wages and salaries and related items
    Other purchases of goods and services
  Interest payments

Table 2-1 *(continued)*

Current expenditures (cont.)
Subsidies and other current transfers
To public enterprises
To other levels of government
To households
To other residents
Transfers abroad
Capital expenditures
Acquisition of new and existing fixed capital assets
Purchases of stocks (inventories)
Purchases of land and intangible assets
Capital transfers
Net lending including net acquisition of equities
Total expenditures and net lending
Memorandum items
Domestic expenditures
Expenditures abroad
Domestic lending
Lending abroad

a. Adapted from *Budget of the United States Government, Fiscal Year 1982*, appendix.
b. Adapted from International Monetary Fund, *A Manual on Government Finance Statistics*, draft (Washington, D.C.: IMF, 1974), pp. 191–93, 208–09.

appears in table 2-2. Headings and subheadings would be added or deleted to reflect the revenue structure of the country.[9]

The budget document should also show the overall deficit or surplus. This is best defined as total revenues less total expenditures; a negative number indicates a deficit, a positive number a surplus. Revenues include receipts from taxes and other sources except borrowing and money creation; expenditures include all outlays except debt repayment. National definitions of the deficit do not always agree with the foregoing statement. Apart from the omissions from the budget discussed earlier, differences may arise from the inclusion of certain proceeds of borrowing in revenues and of certain debt repayments in expenditures. Emphasis is sometimes given to the current account balance rather than the overall balance.[10]

A fairly precise statement of how a deficit will be covered, or a surplus disposed of, should be included. An illustrative listing of the sources of

9. The IMF *Manual on Government Finance Statistics* provides for a separate category of nonrepayable receipts called grants. Although important for a few countries, grants accounted for only about 3 percent or less of total revenue of all non-oil developing countries in 1973–79; International Monetary Fund, *Government Finance Statistics Yearbook*, vol. 5 (1981), p. 33. It may be more informative to consider grants as a means of financing a budget deficit.

10. For a careful examination of different definitions, see Raja J. Chelliah, "Significance of Alternative Concepts of Budget Deficit," International Monetary Fund *Staff Papers*, vol. 20 (November 1973), pp. 741–84.

Table 2-2. *A Classification of Government Revenues*

Tax revenue
  Taxes on net income and profits
    Corporate, company, or enterprise
    Individuals
    Other
  Social security contributions
  Employers' payroll or manpower taxes
  Taxes on property
  Domestic taxes on goods and services
    General sales, turnover, or value-added taxes
    Selective excises
    Profits of fiscal monopolies
    License taxes
    Other
  Taxes on international trade and transactions
    Import duties
    Export duties
    Exchange taxes and profits
    Other
  Miscellaneous taxes
    Poll taxes
    Stamp taxes
    Other

Nontax revenue
  Income from public enterprises
  Administrative fees
  Fines and forfeits
  Sales of government property
  Other

    Total revenues

Source: Adapted from IMF, *Manual on Government Finance Statistics*, pp. 159–61.

financing of a deficit appears in table 2-3. With signs reversed, this could account for the disposal of a surplus—a rarity nowadays. Money creation, an important means of deficit financing, is not shown in the table because it usually takes the form of borrowing from the central bank.

Although most countries now have a functional classification of expenditures, some budget documents still lack that feature. In a few cases, the objects of expenditure are shown in great detail, including a listing of government jobs, but no enlightening summary of the purposes of the outlays is given. A common weakness is the absence of information on the financing of an expected deficit. Another weakness is the failure to clarify the relationship between the economic outlook projected in the budget speech and the budget proper.

Table 2-3. *Financing of a Government Deficit*

Domestic financing
From the central bank or other monetary authority
New borrowing less amortization
Change in deposits[a]
Change in currency holdings[a]
From other banks
New borrowing less amortization
Change in deposits and other liquid claims[a]
From other lenders (net)
Financing abroad
From international development institutions
Loans (net)
Grants[b]
From foreign governments
Loans (net)
Grants[b]
From other lenders
Long-term debt (net)
Short-term debt (net)
Change in deposits, negotiable securities, and other liquid assets[a]
Total financing

Source: Adapted from IMF, *Manual on Government Finance Statistics*, pp. 229–30.
a. A reduction is a source of financing and is recorded as a positive entry; an increase is a negative item.
b. Grants are classified "above the line" (that is, as an item reducing the deficit rather than a means of financing) in the IMF *Manual on Government Finance Statistics*.

Budget Policy

Budget preparation is a two-way process of reaching decisions on the size and composition of expenditures and revenues. It would be unrealistic to attempt to decide the total size of expenditures without considering the availability of revenues. Similarly, the amount of revenue to be raised is influenced by the assessment of needed expenditures and possible sources of deficit financing and their economic consequences. Total expenditures and revenues can be decided only by looking at needed and feasible components. Thus budgeting involves repeated adjustments of preliminary figures for totals and components.

A practical procedure begins with estimates of the yield of existing taxes and nontax revenues and the cost of maintaining existing expenditure programs. Both estimates should take account of forecasts of economic, demographic, and other relevant conditions but should assume no change in tax rates, administration, or expenditure program levels. Some variations in spending rates will usually occur, even with constant program levels, because of demographic changes and the completion of public works projects. It is convenient to make the estimates first on the assumption of constant prices and later to adjust them for expected price changes (to be discussed later). Admittedly, economic forecasts are subject to wide margins of error, particularly in primary-producing countries, but forecasts of some kind cannot be avoided in making budget estimates.

If the prospective revenues are greater than the cost of maintaining existing programs, usually there is scope for tax reduction or for additional expenditures (new programs or improvements in existing programs). If, however, prospective revenues are less than the cost of maintaining existing programs, usually there is need for tax increases or curtailment of spending programs. The word "usually" is included in both formulations to allow for the possibility that any excess or shortfall of revenues will be reflected only in a change in the size of the budget deficit. Commonly, however, adjustments will be needed in the deficit, expenditures, and taxation.

Provisional decisions on total expenditures and taxation can be made most appropriately at a high political level with the help of a policy paper prepared by the budget office. These decisions should be based on judgments about the acceptable weight of taxation, the urgency of major expenditure proposals that have already been discussed, and the scope for borrowing and money creation. They will be subject to modification in the course of detailed consideration of spending proposals and possible tax changes.

Budget Formulation

In well-staffed administrations budgets may be formulated over many months, but in developing countries the process is likely to be compressed within a period of a few weeks. The timing should be set out in a budget calendar. A somewhat idealized version of the process involves the following ten steps.

1. A policy paper is prepared by the budget office for the consideration of the cabinet or the president. If the country has an economic plan, the paper is drafted in consultation with the planning department or jointly

with it. The paper includes projections of revenues and expenditures and outlines major alternative proposals for change during the coming year.

2. The cabinet or the president makes provisional decisions on the total amount of expenditures, on major new spending projects or cutbacks, and on major tax changes.

3. The budget office issues guidelines for the spending departments to follow in making their requests. These instructions are often called the budget circular or the call for estimates.

4. The budget office and the representatives of the spending departments discuss requests and attempt to reach agreement on them.

5. The budget office presents recommendations to the minister of finance, who places them before the cabinet after reviewing them; in a presidential system, the budget office presents its recommendations to the chief executive.

6. Decisions on expenditures and any necessary changes in taxation are made by the cabinet or the president.

7. Spending departments have an opportunity to appeal to the cabinet or the president if they consider their allocations seriously inadequate.

8. Final decisions are made by the cabinet or the president.

9. The budget proposals are submitted to the legislature.

10. The legislature considers and approves the budget by adopting one or more acts. Its freedom to make changes in the expenditure proposals differs considerably among countries.

The procedures followed in developing countries often are less elaborate than this outline suggests. In many countries, the budget office is a unit in the ministry of finance staffed by fewer than ten persons. Spending departments may assign primary responsibility for their presentations to only one or two officers who have other duties as well. The separate steps may not be clearly identifiable. There may be no opportunity for formal appeals by spending departments; however, informal possibilities nearly always exist. The legislative steps may be missing and the budget may be enacted by decree.

An incrementalist approach to reviewing expenditure requests is the most realistic one. It starts with the tacit assumption that the existing tax system and expenditure programs are to be continued with only marginal changes. Attention is focused on relatively small increments, positive or negative. This makes the process far more comprehensible than it would be if all existing revenue sources and expenditure programs were thoroughly reexamined each year; it maintains continuity, and it avoids unproductive conflicts.[11] However, incremental budgeting has the defects of its virtues; taxes and expenditure programs may be continued that would not be approved if all current options were systematically considered. Some proposed reforms intended to improve budget decisionmaking will be discussed later in this chapter.

The traditional methods of the budget office concentrated on the details of spending proposals and stressed frugality. Saving candle ends, as the tactic came to be known, was consistent with the limited functions of the state in a noninterventionist era. Budget offices are still expected to fill the role of economizer, but they are now also expected to give attention to the influence of the budget on the advancement of macroeconomic objectives. The new responsibilities call for attitudes and expertise different from those required in the past.

As a hedge against uncertainty and a means of resisting demands for expenditure increases or tax cuts, budget offices often follow the tactic of conservatively estimating revenues—or deliberately understating the estimates—and assuming that all authorized expenditures will be made promptly. Used in moderation, this tactic allows some scope for meeting unforeseen needs, but carried too far it thwarts financial planning.

Spending departments tend to press for larger expenditures while the budget office urges restraint. The attitude of the spending departments is not necessarily discreditable; officials who are carrying out a program are likely to be keenly aware of further needs in the field and less sensitive than the budget office should be to other demands and to limitations on total resources. Spending departments may inflate their requests in order to leave room for cutbacks. This tactic is particularly prevalent where the budget office follows the practice of reducing all requests, regardless of how well they are supported. The result can be highly unrealistic requests and arbitrary reductions that negate careful consideration of requirements.

Another tactic sometimes adopted by spending departments when they are asked to propose economies is to suggest the elimination of an especially popular or prominent item in order to divert attention from more vulnerable items. If, for example, the ministry of education is asked

11. On incrementalism, see Charles E. Lindblom, "Policy Analysis," *American Economic Review*, vol. 48 (June 1958), pp. 298–312; Lindblom, "Decision-Making in Taxation and Expenditures," in *Public Finances: Needs, Sources, and Utilization*, a Conference of the Universities–National Bureau Committee for Economic Research (Princeton University Press, 1961), pp. 295–329; Aaron Wildavsky, *The Politics of the Budgetary Process*, 3d ed. (Little, Brown, 1979), pp. 13–16, passim; and Wildavsky, *Budgeting: A Comparative Theory of Budgetary Processes* (Little, Brown, 1975), pp. 214–19, passim.

how it would absorb a budget cut, it may reply that some local schools would have to be closed, without conceding that any savings in administrative overhead would be possible.

Still another maneuver is the camel's nose under the tent—or the foot in the door—which involves starting a program or a project on a small scale in the expectation that the growing stream of future expenditures required to carry it on will be authorized to prevent its wasteful or unpopular termination.

In some developing countries, formal approval of the annual budget does not complete the review of spending proposals. Proposals included in the budget may be subjected to further review, and fresh justification may be required. Caiden and Wildavsky call the practice of detailed scrutiny and prior approval of items during the year "repetitive budgeting."[12] They attribute it to the efforts of finance ministries to hedge against the great economic uncertainties to which poor countries are subject. An example cited by these writers is cash flow budgeting in Brazil. The official budget is drafted by the planning ministry and approved by the congress and the president, but the ministry of finance controls its execution. The ministry of finance routinely reduces the allocations to departments and establishes reserves that are released over the year as cash flows are received. Another example (not mentioned by Caiden and Wildavsky) is the Philippines, where at one time the annual budget included a large number of public works projects that could be undertaken only if the secretary of finance found that receipts were sufficient to cover the costs. As it was unlikely that all the projects could be funded, the secretary of finance was in effect charged with remaking the budget, which had originally been prepared by the budget director.

Caiden and Wildavsky criticize repetitive budgeting for its inordinate delay, careless estimating by departments, overtly political criteria for approving expenditures, bias against investment expenditures, and encouragement of lobbying and maneuvering by departments. It often results, they assert, in either an accumulation of claims in the hands of departments or a year-end rush to spend before the authority to do so lapses. These strictures may be justified in some cases, but generally they appear too severe. The practice of controlling the rate of commitments and disbursements during the year, with an eye to cash flows, and of taking account of new developments is essential for orderly financial

12. Naomi Caiden and Aaron Wildavksy, *Planning and Budgeting in Poor Countries* (Wiley, 1974; Transaction, 1980), pp. 71–78.

management. Caiden and Wildavsky propose that repetitive budgeting be replaced by "continuous budgeting"—a recommendation that will be touched on in a later section on budget reform proposals.

Budget Execution

Budget execution is viewed here from the expenditure side. The revenue side is governed mainly by permanent legislation and procedures that can better be considered in connection with tax administration. Budget execution has the legal purpose of ensuring that expenditures are consistent with the limits set out in the annual budget law (or laws) and with the requirements of permanent financial legislation and regulations. It also has the managerial function of promoting efficiency and the macroeconomic function of avoiding or minimizing economic disturbances caused by irregular timing of receipts and disbursements or departures from budget projections. The legal purpose tends to dominate procedures, and to some extent it conflicts with the managerial and macroeconomic functions.

Budget execution is the use of the spending authority granted by the budget law or decree. It includes commitments (that is, contracts or other obligations for hiring personnel and other purchases of goods and services), disbursements to liquidate the commitments, and recording and reporting. Accounting and auditing, though often considered as separate operations, are here regarded as the final stages of budget execution. The budget is unavoidably subject to change during its execution, and such modifications are a normal part of the process.

Countries differ greatly in the degree to which commitments are subject to control by the budget office or another central agency. In some countries, detailed control is exercised by requiring the spending departments to obtain explicit approval before using the budget authorization by entering into commitments. Usually such prior approval does not involve a reexamination of the merits of the expenditure but only a verification that it has been authorized and proper procedures have been observed. (The procedure is often called preaudit.) In other countries, spending departments may make commitments without specific prior approval and are responsible for observing the legal requirements. Prior approval systems tend to be cumbersome but may be expedient where financial discipline is weak.

In many systems, the budget office apportions the annual authorization by time periods (months or quarters) and establishes limits on the amount that can be committed within each period. The purpose of apportionment is to prevent spending departments from making commitments too rapidly, either because of poor management or in the expectation that a supplementary appropriation will be forthcoming if the authorized amount is exhausted before the end of the year. Apportionments (also called allotments) should take account of seasonal factors.

The bulk of disbursements is ordinarily made by central disbursing officers who draw checks on accounts held in the central bank. (The French-influenced countries of Africa and some other countries have independent treasuries that collect and disburse funds on behalf of government agencies and certain other public bodies.) In a few countries, some operating departments, particularly autonomous entities that are not fully integrated in the budget process, maintain separate bank accounts and make their own disbursements. This practice can cause unnecessary borrowing and undesirable macroeconomic effects because it precludes governmentwide cash and debt management. Even if most disbursements are centralized, provision may be made for operating departments to disburse payments in currency or at remote locations. Embassies in foreign countries and overseas purchasing agencies commonly have authority within limits to make disbursements.

Timely information on commitments and disbursements is essential to control the execution of the budget. The ministry of finance also needs information on receipts, cash balances, and debt transactions. Departmental managers should have information on nonfinancial aspects of work programs, which will reveal the rate of progress.

Government accounting systems often are poorly suited to supplying financial information, and they rarely provide nonfinancial information on work programs. Accounting systems tend to be unnecessarily elaborate and to be designed and operated to provide detailed records for audit after the end of the fiscal year rather than to supply current information. Accounts may be completed ("closed") months or years after the end of the period. Computerization should facilitate prompt reporting, but often it has not done so because the system was not appropriately redesigned before computers were put in service.

The reform of government accounting is a technical subject that cannot be discussed here. Countries undertaking accounting reforms have commonly found that success depends on overcoming inertia and resolving rivalries among agencies. Reforms have proved far more contentious and time-consuming than might be expected. Pending the completion of an accounting reform—and perhaps even after a reform—the authorities may rely on preliminary statistical reports for current information. The statistical reports differ from accounts by giving less detail and by including estimates where complete and final figures are not available. Estimates may be used for transactions in remote areas and for many small items without much affecting the totals. Information on cash flows can be obtained from banking sources.

Supplementary statistical reports are necessary in certain countries of francophone Africa and Latin America. These countries keep their accounts open for a complementary period after the end of each fiscal year. Payments made during the complementary period that relate to commitments entered into under authority granted by the budget of the prior year are recorded as expenditures of that fiscal year. Tax collections during the complementary period may be recorded as revenue of the prior year in which the taxes were assessed. The complementary periods vary in length from one or two months up to six months, and they are occasionally extended. The system was designed for legal control, and it is logical from that standpoint. However, it has the disadvantage of producing, after considerable delay, accounts on a mixed cash and accrual basis that cannot be directly used to analyze the macroeconomic impact of the budget. For judging macroeconomic effects, accounts or statistics that report expenditures and revenues when cash is paid or received are more useful.[13]

Changes usually have to be made in the budget during the course of the year to allow for reassessments of needs and resources in the light of current developments. One kind of change is the transfer of spending authority between objects or programs and sometimes between agencies or departments. The degree of formality involved in intradepartmental transfers (sometimes called virements) depends in part on how detailed the provisions of the budget law are and in part on how centralized the system is. If revenues fall short of expectations or if delays are experienced in spending, the budget office may defer or cancel part of the authority of operating departments to make commitments. The apportionment or allotment system makes this feasible. If increases in total expenditures are to be made, supplementary action by the legislature usually will be required

13. For a fuller description, see Petrus J. Van de Ven and Dirk J. Wolfson, "Problems of Budget Analysis and Treasury Management in French-Speaking Africa," International Monetary Fund *Staff Papers*, vol. 16 (March 1969), pp. 140–56; *Manual on Government Finance Statistics*, pp. 114–17. See also Louis Trotabas and Jean-Marie Cotteret, *Droit budgétaire et comptabilité publique*, 2d ed. (Paris: Dalloz, 1978) and Henri Sempé, *Budget et Trésor* (Paris: Cujas, 1973).

in countries in which the original budget was subject to legislative approval. Frequently supplementary appropriations are scrutinized less carefully than the initial budget proposals and hence are a channel for excessive expenditures.

Auditing is the review of transactions after their completion. (This is sometimes called postaudit, as distinguished from preaudit, which is the prior approval of commitments and payments.) Auditing should be carried out by an independent agency not directly involved in the accounting function. This condition, clearly a desirable safeguard against conflict of interest, has not been observed in some Latin American countries where the controller general has both accounting and auditing functions.

The traditional approach, which may be called financial auditing, was intended to check compliance with the budget law and other legal requirements. Reports drawing attention to any irregularities were placed before the legislature or a committee of the legislature. The primary purpose was to prevent the recurrence of such irregularities, with punitive action a secondary purpose where serious abuses were discovered.

More recently, audit agencies in a number of countries have extended their activities to include operations or performance audits—also called comprehensive audits—that comment on the effectiveness and efficiency of programs. In the majority of developing countries, however, auditing has not gone beyond the financial stage, and it appears advisable to give priority to strengthening financial auditing—and the budget office—rather than spreading the limited number of skilled persons over a wider field.

Auditing is often weak or virtually nonexistent in countries without strong legislatures, even though authoritarian governments could benefit as well as democratic ones from financial and operations audits. Auditing can be effective only if the legislature or the executive pays attention to reports and follows up with corrective action.

Budgeting in Inflationary Times

The formulation and execution of the government budget is greatly complicated by inflation, as are the financial plans of enterprises and households.[14] Budget procedures evolved on the assumption that the purchasing power of money would remain stable. Inflation affects both

---

14. This section draws heavily on *Budgetary Reform in the U.K.*

expenditures and revenues and makes inapplicable some traditional methods of forecasting and control. The rate at which prices will rise is uncertain, often varying considerably in the course of a year or from one year to the next during a period of general inflation. Governments, moreover, are reluctant to publicize their best guesses about the future rate of inflation because they do not want to open themselves to criticism and because such official forecasts may become partially self-fulfilling prophecies. The impact of inflation on taxation will be treated in later chapters, and inflation will receive further attention in chapters 9 and 11.

Under inflationary conditions, expenditure plans can best be made initially on the assumption of constant prices. The figures should then be adjusted to allow for expected price changes. This procedure is simple and allows central review and control of price projections, which otherwise would be likely to differ greatly among agencies. Among major objects of expenditure, salaries and wages, transfer payments, and certain interest payments will increase only in response to government action. Prices of most other goods and services and some interest payments will be subject to market forces and will increase with inflation.

In adjusting the constant-price figures for inflation, it is advisable to apply a general price index, except for salaries and wages. (Interest payments on outstanding long-term domestic debt would not need to be adjusted, but this item is unlikely to be large in a developing country, particularly one that has been experiencing inflation for some time.) Probably the projected implicit price deflator for gross domestic product is the most suitable index. It gives a general measure of the opportunity cost of public expenditures and is simpler to apply than sectoral indexes for the specific purchases of government. The use of a general index also encourages departments to seek the best available bargains. For example, if lumber prices rise more rapidly than cement prices, it will be sensible to encourage the substitution of cement for lumber in construction where feasible. To be sure, it may be expedient to allow for extreme changes in relative prices where substitution possibilities are limited in the short run, as in the case of petroleum products after the extraordinary price increases of the 1970s.

Once the price-adjusted projections for the year have been made, they should be converted into allotments for subperiods in the usual way. If the actual rate of inflation during the year diverges significantly from the projected path, it may be necessary to make further adjustments in the allotments. With rapid inflation, it will be expedient to increase salaries and wages to maintain their purchasing power; the failure to do so for long periods in countries experiencing inflation has been unfair to government employees and has frequently diverted them from their official duties to outside activities.

The general price adjustments and changes in salary and wage rates should not be automatic but should be set centrally by the budget office with the approval of the minister of finance and possibly the cabinet or the president. Automatic adjustments at either the planning stage or budget execution stage are dangerous. The United Kingdom formerly budgeted expenditures on a well-conceived constant price basis (with automatic adjustments for price changes), but this greatly weakened control. In 1976 rigid cash limits were imposed on about two-thirds of public expenditure, and control was regained.

The frequency of adjustment should depend on the rate of inflation and the extent of divergence of actual price increases from those assumed. With a divergence of no more than 10 to 15 percent over the course of a year, one correction during the year may be sufficient. With greater divergencies, quarterly or monthly adjustments may be advisable. It may be a good tactic to hold the intrayear price adjustments somewhat below the full increase in the price index in order to force a decrease in the real value of expenditures and thus to moderate inflationary pressures.

As a by-product of the adjustment of expenditures for price changes, historical statistics on expenditures in constant prices should be developed. Although such series are imprecise, they are useful for analysis and public information.

Current and Capital Budgets

A number of developing countries maintain separate current and capital budgets. Some developed countries also follow this practice, but the number doing so has decreased. An illustration of the current/capital division appears in table 2-4. This is a rearrangement of items from tables 2-1 and 2-2, with the addition of a capital consumption allowance. Subheadings could be added as required, of course.

The capital consumption allowance is an estimate of the loss of the value of physical capital assets owing to wear and tear and obsolescence. Many current/capital budget systems omit this item. In that case, the difference between revenue and expenditure in the current budget equals

Table 2-4. *Current and Capital Budgets*

Current (or operations) budget	
Revenues	Expenditures
Taxes	Current purchases of goods and
Fees and fines	services
Income from public enterprises	Interest payments
	Subsidies and transfer payments
	To public enterprises
	Other
	Capital consumption allowance

Revenues − Expenditures = Net current surplus or deficit
= Net saving or dissaving

Capital (investment) budget	
Receipts	Outlays
From current budget	Physical investment (new
Capital consumption allowance	construction and equipment)
Net current surplus (deficit)	Purchase of existing assets
Sales of government property	Net lending (including net
Net borrowing[a]	acquisition of equities)
Grants received from abroad[b]	

Receipts − Outlays = Change in cash balances

Source: Adapted from Ursula K. Hicks, *Development Finance: Planning and Control* (Oxford University Press, 1965), pp. 170–71.

a. Proceeds of new borrowing less loan repayments.

b. Grants received from abroad may be divided between current grants (classified as revenue) and capital grants (classified as capital receipts). The distinction is difficult to make, and all grants are here treated as capital receipts.

gross saving or dissaving; total capital receipts are not affected since the surplus transferred from the current budget is larger by the amount of the excess of gross saving over net saving.

Actual formats are often less logical and comprehensive than that shown in the table, with the consequence that net or gross saving or dissaving and changes in cash balances do not appear as the balances in the current and capital budgets.

In capital budgets, particularly, definitions can be troublesome. Usually physical investment includes buildings and durable equipment except military items. Some construction and transportation and communications equipment, however, can be used for both civilian and military purposes, and questions of judgment arise in classifying them. Government loans often include a subsidy element that casts doubt on their classification as investments. Most important, the physical and financial assets included in capital budgets do not include all outlays that will yield benefits in the future. Education and certain health services are examples of activities that create human capital and produce future returns. Emphasis on such items is a recurring theme of this book.

The purpose of a separate capital budget is not always clear. Four possible purposes may be identified, two of them legitimate and two illegitimate.[15]

First, the capital budget provides a measure of asset accumulation through net or gross saving. By analogy with enterprise and household accounting, saving is often considered highly important. For enterprises, it measures retained profits; for households, it measures additions to wealth. The significance of government saving is not equally clear, and it can easily be misinterpreted. Nevertheless, there is interest in a figure for government saving, partly because it enters into various growth models and partly because of the attention it receives from many foreign observers. Such a figure is a feature of a proper capital budget, but it can be derived as a statistical estimate without a formal separation of capital and current budget accounts.

Second, a separate capital budget and a capital consumption allowance in the current budget can give a truer measure of the annual cost of government programs than a unified budget can in certain circumstances. If, for example, a country constructs a dam and ancillary works that are expected to last for many years and that require outlays equal to a large fraction of annual expenditures, a unified budget may give an exaggerated impression of the cost of irrigation, flood control, and electricity generation during the construction period, and in some sense it may overstate the total cost of government. This issue does not arise with respect to small projects, even if long-lived, provided they are being carried out at a fairly even rate. Lumpy outlays are likely to be relatively more important for small countries and local governments than for large units of government.

Third, the size of outlays in the capital budget, or the amount of net saving in the current budget, is sometimes regarded as an indication of the government's contribution to growth or development. That is a gross misinterpretation. Many current services of government are essential for the maintenance of orderly conditions in which productive activity can be carried on, and any implication that expenditures for these purposes are unproductive should be rejected. It is not even true that capital outlays are

---

15. See Richard Goode and Eugene A. Birnbaum, "Government Capital Budgets," International Monetary Fund *Staff Papers*, vol. 5 (February 1956), pp. 23–46; Ursula K. Hicks, *Development Finance: Planning and Control* (Oxford University Press, 1965), pp. 168–72.

unique in contributing to future production. Functionally, the services of a teacher, like the services of a school building, will produce a return over the lifetime of the pupils. In all fields, expenditures for operations and maintenance must be made in order to obtain the benefits that capital equipment can yield. Much harm has been done by giving unjustified priority to either capital or current expenditures in budgeting.

Fourth, the capital budget has often been viewed as an indicator of the amount that a government may prudently borrow. Indeed, in several countries the capital budget is called the loan account or the below-the-line account or has evolved from such accounts. This attitude is nourished by analogy with enterprise accounting and finance. When an enterprise borrows to finance a productive capital investment, its net position is not impaired as its assets and liabilities increase equally. Future profits from the investment are expected to supply the funds to service the debt. In contrast, government capital outlays, even for highly productive projects, often do not generate future revenues. Governments, unlike enterprises, have a responsibility to take account of the macroeconomic effects of their transactions. Both current and capital expenditures affect aggregate demand for domestic production and imports; the prudent accompanying levels of taxation, government borrowing at home and abroad, and money creation can be decided only by reference to comprehensive totals. It is not safe to assume either that borrowing is always appropriate to cover capital outlays or that it is never appropriate for current expenditures.

Apart from possible erroneous inferences concerning development policy and macroeconomic management, problems arise when the current and capital budgets are not well coordinated. In some countries, the capital budget is prepared by the planning ministry and the current budget by the budget office, with little consultation between the two agencies and no systematic study of the demands that will be placed on the current budget over time for operating and maintenance expenditures as a consequence of capital outlays. In these circumstances, both the substitutability and the complementarity of current and capital outlays are obscured, and rational decisionmaking becomes very difficult.

On balance, there appears to be no real need to introduce a separate capital budget where none exists, and there are some risks in doing so. But neither is there a compelling case for eliminating the current/capital distinction where it is well established and thought to be helpful. What is essential is recognition of the continuing effects of capital expenditures on future needs for current outlays.

Budgeting and Planning

Budgeting is a form of planning. Traditionally directed toward financial planning in a rather narrow sense, the budget process and the budget document increasingly have come to include other kinds of economic information and analysis as well. But development or economic planning is a still broader process. It involves projections of population and indications of how labor, capital, natural resources, and innovations can be combined to produce output. A comprehensive plan will attempt to cover the whole economy and to take account of the external economic environment. Partial plans omit some sectors or industries. Centralized planning is essential if the aim is a high degree of state direction of production and distribution. In other systems, the government may rely primarily on expenditures and taxation, credit policy, and market incentives to induce private enterprises and households to behave in ways that will advance plan objectives. Plans cover several years; five is a favorite number. Plans are usually prepared and monitored by a permanent body, either a ministry or commission.

Planning has been adopted in some form by many developing countries, though plans differ greatly in coverage and detail. The appeal of planning is evident. To many intellectuals it appears almost synonymous with rationality. Political leaders may regard a plan as a modern version of the promises of a better life that they and their predecessors have long been accustomed to holding out to the people. The example of the USSR, whose five-year plans have attracted much attention and admiration in the third world, has contributed greatly to the prestige of planning. Official lenders and aid donors have encouraged planning and have sometimes insisted that recipients support their requests with development plans. The United Nations, the World Bank, and other organizations have supplied extensive technical assistance in planning.

Lately, enthusiasm for planning has cooled. This reflects disappointment over the rate of progress in many developing countries and recognition that the early plans did not make sufficient allowance for obstacles and surprises. Many plans have been poorly conceived and have been based on inadequate economic models. Plans drawn up in the 1950s and 1960s, in particular, tended to give undue priority to industrialization and were often based on naive assumptions about the relation between output and the stock of physical capital (see chapter 10). Some so-called plans were little more than shopping lists of projects for which governments hoped to obtain foreign financing.

Few developing countries, however, have discarded planning altogether. The proper coordination of budgeting and planning remains important. Care needs to be exercised in translating the multiyear plan into the specific provisions of annual budgets. As Waterston has remarked, the nature of the link between the plan and the budget is a test of whether a government is serious about its plan and intends to carry it out.[16] Problems often arise because of poor communication and cooperation between the planning and budgeting staffs. Planners usually are economists, and often they are intrigued by the techniques of input-output analysis and model building. They tend to be spenders and to have a high regard for investment spending. Budget officials may have economic training but usually are concerned primarily with administration and control. They are inclined to take a skeptical or negative attitude toward spending proposals. Organizational rivalries can take root and flourish in these conditions. Undesirable consequences observed at times have included delays in budget preparation, current and capital budgets that bear little relation to each other, budget fragmentation, and inoperative plans.[17]

Coordination between planning and budgeting is essential to the effectiveness of both. One approach is to place both functions in one ministry, usually the ministry of finance. This may be the only practical solution in some cases, particularly in small countries that have few qualified officials. In most cases, however, there are advantages in having separate organizations. Different kinds of expertise and possibly different temperaments are needed for planning and budgeting. A moderate degree of competition between government departments can stimulate new ideas and their critical examination.

The budget office and the planning organization should consult each other fully about the economic assumptions underlying the budget and should collaborate in the preparation of the policy paper that initiates the formulation of the budget. The planning office should participate in the review of proposals for capital expenditures and should be consulted about major changes in subsidies and taxes. Responsibility for the preparation of both current and capital budget proposals should be assigned to the minister of finance or budget director, although the minister of planning

---

16. Waterston, *Development Planning*, p. 201.
17. Caiden and Wildavsky, *Planning and Budgeting in Poor Countries*.

or chairman of the planning commission should be given the opportunity to express separate views.

Some simple changes in approach can encourage cooperation between budgeters and planners. Some countries have found it advantageous to make their fiscal year coincide with the calendar year because the statistics on which the development plan is based and the plan itself cover calendar years. Both planners and budgeters should try to view the annual budget in a medium-term framework. Planners are properly concerned with how far the annual budget will advance the capital investment program visualized for the whole plan period. Budgeters should give special attention to the recurrent costs in future years of capital projects being carried out currently and should use projections of such costs as one basis for choosing among projects.

Proposals for Reform

There has been dissatisfaction with the budget process nearly everywhere, in more developed and less developed countries alike. It is widely believed that total government expenditures have been growing too rapidly. At the same time, outlays for development projects have frequently lagged behind planned rates. Budget procedures have been criticized as outmoded and negative—ineffective both in restraining expenditure growth and in ensuring the best composition of the total.

Many recommendations for reform have been advanced. Although the suggested reforms differ considerably in scope and terminology, the most widely discussed proposals to substitute a new system for conventional budgeting may be classified in three groups: performance budgeting, program budgeting, and zero-base budgeting.

The term performance budget appears to have been publicized (and perhaps originated) by an official U.S. commission that reported in 1949.[18] The proposal called for changing the emphasis in budgeting from inputs, usually measured as money expenditures for specified objects, to outputs, measured in physical terms where feasible. Certain features of the proposal were authorized by law. Despite difficulties, some progress was made in classification and measurement, but budget decisions in the United States did not appear to be much affected.

18. Commission on the Organization of the Executive Branch of the Government (known as the Hoover Commission, after its chairman, former President Herbert Hoover), *Budgeting and Accounting*, Report 7 (Government Printing Office, 1949).

In the 1960s new proposals, incorporating some of the features of performance budgeting and going further, were advanced in several countries. This family of proposals is here called program budgeting. Other terms are planning-programming budget system (abbreviated PPB or PPBS) and in France *rationalisation des choix budgétaires* (RCB). The United Nations opted for the term program and performance budgeting.[19] The terms are not precise, and the proposals they are applied to differ substantially. Elements found in many of the more complete proposals include (1) emphasis on programs to attain objectives rather than on inputs, (2) comparison of a wide range of alternative programs and elements, (3) long-range or medium-term projections, (4) measurement of performance, and (5) supplementary reporting on performance.

Some advocates of program budgeting interpreted it very broadly and, like some supporters of planning, virtually equated their proposals with rational decisionmaking. Generally, there was an effort to gain for budgeting some of the mystique of planning. Great emphasis was placed on classification and economic analysis.

Program budgeting was adopted in some form in a number of countries. Developed countries introducing elements of it include Australia, Austria, Belgium, Canada, France, Japan, New Zealand, Norway, the United Kingdom, and the United States.[20] According to a United Nations survey, program budgeting was adopted in Asia by Korea, Malaysia, the Philippines, and Sri Lanka; in Latin America by Bolivia, Chile, the Dominican Republic, Honduras, Guatemala, Panama, Paraguay, and Venezuela; and in Africa by Botswana, Ghana, and the Ivory Coast. However, the United Nations report states that the introduction of program budgeting "has generally meant more of a cosmetic than substantive change in budgets."[21]

Difficulties were encountered in applying program budgeting, and experience with it has been disappointing. It proved to be hard to define programs and relate them to national objectives. One reason is that an

19. United Nations, Department of Economic and Social Affairs, *A Manual of Programme and Performance Budgeting* (New York: UN, 1965).

20. International Institute of Public Finance, *Nouvelles methodes de choix budgétaires* [New methods of making budgetary choices] (Budapest: IIPF, 1972); David Novick, ed., *Current Practice in Program Budgeting (PPBS): Analysis and Case Studies Covering Business and Government* (Crane, Russak, 1973).

21. United Nations, Department of Technical Cooperation for Development, *Survey of Changes and Trends in Public Administration and Finance for Development, 1975–77* (New York: UN, 1978), pp. 37–40; quotation from p. 38. According to another source, the great majority of Latin American countries adopted program budgeting in whole or in part after 1959, but in some cases the changes seem to have been confined to terminology and improvements in classification. See Victoro J. Arrieche and others, "La técnica del presupuesto por progamas en América Latina," *Tributación* [Santo Domingo, Dominican Republic], vol. 6 (October/December 1980), pp. 41–58.

activity often serves several purposes and is viewed differently by various officials and interest groups. For example, the construction of a dam has wide ramifications. It may provide irrigation, flood control, electric energy, fishing, and recreation. The additional agricultural output may consist of food for domestic consumption, export crops, or raw materials for domestic manufacturing. The project may also stimulate activity in a sparsely settled or poor area. Responsibility for the various aspects of such a project will be assigned to several government departments, and there may be no way of directly relating budgeted expenditures to programs and spending departments.

The measurement of output is fairly straightforward in some activities but virtually impossible for traditional functions such as law enforcement, external relations, and national defense. Many outputs are not desired for themselves but are inputs for a productive process, as for example, the irrigation water and electric energy produced by the dam.

Furthermore, consideration of a wide range of alternative ways of attaining ends is impractical in most cases. The formal analytical techniques visualized by supporters of program budgeting exceeded the capacity of well-staffed civil services and were far beyond the reach of the small and poorly trained staffs of most developing countries. In any case, the techniques could be used only to compare ways of carrying on a particular program and not for the more fundamental choice between programs. There is no formal analysis that can objectively compare the benefits of, say, defense and education, though it may be possible to sharpen thinking about each activity and thus aid marginal choices between the two.

In summary, program budgeting proposals were overambitious; their advocates promised too much and were naive about the nature of budgeting. The United States dropped the formal program budget in 1971 after using it on a governmentwide basis for only five years. At the time, a senior official of the Office of Management and Budget said, "The U.S. experience with these methods suggests that, as yet, they have neither substantially changed nor significantly improved the process of making budgetary choices."[22] This judgment seems too harsh as a general evaluation of the program budgeting movement. Some gains have been

22. William A. Niskanen, "Why New Methods of Budgetary Choices?—Administrative Aspects," in IIFP, *Nouvelles methodes de choix budgétaires*, p. 97. On the U.S. experience, see also Robert L. Harlow, "On the Decline and Possible Fall of PPBS," *Public Finance Quarterly*, vol. 1 (January 1973), pp. 85–105; Allen Schick, "A Death in the Bureaucracy: The Demise of Federal PPB," *Public Administration Review*, vol. 33 (March/April 1973), pp. 146–56.

made in budget classification, output measurement, and the application of analysis to decisions, and efforts are continuing in several countries, though with diminished enthusiasm.[23]

The term zero-base budgeting (ZBB) is fairly recent, but the idea is old. It is that in drawing up a budget the existing level of expenditures should not be taken for granted but should be critically examined. As applied experimentally in the U.S. Department of Agriculture in 1962, ZBB called for reevaluating every program and requiring that it be freshly justified—from a zero base—instead of concentrating on proposed increases or decreases in spending. The fact that a program had been carried on for many years was not supposed to justify its continuation. Officials, however, were unwilling to follow the approach literally. It proved to be impractical for them to spend the time and energy that would have been required for a full annual reconsideration of all activities and politically unrealistic to reopen old controversies.[24]

A modified version of ZBB was introduced throughout the U.S. federal government in 1977. Essentially, it provided for defining a minimum level for each program—ordinarily below the existing level but above zero—and higher levels, which were to be ranked in descending order of priority. Statements of the objectives of programs and supporting details on program levels were to be presented in "decision packages." A cutoff line would be established, and program levels above it would be approved; if the minimum level fell below the line the program would be eliminated. This system, though less ambitious than program budgeting or the earlier version of ZBB, placed heavy demands for information on the spending departments and, if conscientiously followed, would have absorbed senior officials in justifying programs that were highly unlikely to be cut back or eliminated. It appears to have had little effect on budget decisions.

Applied on a more modest scale, ZBB might have been more constructive. There is merit in the idea of systematically setting out a range of possible reductions and increases for certain spending programs and attempting to establish priorities among them. That, in fact, is a feature of the approach suggested earlier in this chapter. Furthermore, it could be useful to demand a thorough review and fresh justification

23. From the extensive literature on program budgeting, see in addition to the items cited in the preceding footnotes, David Novick, ed., *Program Budgeting: Program Analysis and the Federal Government* (Harvard University Press, 1965); Charles L. Schultze, *The Politics and Economics of Public Spending* (Brookings Institution, 1968); Wildavsky, *Budgeting.*

24. See Wildavsky, *Budgeting*, pp. 278–94.

of many programs, but to do so at intervals of several years rather than trying to reexamine every program each year.[25]

An approach that differs radically from other proposals for reform is the suggestion of Caiden and Wildavsky that developing countries adopt "continuous budgeting."[26] These authors argue that, because developing countries are subject to such a high degree of uncertainty, annual budgets cannot incorporate reliable predictions. They suggest that the annual budget exercise be deemphasized. Departments that wished additions to their authorized spending rates would be allowed to request them at any time during the year. The ministry of finance would evaluate the requests in the light of its current appraisal of available resources and competing demands and would then approve the increase or impose cuts. In a sense, the budget period for each department would be shortened, and its duration would be determined mainly by the department's own decision to request an increase in its spending. More significantly, the effort to evaluate all demands and resources simultaneously would be abandoned.

This suggestion stems from a realistic appreciation of the difficulties of comprehensive budgeting, but it seems to retreat too far from the ideal of rational allocation of scarce resources among alternative uses. Continuous budgeting would repudiate comprehensive planning, would assign greater authority to the ministry of finance, and might well aggravate conflicts between the finance ministry and spending departments. This is not to deny that modifications of the budget within the year are often necessary and that the system should provide for them.

The proposals that have been briefly reviewed here were addressed to real deficiencies, and efforts to put reforms into effect have produced some benefits, though much smaller ones than many persons expected.[27] For the majority of developing countries, the most promising route to budget improvement is not through the introduction of a wholly new system but through the incorporation of some new elements into a

25. See Robert W. Hartman, "Budget Prospects and Process," in Joseph A. Pechman, ed., *Setting National Priorities: The 1978 Budget* (Brookings Institution, 1977), pp. 379–85; Frank D. Draper and Bernard T. Pitsvada, *Zero-Base Budgeting for Public Programs* (University Press of America, 1978), and *A First Year Assessment of Zero-Base Budgeting in the Federal Government—Another View* (Arlington, Va.: Association of Government Accountants, 1978).

26. Caiden and Wildavsky, *Planning and Budgeting in Poor Countries*, pp. 315–22.

27. For a temperate assessment of past reform efforts and future possibilities, see two articles by A. Premchand: "Government Budgetary Reforms: An Overview," *Public Budgeting and Finance*, vol. 1 (Summer 1981), pp. 74–85, and "Government Budget Reforms: Agenda for the 1980s," *Public Budgeting and Finance*, vol. 2 (Autumn 1981), pp. 16–24.

conventional framework. Suggestions along that line are summarized in the concluding section of the chapter.

Some Political Aspects of Budgeting

Budgeting is part of politics; it can never be a purely technical exercise. Most of the literature on budgeting implicitly—or explicitly—assumes the existence of a democratic system with clearly defined and separable responsibilities for the executive and legislative branches of government and an informed public opinion with interested and active voters. (Another approach, more popular with economists than with political scientists, is to imply that a philosopher-king is in charge.) A parliamentary system is visualized by most non-American writers, and some Americans hanker after what they perceive as the surer leadership and greater discipline of a parliamentary system. In fact, such conditions do not exist in the great majority of less developed countries. The political regimes of these countries range from stable, well-ordered democracies through a bewildering array of precarious elected governments, military juntas, and other authoritarian governments with or without legislatures and elections.

It is easy to exaggerate the differences in budgeting between countries with authoritarian regimes and those with democratic governments. The economic uncertainties are identical, and the technical problems are almost the same. Nor can the leader of an authoritarian government disregard the pressures exerted by interest groups and spending agencies, though interest groups may be less well organized in most developing countries than in the industrial world. In 1908 Bentley spelled out the limitations on the power of apparent absolute rulers (despots in his usage).[28] Later history and analysis have underscored his conclusions.[29] In budget formulation a nonelected government operating without a legislature may have to pay close attention to the probable reactions of military leaders, the urban elite, large landowners, university students, and even such seemingly powerless groups as truck drivers and residents of shantytowns.

An intelligent leader of any government, whether he gained office by the ballot box or a coup, will wish to make the best use of the limited

28. Arthur F. Bentley, *The Process of Government: A Study of Social Pressures* (Chicago, 1908; Principia Press, 1935), pp. 313–20.

29. For a recent treatment, see Gabriel A. Almond and G. Bingham Powell, Jr., eds., *Comparative Politics Today: A World View*, 2d ed. (Little, Brown, 1980).

resources that he can command, best being defined as most efficient in advancing the objectives that he considers important. These objectives, no doubt, will include some or all of the economic goals mentioned in chapter 1, and also the continuation in office of himself or his political associates. The process of budget formulation and execution need not, in principle, differ greatly between democratic and authoritarian regimes. Organizational features of budgeting may be affected by the governmental system, however.

In most countries, the budget office is part of the ministry of finance, and the minister of finance is usually the most powerful member of the cabinet after the prime minister. Even in countries in which the cabinet does not function in the traditional way, there are advantages in combining expenditure planning and control with taxation, which is nearly always a responsibility of the ministry of finance. In many countries, however, the minister of finance lacks the prestige and power that traditionally attaches to that office, and he may be bypassed by spending departments and interest groups that go directly to those who are thought to wield real power.

In the United States, the location of the budget office in the Executive Office of the President reflects the political realities of the role of the chief executive and his political advisers in budget formulation. Similarly, the recent decision to move the central budget activities of Nigeria to the Office of the President (though not fully implemented at this writing) is consistent with the constitutional system. The budget director in such an arrangement has power and prestige only as he is seen to be acting for the president and enjoys his support.

In a few countries, such as Italy and the Philippines, the budget office is a separate agency. While that arrangement may respond to national history or politics, it is not conducive to strong leadership in budgeting.

Improvements in Budgeting

The budget can be, and should be, at the center of policy formulation and implementation. In few countries, however, does budgeting fully perform the tasks that it could be expected to discharge. Budgeting is especially difficult in developing countries; its shortcomings are numerous, and the menu of reform proposals is extensive. The sweeping innovations of program budgeting or zero-base budgeting appear unworkable in their complete form, and continuous budgeting would be imprudent, though some features of these proposals can be used. Scarce personnel and limited political capital can best be applied to make a series of improvements in existing budget systems.

In many countries, the campaign should begin with strengthening the budget staff by recruitment and training. The staff does not have to be large, but it should include a group of administrative analysts and economists who devote their full time to budgeting, possibly supplemented by some temporary help during the busiest season.

Strenuous efforts should be exerted to reduce earmarking and the use of extrabudgetary accounts and agencies. Fiscal crises may offer opportunities to do this. Further fragmentation of the budget should be strongly resisted. Where a separate capital budget exists, simplistic interpretations of its macroeconomic significance should be rejected, and efforts should be made to coordinate it closely with the current budget. Where it does not exist, a capital budget need not be established.

Development planning and budgeting are different, though related, activities, and they call for different kinds of expertise. But regular communication and cooperation between budgeters and planners are needed to avoid confusion, waste, and frustrations. Both formal and informal methods can help.

Other elements in a realistic program of budget improvement include establishment of a practicable calendar for the principal phases of budget formulation and execution; classification of expenditures on functional and economic lines, as a supplement to object and organizational classifications; publication of an informative budget document covering the recent past and plans for the coming year; timely statistical reporting of receipts, expenditures, and cash balances, which would free policymakers from dependence solely on traditional accounts; reasonable, but not excessive, flexibility in the execution of the annual budget, including, where needed, a systematic adjustment for inflation; improved medium-term projections that pay particular attention to the recurrent costs of investment projects; and, where feasible, the development of work measures and activity analysis for programs. In most countries, these features should not all be introduced at once but should be added over several years.

The success of such a program depends to a great extent on the quality of political leadership. Ignorant or short-sighted leaders may regard budgeting as unimportant or annoying. Enlightened leaders will recognize the advantages of better budgeting and will encourage it.

Summary

Budgeting serves the purposes of policy formulation, policy implementation, legal control, and public information and political accountability. It is complicated by conflicts between the information and procedural requirements of the functions.

Government finance specialists have stressed the desirability of including in the budget all governmental agencies and all financial transactions. Social security systems are frequently omitted, and in some countries expenditures financed by foreign aid or loans and a part of military expenditures are not included. Earmarking of revenues for particular purposes is widespread.

A good budget document includes text and tables designed to serve the multiple purposes of the budget. Expenditures may be classified by department, object purchased, function, and economic character. A statement of the expected sources of financing of a deficit should be included.

Budget preparation requires decisions on the total size and the composition of expenditures and revenues, reached through repeated adjustments of preliminary estimates. The several steps in the process should be set out in a budget calendar. A practical approach concentrates on changes—usually small changes—in existing expenditure programs and taxation.

Budget execution is the use of spending authority granted by the budget law or decree. Broadly interpreted, it includes commitments, disbursements, reporting, accounting, and auditing.

A number of developing countries maintain separate current and capital budgets. This provides a measure of asset accumulation through government saving, and it may give an accurate picture of the annual cost of programs with large, irregular capital expenditures. The size of outlays in the capital budget, however, should not be regarded as an indication of the government's contribution to growth and development or of the amount that can prudently be borrowed.

Budgeting is a form of planning but is less broad than development or economic planning, which is practiced in some form by many developing countries. Proper coordination of budgeting and planning requires frequent consultations between the budget office and the planning organization, especially with respect to the recurrent costs of investment outlays.

Dissatisfaction with the budget process has stimulated recommendations for reform. Performance budgeting, as advocated by an official U.S.

commission in 1949 and adopted in part, was designed to emphasize outputs rather than financial inputs. In the 1960s and 1970s, program budgeting, which also attempted to shift attention from inputs to results, became the leading reform proposal. Program budgeting was adopted in some form by a number of countries, but the results were disappointing because of difficulties in defining programs, measuring output, and analyzing many alternatives.

A third reform proposal is zero-base budgeting, which requires that all spending programs be reexamined and justified each year. The experience of the United States shows that this procedure places excessive demands on spending departments to supply information and on decisionmakers to scrutinize programs that are unlikely to be curtailed or eliminated.

A radically different proposal, intended to cope with the high degree of uncertainty faced by developing countries, would substitute "continuous budgeting" for annual budgeting. Departments' spending plans would be reevaluated whenever they requested increases, and the effort to examine all demands and resources simultaneously would be abandoned. This proposal would depart too far from the ideal of rational allocation of scarce resources among competing uses.

For the majority of developing countries, the most promising route to budget improvement is through the incorporation of revisions into their existing systems rather than through the adoption of a sweeping reform. A realistic program of budget improvement for a developing country might include, in addition to technical and procedural changes, strengthening the budget staff by recruitment and training of a small group of administrative analysts and economists; efforts to reduce earmarking of revenues and the use of extrabudgetary accounts; and steps to promote communication and cooperation between the budget office and the planning agency.

CHAPTER THREE

Government Expenditures

GOVERNMENT EXPENDITURES are made to carry out the essential functions of administering justice and providing national defense and, in the elastic phrase of Adam Smith, to supply certain additional goods and services that are "advantageous to a great society" but that would not be supplied by private enterprises because doing so would not be profitable.

This chapter examines the nature of government expenditures and the influences that determine them. It also considers the economic effects of expenditures. Benefit-cost analysis, a versatile technique for appraising expenditures, is described as well.

The Nature and Objectives of Expenditures

In trying to understand government expenditures, economists have elaborated the technical concept of public goods and have discussed it at length during the past generation. Public goods—actually, they are nearly always services—are supplied under such conditions that it either is not feasible or would be costly to limit their consumption to people who pay for them, as is normal with other goods. For example, the use of an uncrowded city street or rural road is a public good because costly barriers and tollgates would have to be installed in order to limit access to those who paid for the privilege. This characteristic explains why it usually would not be profitable for an enterprise to supply a public good. In contrast, a loaf of bread is a private good because it can easily be sold to buyers who have the exclusive right to consume it. (Private radio and television broadcasting may seem to be anomalies since listeners or viewers cannot be easily excluded, but the operators are selling another service—advertising—that is available only to paying users.) Public goods have another important characteristic: within limits, use by some persons does not prevent use by others as well. So long as the street or road is not congested, additional travelers do not displace the first users. The nonrival nature of the consumption of public goods means that, within the relevant limits, the cost of accommodating additional consumers is zero. Hence it would serve no social purpose to exclude the additional users even if it were feasible to do so.

The two characteristics of nonexcludability and nonrivalry in consumption make a strong case for the state to supply the service without a price or user charge, *provided* it is socially advantageous to have the service available. These characteristics also account for the great difficulty—or impossibility—of ascertaining the demand for the services, measuring output, and allocating usage among beneficiaries.

The traditional minimum functions of justice and defense fit the technical characteristics of public goods well, and this encourages the idea that the concept can be useful in deciding what additional services the state should provide. But it is hard to think of many examples of pure public goods. Flood control, some public health services, and lighthouses may qualify. The varied expenditures of governments in countries at different stages of development and with different political regimes cannot be accounted for by reference to public goods criteria. Pure public goods, in fact, are a polar case of considerable intellectual interest but infrequent occurrence.[1]

Another approach is purely empirical: observe what governments do, without trying to find any underlying explanation of their expenditures. Or, more idealistically, follow John Stuart Mill in taking an attitude that is more prevalent now than it was when he wrote in the middle of the nineteenth century: "The ends of government are as comprehensive as those of the social union. They consist of all the good, and all the immunity from evil, which the existence of government can be made either directly or indirectly to bestow."[2] These approaches, however, seem to give up too quickly the possibility of reasoned criticism of government programs at a time when the appropriate division of responsibilities between government and the enterprise and household sectors is, or should be, a subject of concern.

1. Writings on public goods, many of them highly technical, are extensive. Most modern public finance textbooks treat the subject. See also Peter O. Steiner, *Public Expenditure Budgeting* (Brookings Institution, 1969), reprinted in Alan S. Blinder and others, *The Economics of Public Finance* (Brookings Institution, 1974); Jesse Burkhead and Jerry Miner, *Public Expenditure* (Aldine, 1971), chaps. 2 and 3; Roland N. McKean, *Public Spending* (McGraw-Hill, 1968); J. G. Head, "Public Goods and Public Policy," *Public Finance/Finances Publiques*, vol. 17, no. 3 (1962), pp. 197–221.

2. *Principles of Political Economy*, ed. W. J. Ashley (London:Longmans, Green, 1929), pp. 804–05 (bk. V, chap. ii, sec. 2).

Government expenditures for goods and services may be thought of as a means of supplying services that decisionmakers desire to have provided in appreciably different quantities or qualities from what enterprises would supply through the market. The services may be called collective goods: most of them have a mixture of the attributes of pure public goods and pure private goods.[3] An important characteristic of collective goods is that the benefits they yield accrue not only to the direct users but also to others. Education, vaccination, waste disposal, and certain forms of transportation are examples. They yield, in technical terms, positive externalities. Hence, even in a well-functioning market the amount supplied would be too little because buyers usually would take account only of the benefits that they could appropriate for themselves and their families and would neglect the benefits accruing to others.

The externality feature has more explanatory value than the public goods concept, but it does not attach to all government activities. In developing countries, many expenditures are undertaken because decision-makers think that the market cannot be relied on to meet important needs of consumers and to serve the growth objective adequately. Expenditures are also made to advance the objectives of equitable distribution and national independence. Without questioning the validity of these objectives, analysts can investigate the effectiveness and efficiency of particular government expenditures. As used here, effectiveness is the capacity to attain an objective, and efficiency is the accomplishment of desired results at minimum cost in resources used and other objectives sacrificed. (Economists often equate efficiency with so-called Pareto optimality—a condition that exists when it is not possible to reallocate resources so as to make someone better off without making another worse off. This concept, however, appears to hold little attraction for political leaders or noneconomist intellectuals; most of them take for granted that governments are legitimately concerned mainly with mulcting or restraining some persons to benefit others.)

Especially in regard to expenditures intended to advance macroeconomic objectives, it is useful to ask whether the instrument is both effective and efficient. Government capital expenditures to foster growth or national independence should be compared with tax incentives, protective import duties, and import controls and with other measures to attract domestic

3. Steiner, *Public Expenditure Budgeting*, p. 7.

and foreign investors and encourage production. To promote stabilization, flexible taxation and credit policies may be superior to variable government spending. And to improve income distribution, different forms of government expenditure may be compared with taxation and nonfiscal actions such as land reform. The choice of the mixture of expenditures, tax provisions, and other measures presents important issues of politics, economics, and administration.

Among government expenditures, the choice of expenditures on goods and services or transfer payments and subsidies is significant. Either may be suitable for influencing income distribution and fostering national economic independence. Many economists would argue that transfer payments and subsidies are preferable for these purposes because they leave the recipients free to make their own choices about what goods they will consume or how they will organize production. This reasoning, however, is not necessarily convincing because political leaders and citizens are not neutral in regard to consumption and production patterns. They may, for example, be willing to provide the poor with free medical care or low-cost housing but unwilling to give them an equivalent amount of money to spend as they like. Within limits, such an attitude—whether paternalistic or altruistic—is not at all unreasonable. It reflects a recognition of what Musgrave calls merit wants, which are considered especially worthy though not technically different from private wants.[4]

Transfer payments are used to a much greater extent in industrial countries than in developing countries. Among the latter, transfer payments are more prominent in Europe and certain Latin American countries than in other areas. The difference appears to be due largely to the size of social security expenditures, which usually consist mainly of transfer payments. Statistics for a recent year are summarized in table 3-1. Although there were wide differences among countries within groups, in only two developing countries (Uruguay and Brazil) did central government expenditures for social security and welfare exceed the average percentage ratio for the industrial countries. None of the developing countries covered in the table had a ratio of transfer payments and subsidies to total expenditures and net lending as high as the average for the industrial countries.

Instead of transfer payments for welfare purposes, a good many

---

4. Richard A. Musgrave, *The Theory of Public Finance: A Study in Public Economy* (McGraw-Hill, 1959), p. 13.

Table 3-1. *Transfer Payments and Subsidies and Social Security
and Welfare Expenditures of Central Governments, around 1980*[a]
Percent of total expenditures and lending less repayments

Country group (number)	Transfer payments and subsidies[b]	Social security and welfare expenditures
Industrial countries (18)	43.4	36.1
Oil exporters (6)	11.3	3.5
Other developing countries		
African (26)	8.5	3.4
Asian (9)	9.2	2.6
European (6)	24.2	18.2
Middle Eastern (5)	17.6	8.1
Western Hemisphere (24)	15.9	12.7

Source: International Monetary Fund, *Government Finance Statistics Yearbook*, vol. 6 (1982).
a. Unweighted arithmetic means of country percentages.
b. Transfer payments and subsidies less transfers to other levels of government and transfers abroad.

developing countries provide subsidies for food and other articles of mass consumption through below-cost pricing by public enterprises or by payments to private enterprises. Subsidies are provided for foodgrains, bread, cooking oil and fats, sugar, tea, kerosene, and liquified petroleum gas. Bus and train fares are often subsidized. Many of these subsidies do not show up in the statistics in table 3-1 because financial relations between public enterprises and the central government are not reported in a way that would reveal them.

Governments of developing countries prefer subsidized prices to direct transfer payments to the needy because the subsidies are much simpler to administer. Perhaps subsidies are thought to involve less permanent commitments than other transfer programs, though the experience of many countries has shown that the reduction or elimination of consumer subsidies is politically difficult or even dangerous. Simplicity is obtained at the cost of nonselectivity; the subsidies usually go to the rich and the poor alike. There may seem to be little risk that a subsidy for coarse bread and other basic foods will stimulate consumption by middle- and high-income classes. Cheap bread, however, may be fed to poultry and livestock. Subsidized sugar may be used to distill spirits. Consumer subsidies often primarily benefit urban residents, who may be better off than the majority of the rural population. Frequently subsidies provided through public enterprises escape normal budget controls and reach excessive levels, placing unforeseen demands on the treasury and the banking system.

Influences on Expenditures

Decisions about government expenditures are the outcome of a political process in which little overt consideration is ordinarily given to economic factors such as those reviewed in the preceding section. The views of political leaders and other policymakers are influential, but they are subject to various pressures and constraints. Demands for government spending may originate with interest groups and may be made more powerful by a process of aggregation that consolidates many expressions of interests into a few alternatives.[5] Although forms differ, articulation and aggregation of interests occur to some extent in all political systems. The representative forms of interest groups vary. In traditional systems, tribal, racial, religious, and occupational groups may be important; in transitional systems, political parties, churches, the military, and the bureaucracy are often leading interest groups; in modern systems, labor unions, trade associations, chambers of commerce, and issue-oriented organizations are likely to be prominent. Demonstrations or riots by groups that form suddenly in response to disappointment or frustration are a vigorous expression of interest that may support the continuance of a popular expenditure program. Interest aggregation may be effected by individual leaders or political parties. In democratic systems, the opinions of unaffiliated citizens may influence certain decisions, but generally organized groups are more influential.

Expenditure demands and responses to them are affected by the structure of the economy and by demographic, sociological, geographic, and technological factors. However, the direction of influence is not always obvious. For example, a large agricultural sector could generate demands for spending on programs to benefit agriculture or could be seen as an indication of a need to encourage industrialization. A demographic factor that could be expected to influence the demand for educational spending is the proportion of the population of school age. An increase in longevity might rationally be expected to stimulate demand for education because of the longer period over which the benefits of schooling would be enjoyed. The growth of the proportion of the aged in the population has been associated with greater spending for social security and health in the developed countries and some higher-income developing countries, but

5. Gabriel A. Almond and G. Bingham Powell, Jr., eds., *Comparative Politics Today: A World View*, 2d ed. (Little, Brown, 1980).

the persistence of the extended family and lower standards of health care may prevent a similar result in other countries. Geographic factors affect demands for government expenditures for irrigation, flood control, and transportation. Among the technological developments that have influenced government expenditures, the spread of automobiles and trucks must have been one of the most important, and changes in military technology have also been significant.[6]

The reaction of political leaders and others to the factors mentioned in the preceding paragraph does not occur in isolation. It is conditioned by the climate of opinion and the economic capacity of the country. A considerable amount of attention has been given to economic capacity as indicated by national income or per capita income, but the significance of prevailing opinions has not been sufficiently stressed. Opinions about the adequacy of government expenditures, like tastes for consumer goods, are influenced by communications that cross national and continental boundaries.

Nurkse called attention to an international demonstration effect that causes people in poor countries to wish to emulate the consumption standards of rich countries. This impels them to consume more and save less than they otherwise would and, in Nurkse's view, is a handicap to countries that are latecomers in economic development, giving rise to tendencies toward inflationary pressure and deficits in the balance of payments.[7] The international demonstration effect applies also to government expenditures. Political leaders of low-income countries today will not have the same attitudes toward spending for education, health, and various economic services that existed in the industrial countries when they were at comparable stages of development. And citizens of the poor countries will be unwilling to accept the standards that existed in the past.

A statistical study by Tait and Heller facilitates international comparisons of expenditures and the forces that appear to influence them.[8] The study covers central government expenditures of some ninety countries, including nearly all the industrial countries and a large number of less developed countries. Most of the data are for 1977.

---

6. See Richard A. Musgrave, *Fiscal Systems* (Yale University Press, 1969), pp. 69–90; Alan A. Tait and Peter S. Heller, *International Comparisons of Government Expenditure*, Occasional Paper 10 (Washington, D.C.: International Monetary Fund, 1982).

7. Ragnar Nurkse, *Problems of Capital Formation in Underdeveloped Countries* (Oxford: Basil Blackwell, 1953), pp. 58–75.

8. *International Comparisons of Government Expenditure.*

By regression analysis, the authors related expenditures in functional and economic categories to variables thought likely to influence them. They tested for differences between countries with high and low per capita income, and where discontinuities were found they reported the results separately for the groups. Expenditures were measured as ratios to gross domestic product (GDP). Although the statistics do not establish norms for expenditures, they are enlightening, and they may suggest areas of study.

The Tait-Heller study was most successful in statistically explaining the expenditure ratio for social security and welfare.[9] This category includes expenditures for social security; other sickness, old age, and disability payments; military and civil government pensions; and other welfare expenditures. The per capita income of the country, the percentage of the population over the age of sixty-five, and the share of the labor force employed in industry were all positive and statistically significant influences. No discontinuity between high-income and low-income countries was discovered, which suggests that the low expenditures for this function in most developing countries reflect mainly demographic and economic factors rather than other social and political forces.

The health expenditure ratio was related positively to the percentage of the population over the age of sixty-five and negatively to the population per hospital bed ($R^2 = 0.62$). The latter factor may indicate only that countries with few hospital beds in relation to their population avoid spending for hospitals and do not substitute other health expenditures.

The ratio of educational expenditures to GDP was less well explained ($R^2 = 0.28$). For low-income countries it was strongly associated with per capita income and also positively associated with the enrollment ratio in secondary schools. Surprisingly, the percentage of the population under the age of fifteen was not a statistically significant influence on the ratio.

Expenditures for roads and other forms of transportation and for communications were positively related to the rate of growth of the urban population and negatively related to both the share of manufacturing and the share of agriculture in GDP ($R^2 = 0.23$). The expenditure

9. The value of R^2 is 0.80, which means that 80 percent of the variance in the ratio was associated with the variables in the regression equation. This is consistent with the hypothesis that the differences among countries were caused by those factors but does not prove that was so.

ratio for housing and community amenities was positively related to per capita income in low-income countries but not in high-income countries ($R^2 = 0.21$).

Expenditures for other economic services and for defense were not well explained by the Tait-Heller study (all R^2s were below 0.20). The defense expenditure ratio varied widely among countries. Israel, Oman, Jordan, Syria, and Iran had ratios to GDP of 10 percent or more in 1977, no doubt influenced by the recent history of war in the region. In contrast, the following countries spent less than 1 percent of their GDP on defense: Bangladesh, Barbados, Mauritius, the Bahamas, Fiji, Mexico, Sri Lanka, Costa Rica, Madagascar, El Salvador, Jamaica, and Nepal.

Wages and salaries are an important and often controversial part of government spending. For sixty-five countries, Tait and Heller found that the ratio of government wage and salary payments to GDP was positively related to the educational expenditure ratio, reflecting the importance of teachers' salaries. Spending on economic services in the fields of mining and manufacturing was also associated with relatively high expenditures for wages and salaries. Wage and salary payments make up a greater share of total government expenditures in developing countries than in industrial countries. If, however, subsidies and transfer payments are excluded from the total, this is no longer true. In 1977 wages and salaries accounted for 38 percent of total expenditures for goods and services and interest in fifty-seven developing countries and for 41 percent of the comparable total in ten developed countries (unweighted arithmetic means of percentages).

The pay of government employees is much higher in relation to average income in the less developed countries than in more developed countries. Nevertheless, government wage rates in less developed countries are lower than in the modern sector as a whole, which of course constitutes a much smaller part of the economy in these countries than in the more developed ones.[10]

Do ideology and the character of the political system have predictable influences on government spending distinguishable from those of the economic, demographic, and other "objective" factors? This question appears to have been little studied in regard to developing countries. A careful study by Pryor, published in 1968, compared public consumption

---

10. Alan A. Tait and Peter S. Heller, "Government Employment and Pay: Some International Comparisons," unpublished paper, International Monetary Fund, 1982.

expenditures (defined as government current expenditures for goods and services and transfer payments) in seven market economies and seven centrally planned economies, all of which are industrial or semi-industrial countries. The author found that the nature of the economic system played a statistically significant role in accounting for differences in public consumption expenditures for education but not in expenditures for defense, welfare, and health.[11] A recent unpublished study by Tait and Heller covering a large number of countries found that neither the degree to which an economic system is socialist nor the nature of the political regime was a statistically significant influence on the size of general government employment.[12] A more limited study of the impact of military regimes and military coups in sixty-six less developed countries reported that the nature of the regime and the occurrence of successful coups were "not very helpful" in predicting military spending.[13]

The Growth of Expenditures

In most countries for which statistics are available for a long span of years, there has been a tendency for government expenditures to grow at faster rates than population and national income. Adolph Wagner, a German economist in the nineteenth century, formulated a "law" of increasing state activity and expenditures that he asserted applied in "progressive" states. Although there is some doubt about Wagner's exact meaning, his generalization can best be interpreted as predicting an increase in the ratio of government expenditures to national income as per capita income rises in the course of industrialization. He attributed this to growing administrative and protective actions of government in response to more complex legal and economic relations and increased urbanization and to rising cultural and welfare expenditures. He apparently considered the latter services luxuries, characterized by income-elastic demand, that is, demand that rises faster than income. Wagner also expected growth in

11. Frederic L. Pryor, *Public Expenditures in Communist and Capitalist Nations* (Irwin, 1968), pp. 285–92, passim. The market economies were the United States, West Germany, Austria, Ireland, Italy, Greece, Yugoslavia; centrally planned economies included Czechoslovakia, East Germany, the USSR, Hungary, Poland, Romania, and Bulgaria.

12. Tait and Heller, "Government Employment and Pay."

13. Gary Zuk and William R. Thompson, "The Post-Coup Military Spending Question: A Pooled Cross-Sectional Time Series Analysis," *American Political Science Review*, vol. 76 (March 1982), pp. 60–74, quotation from p. 71.

public enterprises, but that would not necessarily involve increasing government expenditures in the strict sense.[14]

There have been numerous attempts to test Wagner's law. Although findings differ, they generally confirm the tendency of the share of total government expenditures in national income to rise. This tendency can be seen in the following figures for the ratio of total government expenditures (of all levels of government) to gross national product or gross domestic product (in percent) in five industrial countries in about 1890 and 1970:[15]

	1890	1970
Canada	9	32
France	14	49
Germany	13	32
United Kingdom	9	33
United States	7	30

(The figures for the two dates and the five countries are not strictly comparable because of differences in concepts and coverage.) Some interruptions or reversals of the rising trend have occurred, but for the eighty years as a whole the movement is dramatic. Since total expenditures include transfer payments as well as expenditures for goods and services, the ratios indicate the share of output that is allocated through the budgetary process rather than the share directly used by government, which consists of expenditures for goods and services. The ratios, nevertheless, are an incomplete measure of the extent of state intervention in the

14. Only brief excerpts from Wagner's writing have been translated into English. A convenient German-language summary of his discussion of the law appears in Herbert Timm, "Das Gesetz der wachsenden Staatsausgaben," *Finanzarchiv*, vol. 21 (January 1961), pp. 201–47. A good English-language review can be found in Richard M. Bird, *The Growth of Government Spending in Canada*, Canadian Tax Papers 51 (Toronto: Canadian Tax Foundation, 1970), pp. 69–88; essentially the same material appears in Bird's article, "Wagner's 'Law' of Expanding State Activity," *Public Finance/Finances Publiques*, vol. 26 (1971), pp. 1–26.

15. The sources for the ratios for the earlier year are as follows: for Canada, Bird, *Growth of Government Spending in Canada*, p. 266; for France, Christine Andre and Robert Delorme, "L'évolution de longue période des dépenses publiques en France: 1872–1971," in Horst Claus Recktenwald, ed., *Tendances à long terme du secteur publique/Secular Trends of the Public Sector*, Proceedings of the Thirty-Second Congress of the International Institute of Public Finance, 1976 (Paris: Cujas, 1978), p. 66; for Germany (1891), Musgrave, *Fiscal Systems*, p. 101; for the United Kingdom, Alan T. Peacock and Jack Wiseman, *The Growth of Public Expenditure in the United Kingdom* (Princeton University Press for the National Bureau of Economic Research, 1961), p. 9; and for the United States, Bureau of the Census, *Historical Statistics of the United States, Colonial Times to 1970* (Government Printing Office, 1975), pp. 224–1120. For 1970, all ratios except for France are from Morris Beck, *Government Spending: Trends and Issues* (Praeger, 1981), p. 68; the ratio for France is from Andre and Delorme, "L'évolution de longue période des déspenses publiques en France."

economy since they fail to reflect the influence of regulations affecting production and consumption in other sectors.

Further statistical evidence is provided by Beck's estimates of the income elasticity of government expenditures in constant prices over the period 1950–77 for twelve industrial countries, including the five mentioned above and Austria, Denmark, Finland, Ireland, the Netherlands, Sweden, and Switzerland.[16] The elasticities (measured as the percent increase in government expenditures divided by the percent increase in GDP, both in constant prices) range from 1.4 for the United Kingdom to 2.7 for Sweden; the median value is 1.8.[17]

Wagner's generalization may not be a genuine law in the sense of offering a firm basis for predicting the behavior of individual countries. Among industrial countries, large differences between countries and between periods in the same country can be observed. And it is not clear to what extent developing countries can be expected to follow the same course as the industrial countries. Wagner's law seems to have been intended to apply only to industrial countries, but that does not rule out the possibility of a wider application.

Most of the studies of developing countries that might test Wagner's law are cross-section studies rather than the more relevant time-series (historical) studies. Cross-section studies cover an array of countries at different income levels at one time and have been used to infer the behavior of a single country as its income rises over time. These studies, however, cannot properly separate income from other national characteristics and opinions that influence the growth of government spending.

In one of the best of the few time-series studies of developing countries, covering the late 1950s and 1960s, Enweze found positive income elasticities for total expenditures in thirteen out of fifteen countries and positive elasticities for most of the principal functional categories in the majority of the fifteen countries.[18] A study of Brazil by Mahar and Rezende covering

---

16. Beck, *Government Spending*, p. 68.

17. By analogy with the terminology of tax analysis, it would be preferable to use the term expenditure buoyancy, since expenditures reflect any automatic, or quasi-automatic, responses to income growth and also discretionary changes. To avoid confusion, however, I have followed the practice of other writers and referred to elasticity.

18. Cyril Enweze, "Structure of Public Expenditures in Selected Developing Countries: A Time Series Study," *Manchester School of Economic and Social Studies*, vol. 41 (December 1973), p. 445. Two other time-series studies, showing mixed results, are Irving J. Goffman and Dennis J. Mahar, "The Growth of Public Expenditures in Selected Developing Nations: Six Caribbean Countries, 1940–65," *Public Finance/ Finances Publiques*, vol. 26 (1971), pp. 57–74; and Joseph E. Pluta, "Wagner's Law, Public Sector Patterns, and Growth of Public Enterprises in Taiwan," *Public Finance Quarterly*, vol. 7 (January 1979), pp. 25–46.

a fifty-year period reported that total government expenditures grew at irregular rates from 12.5 percent of GNP in 1920 to 32.2 percent in 1969. All major categories of expenditures grew faster than GNP. Among expenditures for goods and services, consumption expenditures were more elastic than fixed capital outlays.[19]

Historical statistics on government finance are as yet less plentiful for developing countries than for industrial countries. From national income account statistics, however, it is possible to obtain fairly long series on government consumption expenditures in a large number of developing countries. In the majority of these countries, government consumption has been growing faster than GDP. Table 3-2 shows for seventy-five developing countries the annual growth rates of GDP and government consumption (both measured in constant prices) in 1960–70 and 1970–80. Since estimates were not available for all the countries for both periods, there are 134 pairs of observations in the table. Among the 129 cases in which GDP was increasing, government consumption was increasing more rapidly than GDP in 88 cases (68 percent of the total); it was increasing at the same rate or less rapidly in 35 cases (27 percent of the total); and it was decreasing in 6 cases. In the five cases in which GDP was decreasing, government consumption was increasing in three cases and decreasing more rapidly than GDP in two cases.

Although the statistics omit important parts of government expenditures—capital outlays, transfer payments and subsidies, interest payments, and net lending—they shed light on the fiscal problems that many developing countries experienced during the 1960s and 1970s. It seems highly likely that many developing countries will continue to face demands that will cause government expenditures to grow faster than national income. In addition to expenditures for goods and services, transfer payments may well increase as social and economic changes, together with the international demonstration effect, push countries to adopt and expand social security systems. Transfer payments have been an important component of the growth of government spending in industrial countries in recent decades. Although, according to Beck, total government expenditures, measured in constant prices, grew more rapidly than GDP in all of the twelve industrial countries that he studied, government consumption grew less rapidly than GDP in six of the countries.[20]

19. Dennis J. Mahar and Fernando A. Rezende, "The Growth and Pattern of Public Expenditure in Brazil, 1920–69," *Public Finance Quarterly*, vol. 3 (October 1975), pp. 380–99.
20. *Government Spending*, p. 79.

A factor that seems to have contributed to the rise of government expenditures in relation to national income in industrial countries and that may also operate in developing countries in the future is a faster rate of increase in the prices of government purchases than of other prices.[21] This could come about if the productivity of government employees does not grow as rapidly as productivity in other sectors while wages and salaries in both sectors move up in response to increasing productivity in the nongovernmental sector.[22] Whether that is likely to be the case in developing countries is unclear. Although activities such as teaching, general administration, and cultural services lend themselves less easily to mechanization than work in much of the enterprise sector, the use of computers and improved communications and transportation have undoubtedly increased the output of many government employees. The virtual impossibility of accurately measuring productivity in many government activities implies that increases in prices cannot be distinguished from increases in quantities and improvements in quality. In national income and product accounting, no allowance is made for changes in productivity in the government sector, which in effect are considered to be zero.

The growth of government spending, of course, is limited by the capacity to finance it. Often it is asserted that this constraint is more binding in less developed countries than in more developed ones and that total spending in the former is limited by fiscal capacity whereas in the latter countries it responds primarily to demands for services and transfers. Although the generalization appears plausible, it exaggerates the difference between groups of countries. Both the demand for services and the supply of resources affect government expenditures in all countries. Economic and other limitations on taxation, borrowing, and money creation will be discussed in later chapters.

The Distribution of Benefits and the Effects of Expenditures

It would be desirable to have theories about the distribution of the benefits and associated effects of government expenditures parallel to those

---

21. According to Beck, the median ratios of total government expenditures to GDP in twelve industrial countries increased from 21.2 percent to 33.1 percent in current prices between 1950 and 1970 and from 21.2 percent to 29.2 percent in constant 1950 prices (ibid., p. 65).

22. Although other writers have commented on the subject, the hypothesis was stated clearly and fully by William J. Baumol and is often associated with his name. See his article, "Macroeconomics of Unbalanced Growth: The Anatomy of Urban Crisis," *American Economic Review*, vol. 57 (June 1967), pp. 415–26.

Table 3-2. *Annual Growth Rates of Gross Domestic Product and Government Consumption in Seventy-Five Developing Countries, 1960–70 and 1970–80*[a]

Percent

Country[b]	Gross domestic product		Government consumption[c]	
	1960–70	1970–80	1960–70	1970–80
Kampuchea, Democratic	3.1	...	2.6	...
Chad	0.5	−0.2	4.4	−1.7
Ethiopia	4.4	2.0	4.7	3.2
Somalia	1.0	3.4	3.7	10.8
Mali	3.3	4.9	6.2	7.5
Burundi	4.4	2.8	19.2	3.6
Rwanda	2.7	4.1	1.1	14.0
Upper Volta	...	3.5	...	7.3
Zaire	3.4	0.1	8.5	−2.2
Malawi	4.9	6.3	4.6	2.5
Mozambique	4.6	−2.9	6.8	−4.0
India	3.4	3.6	−0.2	4.2
Sierra Leone	...	1.6	...	4.3
Central African Republic	1.9	3.0	2.2	−2.6
Pakistan	6.7	4.7	7.3	4.3
Benin	2.6	3.3	1.7	2.0
Niger	2.9	2.7	2.0	3.0
Madagascar	2.9	0.3	2.7	0.2
Sudan	1.3	4.4	12.1	−4.2
Togo	8.5	3.4	6.7	10.1
Ghana	2.1	−0.1	6.1	0.8
Kenya	6.0	6.5	10.0	9.0
Lesotho	...	7.9	...	15.2
Indonesia	3.9	7.6	0.9	12.9
Yemen Arab Republic	...	9.2	...	10.8
Mauritania	...	1.7	...	15.1
Senegal	2.5	2.5	−0.2	3.0
Angola	4.8	−9.2	9.1	3.0
Liberia	5.1	1.7	5.6	2.8
Honduras	5.3	3.6	5.3	7.6
Zambia	5.0	0.7	11.0	1.4
Bolivia	5.2	4.8	8.9	7.3
El Salvador	5.9	4.1	6.4	6.1
Cameroon	3.7	5.6	6.1	5.8
Thailand	8.4	7.2	9.7	9.2
Philippines	5.1	6.3	5.0	7.2
Nicaragua	7.3	0.9	2.2	9.7
Papua New Guinea	6.5	2.3	6.5	−0.6
Congo, Peoples Republic	2.7	...	5.4	...
Morocco	4.4	5.6	4.4	14.7
Peru	4.9	3.0	6.3	6.2

Table 3-2. *(continued)*

Country[b]	Gross domestic product		Government consumption[c]	
	1960–70	*1970–80*	*1960–70*	*1970–80*
Nigeria	3.1	6.5	10.0	11.3
Jamaica	4.4	– 1.1	8.6	6.7
Guatemala	5.6	5.7	4.7	6.4
Ivory Coast	8.0	6.7	11.8	8.1
Dominican Republic	4.5	6.6	1.9	2.2
Colombia	5.1	5.9	5.5	4.9
Ecuador	...	8.8	...	13.5
Paraguay	4.2	8.6	6.9	5.6
Tunisia	4.7	7.5	5.2	9.5
Syria	...	10.0	...	16.1
Lebanon	4.9	...	5.9	...
Turkey	6.0	5.9	6.7	6.4
Korea, Republic of	8.6	9.5	5.5	8.3
Malaysia	6.5	7.8	7.5	9.9
Costa Rica	6.5	5.8	8.0	5.9
Panama	7.8	4.0	7.8	5.8
Algeria	4.3	7.0	1.5	10.8
Brazil	5.4	8.4	3.5	8.1
Mexico	7.2	5.2	9.5	9.9
Chile	4.5	2.4	4.7	0.9
South Africa	6.3	3.6	7.0	4.9
Portugal	6.2	4.6	7.7	8.7
Argentina	4.2	2.2	1.2	12.1
Yugoslavia	5.8	5.8	0.6	4.6
Uruguay	1.2	3.5	4.4	3.6
Iran	11.3	...	16.0	...
Iraq	6.1	...	8.1	...
Venezuela	6.0	...	6.3	...
Trinidad and Tobago	4.0	...	7.1	...
Greece	6.9	4.9	6.6	6.9
Singapore	8.8	8.5	12.6	6.4
Israel	8.1	4.1	13.8	3.3
Libya	...	2.2	...	21.6
Kuwait	...	2.5	...	12.8

Source: World Bank, *World Development Report 1982* (Oxford University Press, 1982), pp. 112–13, 116–17. Ellipses indicate data are not available.

a. In some cases, rates are for 1961–70 and 1970–79.
b. Countries are listed in ascending order of estimated per capita GNP in 1980.
c. Consumption of all levels of government.

about taxation (to be briefly reviewed in chapter 4). The expenditure side, however, is much less well developed. Lately, more attention has been given to the incidence of expenditures, and quantitative studies have been made, though they are still far fewer than studies of the distribution of taxes. The empirical studies of expenditures have preceded the elaboration of deductive analyses and have stimulated the development of theories on the subject, whereas in the tax field there was a long history of theorizing about incidence and effects before many quantitative studies were done.

Following De Wulf, we may distinguish four ways of looking at the distributional implications of government expenditures: (1) money flow or impact, (2) on whose behalf the expenditures were made, (3) expenditure incidence, and (4) benefit incidence.[23]

The money flow or impact approach accounts for expenditures by attributing them to the recipients of the payments. This is straightforward for transfer payments, but it is not clearly justifiable to regard salaries and wages as benefits to government employees and other purchases as benefits to contractors and their employees and suppliers. This approach is often followed in studies that attempt to allocate benefits among regions or between urban and rural areas. It appears to have some appeal to politicians, who may be as interested in what budget analysts think of as inputs as they are in what the analysts classify as outputs.

Strictly viewed, compensation of government employees and payments to contractors are benefits to them only to the extent that they exceed the amount that the recipients could earn in their next-best employment or business activity. When government purchases are relatively small, when the economy is reasonably competitive, and when favoritism and corruption are avoided, the margin may be narrow except for a few highly specialized persons or items; but absent these conditions, the difference may be great. In many underdeveloped countries, the government is by far the largest employer of university graduates. Some construction firms may work almost exclusively on government contracts. In such cases, the money flow approach has a good deal of validity. Where corruption exists, some persons on the payroll may rarely report for duty and contracts may be padded, and the special benefit element is larger. Only a bold analyst, however, would attempt to quantify precisely the benefits properly attributable to the recipients of government payments for goods and services.

Assignment of benefits to those on whose behalf the expenditures were made is the common-sense approach and the one most often followed in empirical studies. According to this approach, for example, educational expenditures are allocated to the families of pupils and health expenditures to those who receive medical treatment. There are two objections. First,

23. Luc De Wulf, "Incidence of Budgetary Outlays: Where Do We Go From Here?" *Public Finance/ Finances Publiques*, vol. 36 (1981), pp. 55–76.

what is allocated is costs rather than benefits. Conceptually, benefits may be greater or less than the costs incurred, although it may be hard to obtain a separate measure of benefits. (Dissatisfaction with the traditional concentration on measuring inputs rather than outputs is one of the reasons for interest in some of the budget reform proposals discussed in chapter 2.) Second, the approach fails to account adequately for the external benefits of education, health services, and many other activities. Usually no allowance is made for such externalities; sometimes part of the cost is arbitrarily classified as a public good.

Expenditure incidence concerns the effects of government spending on prices, wages, profits, land values, and so on. As already mentioned, government salary scales may set the earnings standard for all university graduates. Even where that is not true, government demand is likely to affect the relative pay of teachers, architects, engineers, accountants, statisticians, and economists. Expenditures to increase agricultural productivity or to support prices of farm products may result in an increase in the value of agricultural land, thus benefiting landowners rather than tenants and farm workers, just as certain taxes may be capitalized in the form of a decrease in land values.

The usual way of conceptualizing benefit incidence is to ask how much beneficiaries would be willing to pay for government services if they had to buy them. But it is hard to answer that question. Most treatments are nonquantitative, abstract, and hedged in by restrictive assumptions. For certain public works projects and a few services, it may be possible to develop plausible estimates of the market value of the output and to attribute it to beneficiaries. Something will be said about that technique in the following section on benefit-cost analysis. It cannot be applied, however, to the administration of justice, to national defense, and to numerous other programs. Even where the technique can be applied, it is subject to criticism. One objection is that market values reflect the existing distribution of purchasing power; hence, their use in a justification of a government activity gives the greatest weight to preferences of the affluent and ignores the objective of a more equitable income distribution. Another criticism is that people's preferences may not be based on experience or good information. A person cannot reliably value schooling, clean water, or an attractive public park if he has never come in contact with them.

Of the four approaches, the first two—money flow and identification of intended beneficiaries—can be followed at present in statistical studies covering a large fraction of government expenditures, despite qualifications of the kind mentioned. The other two approaches—expenditure incidence and benefit incidence—may aid understanding but appear to offer only limited possibilities of quantification.

Almost by definition, there is no clear and uncontroversial way of allocating to individuals the benefits of pure public goods and mixed goods for which externalities are especially significant.[24] Authors of quantitative studies have either omitted these items or have adopted an arbitrary assumption about the distribution of benefits. Among the assumptions are allocation on an equal per capita basis and on the basis of income. These assumptions tell more about attitudes toward the state than about measurable benefits. General public services and defense make up the bulk of the expenditures for which benefits cannot be allocated. In 1977–78 these items represented 18 percent and 14 percent, respectively, of central government expenditures in a large sample of developing countries.[25]

Any attempt to allocate the benefits of all other expenditures comes up against another insurmountable obstacle. It is not possible to say with any certainty what conditions would exist in the absence of the government expenditures. Surely, production, prices, and income would differ greatly from what they now are. For expenditures, there appears to be no suitable parallel to the differential incidence assumption that is commonly adopted in tax studies (see chapter 12). A more feasible and more useful objective is to quantify and allocate the effects of comparatively small increases or decreases of expenditures for various functions.

The findings of statistical studies of benefits of government expenditures and of net budget incidence will be noted in chapter 12.

Benefit-Cost Analysis

Any careful appraisal of an expenditure proposal is a form of benefit-cost analysis. It is preferable, however, to reserve the term for a systematic

24. Theoretical measures have been proposed, but in my judgment they do not yield useful empirical estimates. See Henry Aaron and Martin McGuire, "Public Goods and Income Distribution," *Econometrica*, vol. 38 (November 1970), pp. 907–20; and Shlomo Maital, "Apportionment of Public Goods Benefits to Individuals," *Public Finance/Finances Publiques*, vol. 30 (1975), pp. 397–416.

25. Unweighted arithmetic means of percentages, all developing countries for which the information is given in International Monetary Fund, *Government Finance Statistics Yearbook*, vol. 4 (1980).

and formal evaluation of certain kinds of expenditures. The techniques are particularly suitable for long-lived projects that produce marketable output, that is, goods or services that are sold or that could be sold. Most of the following discussion relates to such applications, but toward the end of the section some remarks will be made on the possibility of extending the method to other expenditures.

Benefit-cost analysis is similar in important respects to the appraisal of an investment by an enterprise but goes beyond financial profitability and attempts to take a broader view of benefits and costs. It appeals to economists because it uses tools with which they are familiar, and they have written extensively on the subject.[26]

Some of the literature implies that the analysis can do more than should be expected of it. It can be an important aid to decisionmaking, but it cannot turn an inherently political process into a purely technical one. Although nonfinancial factors can be introduced into benefit-cost analysis, judgmental elements will remain in the decision process. Efforts to include every conceivable consideration are more likely to discredit benefit-cost analysis than to win general acceptance for it. Another limitation is that the analysis is suitable for relatively small projects but not for projects so large that they would change the whole structure of the economy and bring about entirely new sets of costs and prices. As usually conceived, it would not be applicable to a project such as the high dam at Aswan, Egypt.

The net social benefit of a project is equal to the excess of benefits over costs. For long-lived projects, both benefits and costs will occur over a period of years, and it is necessary to summarize the two streams. This is ordinarily done by estimating the present or discounted value of future benefits and costs:

$$NSB = PV(B - C)$$
$$= \sum_{t=0}^{H} \frac{Bt}{(1 + r)^t} - \sum_{t=0}^{H} \frac{Ct}{(1 + r)^t},$$

where NSB is net social benefit, PV is present value, B is benefits, C is costs, r is the rate of discount, t is time in years, and H is the time horizon.

Benefits and costs must be stated in money terms. If both benefits and

26. See Stephen A. Marglin, *Public Investment Criteria: Benefit-Cost Analysis for Planned Economic Growth* (MIT Press, 1967); I. M. D. Little and J. A. Mirrlees, *Project Appraisal and Planning for Developing Countries* (Basic Books, 1974); Lyn Squire and Herman G. van der Tak, *Economic Analysis of Projects* (Johns Hopkins University Press for the World Bank, 1975); Edward J. Mishan, *Cost-Benefit Analysis*, 2d ed. (Praeger, 1976); and Edward M. Gramlich, *Benefit-Cost Analysis of Government Programs* (Prentice-Hall, 1981).

costs are equally affected by a rise in the general price level, inflation may safely be ignored and the analysis conducted on the assumption of a constant price level. An allowance for inflation should be made if it can be foreseen that the prices for benefits and for costs will be differently affected, but that is rarely possible.

The rest of this section describes the variables in the equation in more detail and discusses how benefit-cost analysis can be used in setting priorities for competing projects.

Benefits

Benefits, broadly viewed, comprise all contributions to the attainment of objectives. In practice, this means the objectives accepted by decision-makers. Benefits from the kind of projects under consideration may include increases in consumable output, improvements in the distribution of welfare among consumers, and gains in the capacity for national independence. The increase in consumable output made possible by a project may be provisionally identified with the increase in net domestic product (gross domestic product minus an allowance for capital consumption). Purely financial benefits, such as increases in land values, are not social benefits and usually are not included in a formal analysis. But they affect the distribution of wealth and may influence the attitudes of political leaders and others toward projects.

Where the service is an input of producers, the usual approach is to estimate the market value of the increase in output that it makes possible. For example, the value of irrigation water is estimated as the market value of additional agricultural output, less the cost of fertilizer, labor, and other inputs. The value of the services of a road might be approximated by estimating the savings of transportation costs for existing movements of travelers and freight and adding an allowance for the amount that users would be willing to pay for moving any additional traffic generated by the road. The first component can be estimated fairly well if data on traffic and vehicle operating costs are available, but valuing the second component is unavoidably speculative.

For various reasons, the market value of the net additional output attributable to a project may be considered inappropriate or subject to adjustment in measuring benefits. One reason, long recognized by economists and linked to the concept of consumers' surplus, is that a large increase in output may result in a fall in the price. In that case, consumers would have been willing to pay close to the old, higher price for part of the additional output, intermediate prices for other parts of the output, and the new market price for the marginal part. Valuing the whole of the additional output at the new, lower price will yield an underestimate. This will not hold for exports or goods that substitute for imports, provided, as is usually so, the production of the developing country is a small fraction of world production and trade; for such goods the market price will not be affected unless direct controls on exports or imports are changed. While such insights are valid, it is not easy to reflect them in estimates of benefits.

Government decisionmakers may wish to adjust or reject the market-value measure of benefits because they have objectives other than increasing output so valued. They may favor projects that generate income that is especially likely to be saved and invested or to contribute to tax revenue. They may value some goods and services more highly than individual consumers do. Possible examples are items that enhance national culture, prestige, or public health. These may be thought of as cases in which collective goods are supplied jointly with ordinary goods. Another possibility is that decisionmakers may attach special importance to goods and services consumed by the poor or by residents of backward areas. Finally, they may wish to encourage production that serves the purposes of national independence or self-sufficiency, for example, goods that substitute for imported food or other essentials. Market values reflect the tastes of individual consumers, which decisionmakers may regard as uninformed or shortsighted, and the existing distribution of purchasing power, which they may consider unjust.

A formal way of taking account of the considerations just recited is to assign numerical weights that will enhance the value of the preferred forms of output. This may be termed the use of shadow prices or accounting prices to substitute for market prices.[27] The formal method appeals to economists but may be repugnant to politicians who dislike its explicitness and who tend to regard national prestige, cultural gains, and some other benefits as unquantifiable. Politicians of this persuasion are inclined to insist that judgment is superior to quantitative methods.

Neither the mechanical application of formal evaluation methods nor reliance on unaided judgment deserves general endorsement. Economists and other experts should try to extend quantification as a means of introducing more objectivity but should avoid discrediting their methods by putting numerical values on a long list of intangibles. A possible extension would be the assignment of distribution weights favoring benefits

27. Squire and van der Tak examine this technique in detail in their *Economic Analysis of Projects.*

to low-income groups (chapter 12). Politicians should recognize that quantification can help them analyze their preferences and make consistent decisions.

So-called secondary benefits, that is, gains associated with the processing of the direct output, are sometimes attributed to a project. For example, irrigation may allow more cotton to be grown. The net value of the raw cotton (gross value minus farmers' production costs other than water charges) is the direct benefit. The value of textiles made from the cotton may be classified as a secondary benefit. But to add secondary benefits of this kind results in double counting and overstates benefits. The value of the cotton reflects its contribution at all stages of production, if cotton is priced in a properly functioning market. While market imperfections exist in less developed countries, benefit-cost analysis should aim at assigning correct prices to the additional output made possible by projects rather than elaborating the misleading idea of secondary benefits. This does not mean that the minor direct benefits of multipurpose projects should be overlooked.

Costs

Costs are basically the negatives of benefits—forgone opportunities. Usually they are valued by the prices paid for inputs, consisting of capital costs and operating costs. (Interest costs and depreciation allowances need not be separately reckoned, as the former are reflected in discounting and capital costs are entered as the outlays are made.) Market prices, however, may be thought to be inaccurate measures of social opportunity costs—the true cost to the society of forgoing other uses of the same resources—and shadow prices or accounting prices may be substituted.[28]

An important item for which a shadow price may be appropriate is labor. The wages actually paid to construction workers are influenced by government practices and custom and may exceed the social opportunity cost of using labor, especially when unemployment or underemployment exists. A lower shadow wage—or conceivably a zero shadow wage—may be substituted for actual wages in the benefit-cost analysis in order to avoid overstating social costs. Caution is advisable, however. Underemployment usually is less pervasive than is often assumed (see chapter 10). To the extent that it exists, underemployment mainly affects unskilled laborers, who are not in as much demand as the skilled or semiskilled workers

28. Treated in detail in Little and Mirrlees, *Project Appraisal and Planning.* See also Squire and van der Tak, *Economic Analysis of Projects,* and the other general expositions of benefit-cost analysis.

needed for projects. Furthermore, workers will consume more if they earn more; this additional consumption absorbs resources and thus increases social opportunity costs.

Shadow pricing may also be applied to the exchange rate used for valuing the cost of imported materials and equipment (as well as the value of output that is exported or that substitutes for imports). Many developing countries maintain overvalued exchange rates, supported by foreign exchange restrictions and direct controls on imports, with informal rationing of imported goods. In such cases, a shadow exchange rate should replace the official exchange rate, resulting in higher figures for the local currency cost of imported components of projects and for the value of certain outputs. (A still better solution would be to change the exchange rate, but that decision is outside the control of expenditure analysts.) Wherever shadow prices are used, they should be centrally determined, ordinarily by the planning agency, to ensure consistency among departments.

Discount Rates

Future benefits and costs must be discounted when a project is being analyzed. Future benefits are less valuable than present benefits, and future costs less onerous than present costs. Traditionally this time preference was regarded as an attitude associated with impatience and the necessity of rewarding abstinence to induce saving. It can also be explained on the grounds that present output (benefits) can be invested and used to produce more goods later, whereas that potential gain is not available with respect to output (benefits) that will only be realized in the future. In financial markets, these factors are reflected in interest charged to borrowers and paid to lenders. Discounting is an established part of project appraisal and figures in negotiations between developing countries and foreign official lenders.

The choice of the actual rate of discount (r in the general formula for calculating net social benefit) has great practical importance in valuing future benefits. Many projects that would appear advantageous if future benefits were not discounted look quite different with discounting.

A high discount rate favors projects that yield benefits quickly, whereas a low discount rate makes projects involving initial high capital costs and benefits extending over a long period more attractive. At a 5 percent discount rate, for example, a stream of benefits of $5 a year for ten years has a present value of $38.61, and a stream of $1 a year for fifty years has a present value of $18.26. At a 10 percent discount rate, the present values of the two streams are $30.72 and $9.91, respectively. At a 5 percent discount rate, the shorter stream is worth 2.11 times the longer one, whereas at a 10 percent discount rate the shorter stream is 3.10 times as valuable.

The selection of a discount rate is a complex and controversial matter. The economic literature is extensive, but much of it is highly abstract and is oriented toward economies with institutions very different from those of most developing countries.[29] Theorists have outlined a set of conditions in which the government's discount rate should be determined by consumers' time preference and the rate of return on enterprise investment. Indications of consumers' time preference would be obtained by observing what rates of interest people receive on their savings and what rates they pay for consumer credit. In an idealized financial market these rates and the rate of return on enterprise investment would be equal at the margin, with allowances for differences in risk and transaction costs and for income taxes. It follows that, regardless of how government investment were financed, it would displace immediate consumption or investment that households and enterprises would voluntarily exchange for future consumption or investment only if they received a premium equal to the rate of interest. Hence, it is concluded that in those circumstances deferred benefits from a government project should be discounted at the market rate of interest.

No one believes that the idealized conditions just described actually exist in any country. There is a wide gap between the rates of interest received by individual savers and the rates payable on consumer credit even in the countries, such as the United States, where consumer credit is most readily available. In developing countries, the rates payable on savings deposits usually are low (often negative in real terms when allowance is made for inflation), and often consumer loans can be obtained only from money lenders at exorbitant interest rates. In all countries, the rates of return on enterprise investments differ widely and are influenced by monopoly elements and other market imperfections. The practical question is whether any useful guidance can be obtained

---

29. In addition to the general references cited in preceding footnotes, see Raymond F. Mikesell, *The Rate of Discount for Evaluating Public Projects* (Washington, D.C.: American Enterprise Institute for Public Policy Research, 1977). This monograph contains an extensive bibliography and a review of previous contributions. Several papers, most of them highly technical, appear in Robert C. Lind and others, *Discounting for Time and Risk in Energy Policy* (Washington, D.C.: Resources for the Future, 1982).

by observing rates of interest and rates of return on enterprise investment; on this, opinions differ.

Instead of seeking to ascertain consumers' preferences, government officials may feel that it is their responsibility to determine a social rate of time preference. In a sense they do that when they embark on programs to increase investment and speed up growth rates. Individuals may be shortsighted, and governments may be justified in applying a low discount rate to future benefits in order to give weight to the interests of future generations. An opposing consideration is that, because of technological progress, future generations are likely to be richer than the present generation and hence to have less urgent needs for consumption. Nor is it clear that governments always take a long view. Some do; the big push toward industrialization in the USSR in the late 1920s and the 1930s imposed heavy sacrifices to increase investment at a time when consumption was low, and ambitious investment programs in a number of less developed countries forty to fifty years later seem to imply a similar low discount rate for future benefits. This attitude, of course, favors investment in both the enterprise sector and the government sector and does not suggest a lower discount rate for government projects than for enterprise investment. But rapid industrialization programs do not necessarily reflect such economic calculations. They may be motivated partly by desires for power and prestige and may be expected to yield short-term political gains. A common complaint against politicians in democratic systems, which may apply also in other regimes, is that they have short time horizons and lack patience in the pursuit of macroeconomic policies. These considerations offer little help in the choice of a discount rate.

Perhaps the best approach for the government of a developing country is to relate its discount rate to its decisions on borrowing and capital subscriptions to nonfinancial public enterprises. The discount rate should be at least as high as the interest rate on external borrowing, provided that the government is borrowing abroad or would like to do so. This rate is significant even for projects financed entirely from domestic sources because forgoing one of these projects presumably would release funds for other projects and thus reduce the need for external borrowing (though domestic and foreign financing are not perfect substitutes; see chapter 8). Moreover, the discount rate for government projects should not be lower than the return that state enterprises could earn on additional capital subscriptions or loans from the treasury. Otherwise, a gain could be realized by shifting resources from government projects to public enterprises. This reasoning applies better to small projects than to large ones whose financing might entail changes in taxation and other government expenditures.

A qualification should be added immediately. Interest rates on loans have come to reflect the expected rate of decrease in the purchasing power of the currency in which they are denominated, owing to inflation. A 12 percent interest rate may reflect, say, a 5 percent real interest rate and (approximately) a 7 percent expected inflation rate. If, as is the usual practice, future benefits are valued in constant prices, the application of a discount rate reflecting expected inflation will produce inconsistent results. To be consistent, the discount rate should be expressed in real terms. But the exact adjustment required to allow for inflation is unknown. Perhaps it is best to err on the side of caution and apply a fairly high real rate. It would be excessively conservative, however, to apply the market rate without adjustment.

The selection of the discount rate for benefit-cost analysis should be treated as the important matter of public policy that it indeed is. A rate should be proposed by the planning department in consultation with spending departments and should be adopted by a high political authority. The decision can be based partly on the objective indicators mentioned above but will also have to rely on judgment. The same discount rate should apply throughout the government. Externalities, distributive equity, and other sociopolitical considerations can be allowed for better in estimates of benefits and costs than by applying a variety of discount rates. A rate that cannot be rigorously justified is better than a zero rate (no discounting) or different rates for different projects. The rate should be reviewed from time to time.

The Time Horizon

The general formula for discounting future benefits and costs includes, in addition to the discount rate, an element H for the time horizon. The time horizon is the extreme limit to which the calculations are carried. Beyond that date any further benefits or costs are considered unforeseeable and are disregarded. The adoption of a time horizon embodies the idea that uncertainties about matters such as tastes, resource availability, and technology increase with the length of the period for which forecasts are made and finally become so great that they overwhelm the foreseeable elements. A time horizon is applicable mainly to long-lived projects such as large dams but may also be pertinent to projects in fields in which technology is changing rapidly. Time horizons appropriately differ among projects. They, in effect, set a limit to the useful life of a project arbitrarily rather than on the basis of presumed physical durability.

Adoption of a time horizon seems preferable to the alternative of raising the discount rate to allow for risk and uncertainty. The latter technique assumes that risk and uncertainty increase at a uniform compound rate over time, which is implausible and which heavily penalizes long-term projects. An approach that may be revealing is to present benefits and costs in ranges rather than as single figures. Combining a low figure for benefits with a high figure for costs will yield a cautious or pessimistic evaluation, whereas the opposite combination will yield an optimistic evaluation.[30] This method, however, can easily produce a very wide range of values for net benefits, and partly for that reason it is unpopular with decisionmakers.

Setting Priorities

Government expenditures are always subject to budget limitations established by political decisions. Although the budget limitation may be relaxed to accommodate good project proposals, it will never be determined solely by the availability of good projects. It cannot be assumed that all projects that withstand benefit-cost analysis will be authorized.

In choosing among projects, the best rule is to try to maximize net social benefits within the limit on expenditures. Projects should be arrayed, including different-sized versions of particular projects, to reveal the group having the greatest present value of net benefits. It might be impracticable to select projects that would exactly exhaust a fixed budget limit, but usually there is some flexibility in the budget limit.

Comparison of ratios of discounted value of benefits to discounted value of costs may appear to be a convenient way of ranking projects. While projects with benefit-cost ratios below 1.0 should be rejected, the projects with the highest ratios are not necessarily the most advantageous. Consider two projects. Project A is estimated to involve benefits of 100 and costs of 50, yielding a benefit-cost ratio of 2.0. Project B is expected to have benefits of 200 and costs of 125, yielding a benefit-cost ratio of 1.6. Although the benefit-cost ratio is lower for B, the absolute amount of net benefit is greater. If the two projects are mutually exclusive (say, two different scales for a dam), it will be better to choose B, provided financing is available.

30. See Little and Mirrlees, *Project Appraisal and Planning*, pp. 131–37, 306–31.

The superiority of B, however, depends on its larger size; for projects of equal size, the one with the highest benefit-cost ratio will always be best.[31]

Another technique that is sometimes recommended for choosing among projects is to select those that are estimated to yield the highest internal rate of return. The internal rate of return is the discount rate that makes expected benefits and cost equal over the time horizon—in other words, the discount rate that reduces net benefits to zero. There are pitfalls, however. Like the benefit-cost ratio, the internal rate of return may be misleading when projects of different sizes are compared. Furthermore, the internal rate of return may favor short-lived projects that yield high returns for a few years over long-lived projects with lower annual rates of return but greater discounted net benefits. The calculations can produce mathematically ambiguous results with multiple solutions.[32]

In addition to the appraisal of physical investment projects, benefit-cost analysis has been used to evaluate other kinds of expenditures and broad expenditure programs. The largest number of empirical estimates relate to the social rate of return on the cost of education.[33] Plausible results also have been obtained for certain research and health programs.[34] An early application was an estimate of the rate of return on the research costs of perfecting hybrid corn (maize). It involved the cumulation of research costs, increased by a rate of interest, the estimation of the value of the additional future production of corn, and the establishment of a rate of return equal to an estimate of the perpetual flow of net social benefits in relation to the accumulated research costs.[35] Although experimentation with such techniques may be informative, probably most developing countries should concentrate at present on the extension and improvement of benefit-cost analysis for conventional projects yielding benefits primarily in the form of marketable output.

31. On ranking methods, see Burkhead and Miner, *Public Expenditure*, pp. 215–24.

32. See Gramlich, *Benefit-Cost Analysis of Government Programs*, pp. 92–93. For tabular methods of calculating present values and internal rates of return, see World Bank, *Compounding and Discounting Tables for Project Evaluation* (Washington, D.C.: World Bank, 1973). This useful publication contains tables for annual interest rates up to 50 percent.

33. George Psacharopoulos, "Returns to Education: An Updated International Comparison," *Comparative Education*, vol. 17 (1981), pp. 321–41.

34. For examples and general discussions, see Robert Dorfman, ed., *Measuring Benefits of Government Investments* (Brookings Institution, 1965); Samuel B. Chase, Jr., ed., *Problems in Public Expenditure Analysis* (Brookings Institution, 1968); and Gramlich, *Benefit-Cost Analysis of Government Programs*. These treatments are all oriented toward the United States but they have methodological value.

35. Zvi Griliches, "Research Costs and Social Returns: Hybrid Corn and Related Innovations," *Journal of Political Economy*, vol. 66 (October 1958), pp. 419–31. These calculations did not take account of an important kind of externality—the benefits from growing hybrid corn outside the United States.

Summary

The concept of public goods, developed as an aid to understanding government expenditures, focuses attention on a polar case in which it is difficult or expensive to exclude users and additional consumers can be supplied at no or very low marginal cost. A more enlightening explanation of spending is that governments tend to supply services that decisionmakers value but think would be insufficiently provided by the market alone. Such services may yield external benefits or may be expected to advance the objectives of growth and development, stability, equitable distribution, or national independence. Transfer payments, which are a preferred means of influencing income distribution in developed countries, are as yet little used in the majority of developing countries. Consumer subsidies through below-cost pricing by public enterprises are a partial substitute but have serious disadvantages. They encourage waste; they usually are not restricted to needy persons; and they frequently escape normal budget controls.

The pattern of government spending is affected by interest groups and by economic, demographic, sociological, geographic, and technological factors. The international demonstration effect induces less developed countries to model their spending after that of more developed countries. Statistical studies shed some light on the particular factors that seem to influence expenditures for various functions and economic categories but do not fully explain them.

In most countries for which statistics are available, government expenditures have tended to grow at a faster rate than national income, in accordance with the usual interpretation of Wagner's law. Several factors related to the demand for government services, their cost, and fiscal capacity presumably account for this phenomenon.

Theories and statistics on the distribution of benefits and the effects of government expenditures are much less well developed than theories of tax incidence and estimates of the distribution of the tax load. Available estimates relate to money flow or the allocation of costs to intended beneficiaries. The studies do not deal adequately with the effect of externalities, the impact on prices and income shares, the distinction between benefits and costs, and the differences between intended and actual beneficiaries. Expenditures for general government and defense, equal to about one-third of total expenditures in developing countries, have to be omitted from statistical studies or arbitrarily allocated.

Benefit-cost analysis is useful for designing projects that yield marketable output and selecting among them. Despite many uncertainties that surround it, the analysis has the great merit of forcing more systematic consideration of project proposals and is likely to cause some of the poorest ones to be dropped. The methods may also be of some assistance in evaluating certain nonproject expenditures. Formal analysis, however, is only one input into the political process of reaching decisions on government expenditures.

CHAPTER FOUR

Taxation: A General Discussion

A TAX is a compulsory contribution to government made without reference to a particular benefit received by the taxpayer. These characteristics distinguish it from a price, which is a voluntary payment for a good or service. The distinction is politically and economically important. The absence of a perceived direct benefit causes taxation to be regarded as burdensome in a way that prices are not, even by persons who recognize that the state provides benefits for the community and who approve its policies. Generally, the amount of tax paid by a person will not affect the benefits that he receives individually, and it will be too small to have an appreciable effect on total benefits. Hence, an individual could rationally, if selfishly, advocate reducing his own taxes even though he wished government services to be maintained or expanded.

This chapter discusses the purposes of taxation, principles of tax design, shifting and incidence of taxes, taxable capacity and tax effort, the relation between the tax structure and the stage of development, tax elasticity, and limits to taxation. It will be followed by three chapters dealing with the main forms of taxation.

The Purposes of Taxation

The primary purpose of taxation is to divert control of economic resources from taxpayers to the state for its own use or transfer to others. Taxation not only restrains total spending by households and enterprises but influences the allocation of economic resources, recognizes social costs that are not reflected in market prices, and affects the distribution of income and wealth.

Taxes are usually paid in money and represent a forced surrender of purchasing power. Exceptionally, however, they are collected in kind, as were agricultural taxes in Japan and Korea immediately after World War II and as are taxes on oil companies in a number of producing countries. Governments also make nonmonetary exactions that resemble taxes when they require services to be performed or goods to be delivered for less than full compensation. Examples are compulsory military service, below-market procurement prices set by an official marketing board for agricultural crops, and compulsory surrender of foreign exchange to the central bank at an unfavorable rate.

The functions of taxation are most clearly seen in relation to direct taxes, which are assessed on income or property with the expectation that the persons from whom the tax is collected will be the ones who actually lose purchasing power. Indirect taxes, including excises, customs duties, and sales taxes, are collected from producers or sellers in the expectation that they will be passed on to consumers. These taxes divert purchasing power from final consumers by driving a wedge between the sum of the payments to producers and distributors and the price. In practice, expectations about who will pay are not always realized, and the difference between direct and indirect taxes is less sharp than the definitions indicate.

Taxation is necessary because it would be neither feasible nor desirable to finance government solely by charges for services. For public goods, charges for services are infeasible, and for mixed public-private goods, they are undesirable because pricing could not perform all the allocative and distributive functions of taxation. Nevertheless, there are economic and political constraints on taxation, and it is prudent to consider the possibility of charging prices for goods and services provided by the public sector wherever there are no compelling policy or practical objections to doing so.

Principles of Tax Design

There are three major principles of tax design: equity, efficiency, and administrative feasibility. The principle of equity requires that taxation conform to the community's sense of fairness. Economic efficiency, as used here, means that taxation should not impose avoidable real costs on the community; it should not unnecessarily interfere with the attainment of the prime economic objectives of growth, stability, equitable distribution, and independence and if feasible should promote them. Administrative feasibility implies that revenue is collected without excessive costs for the government or for taxpayers.

Although the principles are widely accepted in general terms, differences of opinion and conflicting interests affect their specific interpretation and application. Particular measures may be both praised and condemned by appeal to the general principles.[1] Furthermore, inconsistencies or competition between the principles may occur. Preoccupation with equity may lead to harmful economic effects and excessive costs of administration and compliance. Attempts to promote growth and economic independence may result in unfairness. Giving priority to administrative feasibility may cause the rejection of innovations that would improve equity and economic efficiency. As in other areas, tradeoffs or compromises are necessary in designing a tax system. The principles, nevertheless, offer a needed framework for organizing analysis and arguments.

In some less developed countries preeminence is given to raising adequate amounts of revenue. This approach stresses the use of available "tax handles"—opportunities to obtain revenue with relative ease—by concentrating on import and export duties and traditional excise taxes. In substance, it emphasizes administrative feasibility with some admixture of political expediency. It is less pragmatic than it may appear, however, because other concerns are neglected and because revenue needs might be better served by an elastic tax system including some nontraditional taxes.

The principle of equity will be examined in the next section. Economic efficiency and administrative feasibility will figure in the discussion of other general themes and in later chapters on the major forms of taxation.

Equity

Although specific beliefs about fairness in taxation differ among countries and social and economic classes, some general propositions seem to be widely accepted. A fundamental one is that persons who are similarly situated should be taxed equally and those who are differently situated in relevant respects may be taxed differently. To be fair, taxes should be imposed according to general and objective rules that are recognized as reasonable and just. The amount of taxes to be paid should be certain and should not be set by negotiation or arbitrary exaction.

A standard of equity that has long been discussed is the benefit principle. Taxes are justifiable because the state provides benefits. This, however, is

1. On "conflict and harmony" in taxation, see Roy Blough, *The Federal Taxing Process* (Prentice-Hall, 1952), pp. 3–16; on "consensus and conflict criteria," Carl S. Shoup, *Public Finance* (Aldine, 1969), pp. 21–47.

a broad rationalization of taxation rather than a guide for its allocation among individuals. The benefit theory may underlie a widely accepted rule of tax jurisdiction—a state may tax only residents or citizens or transactions that have a direct connection with its territory and that thus benefit from its protection. Possibly, however, a more realistic interpretation is that states can in practice collect taxes only when they have some control over the taxpayers or the transactions. Within a country, the benefit principle may be applied on a regional or sectoral basis to justify taxing groups who receive identifiable services from government.

For allocation among individuals, the benefit theory has limited application to certain taxes, such as gasoline taxes, the proceeds of which are used to provide special benefits to the taxpayers in at least rough proportion to the amount they pay. But it breaks down as a general principle. A technical reason is that individuals cannot be induced to reveal their true evaluation of the benefits they gain from public goods and mixed goods. More basically, government cannot be limited to actions that receive unanimous approval or at least the consent of all those directly affected. Government involves compulsion—actual or potential coercion. Political leaders who undertook to tax people in accordance with the benefits they derive from the state would encounter an old conundrum: Who benefits most, the rich and powerful whose possessions are protected, or the poor and weak who would otherwise be the victims of the strong and their own poverty?

Ability to pay has more appeal as a principle of tax equity. It implies that those with equal abilities to support government should pay equal amounts and that those with unequal abilities should pay different amounts bearing a reasonable relation to their abilities. The former aspect is often called horizontal equity, the latter, vertical equity.

Ability to pay is primarily a matter of economic capacity. That can be measured by income, wealth, or consumption. The merits of these measures are discussed in later chapters on the principal forms of taxation. Taxpaying ability is affected also by a person's needs. Needs may be recognized by personal exemptions, allowances for dependents, and other adjustments of direct taxes and by selectivity in indirect taxes.

The ability-to-pay principle could be implemented by imposing taxes that are proportional to the agreed measure. For simplicity, the measure of ability may be called the base, though in strict usage the base of an indirect tax is the object or transaction that is taxed. Thus if income is the accepted measure or tax base, a person with twice as much income as another would pay twice as much in taxes. Usually, however, ability to pay is thought to increase more rapidly than the base and progressive tax rates are considered fair. With progressive rates, the person with twice as much income will pay more than twice as much in taxes.

Although contrary to the ability-to-pay principle, regressive taxation—which increases less rapidly than the base and thus constitutes a larger percentage of the base for the poor than for the rich—characterizes many taxes and entire tax systems. Indirect taxes, which are a major revenue source in developing countries, tend to be regressive with respect to income for two reasons. First, total consumption expenditures of households are a declining fraction of income for successively higher income classes.[2] Second, expenditures on some heavily taxed items such as tobacco and beer often are a declining fraction of total consumption as income rises. However, careful selection of objects of indirect taxation and tax rates can result in a distribution of indirect taxes that is broadly proportional or progressive with respect to income or total consumption. A pronounced degree of progressivity can be obtained only by direct taxes and in practice has seldom been achieved.

There have been many lengthy discussions of the reasons for accepting tax progressivity and of the appropriate degree of progressivity. Three justifications for progressivity may be succinctly stated. First, a minimum standard of living should be free of taxation, partly for humane reasons and partly because infringement on it will impair people's capacity to work. The exemption of a minimum amount of income or consumption will necessarily imply some progression because the amount of tax will increase faster than the base even if the rate on the taxable part is uniform. But this implies only a mild degree of progressivity.

Second, the satisfactions from successive units of income, wealth, or consumption diminish as the number of units a person has increases. From the late nineteenth century, this generalization was known as the principle of diminishing marginal utility. Elaborate theorizing about it and the implications for tax progressivity was carried out, but this fell into disfavor by the 1930s. The hedonistic psychology on which the theory was based came to be considered naive and the satisfactions enjoyed by individuals not cardinally measurable and comparable. Lately, there has been some reaction against these views, but the earlier theorizing on progressive taxation has not been rehabilitated. Actually, the idea of progressive taxation does not depend on economic theory but on a social or political

2. There is dispute about this generalization. See chapter 10.

judgment about the importance of successive increments of income, wealth, or consumption.

A third, and related, justification of tax progressivity is that reduced inequality is politically and ethically desirable in itself. Some combination of the three justifications underlies the widely accepted, though vague, objective of equitable distribution.

Shifting and Incidence

A tax is said to be shifted when the enterprise or person who originally pays it passes it forward to buyers or backward to suppliers of goods and services used in the production process. The incidence of the tax is the place at which it comes to rest. Indirect taxes in the form of excises, customs duties, and sales taxes are expected to be shifted forward to consumers because they are, for producers and distributors, an additional cost of doing business. In contrast, a direct tax on income and profits usually is assumed not to be shifted because it represents a share of the difference between costs and prices rather than an additional cost. Producers no doubt would wish to shift forward the income tax but may not be able to do so. Whereas the amount of indirect tax per unit sold is uniform, the amount of income or profits tax per unit depends on the profitability of the producer; any attempt to raise prices to recoup the income tax would involve differing increases and might cause the most profitable firms to lose sales to others.[3]

These generalizations need some explanation and are subject to qualifications. Tax shifting results from market forces and is constrained by them. This does not mean that it is a quasi-mechanical process involving no volition on the part of producers; rather, shifting results from producers' decisions that are shaped by market forces. The imposition of a new excise tax usually will bring about a prompt increase in prices. If prices did not rise, production or importation of the taxed goods would become unremunerative and would decline, causing a price increase. If, as sometimes

---

3. Shifting and incidence are covered in all introductory public finance textbooks. For more advanced treatments, which nonetheless lack consideration of the special conditions of developing countries, see George F. Break, "The Incidence and Economic Effects of Taxation," in *The Economics of Public Finance* (Brookings Institution, 1974), pp. 119–237; Richard A. Musgrave, *The Theory of Public Finance: A Study in Public Economy* (McGraw-Hill, 1959), pp. 205–401; Anthony B. Atkinson and Joseph E. Stiglitz, *Lectures on Public Economics* (London: McGraw-Hill, 1980), pp. 23–226.

happens, the initial price rise exceeds the amount of the tax, prices can be expected to fall later or to rise less rapidly than they otherwise would.

Basically, tax shifting occurs because those engaged in the production and distribution of the taxed items will withdraw from these activities rather than absorb the tax, while buyers will pay higher prices rather than do without the taxed goods or services. In more formal terms, these conditions indicate that supply is somewhat elastic whereas demand is somewhat inelastic. The greater the elasticity of supply and the less the elasticity of demand, the greater is the degree of tax shifting.

Those who withdraw from a taxed activity need not become idle; more likely, they will move to an untaxed or less taxed field. A tax on beer, for example, may cause bottlers to produce less beer and more soft drinks, or a tax on the sale of agricultural commodities may cause farmers to retain more of their output for home consumption or barter. Generally, the more specialized are the land, capital equipment, and labor employed in the production of the taxed items—and hence the wider the margin between their earnings in their customary uses and their next-best opportunities—the less elastic is the supply and the greater is the probability that producers will have to absorb part of a tax.

Other things being equal, a tax of narrow coverage will leave open many untaxed alternatives, and this will make withdrawal from the field easy and thus facilitate forward shifting. But narrow coverage also makes it easy for consumers to find substitutes, which results in an elastic demand and difficulty in shifting. The outcome could be the disappearance of a taxed item. For example, a tax on large cigarettes that did not apply to small cigarettes might well eliminate large cigarettes, because producers or importers could easily switch to small cigarettes and consumers would buy small cigarettes rather than pay more for large ones. Both supply and demand are more elastic in the long run than in the short run because producers and consumers have time to adjust their behavior and because new enterprises and households enter the market.

The presumption that an excise tax is more easily shifted than an income tax is due partly to the tacit assumption that the latter applies to income from all sources whereas the excise tax strikes a fairly narrow range of activities. An income tax on profits from a single product would be shifted because enterprises would produce less of that item and more of others, over time if not immediately.

The usual theory of tax shifting applies to taxes yielding amounts that are small in relation to national income. For a broad sales tax of large yield to be shifted forward in higher prices, an increase in the quantity of money usually will be required. Ordinarily it is assumed without discussion that the central bank will allow the increase to occur, but the significance of this assumption should not be overlooked. Absent such accommodation, the sales tax would result in some combination of an increase in the velocity of circulation of money and a compression of producers' and distributors' profit margins with some backward shifting to workers and others.

Sometimes it is asserted that the theories of tax shifting, while possibly applicable to industrial countries, have little relevance for less developed countries. The agricultural sectors of the latter countries are said to be tradition-bound, with farmers ill informed about opportunities and insensitive to market incentives. In the nonagricultural sector, market imperfections, including the absence of vigorous competition, are said to make forward shifting of all taxes easy and, indeed, to allow taxes to be passed on to consumers with a markup (sometimes called pyramiding).

Granted that tax shifting does not always occur in exactly the way visualized by theorists or government officials, these criticisms are overdrawn. Many studies as well as casual observations indicate that farmers and others in developing countries are often better informed and nearly always are more responsive to economic incentives than those who adopt the rather supercilious attitude toward them suppose. Further comments on this important question will be made in later chapters.

For various reasons, including the small size of the market in many developing countries and government restrictions on imports, competition in the pricing of manufactured goods is often weak. This may occasionally allow a degree of tax pyramiding to occur, but it does not upset the generalizations set out in the preceding paragraphs. The theories apply to monopolistic or quasi-monopolistic conditions as well as to competitive markets, provided producers and distributors act to maximize their profits and are reasonably alert to opportunities of doing so.

Two conditions that tend to be more important in developing countries than in industrial countries and that have a bearing on tax shifting are the larger size of the nonmarket or nonmonetized sector and the greater prevalence of small firms engaged in handicraft production and retailing. As already mentioned, taxes on market transactions can sometimes be avoided by diverting activities to subsistence production or barter. While such reactions are not unknown in industrial countries, the scope for them is greater in developing countries. Price increases in the market sector may be heightened, and tax yields may suffer. The difficulty of taxing small firms, which often results in either their exemption or evasion of taxes, can limit the possibilities of tax shifting by larger firms because of the risk of losing sales to the small firms.

The effect of international trade on tax shifting must also be considered. In general, it may be assumed that the supply of imported goods is almost perfectly elastic to any one developing country, that is, within broad limits the price is not affected by the quantity imported and foreign suppliers will turn to other markets if offered less than the prevailing price. That means that, regardless of the elasticity of demand, a tax on imports will be borne entirely by enterprises or consumers in the importing country. If imports are limited by direct controls or exchange restrictions and there is no consumer rationing or effective price control at the retail level—a not unusual set of conditions in developing countries—a tax on imports may be absorbed largely by importers and distributors. In that case, it is likely to be progressive in relation to income.

With regard to exports, it may be assumed that in many cases the foreign demand for the goods of any one developing country is almost perfectly elastic because alternative sources of supply are open to foreign buyers. In those conditions, any tax on exports will have to be borne by producers in the exporting country. Where the exporting country accounts for a considerable part of world production of a commodity, demand for its exports will be less elastic, and this can have a bearing on the incidence of a tax on production or exports. This subject will be discussed in chapter 7.

International movements of capital and labor also affect tax shifting and incidence. Governments of developing countries are fully aware that their taxes may influence the inflow of capital from abroad. They tend to be less sensitive to the possibility that taxes on income and profits can induce residents to invest abroad, thus curtailing the amount of capital available in the taxing country and pushing up profit and interest rates. Controls on capital exports may inhibit capital outflow but do not wholly prevent it. A tax withheld from interest payments to foreign lenders usually will cause an increase in the rate payable by domestic borrowers to cover the tax, because the supply of loans from abroad is perfectly elastic or virtually so. Although people are less mobile than capital, a small number of technical experts and managers have long been able to negotiate tax exemption or reimbursement for income taxes as an inducement to come to developing countries. Many professional persons and skilled workers are ready to migrate to foreign countries where earnings are higher. Taxation, of course, is one factor determining net earnings, and differences in taxation can influence migration and hence labor supply and salary and wage rates.

Another international aspect of taxation that has been neglected in the public finance literature, though not in international trade theory, is the significance for tax shifting and incidence of changes in the foreign exchange value of the currency. Something will be said about that in chapter 6.

Taxable Capacity and Tax Effort

The level of taxation is customarily measured by the ratio of tax revenue to gross national product (GNP) or gross domestic product (GDP), which for brevity may be called simply the tax ratio. The tax ratio is determined by the demand for government expenditures, as influenced by factors discussed in chapter 3; the availability and willingness to use nontax sources of finance, including borrowing and money creation; and the taxable capacity of the country. Taxable capacity depends on the ability of people to pay and the ability of the government to collect. Tax effort is the degree to which taxable capacity is used.[4]

An appreciation of taxable capacity and tax effort can assist a government in formulating policy and aid donors and foreign lenders in appraising the government's performance. While the factors affecting taxable capacity cannot be precisely measured and evaluated, the idea is essentially quantitative, and numerical estimates, however rough, give a concrete basis for discussion and debate. Once taxable capacity has been quantified, tax effort can be measured.

The first element in taxable capacity, people's ability to pay taxes, seems to depend primarily on their per capita income or possibly per capita income in excess of the subsistence level. The ability of the government to collect taxes depends largely on administrative effectiveness as determined by the number, skills, and dedication of the revenue staff and the cooperativeness of taxpayers as influenced by social and political attitudes. These intangible factors do not lend themselves to quantification. Statistical studies, therefore, have concentrated on tax handles, that is, objects of

4. Compare Raja J. Chelliah, "Trends in Taxation in Developing Countries," *International Monetary Fund Staff Papers*, vol. 18 (July 1971), pp. 292–93.

taxation or economic sectors that can be reached with relative ease. Tax handles include international trade, mineral production, and transactions of large enterprises. By hypothesis, taxable capacity is positively related to the shares of these items in GDP and negatively related to the shares of agricultural production and transactions of small enterprises. Another variable that may have a bearing on the feasibility of collecting taxes is the extent to which transactions and income arise in the monetized sector as distinguished from the subsistence and barter sectors.

A series of studies at the International Monetary Fund have investigated the statistical relationship between the variables and actual tax ratios in developing countries.[5] The actual tax ratio, of course, reflects both taxable capacity and tax effort. If the variables that affect taxable capacity but not tax effort could be isolated, taxable capacity could be estimated as either an absolute amount of tax revenue or a tax ratio. The residual difference between estimated taxable capacity and actual revenue or tax ratio would provide a measure of tax effort. This would be equivalent to assuming that taxable capacity is measured by the revenue or tax ratio obtained when a country uses its tax bases with the average degree of intensity.[6]

There are difficulties, however. Perhaps the most serious one is that some of the variables probably affect both taxable capacity and tax effort. For example, per capita income may reasonably be viewed as a determinant of taxable capacity, but equally as an influence on the demand for government service and, indirectly, the willingness to tax. This difficulty could be circumvented if it could be assumed that, in developing countries, *on the average* the amount of taxation is set by governments' judgments of taxable capacity rather than by the (greater) demand for expenditures. As chapter 3 notes, this proposition may appear plausible, but it seems more likely that actual tax ratios respond to influences from both sides, just as prices are determined by both supply and demand. A second difficulty is that the residual differences between estimated taxable capacity and the actual tax ratio comprise errors of estimation as well as differences

5. Jorgen R. Lotz and Elliott R. Morss, "Measuring 'Tax Effort' in Developing Countries," International Monetary Fund *Staff Papers*, vol. 14 (November 1967), pp. 478–99; Lotz and Morss, "A Theory of Tax Level Determinants for Developing Countries," *Economic Development and Cultural Change*, vol. 18 (April 1970), pp. 328–41; Chelliah, "Trends in Taxation in Developing Countries," pp. 254–331; Roy W. Bahl, "A Regression Approach to Tax Effort and Tax Ratio Analysis," International Monetary Fund *Staff Papers*, vol. 18 (November 1971), pp. 570–612; Raja J. Chelliah, Hessel J. Baas, and Margaret R. Kelly, "Tax Ratios and Tax Effort in Developing Countries, 1969–71," International Monetary Fund *Staff Papers*, vol. 22 (March 1975), pp. 187–205; and Alan A. Tait, Wilfrid L. M. Grätz, and Barry J. Eichengreen, "International Comparisons of Taxation for Selected Developing Countries, 1972–76," International Monetary Fund *Staff Papers*, vol. 26 (March 1979), pp. 123–56.

6. Bahl, "A Regression Approach to Tax Effort and Tax Ratio Analysis," pp. 571–73.

in tax effort. There is no way of exactly separating these components, though qualitative considerations may be helpful. Finally, there are the common difficulties of obtaining reliable data, of possible interrelations (collinearity) between the independent variables, and of biases in the statistical techniques.

The undeniably formidable nature of the difficulties has prompted caution in the interpretation of tax effort analysis but has not caused its abandonment. Ministers as well as outside experts are interested in comparisons of the weight of taxation in different countries. Tax effort analysis represents an attempt to go beyond simple comparisons of tax ratios (which may be regarded as a rudimentary way of recognizing differences in taxable capacity) to a comparison that takes account of measurable variables that significantly affect taxable capacity. The authors of a recent study propose that the neutral term "international tax comparison" be substituted for tax effort in order to lessen the risk of misinterpretation.[7]

The findings of the IMF staff studies, which will be summarized in general here, relate the tax ratio to some combinations of per capita income; the openness of the economy as measured by the relative size of foreign trade; and economic structure, particularly the relative sizes of agriculture and mining.[8]

When both more developed and less developed countries are taken together, per capita income is found to be positively related to the tax ratio and statistically significant. This variable and a measure of openness explain a large fraction of the variance of the tax ratio ($R^2 = 0.61$ for a sample of seventy-two countries). However, when the developing countries are studied as a separate group, the influence of per capita income becomes doubtful. It appears that the result for all countries is dominated by the fact that tax ratios are generally higher in developed countries than in less developed countries, though the relationship between per capita income and the tax ratio within each of the two groups is weak. Per capita income, nevertheless, has strong intuitive appeal as a determinant of taxable

---

7. Tait, Grätz, and Eichengreen, "International Comparisons of Taxation," p. 126.

8. For studies other than those of the IMF, see Jeffrey G. Williamson, "Public Expenditure and Revenue: An International Comparison," *Manchester School of Economic and Social Studies*, vol. 29 (January 1961), pp. 43–56; Harley H. Hinrichs, "Determinants of Government Revenue Shares among Less Developed Countries," *Economic Journal*, vol. 75 (September 1965), pp. 546–56; Hinrichs, *A General Theory of Tax Structure Change during Economic Development* (Harvard University Law School, 1966), pp. 7–31; Richard S. Thorn, "The Evolution of Public Finances during Economic Development," *Manchester School of Economic and Social Studies*, vol. 35 (January 1967), pp. 19–53; and Kilman Shin, "International Differences in Tax Ratio," *Review of Economics and Statistics*, vol. 51 (May 1969), pp. 213–20.

capacity, and there has been a tendency to retain it in the estimating equations despite its failure to pass the usual tests of statistical significance.

Foreign trade offers a tax handle that has long been used to extract revenue. Measured usually as the ratio of the sum of exports and imports to GNP or GDP, it is positively related to the tax ratio and is statistically significant by customary standards in most formulations.

Mining is another tax handle, owing to a combination of factors: mineral deposits belong to the sovereign in many countries; mining generates economic rent; and frequently it is carried on by large-scale foreign enterprises. The IMF studies confirm that the share of mining (including petroleum production) in GDP is positively related to the tax ratio and is statistically significant.

Agriculture, on the other hand, is notoriously hard to tax, for administrative and technical reasons and in some countries because of political sensitivities. In most formulations, the share of agriculture has the expected negative relationship to the tax ratio, but the coefficient is not always statistically significant.

There is some evidence that, as expected, the degree of monetization may be positively related to the tax ratio, but difficulties in measurement and in distinguishing the influence of this variable from that of per capita income have caused monetization to be dropped from recent studies.

For a sample of sixty-three developing countries in 1972–76, various equations including the economic variables mentioned above statistically explain about two-fifths to three-fifths of the variance in tax ratios. While these figures may seem low, they are impressive in the light of the complexity of forces that bear on taxation and the results obtained in other studies of economic and political behavior.[9]

9. Three equations fitted by Tait, Grätz, and Eichengreen give the following results for sixty-three developing countries, 1972–76:

$$T/Y = 7.1134 + 0.0024(Y_p - X_p) + 0.5700N_y + 0.2218X_y'$$
$$ (4.82) \quad\ (0.94) (9.31) (4.17)$$
$$\overline{R}^2 = 0.581$$

$$T/Y = 7.3663 + 0.003(Y_p - X_p) + 0.3025X_y$$
$$ (4.41) \quad\ (0.94) (6.19)$$
$$\overline{R}^2 = 0.375$$

$$T/Y = 9.1859 + 0.3550N_y - 0.0240A_y + 0.1903X_y$$
$$ (4.88) \quad\ (5.51) (-0.61) (4.30)$$
$$\overline{R}^2 = 0.593$$

where T/Y is the tax ratio, excluding social security taxes, in percent; Y_p is per capita GNP in U.S. dollars; $(Y_p - X_p)$ is per capita nonexport income in U.S. dollars; N_y is the share of mining (including petroleum) in GDP; X_y is the export ratio; X_y' is the export ratio excluding mineral exports; and A_y is the share of agriculture in GDP. The figures in parentheses are the ratios of the regression coefficients to their standard

By comparing estimated tax ratios with actual ratios, indexes of tax effort or international tax comparison indexes have been calculated. Although the numerical value of the indexes is sensitive to the choice of estimating equation, the sample selected, and the time period covered, the ranking of countries is generally similar. If countries are divided into three groups—those with low, medium, and high indexes—this grouping proves to be stable regardless of the method of deriving the indexes. Table 4-1 shows the classification of sixty-three developing countries in a study by Tait, Grätz, and Eichengreen.

It is important to emphasize that a low index of tax effort does not indicate that the country should raise taxes, nor does a high index indicate that taxes should be lowered. Such a decision should emerge from a careful consideration of expenditure needs, alternative sources of finance, the effects of the particular taxes that would be changed, administrative capability, and the political acceptability of the program. What tax effort analysis can do is suggest where to begin in addressing a budget problem. A country with an excessive budget deficit may reasonably focus attention particularly on possible tax increases if the tax effort index is low but may first seek expenditure reductions if the tax effort index is high. Tax effort analysis, if cautiously used, meets the widely felt need for a standard for comparing tax burdens of countries. Some critics, however, argue that conditions differ so greatly among countries that general theorizing and quantitative comparisons are not helpful in evaluating policies in a particular country.[10]

Tax Structure and the Stage of Development

Many writers have commented on the relationship between the stage of development and the tax structure. The notion of a representative or model tax system for groups of countries at the same stage of development has attracted attention. The authors who have most fully expounded on the subject are Hinrichs and Musgrave.[11]

---

errors; $\bar{R}^2$ is the adjusted coefficient of determination. All the regression coefficients are significant at the 99 percent confidence level except for nonexport income in the first and second equations and the agricultural share in the third equation. See "International Comparisons of Taxation," pp. 128–29.

10. See Richard M. Bird, "Assessing Tax Performance in Developing Countries: A Critical Review of the Literature," *Finanzarchiv*, vol. 34 (1976), pp. 244–65. See also the discussion of methodological difficulties in Bruce R. Bolnick, "Tax Effort in Developing Countries: What Do Regression Measures Really Mean?" in J. F. J. Toye, ed., *Taxation and Economic Development* (London: Cass, 1978), pp. 62–80.

11. Hinrichs, *General Theory of Tax Structure Change*; Richard A. Musgrave, *Fiscal Systems* (Yale University Press, 1969), pp. 125–67.

Table 4-1. *Index of International Tax Comparison or Tax Effort for Sixty-Three Developing Countries, 1972–76*

Low index	Medium index	High index
Afghanistan	Burundi	Algeria
Bangladesh	Chile	Benin
Bolivia	Colombia	Brazil
Burma	Costa Rica	Cameroon
Central African Republic	Dominican Republic	Congo
Ecuador	Ethiopia	Guinea
Egypt	Gambia	Guyana
El Salvador	Ghana	India
Guatemala	Iraq	Ivory Coast
Honduras	Jamaica	Kenya
Indonesia	Jordan	Malaysia
Liberia	Korea	Mali
Malawi	Pakistan	Morocco
Mexico	Peru	Sudan
Nepal	Rwanda	Taiwan
Nicaragua	Senegal	Tanzania
Panama	Sierra Leone	Tunisia
Paraguay	Sri Lanka	Turkey
Philippines	Swaziland	Upper Volta
Syrian Arab Republic	Thailand	Zaire
Togo	Yemen Arab Republic	Zambia

Source: Alan A. Tait, Wilfrid L. M. Grätz, and Barry J. Eichengreen, "International Comparisons of Taxation for Selected Developing Countries, 1972–76," International Monetary Fund *Staff Papers*, vol. 26 (March 1979), p. 143. The indexes are those estimated from the first equation cited in note 9 of this chapter.

Both Hinrichs and Musgrave stress tax handles as determinative, at least in the early stages of development. Both attempt to test their hypotheses by historical accounts and cross-section studies. As more and better cross-section statistics become available through the government finance statistics program of the International Monetary Fund, further statistical studies will be worthwhile, despite weaknesses in the approach to be mentioned.

According to Hinrichs, countries tend to move in the course of development from an early period in which the ratio of direct to indirect tax revenue is high through stages in which indirect taxation becomes more important and finally to a stage in which direct taxes are again dominant. At an early stage of development, traditional societies derive government revenue primarily from nontax sources and from "traditional direct taxes" in the form of taxes on land, livestock, agricultural output, and water rights and poll taxes. During the transition to modernity, these sources diminish in importance compared with indirect taxes. Openness to foreign trade favors the use of customs duties and a high overall tax ratio. As development proceeds, Hinrichs visualizes a rise in the share of revenue from internal indirect taxes, which becomes feasible as monetization and domestic production increase. Modern direct taxes are introduced but at first their yield is smaller and less elastic than that of foreign trade taxes and domestic consumption taxes. At advanced stages of development, taxes on foreign trade diminish in importance while modern direct taxes grow.

In Hinrichs's view, countries at the highest stages of development have the greatest opportunity to adapt their tax systems to their political preferences, whereas in earlier stages, governments are more constrained by the size of alternative tax bases and their administrative capabilities. Generalizing on the choice of tax base, Hinrichs writes, "Looking at tax revenue history in broad perspective, one may be more than halfway justified in saying that the structural movement has been from taxation on (1) agriculture, to (2) foreign trade, to (3) consumption, to (4) net income, individual and business."[12]

Musgrave sees representative tax structures as being shaped by economic factors, which account for the size of different tax bases, and by political and social factors, which influence opinions on tax equity. Government centralization is favorable to direct taxes on income and wealth because of its administrative advantages in assessing these taxes. In the early stage of development, revenue tends to be obtained from land taxes, import and export duties, and a few excises. Income taxes apply mainly to civil servants and employees of large enterprises. Later, general income taxes become feasible and attract support because of egalitarian sentiments, democratic politics, and government centralization. Like Hinrichs, Musgrave thinks that governments of countries at an advanced stage of development have far more scope for exercising choice in the design of their tax systems than governments of countries at earlier stages have. He suggests that "'model tax structures' applicable to groups of countries with more or less similar characteristics regarding availability of tax bases and levels of per capita income" could be devised to appraise tax systems and identify needed changes.[13]

The generalizations of Hinrichs and Musgrave gain some support from statistics that have become available since they wrote. Table 4-2 brings together data on the composition of central government revenues in more

12. *General Theory of Tax Structure Change*, p. 106.
13. *Fiscal Systems*, p. 166.

Table 4-2. *Composition of Central Government Revenues,*
around 1980[a]

Percent

Country group (number)	Taxes			Social security contri- butions	Nontax revenues
	Income and profits	Domestic goods and services	Inter- national trade		
Industrial countries (20)	33.3	26.0	3.7	25.0	9.0
Semi-industrial countries (15)	25.3	30.6	14.5	13.0	11.1
Middle-income countries (55)	23.7	23.1	28.9	4.1	14.9
Least developed countries (14)	17.0	21.7	41.6	1.6	13.0

Source: International Monetary Fund, *Government Finance Statistics Yearbook,* vol. 6 (1982).
a. Unweighted arithmetic means of the percentages for each country in the group. Data will not add to 100 percent because of the omission of property taxes and other minor taxes and rounding. For country classification, see note 14.

than a hundred countries for fiscal years around 1980.[14] Taxes on income and profits are distinctly more important in the industrial countries than in the developing countries, and among the latter countries these taxes contribute the smallest percentage of revenues in the least developed countries. The contribution of taxes on international trade and transactions is inversely related to the level of income and the degree of industrialization. The degree of reliance on domestic taxes on goods and services is greatest in the semi-industrial countries. Social security contributions, as expected, are most significant in the industrial and semi-industrial countries.

The major oil-exporting countries are omitted from table 4-2. Among the five of these countries for which information is readily available (Iran, Kuwait, Nigeria, Oman, and Venezuela), identifiable oil revenues accounted for 63.5 percent of total central government revenues. The share probably was higher in some of the oil-exporting countries for which information is not available.

As with studies of expenditures, it is doubtful whether cross-section studies of tax structures can predict the course of change. The use of the terms "early" and "late" stages of development may be misleading in regard to cross-section studies; countries that are now at lower stages of development may or may not later come to resemble the countries that are now at advanced stages. Changes in tastes or fashions apply to taxation as

14. The classification of countries is that given in chapter 1, footnote 6. Among industrial countries, Japan and the six nonmarket countries are omitted because of lack of data. Romania, Bahrain, and the major oil exporters are omitted because their revenue systems differ greatly from those of the other countries and because of my doubts about the consistency of the classification of revenues of the oil exporters. All other countries for which data are given in the IMF yearbook are included.

well as consumption. Technological changes occur, such as the introduction of the value-added tax. Another issue is whether statistical regularities have normative significance. The case for using a statistically derived model or representative tax system is similar to—but perhaps weaker than—that for tax effort analysis: It may offer a better beginning point than a purely subjective or deductive appraisal by either experts or politicians.[15]

Tax Elasticity

An important aspect of the tax structure is the elasticity of yield. This is the relation between the proportional changes in tax revenue and in a broad measure of national income or output, usually GNP or GDP. An elasticity of unity means that each 1 percent change in GNP (if that is the chosen standard) will be accompanied by a 1 percent change in tax revenue; an elasticity of less than 1 means that the percentage change in revenue will be less than the percentage change in GNP; and an elasticity greater than 1 means that the percentage change in revenue will exceed that in GNP. Commonly a system or a particular tax is said to be elastic if the measure exceeds 1 and inelastic if it is less than 1. In strict usage, elasticity has come to refer only to the changes in tax revenue that occur automatically without any alteration in tax rates or administration and without the introduction or elimination of taxes. This is sometimes called built-in elasticity. It should be distinguished from buoyancy, which reflects both the automatic response of revenue and discretionary changes in the tax system or tax administration.

In a period of economic growth, an elastic tax system is highly advantageous for the government. As brought out in chapter 3, government expenditures usually tend to increase faster than income. Politically it is much easier to obtain additional revenue from the automatic response of an elastic tax system than by frequently raising tax rates or imposing new taxes. It is also more convenient for tax administrators, and it lessens economic uncertainty associated with tax changes. In inflationary conditions it is particularly desirable that tax revenue keep pace with government expenditures. A lag in tax revenue, of course, will increase the deficit, which may lead to more financing by money creation and perpetuation of

---

15. For a critical review of the theories and statistical studies, see Vito Tanzi, "The Theory of Tax Structure Change during Economic Development: A Critical Survey," *Revista di Diritto Finanziario e Scienza delle Finanze*, vol. 32 (1973), pp. 199–208.

the inflationary spiral. If the elasticity of tax revenue exceeded that of government expenditures, the deficit would be reduced and inflation would be slowed. That outcome, however, is unlikely when inflation is rapid, and some critics would argue that it would be undesirable because a constraint on the growth of the budget would be loosened.

The elasticity of the tax system is a weighted average of the elasticities of the component taxes. The elasticity of a particular tax may be decomposed into two elements—the elasticity of the base and the elasticity of yield with respect to the base.[16] Hence the elasticity of the system can be enhanced by taxing items or sectors that are growing as fast as or faster than GNP and by applying taxes that are proportional or progressive with respect to the base. Thus an excise tax on luxury consumption items at a uniform ad valorem rate will be elastic because of the behavior of the base. Over fairly long periods, the bases of a broad sales tax and of a general income tax will tend to grow faster than GDP because the share of the nontaxed subsistence sector will decline in the course of development. In the short run, the yield of an income tax should be more elastic than that of a sales tax because of its personal exemptions and progressive rates. Elasticity is often held down by the exemption of growing sectors and by the application of specific rates (fixed amounts per physical unit) rather than ad valorem rates.

Ordinarily, the elasticity of the tax system is expected to be lower in less developed countries than in more developed countries because of the greater role of specific excises, customs duties, and stamp taxes and the lesser contribution from progressive income and profits taxes in the systems of the less developed countries.

The most informative measure of the elasticity of a tax system can be built up from separate estimates of the two elements for each of the major groups of taxes.[17] The first step is to select a period for study and to assemble data on the bases of the major taxes (or proxies for the bases if direct information is not available, as it often is not) and on the yield of the taxes at unchanged rates. For some taxes, figures on the yield at constant rates can be estimated by simply applying the rates to the bases, but for

16. Elasticity of tax, Ti, is as follows:

$$Ti = [(\Delta Bi/Bi)/(\Delta Y/Y)] \times [(\Delta Ti/Ti)/(\Delta Bi/Bi)]$$
$$= (\Delta Ti/Ti)/(\Delta Y/Y)$$

where Bi is the base of Ti, Y is GNP, and the deltas indicate increases.

17. See Charles Y. Mansfield, "Elasticity and Buoyancy of a Tax System: A Method Applied to Paraguay," International Monetary Fund *Staff Papers*, vol. 19 (July 1972), pp. 425–46.

income taxes and other taxes with complex rate structures a more intricate procedure is necessary. The elasticities of the bases and of tax yields in relation to the bases can then be estimated by fitting double logarithmic equations.[18] For some purposes it is enlightening to relate the tax base to a broad measure of economic activity other than GNP or GDP. For example, the base of a sales tax might be related to total household consumption or the base of import duties to total imports. For estimating the elasticity of the tax system as a whole, however, the separate elasticities of all the components must be measured by the same standard, and GNP or GDP is nearly always the most suitable.

Empirical studies confirm some but not all of the expectations about the elasticity of particular taxes and tax systems in developing countries.[19] In Colombia, the base of a hypothetical sales tax, excluding food, was estimated to have an elasticity of 1.3 with respect to GDP over the period 1925–65. In Paraguay and Peru, the elasticities of the bases of some of the principal excises, such as those on alcoholic and nonalcoholic beverages, were found to be fairly high during the 1960s, but the tax yields were inelastic because of the low response of the taxes (which were largely specific in nature) to their bases. In Honduras, Nicaragua, and Costa Rica, the elasticities of yield of excise, consumption, and sales taxes were in the 1.4–1.5 range in 1955–74, but the low elasticity of import duties held down the overall elasticity of indirect taxes to 1 or lower. Surprisingly, income taxes in Paraguay and Peru were found to be not significantly more elastic than excises and other taxes on production and expenditures, presumably because of exemptions and exclusions granted as incentives and possibly also because of poor enforcement. In Malaysia, Zambia, and Central America, however, income taxes, as expected, were found to be

18. The equations are $\log Bi = \log a + b \log Y$ and $\log Ti = \log c + t \log Bi$. The coefficients b and t are the elasticities of the base with respect to GNP and the elasticity of the tax yield with respect to the base, respectively. The elasticity of Ti with respect to Y is bt. The objective is to find the relationship between changes in tax yield and GNP, not to make the best statistical estimate of tax yield. It is important that the coefficients be statistically significant and the coefficient of determination be reasonably high, adjusting for the number of degrees of freedom, which is usually small.

19. Jonathan Levin, "The Effects of Economic Development on the Base of a Sales Tax: A Case Study of Colombia," International Monetary Fund *Staff Papers*, vol. 15 (March 1968), pp. 30–99; Mansfield, "Elasticity and Buoyancy of a Tax System"; Nurun N. Choudhry, "A Study of the Elasticity of the West Malaysian Income Tax System," International Monetary Fund *Staff Papers*, vol. 22 (July 1975), pp. 494–509; D. Sykes Wilford and W. T. Wilford, "Estimates of Revenue Elasticity and Buoyancy in Central America, 1955–74," in Toye, *Taxation and Economic Development*, pp. 83–101; Amaresh Bagchi and M. Govinda Rao, "Elasticity of Non-Corporate Income Tax in India," *Economic and Political Weekly*, vol. 17 (September 4, 1982), pp. 1452–58; William J. Byrne, "The Elasticity of the Tax System of Zambia, 1966–1977," *World Development*, vol. 11 (February 1983), pp. 153–62; and an unpublished paper on Peru by Sheetal K. Chand and B. A. Wolfe (1973) of the International Monetary Fund staff.

an elastic revenue source. For India, some studies reported low elasticities for the income tax; however, a recent careful analysis estimates the elasticity of the noncorporate income tax at approximately 1.1 in 1965–66 to 1978–79. For income taxes, it may be important to distinguish between the elasticity of liabilities or assessments and the elasticity of collections. Lags between the accrual of liability or assessment and collection, which are lengthy in some countries, become especially significant in periods of inflation.

Limits to Taxation

The idea that there is a limit to the amount of tax revenue that can be raised by a government is plausible and has long been a subject of comment and occasional systematic exposition.[20] In a sense, the limit to taxation is reached when a country is fully using its taxable capacity, and the same factors that influence taxable capacity also establish the tax limit. As explained in an earlier section, however, estimates of taxable capacity have been based on relative criteria. They represent an attempt to ascertain a norm from average behavior rather than a limit. In the section on taxable capacity and tax effort, emphasis was placed on the ability of people to pay, as indicated by per capita income, and the availability of tax bases or tax handles. Here, the focus of attention will shift to the economic, political, and administrative consequences of heavy taxation.

Tax limits may operate because excessive taxation impairs productive capacity, weakens economic incentives, arouses resistance or evasion, or imposes insupportable administrative burdens. An absolute limit would prevail if these reactions were so adverse that no additional revenue could be obtained. Absolute limits, however, are rarely encountered. Usually a limit reflects a judgment by decisionmakers that the harm done by raising taxes beyond that point would outweigh the advantages of greater government expenditures or the disadvantages of additional borrowing or money creation.

Taxation may reduce productive capacity by destroying capital or by infringing on the consumption needed to maintain the energy and abilities

---

20. This section draws on my paper "Limits to Taxation," in Karl W. Roskamp and Francesco Forte, eds., *Reforms of Tax Systems*, Proceedings of the Thirty-Fifth Congress of the International Institute of Public Finance (Wayne State University Press, 1981), pp. 41–54. Some passages are taken from that paper. See also A. R. Prest, "The Taxable Capacity of a Country," in Toye, *Taxation and Economic Development*, pp. 13–32.

of workers. The danger of destroying existing capital and retarding saving and capital accumulation was regarded as the main economic limitation on taxation in early comments. A system that relied on progressive taxes on income and wealth was thought to be subject to a lower limit on the tax ratio than one that depended mainly on taxes on mass consumption. A few neoclassical writers, notably Marshall, recognized that part of consumption was productive in the sense that it preserved and enhanced the capabilities of workers.[21] This perception suggests that restraint in imposing consumption taxes may be advisable for economic as well as humane reasons. Productive consumption is likely to make up a greater share of total consumption and income in poor countries than in rich ones.

Although the willingness to produce cannot be sharply distinguished from the ability to do so, it is useful to consider both the damage to economic incentives and the impairment of productive capacity. High taxes may make people less willing to work, to assume managerial responsibility, to make innovations, to save, and to invest because the taxes reduce the economic rewards of carrying out such activities. However, that effect does not necessarily follow. Economic theory analyzes the impact on incentives under two headings—the substitution effect and the income effect. The substitution effect of taxation normally causes people to reduce their productive activities because the rewards for substituting them for leisure or a quiet life are diminished. The income effect pushes in the opposite direction. A person whose disposable income is lowered by taxation may be impelled to greater activity in order to make up for the income loss and to maintain or reach a desired standard of living. The relative strengths of the two effects cannot be predicted a priori. It can be said that the substitution effect attaches closely to marginal tax rates, whereas the income effect pertains to average rates. Hence, for equal yields, the more progressive a tax the more likely it is that the substitution effect will dominate and incentives will be damaged.

The use to which the government puts the revenue has an effect on the economic limit to taxation. There is clearly less risk of harming productive capacity by capital destruction when the government spends for investment than when resources are used for military or welfare purposes. If government spending promotes better health and education and supplements the income of the poor, heavy taxes on the population are far less likely to impair the productive capacity of labor than if the revenue is used to finance ill-chosen prestige projects and an idle bureaucracy. From this

21. Alfred Marshall, *Principles of Economics*, 8th ed. (London: Macmillan, 1938), p. 229.

standpoint, the tax limit could be very high in a country in which investment and a large part of consumption were socialized. But the incentive effects are different. Government use of tax revenue to subsidize or provide free goods and services that people would otherwise buy for themselves, such as food, housing, and medical services, will accentuate the adverse effects on incentives because there will be less need to earn income.

Taxation is limited also by the resistance that may be aroused when taxes rise rapidly and are regarded as excessive. Resistance may take the form of increased evasion, especially of import and export duties and direct taxes on income, profits, and wealth. While there is evidence that smuggling is related to tax rates as well as to geographic and other factors, evasion of internal taxes is a complex phenomenon that is not closely linked with tax rates. Other more subtle forms of resistance may be equally or more important. One of these is the diversion of activities from commercial or organized markets to other channels that are less exposed to taxation. As already mentioned, farm production in developing countries is especially open to such displacement. Similarly, trade may be taken over by small vendors who are exempt from sales taxes. Although the net economic loss is smaller than the loss of the tax base, economic efficiency suffers.

Migration and capital flight to countries with lower taxes are strong forms of resistance. Although many barriers to the movement of people and capital exist, there are fewer now than in the past and the remaining restrictions have become less effective with improved communications and transportation. Governments' worries about capital outflow may have a moderating influence on tax rates and may also motivate special incentive measures.

Another form of resistance to taxation shows itself in inflation. Although the failure to impose sufficient taxation in relation to expenditures is a much more common cause of inflation, high taxes themselves can aggravate inflation. The most prominent manifestation occurs when workers obtain wage increases to compensate them for higher taxes. This behavior is most evident with respect to indirect taxes that enter into the prices of consumer goods. When wages are formally linked with the cost-of-living index, the adjustments are more or less automatic. Proposals to avoid such reactions by excluding indirect taxes from consumer price indexes generally have not been accepted. To be sure, wage demands could be discouraged and their inflationary effects largely neutralized by firm monetary restraint. But governments are reluctant to face the strife, unemployment, and disruption of production that would be likely if strong and insistent wage demands met unyielding monetary limits. The risk of compensating wage increases is less threatening in the majority of developing countries than it is in many industrial countries because organized labor is less powerful. Some developing countries, however, face the problem in acute form.

Are tax limits lower in democracies than in countries where political power is concentrated in a few hands? There is no convincing evidence that they are. Even dictatorial regimes must take account of economic incentives, and voluntary compliance with taxation may be harder to obtain in countries with such governments than in more democratic ones.

Centrally planned economies may be thought to have higher tax limits than private enterprise economies, but it is hard to make a valid comparison because of pervasive differences. Taxes and other receipts are not always clearly separated in the centrally planned economies because the roles of the state as a supplier of production factors and as the provider of general government services are not distinguished.

These considerations leave the nature of tax limits uncertain and provide little help in deciding whether a country is approaching a limit. The economic effects of the principal forms of taxation will be examined in more detail in the chapters devoted to them. Here it may be noted that, despite persuasive deductive arguments that progressive taxes are more harmful to incentives than proportional or regressive taxes, observation does not support an inference that tax limits can be raised by deemphasizing direct, progressive taxes. Among both industrial and developing countries, those with the highest overall tax ratios tend to rely most on generally progressive income and profits taxes. Table 4-3 demonstrates this for sixty-two developing countries in 1972–76. Perhaps the political attractions of progressivity have outweighed its economic disadvantages. Or there may be an association between the values and political attitudes that favor active governments and those that support progressive taxation.

For whatever reasons, decisionmakers in many developing countries have recently come to regard as serious the difficulties and disadvantages of further tax increases. But pressures for additional government spending are strong. Opportunities for borrowing at home are severely limited in most developing countries. The result has been, and may continue to be, more borrowing abroad and more financing by money creation, together with some constraint on the growth of expenditures.

Summary

Taxes seem burdensome because of the absence of a perceived connection between the amounts paid and benefits received by individuals. Their

Table 4-3. *Tax Ratios and Composition of Tax Revenue in Sixty-Two Developing Countries Classified by Overall Tax Ratio, 1972–76*
Unweighted arithmetic means, in percent

	Highest 15 countries	Middle 32 countries	Lowest 15 countries
Ratio of tax revenue to GNP			
All taxes	25.70	15.39	8.79
Income and profits taxes	9.62	3.76	1.95
Social security contributions[a]	0.87	0.50	0.14
Property taxes	0.33	0.24	0.22
Taxes on goods and services	13.72	9.90	5.76
Other taxes	1.15	0.99	0.73
Composition of tax revenue[b]			
All taxes	100.00	100.00	100.00
Income and profits taxes	37.43	24.43	22.18
Social security contributions[a]	3.39	3.25	1.59
Property taxes	1.28	1.56	2.50
Taxes on goods and services	53.39	64.33	65.53
Other taxes	4.47	6.43	8.30

Source: Tait, Grätz, and Eichengreen, "International Comparisons of Taxation," pp. 155–56. Turkey, which is included in the study from which these data are taken, is omitted.

a. Information on social security contributions may be incomplete; according to the source, they "were included for those countries for which data were available."

b. Derived from group averages of ratios to GNP.

primary purpose is to restrain total spending by enterprises and households, and they also serve allocative, regulatory, and distributional functions.

The major principles of tax design are equity, efficiency, and administrative feasibility. Inconsistencies and competition between the principles frequently occur.

Forward shifting of taxes through price increases is favored by elastic supply and inelastic demand. These conditions exist when producers have untaxed alternatives and consumers are unwilling or unable to substitute other items for those taxed. The existence of a sizable subsistence sector in many developing countries contributes to the elasticity of both supply and demand in the market sector with the probable result that market prices will be pushed up by taxation but revenue yield will suffer. For most developing countries and most commodities, the supply of imports and the demand for the country's exports are highly elastic. Hence, taxes on imports or exports will be borne largely by residents rather than foreigners. International movements of capital and skilled professional persons cause their supply to be more elastic than it would be in a closed economy and are conducive to increases in profit and interest rates and earnings to compensate for taxes, especially in small, fairly open economies.

The taxable capacity of a country depends on the ability of the people to pay and the ability of the government to collect. Statistical estimates for developing countries have attempted to measure both by some combination of per capita income, the size of foreign trade, and the relative sizes of mining and agriculture. Agriculture has been found to be negatively related to the tax ratio, and the other variables positively related to the tax ratio, though not all are statistically significant by the usual tests. A country may be classified as having a high or low tax effort—or international tax comparison index—according to whether its actual tax ratio is above or below the predicted ratio for a country with its characteristics. The index does not indicate whether taxes should be raised or lowered, but it provides information that both political leaders and technicians have found helpful in suggesting where to begin in addressing fiscal problems.

The conception of representative or model tax systems for countries at different stages of development has attracted attention. Cross-section comparisons of tax structures, like the analysis of taxable capacity and tax effort, have some value in appraising a tax system, but it is doubtful whether they can predict the evolution of systems.

The yield of an elastic tax system will automatically increase at a faster rate than national income. This characteristic is convenient because government expenditures tend to grow faster than income and the imposition of new taxes or increases of tax rates have political and administrative costs. The elasticity of tax systems probably is lower in less developed countries than in more developed countries because of the greater role of specific excises and customs duties and the smaller contribution from income and profits taxes in the less developed countries.

The amount of the tax revenue that a country can raise is limited because excessive taxation impairs productive capacity, weakens economic incentives, arouses resistance, and imposes insupportable administrative burdens. Resistance may take the form of tax evasion; diversion of activity to the subsistence sector and to small, hard-to-tax enterprises; emigration and capital flight; and inflationary wage demands. It has been asserted that the tax limit will be higher if direct, progressive taxes are avoided or deemphasized. This proposition, however, is contradicted by the fact that the developing countries with the highest overall tax ratios rely to the greatest extent on income and profits taxes.

CHAPTER FIVE

Taxation of Income and Wealth

FOR A long time taxes on income and wealth have been considered the best forms of taxation because they accord best with ability to pay. Limitations on their successful use in developing countries have been recognized, but these countries have sought to overcome the obstacles and have increased their reliance on income taxes.

This chapter deals with taxes on individual income and on corporation (company) profits and more briefly with taxes on wealth in the form of individual net worth, urban property, agricultural land, estates, inheritances, and gifts. International aspects of income taxation are discussed in connection with the corporation income tax, where they are of the greatest practical importance, though they relate also to individual income taxation. A separate section is devoted to the distortions of income taxes caused by inflation and ways of mitigating them.

Recently, many writers, reviving old doctrines, have argued that consumption taxes are more equitable than income and wealth taxes and preferable on economic grounds. The issues related to that contention will be addressed in chapter 6.

Theoretically, income and wealth taxes may be useful in market economies but should not be needed in centrally planned economies. With comprehensive central planning, the distribution of personal income and enterprise profits would be determined in principle by setting prices, wages, and social services to attain the desired standards of equity and economic efficiency. In contrast to a market economy, a centrally planned economy would not need to correct the distribution of income or modify profit rates by taxation. Actually, the conditions are not fully realized in the countries classified as centrally planned economies. Income taxes are used in Eastern Europe, though their role is much smaller than in other areas. The People's Republic of China imposes income taxes, but they are designed to apply mostly to foreign individuals and companies and to joint enterprises.

Because of its high personal exemptions, the individual tax adopted in 1980 was expected to apply to only about twenty Chinese, all of whom were performers, artists, or writers.[1]

The Individual Income Tax

The individual income tax has appeal as a "modern" tax. It applies to a recognized measure of ability to pay. As a direct tax, it can take account of the taxpayer's needs as indicated by the number of his dependents and other personal circumstances. It is adaptable to progressive rates. Although not completely neutral in its economic effects, a good individual income tax involves fewer unintended and nonfunctional discriminations between households and enterprises than result from most excise taxes, import duties, and sales taxes. Finally, the yield of the individual income tax can be highly elastic.

These advantages pertain to a well-designed and well-administered tax. In practice, the individual income taxes of many countries depart from the ideal in important respects. Like other sophisticated devices, an income tax will function poorly and may do harm if it is not carefully designed and properly applied.[2]

Conditions for Use as a Major Revenue Source

All countries can make some use of the individual income tax, but it can be a major revenue source only if certain prerequisites are satisfied. A list of conditions proposed in 1951 included the following: (1) the existence of a predominantly money economy; (2) a high standard of literacy; (3) prevalence of honest and reliable accounting; (4) a large degree of voluntary compliance on the part of taxpayers; (5) a political system not dominated by wealthy groups acting in their self-interest; and (6) honest, reasonably efficient administration.[3]

---

1. *IMF Survey*, September 15, 1980, p. 294; Richard D. Pomp, Timothy A. Gelatt, and Stanley S. Surrey, "The Evolving Tax System of the People's Republic of China," *Texas International Law Journal*, vol. 16 (Winter 1981), p. 40.

2. The terms individual income tax and personal income tax are often used interchangeably, but that is technically inexact since corporations and other legal entities are persons in a legal sense.

3. Richard Goode, "Reconstruction of Foreign Tax Systems," *Proceedings of the Forty-Fourth Annual Conference on Taxation*, National Tax Association, 1951, pp. 213–15; reprinted in Richard M. Bird and Oliver Oldman, eds., *Readings on Taxation in Developing Countries* (Johns Hopkins University Press, 1964), pp. 170–72; and in the revised edition of that volume (Johns Hopkins University Press, 1967), pp. 122–24. See also Richard Goode, "Personal Income Tax in Latin America," in *Fiscal Policy for Economic Growth in Latin America*, Papers and Proceedings of a Conference Organized by the Joint Tax Program of the Organization of American States, the Inter-American Development Bank, and the Economic Commission for Latin America (Johns Hopkins University Press, 1965), pp. 159–60.

These generalizations have been frequently cited but have not been rigorously tested; probably they could not be so tested, because all except the first two are essentially matters of judgment. A critic has argued that the suggested requirements are too severe and that they refer to utopian conditions. He is skeptical of the existence of voluntary compliance anywhere and maintains that in Latin America and other areas where wealth is highly concentrated large amounts of revenue can be obtained from a vigorously enforced tax on a few persons.[4]

Admittedly, high degrees of monetization and literacy are most pertinent to a mass tax, and an income tax need not apply to a large proportion of the population in order to be an important revenue source. As recently as 1939, the U.S. income tax covered only 5 percent of the population and produced about 18 percent of central government tax revenue.[5] But voluntary compliance, reliable accounting, and good administration appear to be especially necessary for the equitable operation of a measure as complex as the individual income tax. Although these conditions are hard to evaluate objectively, their prevalence, as reported by informed observers, seems to be positively correlated with the relative contribution of the income tax. It is doubtful, moreover, whether heavy progressive taxes on a small part of the population will be enacted and enforced in countries where income and wealth are highly concentrated. Sudden upheavals accompanied by expropriation may be more likely than persistent application of such taxes.

The opinion that the individual income tax, though equitable in principle, is particularly difficult to apply fairly is not new. Writing in the middle of the nineteenth century, John Stuart Mill asserted that the income tax was likely to be so unequally assessed and so widely evaded that it should "be reserved as an extraordinary resource for great national emergencies, in which the necessity of large additional revenue overrules all objections."[6] Great Britain did not heed Mill's advice, and in time the British income tax became a major source of peacetime revenue and a model of compliance with statutory provisions.

---

4. Vito Tanzi, "Personal Income Taxation in Latin America: Obstacles and Possibilities," *National Tax Journal*, vol. 19 (June 1966), pp. 156–62; reprinted in Richard M. Bird and Oliver Oldman, eds., *Readings on Taxation in Developing Countries*, 3d ed. (Johns Hopkins University Press, 1975), pp. 233–39.

5. The coverage is the number of taxpayers and their dependents; see Richard Goode, *The Individual Income Tax*, rev. ed. (Brookings Institution, 1976), p. 4. The share of tax revenue is for the fiscal year ended June 30, 1940, and is derived from U.S. Bureau of the Census, *Historical Statistics of the United States, Colonial Times to 1970* (Government Printing Office, 1975), p. 1105.

6. *Principles of Political Economy*, ed. W. J. Ashley (London: Longmans, Green, 1929), pp. 829–31 (bk. V, chap. iii, sec. 5). The notes indicate no change in the language after the first (1848) edition.

The conclusion is not that less developed countries should eschew the income tax. Prevailing political sentiments demand its use. Rather, the governments of countries at early and middle stages of development should not count on making the individual income tax a major revenue source. After gaining experience with a tax of limited coverage and moderate rates, these countries can extend and increase it. The process need not take as long as it did in the industrial countries.

Global, Schedular, and Mixed Systems

Individual income taxes may be classified as global (or unitary), schedular, or mixed systems. In a pure global tax, income from all sources is aggregated and is subject to a single rate or set of graduated rates, after allowance for personal exemptions and deductions. In a pure schedular system, each of the principal income flows—salaries and wages, dividends, rent, business profits, and so forth—is subject to a separate tax. Rates may differ among schedules but are not graduated; personal exemptions are not allowed, and the only deductions permitted are for costs of obtaining income. A mixed system combines some features of global and schedular taxes.

Pure global or pure schedular systems are now rare. Most nominally global systems apply lower effective rates to capital gains and part of earned income (income from personal effort) than to income from other sources. Mixed systems frequently have evolved from pure schedular systems through the addition of a global complementary tax and provision for personal exemptions and graduated rates in some of the schedules. Mixed systems are often called global or schedular according to their predominant characteristics. Further terminological confusion may arise because laws that impose basically global taxes, such as those of the United Kingdom and the United States, refer to schedules for the determination of the components of total income.[7]

Global systems now exist in the industrial countries, but in France, Belgium, and Italy, they replaced schedular systems only in the past twenty-five years. Among developing countries, the colonial heritage is still

---

7. For a detailed discussion of various features of schedular and global systems, see a series of articles by Sylvain R. F. Plasschaert in *Bulletin for International Fiscal Documentation*, vol. 30, March 1976; vol. 31, December 1977; vol. 33, May 1978; vol. 34, July 1980; vol. 35, June, August, and September 1981. Plasschaert is also the author of an unpublished paper, "Administrative Feasibility and Efficiency," about schedular and global systems (1980). I have benefited from consulting an unpublished paper by A. M. Abdel-Rahman of the International Monetary Fund, "Reforming Personal Income Taxation—from Schedular Income Taxes to a Global Unitary Income Tax," which was presented at an international seminar on taxation and development in Paris, September–October 1982.

influential. Global systems are found in former British colonies and protectorates, while mixed or schedular systems prevail in most of French-speaking Africa, Egypt, a few Latin American countries, Syria, Lebanon, and Portugal.

Most income taxes originated as schedular taxes, and schedular and mixed systems persist partly because of inertia. An advantage claimed for them is ease of administration. This is valid for a pure schedular system because the full tax on recurrent income items including salaries and wages, dividends, interest, pensions, and rents can be collected by withholding at the source, without an individual return. In a mixed system, however, a comprehensive individual return usually is required, and complications may arise in assigning certain items to the appropriate schedule. A mixed system, nevertheless, may have administrative advantages if the complementary tax applies to only a small minority of all taxpayers, and if both the schedular and complementary taxes on persons receiving only salaries and wages are fully discharged by withholding, without an individual return, as is the practice in some countries. Although withholding is also used in global systems, individual returns and final computation of tax are required to adjust for differences between the amount withheld and the individual's liability.

Another advantage sometimes claimed for a schedular system is that rates can be adjusted to compensate for underreporting and tax evasion. For example, the rates may be higher on business profits and professional earnings than on salaries and wages because it is presumed that the former will be less fully reported than the latter. Such a procedure could achieve substantially uniform effective taxation, however, only if the degree of evasion were the same for all recipients of a particular kind of income—a most unlikely condition. The rationalization of rate differentiation serves as an excuse for taxpayers to underreport income and for officials to condone it. Acquiescence in different degrees of cheating roughly compensated by rate differences is incompatible with a strong income tax.

The special advantages of income taxation—progressivity and recognition of the taxpayer's personal circumstances—can be fully attained only by a global or unitary tax. Its superiority has come to be widely conceded. In francophone Africa, Chad, Gabon, and the Congo have adopted global taxes, though recipients of salaries and wages continue to benefit from some special provisions. The majority of Latin American countries now have unitary taxes. Unless a country is prepared to introduce a thoroughly revised set of rates and to strengthen administration, replacement of a schedular or mixed system by a global tax may well result in a revenue loss because of the granting of personal exemptions for recipients of all kinds of income. Hence, the speed at which the goal of a predominantly global system should be approached is a matter on which opinions will differ.

Rates and Exemptions

In schedular systems and in some global income tax laws, income subject to tax is defined by enumerating the sources, usually with the addition of a catchall phrase to cover items not specifically mentioned. Especially for a global tax, it is helpful to agree on a general definition of income, which can be used in deciding whether particular items should be included in taxable income. The great majority of tax specialists now favor the accretion concept, according to which income is the algebraic sum of an individual's consumption and the change in his wealth (or net worth).[8] Some items that clearly fall within the definition are commonly not taxed because of administrative difficulty (for example, imputed consumption and unrealized capital gains) or policy reasons (for example, profits that are exempt to encourage new enterprises).

In many developing countries the beginning rate of the global income tax or the complementary tax may be too low and the top rate too high. A beginning rate as low as 3 to 5 percent, applying to income in excess of personal exemptions, results in liabilities for many taxpayers that are too small to repay the cost of assessment and collection. An initial rate of at least 6 to 10 percent usually is more appropriate. Because of the personal exemptions, the effective rate, of course, will be much lower for those subject only to the initial rate. Top rates often are unrealistically high, occasionally exceeding 90 percent. Excessive rates are likely to discourage effort and investment and to provoke avoidance and evasion. Top rates may be more significant because of their political symbolism and their influence on rates lower down the scale than because of their revenue yield. Just how high they should be is a question to which no general answer can be confidently given.

Tax rates cannot be appraised without taking into account personal exemptions. Global taxes and complementary taxes provide an exemption or personal allowance, which frees from tax a certain amount of income, and they usually grant additional exemptions or allowances for a dependent

---

8. Also called the Schanz-Haig-Simons concept. See Richard Goode, "The Economic Definition of Income," in Joseph A. Pechman, ed., *Comprehensive Income Taxation* (Brookings Institution, 1977), pp. 1–36.

spouse and for children and other closely related dependents. Personal exemptions would result in progressive tax liabilities even if rates were not graduated; for many taxpayers the exemptions contribute more to progressivity than rate graduation does. The exemption level determines how many individuals will be subject to a tax, a matter that should be carefully considered in the light of the tax department's capacity to process returns. It is rational to set exemptions higher in relation to average income in less developed countries than they are in most industrial countries because in the former administration usually is weaker and the salaries of tax officials, which are a major component of administrative costs, are typically much higher relative to average income.

Provisions for personal exemptions are modeled on the Western nuclear family consisting of husband, wife, and children with the occasional addition of other dependents who are closely related by blood or marriage. The provisions are not well adapted to the extended family system of Africa and much of Asia in which obligations to dependents are much more extensive but somewhat less precise. To be sure, the extended family tends to be less prevalent in the modern sector, to which the income tax mainly applies, than in the traditional sector. Nevertheless, several African countries have considered it prudent to fix a low limit on the number of dependents for whom exemptions will be allowed. In India, the Hindu undivided family—comprising the male descendants of a common male ancestor, together with the wives and unmarried daughters dependent on them—is taxed as an entity, without adjusting the personal exemption to the number of members. In Islamic countries, ordinarily an exemption is allowed for only one wife.

An example of the transplantation of an important income tax feature to an environment different from that in which it was conceived is the quotient system that several francophone countries of Africa have taken over from France. In that system the rate applicable to aggregate income under a unitary tax or the complementary tax is determined by dividing the income by a factor related to the number of family members. The divisor usually is the number of family members, with husband and wife counted as one each and children as one-half each. It may be subject to a fixed maximum. This splitting of taxable income reduces the exposure to high rates in graduated schedules and lessens tax liability and progressivity. A motive for its adoption in France was a desire to stimulate a lagging birthrate, an effect that would be inappropriate in Africa and that presumably is not sought. The quotient system seems quite unsuitable for the developing countries.

Forfaits and Similar Assessment Methods

Where adequate accounting records are not available, tax officials may resort to other evidence to make best-judgment or administrative assessments of income, or the law may provide, as an alternative to conventional assessment methods, a *forfait* system that determines income by indirect or external indicators. There are important legal differences between these two assessment methods, but in practice they may be similar.[9]

The Israeli *tachshiv* is an example of the use of economic analysis to assist officials in making best-judgment assessments in cases where comprehensive and reliable information is not available from books of account. *Tachshivim* are standard assessment guides that are prepared for various trades and professions by economists of the tax department and continually brought up to date. In 1977 they were said to cover about a hundred economic sectors.[10]

France, in its *forfait* system, appears to have gone farthest in legally establishing alternative bases of assessment, using indicators to determine estimated income rather than to check assessments ostensibly based on conventional records. *Forfaits* are used in France for assessing the income tax of farmers, unincorporated business enterprises, and professional persons whose gross receipts fall below stipulated levels. For agriculture, *forfaits* reflect average rates of return per hectare for different types of farming and different regions, as estimated by the agriculture department. For other *forfaits*, French tax inspectors have at their disposal a monograph for each important trade or economic activity that includes descriptive material and information on gross profit margins for various activities or products. The monographs are prepared on a regional or national basis by the research division of the tax department, and representatives of business or professional organizations are invited to comment on them. In addition, the French tax administration has statutory power to assess income tax by reference to certain external indicators of the taxpayer's style of life, each

---

9. The following paragraphs include some passages from my paper, "Some Economic Aspects of Tax Administration," International Monetary Fund *Staff Papers*, vol. 28 (June 1981), pp. 249–74. For more details on the *forfait* system and the use of indirect indicators, see that paper and Arye Lapidoth, *The Use of Estimation for the Assessment of Taxable Business Income*, Selected Monographs on Taxation 4 (Amsterdam: Harvard Law School International Tax Program and International Bureau of Fiscal Documentation, 1977); Harvard Law School, *Taxation in France*, World Tax Series (Chicago: Commerce Clearing House, 1966), pp. 345–68; Louis Trotabas and Jean Cereze, *L'imposition forfaitaire des benefices industriels et commerciaux* (Paris: Librairie Generale de Droit et de Jurisprudence, 1958).

10. Lapidoth, *Use of Estimation for the Assessment of Taxable Business Income*, pp. 124–47; Harold C. Wilkenfeld, *Taxes and People in Israel* (Harvard University Press, 1973), pp. 144–50.

of which is assigned a specific value. The external indicators are derived primarily from household consumption surveys of the national statistical institute. They include the rental value of the person's principal and secondary residences; ownership of cars, motorcycles, boats, aircraft, racehorses, and saddle horses; and employment of servants.

Forfait assessments are used in a number of francophone countries in Africa, though in less elaborate form than in France. Whether for formal *forfaits* or merely for administrative aids, there is scope for productive research in developing countries to extend and improve indirect or external indicators of net income.

Of course, reliance on indirect indicators is less satisfactory than assessment of the income tax by reference to reliable accounting statements or other direct information. A *forfait* system or rigidly applied set of guidelines tends to convert the levy into a tax on the indicators rather than a tax on the nominal base, and the de facto tax may have economic effects quite different from those normally attributed to an income tax. But there may be no good alternative during the lengthy period required to promote reliable bookkeeping and voluntary compliance with sophisticated tax laws. The temptation to turn the tax assessment into a purely negotiated amount, with little reference to objective indicators, should be strongly resisted.

Forfait systems usually allow taxpayers to "graduate" to the normal regime by establishing satisfactory accounts. There is, of course, a risk that those whose assessments would be higher under the normal regime will be deterred from improving their accounts. As a safeguard, it may be advisable gradually to restrict eligibility for the *forfait* system and to keep *forfaits* rather high.

The African Personal Tax

The African personal tax is a simplified form of income taxation that evolved out of the hut taxes or poll taxes that were imposed during the colonial period to raise revenue and also to push Africans into the market economy by giving them a need for money. In Northern Nigeria, the personal tax predated British rule. The tax was widely used in British colonies and protectorates, and it also spread to francophone areas.

African personal taxes varied in form and name. Usually, they applied to men, with exemptions for youths and the disabled, elderly, or destitute. In British-influenced areas, typically there was a minimum tax, and some men were subject to higher taxes graduated according to a slab system.

(Persons falling within a category or a range of income or wealth all paid a fixed total tax, whereas in a bracket system different rates are applied to the exact amount of income falling within each bracket and the total tax is computed by summing the liabilities in the brackets.) Either formally or de facto, the African personal tax and the regular income tax applied to different groups, the personal tax being paid by Africans whose income was below the exemptions for the regular tax. There was a high degree of local participation in the assessment of the personal tax, regardless of whether the revenue was for national or local use. Rolls were drawn up by local officials, and assessments were made by local committees of laymen. A sophisticated system in effect in Uganda in the 1960s took account of the number of cattle and coffee trees and other items of wealth owned by the assessee. In other cases, assessments were based on the committee's appraisal of the individual's economic status taking account of apparent consumption and wealth. Among francophone countries, personal taxes sometimes took account of earnings or sales, and in other cases they were fixed at amounts varying according to the prosperity of the region.

The personal taxes were continued after independence in most countries, but they have become less important. They appear to have been reasonably effective in tapping the limited ability to pay of low-income groups. They are fairer than poll taxes, and they seem to be well adapted for use as a local revenue source outside the large cities in Africa and possibly in other areas.[11]

The Corporation Income Tax

As used here, the word corporation is intended to cover a variety of business enterprises, all of which are entities having a legal personality, distinct from their owners. The Anglo-American tradition, which has been followed by members of the Commonwealth, is to recognize three types of enterprise: sole proprietorships, partnerships, and corporations or companies. Only the third type has a separate legal personality. That means, among other things, that the owners are not liable for the debts of the enterprise, and the life of the enterprise is independent of the lives of its

11. John F. Due, *Taxation and Economic Development in Tropical Africa* (MIT Press, 1963), pp. 61–82; Edward A. Arowolo, "The Taxation of Low Incomes in African Countries," International Monetary Fund *Staff Papers*, vol. 15 (July 1968), pp. 322–41; Ministère des Relations Extèrieures, Ministère de la Coopération et du Développement, *Evolution de la fiscalité dans 13 pays d'Afrique Noire Francophone*, Etudes et Documents 48 (Paris: Government of France, July 1982), pp. 97–99.

shareholder-owners. (The simplicity of this picture is blurred by the existence of limited partnerships and unincorporated associations, which resemble corporations in certain respects.) Civil law countries usually have a more elaborate classification of enterprises; here all those that are considered legally distinct from the natural persons who own them are called corporations.

All countries apply taxes to corporations, including in most cases income taxes. State-owned corporations are usually subject to tax in the same way as other corporations, though their compliance is often poor. Civil law countries may tax as separate entities some enterprises that do not qualify as corporations even in the extended sense.

Why are corporations taxed as such, instead of confining income taxation to natural persons? As usually formulated, the principle of ability to pay applies to natural persons but not to legal entities; taxes on corporations ultimately come from the income or wealth of individuals, although their incidence may be obscure. An important reason for taxing corporations is that significant amounts of revenue can be conveniently obtained by doing so. It has been argued that the tax is justified as a charge for the privilege of doing business in the corporate form, which makes possible the assembly of capital from many investors and large-scale activities. In the absence of special provisions to be discussed later, a corporation tax is needed to prevent retained profits from escaping taxation, because they would not be included in the income of shareholders. Even distributed profits might escape taxation. In many civil law countries, shares may be issued in bearer form, making it impossible to identify the owners, and for registered shares it may be difficult to locate the owners and make sure that they include dividends received in their taxable income. Since nonresident shareholders are not subject to the individual income tax of a country in which the corporation does business, the host country must collect a corporation tax if it is to share in the revenue from taxes on the profits realized within its territory.

Income Measurement and Rates

Taxable corporate income is usually defined according to commercial accounting principles. These principles are intended to indicate the amount that could be distributed to shareholders without impairing the capital of the enterprise. Hence, payments of interest and rents but not dividends are deductible. The measurement of capital consumption or amortization, in the form of depreciation allowances, involves judgments about the normal useful life of equipment and buildings and the appropriate distribution of the allowances over the life of the assets. Special complications arising in periods of inflation will be discussed in a later section. Other issues of some importance, particularly for small and medium-sized companies owned and controlled by a few shareholders, are how much may properly be deducted from the taxable income of the company by way of compensation for shareholders who are officers and how benefits in the form of houses, cars, club memberships, and the like for such officers shall be treated in assessing taxes on both the company and the individuals.

Graduation of corporation income tax rates does not have the same justification as progressive individual income tax rates. While all individuals may reasonably be regarded as similar and thought to use increments of income for successively less urgent purposes, no analogous presumption can be made about corporations. Clearly, they differ enormously in number of shareholders, amount of capital, and size of profits. Technological requirements demand, for example, that a small steel mill have an invested capital that would be extraordinarily large for a clothing manufacturer. Except among a few populists, there would be little support for graduation of corporate tax rates over a wide range, thus penalizing large companies.

An alternative form of graduation would cause tax rates to increase not with the absolute size of profits but with the rate of return on invested capital. It is supported on the grounds that enterprises that enjoy high rates of profits may be monopolies or quasi monopolies and may be presumed to have greater taxpaying capacity than those realizing lower rates of return. A rate schedule of this kind has been used for supplementary taxes in India and a few other countries. It is subject to the disadvantage that the tax department has not only to ascertain income but to establish the value of the invested capital, which may be especially difficult in inflationary times. An economic objection is that the graduated tax tends to discriminate against especially risky investments as well as monopolies.

Generally, the corporation income tax applies a flat rate to large companies. In setting the rate, governments of less developed countries ordinarily try to avoid discouraging investment from abroad and therefore choose a rate no higher than those prevailing in the main industrial countries and close to the rates in neighboring countries. Reduced tax rates are often applied to small corporations, though it is hard to rationalize the practice. If this practice is instituted, it is advisable to introduce safeguards against splitting up corporations into nominally independent enterprises while continuing to operate them as parts of larger business.

Economic Effects

As explained in chapter 4, the majority opinion among public finance specialists has been that a general tax on net profits cannot be shifted forward or backward in the short run and that hence it rests on enterprises and their owners. This proposition has been rejected by many businessmen and some economists who maintain that the corporation income tax is immediately passed on to consumers in the form of higher prices. The question has been extensively debated in industrial countries, and it has been the subject of a number of statistical studies, which have reached conflicting results. Similar studies have been made for India, also with conflicting results.[12]

The statistical studies have encountered severe difficulties in identifying and measuring the relevant independent variables and in isolating their influence. Part of the problem is that nominal and effective rates of corporate tax have varied over time in ways that suggest that they have been influenced by some of the same forces that are presumed to affect profits. As a result, it is difficult, and perhaps impossible, to determine whether the tax or the other factors caused gross profits to vary so as to suggest forward shifting to buyers through price increases. In my opinion, the statistical studies have not destroyed the deductive conclusion that the initial incidence of the corporation income tax is mainly on profits.

12. Among a large number of studies, see Marian Krzyzaniak and Richard A. Musgrave, *The Shifting of the Corporation Income Tax* (Johns Hopkins University Press, 1963); Richard Goode, "Rates of Return, Income Shares, and Corporate Tax Incidence," in Marian Krzyzaniak, ed., *Effects of Corporation Income Tax* (Wayne State University Press, 1966), pp. 207–46; John G. Cragg, Arnold C. Harberger, and Peter Mieszkowski, "Empirical Evidence on the Incidence of the Corporation Income Tax," *Journal of Political Economy*, vol. 75 (December 1967), pp. 811–21; Robert J. Gordon, "Incidence of the Corporation Income Tax in U.S. Manufacturing, 1925–62," *American Economic Review*, vol. 57 (September 1967), pp. 731–58; William H. Oakland, "Corporate Earnings and Tax Shifting in U.S. Manufacturing, 1930–1968," *Review of Economics and Statistics*, vol. 54 (August 1972), pp. 235–44; Karl W. Roskamp, "The Shifting of Taxes on Business Income: The Case of West German Corporations," *National Tax Journal*, vol. 18 (September 1965), pp. 247–57; Richard Dusansky and J. Ernest Tanner, "The Shifting of the Profits Tax in Canadian Manufacturing, 1935–65," *Canadian Journal of Economics*, vol. 7 (February 1974), pp. 112–21; J. M. Davis, "An Aggregate Time Series Analysis of the Short-Run Shifting of Company Taxation in the United Kingdom," *Oxford Economic Papers*, vol. 24 (July 1972), pp. 259–86; Gurcharan S. Laumas, "The Shifting of the Corporation Income Tax—A Study with Reference to Indian Corporations," *Public Finance/Finances Publiques*, vol. 21 (1966), pp. 462–73; V. Ganapathi Rao and K. S. Hanumanta Rao, "The Incidence of the Corporate Income Tax in the Short Run: The Case of Indian Corporations," *Public Finance/Finances Publiques*, vol. 26 (1971), pp. 586–606. Krzyzaniak and Musgrave, Roskamp, Dusansky and Tanner, and Laumas conclude that the tax is fully or largely shifted in the short run; the other econometric studies find little evidence of short-run shifting. My paper contains a detailed criticism of the Krzyzaniak-Musgrave study, which initiated the series. A review of studies and an extensive bibliography appear in Balbir S. Sahni and T. Mathew, *The Shifting and Incidence of the Corporation Income Tax* (Rotterdam University Press, 1976).

A corporation income tax that comes mainly out of profits in the short run could nevertheless affect relative prices, and possibly the general price level, in the long run. In the absence of full integration of corporate and individual income taxes, corporate profits would be taxed more heavily than other income from capital. This would tend to cause new investment to be directed toward unincorporated enterprises, real estate, and other uses. Before-tax rates of return would rise in the corporate sector and fall in other sectors, and this process would continue until the various forms of investment were again equally attractive at the margin, with allowance for risk, convenience, and other factors.

In a closed economy (that is, one that participated in neither international trade nor international capital flows), there would be some reduction in the rate of return on all kinds of capital and an increase in the relative prices of goods and services in which the corporate form of doing business was especially advantageous. The total amount of investment probably would diminish, depending on the elasticity of saving and investment with respect to the rate of return; the reduction might not be great. This process would be limited by the possibility of substituting borrowed capital for share capital in corporations since the interest paid on borrowed capital is deductible in arriving at taxable income. The behavior of the general price level would depend primarily on the quantity of money and other macro-economic variables.

In fact, of course, countries are not closed economies, and allowance must be made for the influence of international trade and capital flows. Generally, the existence of international trade limits shifting opportunities, whereas in some cases international capital flows enhance the possibilities.

For a small country, the prices of export products are fixed in international markets, and there is almost no possibility of shifting a profits tax to foreign consumers even in the long run. Exceptions are commodities of which the taxing country produces a large part of the world supply. In the case of manufactured goods for home consumption, there is hardly any possibility of forward shifting by domestic producers when the market is supplied partly by them and partly by imports; a price increase by domestic producers will cause them to lose trade to imports. Price increases are most feasible for goods that are produced entirely at home for sale in a highly protected market.

When the profits tax of any one developing country exceeds the tax in capital-exporting countries or in other capital-importing countries, investment from abroad will be discouraged and capital outflows encouraged. Gross profit rates in the high-tax country will tend to rise, which will partly compensate for the effect on after-tax profits, and wages may be held down because workers will produce with a smaller capital stock. In contrast, a tax roughly equal to those in other capital-importing countries may have little influence on capital flows and hence may exert no effect on gross profit rates through this channel. In the long run, it seems likely that resident owners of capital and foreign investors will bear a large part of the corporate tax, for two reasons. First, only the excess of taxation at home over taxation abroad will affect capital flows. Second, the equalization of after-tax profit rates through international capital flows is incomplete. There is some evidence that differences in profit rates among countries persist for lengthy periods of time.

Many governments of developing countries have tried to mitigate the discouragement to investment caused by the corporation income tax by adopting special incentive schemes. These will be examined in chapter 10.

A tax-induced reallocation of capital between the corporate sector and other domestic uses may cause a loss of economic efficiency by reducing production in large-scale enterprises in the modern sector and increasing activity of smaller firms and traditional sectors. Concern about the possibility of such results may cause governments of developing countries to be cautious in their use of the corporation income tax.

Economic theorists, taking a different view of efficiency, have argued that the reallocation of production will result in a mix of goods that will be less satisfying to consumers than the mix that would be produced with a neutral tax system. Harberger quantified the loss for the United States on the basis of a number of restrictive assumptions,[13] and his methods have attracted much attention from other economists. Similar welfare losses could be ascribed to other taxes that alter relative prices and production patterns—particularly to excises and import duties but to a greater or lesser degree to virtually all taxes. Government officials of the United States and other industrial countries, however, have

---

13. Arnold C. Harberger, "The Incidence of the Corporation Income Tax," *Journal of Political Economy*, vol. 70 (June 1962), pp. 215–40; reprinted in Harberger, *Taxation and Welfare* (Little, Brown, 1974), pp. 135–62. Among the many papers stimulated by the Harberger article, special mention should be made of a highly technical one: John B. Shoven and John Whalley, "A General Equilibrium Calculation of the Effects of Differential Taxation of Income from Capital in the U.S.," *Journal of Public Economics*, vol. 1 (November 1972), pp. 281–321, which generally confirms Harberger's findings using a different method.

displayed little interest in estimates of such losses, and it is likely that officials of developing countries will be even less inclined to accept the premise that the market-directed allocation of resources under a hypothetical neutral tax system would be inherently efficient and departures from it costly.

Part of the profits earned on successful ventures compensate investors for assuming risk. If the corporate tax infringes on this necessary return, investment will be curtailed. Narrowing of the normal spread between rates of return on more risky and less risky ventures will tend to divert investment from the former to the latter. This may be undesirable because the more risky activities may be more innovative and hence may contribute more to development.

The discouragement of investment, however, is less severe than may appear because the tax often reduces the net loss suffered on an unsuccessful investment as well as the net profit realized on a successful one. If all losses could be immediately offset against taxable profits from other activities and if the tax rate were proportional, then losses, gains, and the net amount at risk would all be reduced by a percentage equal to the tax rate, and there would be no bias against risk taking.[14] In practice, these conditions are not fully realized. A company may lack sufficient income to absorb losses, and in some cases (as when the tax rate varies with the rate of return on capital) the corporate tax is graduated. Most countries enhance opportunities for offsetting losses by allowing them to be carried back against prior income or forward against future income. Loss offsets are likely to be more available for established, diversified enterprises than for new ventures.

Two economic characteristics of a corporation income tax that may be regarded as advantages are its long-term elasticity of yield and its broadly progressive effect on the distribution of the tax load among individuals. The latter characteristic (which attaches only to the unshifted part of the tax) is attributable to the fact that owners of corporate shares on the average have relatively high incomes. But the progressivity obtainable by the corporate tax is much less precise than that produced by the individual income tax because of wide differences in the shareholdings of individuals in the same income class and because of the ownership of shares by insurance companies, provident funds, and other financial institutions.

---

14. Evsey D. Domar and Richard A. Musgrave, "Proportional Income Taxation and Risk-Taking," *Quarterly Journal of Economics*, vol. 58 (1944), pp. 388–422.

The Integration of Corporate and Individual Income Taxes

The corporation income tax has been frequently attacked as arbitrary and unfair because it results in corporate profits being taxed differently from other income. Most often critics point to what they call the double taxation of distributed profits that is attributable to the combined effects of the corporation income tax and the inclusion of dividends in the taxable income of shareholders. But retained profits will be taxed more lightly than the income of shareholders if the shareholders are subject to marginal individual income tax rates higher than the corporate rate. Possible economic distortions due to tax discrimination against the corporate form of enterprise have already been mentioned. The separate application of corporation and individual income taxes (sometimes called the classical system), nevertheless, is practiced in the United States and the Netherlands and in the francophone countries of Africa, most of the Latin American countries, the Philippines, and some members of the Commonwealth.

Many leading industrial countries and some developing countries have adopted provisions for partial or complete integration of corporation and individual income taxes. Complete integration can be achieved only by disregarding for tax purposes the legal separateness of a corporation and its shareholders. All profits, regardless of whether distributed as dividends or retained by the corporation, would be allocated to shareholders, included in their taxable incomes, and taxed at the usual individual rates. This method is used by a number of countries in taxing small corporations with simple capital structures and few registered shareholders. It would be impracticable for corporations with complex capital structures and many shareholders and for all corporations that issue bearer shares or have nonresident shareholders.

Partial integration can be achieved by reducing taxes on dividend income in either of two ways. One method is the split-rate or dividends-paid credit system, which applies a reduced corporate tax rate (possibly zero) to distributed profits and requires that dividends received by shareholders be taxed like other income under the individual income tax. The other method is the withholding or imputation system, according to which shareholders are given credit for all or part of the corporate tax on the profits from which dividends are paid (that is, corporate tax is imputed to shareholders). Shareholders report for tax purposes dividends plus the withheld or imputed tax; they are taxed at the usual individual rates on the total and apply the credit against their individual liability.

The two systems would be equivalent in a closed economy, but they differ when some or all shareholders reside outside the country that taxes the corporation. A country following the split-rate system would collect no individual income tax on dividends received by nonresidents and hence would sacrifice corporate tax revenue without realizing partly compensating individual income tax revenue. A country following the imputation system would protect its revenue by collecting tax from the corporation and might decline to grant tax credits to nonresident shareholders.

The government's advantage in regard to nonresident shareholders appears to have weighed heavily in the favor of the imputation system. The split-rate system is little used, while the imputation system is in effect in a number of countries and has been officially proposed as the standard for the European Economic Community. A version of the imputation system was in effect for a long time in the United Kingdom (it was dropped for a time but has been reinstituted in a modified form) and was transplanted to the colonies. Some members of the Commonwealth continue it and even allow credits to nonresident shareholders, but the system has been discontinued by other Commonwealth countries (including India, Kenya, Tanzania, Uganda, and Zambia).

The adoption of a partial integration or dividend relief system ordinarily involves a revenue loss. At its introduction, partial integration gives windfall gains to shareholders who bought their shares without anticipating the tax relief. Extension of the system to all nonresident shareholders is probably not feasible, but for resident shareholders the imputation system does not entail insuperable complications. Either a split-rate system or an imputation system tends to encourage the distribution of dividends by reducing or eliminating their so-called double taxation. Many economists argue that this helps develop the capital market and results in a more efficient allocation of investment. Others disagree on the grounds that retained profits often finance expansion by successful enterprises that have superior management and because shareholders will use dividends partly for consumption rather than investment in other enterprises. Countries that have partial integration systems may wish to continue them to avoid the risk of discouraging investment, but for other countries the adoption of such a system does not qualify as a high-priority reform.[15]

15. For further discussion of integration methods and related matters, see Richard Goode, *The Corporation Income Tax* (Wiley, 1951); Charles E. McLure, Jr., *Must Corporate Income Be Taxed Twice?* (Brookings Institution, 1979); and George E. Lent, "Corporation Income Tax Structure in Developing Countries," International Monetary Fund *Staff Papers*, vol. 24 (November 1977), pp. 722–55.

Further International Aspects

Important technical questions arise in the measurement of the income of a branch or subsidiary of a foreign corporation. These relate to the valuation of flows of goods and services between the affiliates. Branches or subsidiaries of multinational corporations that operate in developing countries commonly buy a variety of materials, components, and supplies from the parent company or other affiliates and sell finished or semifinished products to them. As much as half of the total exports of developing countries consist of such trade within multinational groups; excluding petroleum the fraction may be about one-fourth. In addition to petroleum, this kind of trade is especially important for other minerals, tea, coffee, bananas, sugar, palm oil, and rubber.[16] Royalties for the use of patents and know-how and management fees often flow from developing countries to foreign parent companies, and interest on loans is sometimes paid to parent companies or other affiliates. The valuations placed on these flows are called transfer prices.

According to generally accepted accounting and legal standards, transfer prices should be set on an objective, "arm's length" basis and should equal the prices that would be paid by a willing buyer to a willing and unaffiliated seller. If the arm's length principle is not observed income will be misstated. Thus, if a branch or subsidiary in a developing country is charged too much for its purchases and paid too little for its sales, its profits will be siphoned off to the foreign parent or other affiliate. By manipulation of transfer prices, an affiliated group of companies could arrange for profits to be reported in low-tax countries rather than high-tax countries. Manipulation of transfer prices could also enable a company to remit profits abroad without attracting attention and possibly in violation of exchange controls.

The tax departments of developing countries find it difficult to ascertain whether transfer prices are equal to arm's length prices. For basic commodities, including most of those for which intrafirm trade is especially large, market prices are known and transfer prices can be compared with them. Although it is likely to be excessively expensive to check more than a small fraction of transactions, the possibility of checking may induce caution on the part of enterprises. For less standardized items—particularly those involving high technology and brand identification, including phar-

16. Gerald K. Helleiner, ed., *A World Divided* (Cambridge University Press, 1976), p. 22.

maceuticals, certain chemicals, and many component parts—objective evidence on arm's length prices is scarce or unavailable. Even well-staffed tax departments of industrial countries encounter difficulties in checking transfer prices. For example, a study by the General Accounting Office of the United States concluded that the Internal Revenue Service "can seldom find an arm's length price on which to base adjustments but must instead construct a price." The study characterized the enforcement process as "difficult and time-consuming for both IRS and taxpayers."[17]

Some studies have reported substantial overpricing of developing countries' imports of pharmaceutical, chemical, and metallurgical products, but the findings are controversial because of differences of opinion about the extent to which allowances should be made for overhead costs, research and development costs, and other factors. Officers of multinational corporations naturally deny that tax considerations determine transfer prices, and there is disagreement about how common manipulation is.

Some constraints other than the vigilance of tax officials limit manipulation. From the management side, it may be eschewed because it would prevent the operation of autonomous profit centers, which are regarded as a desirable means of decentralization to improve management and efficiency. Overstatement of the value of imports may increase customs duties. Possible gains may be too small to make manipulation worthwhile if differences in tax rates are not great. A common opinion among experts is that manipulation is less frequent among small firms, which lack sophistication, and very large firms, which operate on the basis of general instructions and rules of thumb, than among medium-sized multinationals.[18]

Payments for services involve even more difficult issues than transfer prices for goods. Less developed countries tend to take a restrictive attitude toward the deduction of payments to parent companies and in some cases toward payments to other nonresidents. Deductions for payments of

---

17. Comptroller General of the United States, *IRS Could Better Protect U.S. Tax Interests in Determining the Income of Multinational Corporations*, Report to the Chairman, House Committee on Ways and Means, September 30, 1981, p. v.

18. On transfer pricing and related issues, see George F. Kopits, "Taxation and Multinational Firm Behavior: A Critical Survey," International Monetary Fund *Staff Papers*, vol. 23 (November 1976), pp. 624–73 (which contains an extensive bibliography); Organization for Economic Cooperation and Development, Committee on Fiscal Affairs, *Transfer Pricing and Multinational Enterprises* (Paris: OECD, 1979); Sylvain Plasschaert, *Transfer Pricing and Multinational Corporations: An Overview of Concepts, Mechanisms and Regulations* (Westmead, England: Saxon House, 1979); Sanjaya Lall, "Transfer Pricing and Developing Countries: Some Problems of Investigation," *World Development*, vol. 7 (January 1979), pp. 59–71; and Isaiah Frank, *Foreign Enterprise in Developing Countries*, Supplementary Paper of the Committee for Economic Development (Johns Hopkins University Press, 1980), pp. 96–100.

royalties or license fees to parent companies are limited or disallowed by several developing countries, including India, Brazil, and other Latin American countries.[19] A number of countries regard all loans by parent companies to subsidiaries as equity investments and do not allow deductions for interest paid on them.[20] Such loans appear to be fairly small, as most multinationals encourage their subsidiaries to borrow locally when possible and make loans only when other sources of finance are not available.

No fully satisfactory solution of the problems of transfer pricing is likely since there are technical difficulties, differences of views among the parties, and conflicting interests. An alternative to the prevailing approach would be for each national tax department to treat all affiliated companies in a group as a unit and to attribute to the local branch or subsidiary a share of the unit's total profits on the basis of a formula that would take account of the location, within the country and outside, of production factors and the origin of receipts. This unitary method is used by most states of the United States in taxing domestic corporations, with an allocation formula including the value of tangible property, payrolls, and sales receipts. Its international application has been advocated as simpler and less open to abuse than the separate entity, arm's length method and more conducive to international tax harmony.[21]

Although the unitary method has some appeal, it seems impractical for general use. The appropriate definition of a business unit is unclear since multinational corporate groups differ widely in the degree of common ownership and control, variety of products, and extent of integration of operations. The national tax department of a developing country might find it quite infeasible to determine the profits and allocation factors for large multinational corporations and might make heavy demands for information from the companies. Even if these difficulties could be overcome—perhaps by some form of international cooperation—the allocation of profits would remain controversial. Since

19. Such restrictions are sanctioned by the model double taxation conventions of the OECD and the United Nations (article 7).

20. An alternative approach, which avoids the need to distinguish parents from other creditors, is to limit the total interest deduction to that attributable to an amount of debt not exceeding a stated fraction of total equity plus debt. This approach may be especially suitable for concession agreements or mineral production contracts.

21. Geoffrey John Hurley, "International Division of the Income Tax Base of Multinational Enterprise: An Overview," *Tax Notes*, vol. 13 (December 28, 1981), pp. 1563–70. See also Peggy B. Musgrave, "International Tax Base Division and the Multinational Corporation," *Public Finance/Finances Publiques*, vol. 27 (1972), pp. 394–413.

rates of profit in relation to invested capital, labor costs, and sales receipts arguably vary significantly among countries, no one allocation formula would be equally attractive to all countries. If different formulas were applied, or if some countries used the unitary method and others the separate entity method, double taxation would result.

The best course for individual developing countries is to improve their present assessment methods, sometimes calling on the services of private accounting firms. Cooperation between tax officials in different countries would be helpful to exchange information and to ensure consistent treatment of transactions.[22]

Countries with especially weak tax administrations may wish to consider adoption of a minimum corporate income tax as a safeguard against extreme forms of abuse of transfer pricing. Several francophone African countries apply such a provision, requiring corporations to pay the higher of either the regular corporation income tax or a minimum tax, which is a fixed amount or a percentage of turnover. Usually, the minimum tax is payable at the beginning of the year and is credited against the regular corporate tax.[23] A minimum tax may be justifiable as an administrative expedient or as a benefit levy, but clearly it differs in economic character from a profits tax.

International double taxation of income, or escape from taxation, may occur because countries choose different bases for asserting their jurisdiction to tax. There are two principal bases—the source or territorial, according to which a country taxes income arising within its borders, and the residence, according to which the worldwide income of residents is taxed. If, for example, the XYZ Corporation is resident in country A and carries on all its operations in country B, its income would be taxed twice if A followed the residence principle and B the source principle. Residence is a term of art that need not be discussed here except to say that some countries consider the residence of a corporation to be the place in which it is incorporated and has its head office while others consider the residence to be the place from which effective management and control are exercised. Resident corporations may be called domestic corporations and nonresident ones foreign corporations.

22. United Nations, Department of International Economic and Social Affairs, *International Co-operation in Tax Matters*, Report of the Ad Hoc Group of Experts on International Cooperation in Tax Matters (New York: UN, 1983).

23. This paragraph draws on an unpublished paper written in 1978 by A. M. Abdel-Rahman of the International Monetary Fund, "The Minimum Corporate Income Tax: The Experience of French-Speaking African Countries."

Broadly, capital-exporting countries including the United States, the United Kingdom, and Japan tax residents on their worldwide income, whereas capital-importing countries emphasize the source principle. Another interpretation is that the residence principle is congenial to countries with a global income tax tradition, whereas the source principle often appeals to countries with a history of schedular income taxation.

All countries recognize the source principle and subject income originating within their boundaries to their tax laws. A few (including Argentina, the Dominican Republic, Haiti, Panama, and Venezuela) follow it exclusively. Most countries, however, apply some combination of residence and source principles. France, Belgium, the Netherlands, and Switzerland tax resident individuals on their worldwide income but exclude from the taxable income of domestic corporations much or all of their foreign-source income. The United States, Mexico, and the Philippines also assert a third basis of jurisdiction and make all citizens liable for tax on their worldwide income even though they reside abroad.

Although neither general rules of international law nor any supra-national authority exists to prevent double taxation, it is widely conceded to be inequitable and economically undesirable. Hence, relief is provided by unilateral action and treaties. Countries that apply the residence principle usually allow the country of source priority in taxing income. Many countries (including the United States, Japan, the United Kingdom, and the Federal Republic of Germany) allow resident corporations and individuals a credit—that is, a deduction from tax—for tax on foreign income assessed in the country of source, up to the amount of their own tax on the income. To illustrate, if a resident company of one of these capital-exporting countries is subject to a marginal income tax rate of 50 percent, it is eligible for a full credit for a foreign tax of no more than fifty dollars on each hundred dollars of income from a foreign source and for a fifty dollar credit for a higher foreign tax. Hence, a foreign tax at a rate no higher than the domestic tax costs a resident individual or corporation nothing but merely allows the source country to obtain revenue at the expense of the treasury of the capital-exporting country. This arrangement encourages capital-importing countries to tax the profits of foreign corporations. In contrast, a tax levied by the source country on profits of a corporation resident in France or another country following the territorial principle will reduce the company's net profits.

For corporations in countries following the residence principle, there is an important difference between carrying on operations abroad through branches and through separately incorporated foreign subsidiaries. The income of foreign branches is subject to tax as it accrues and is eligible for foreign tax credit. The income of a foreign subsidiary usually is taxed in the residence country of the parent corporation only when it is remitted to the parent, and a foreign tax credit is allowed at that time.

Developing countries have complained about the practices of the capital-exporting countries that tax worldwide income. Although the foreign tax credit will alleviate double taxation, the opportunity for a capital-importing country to attract investment by offering a low tax rate or a special tax incentive will be curtailed (see chapter 10). As a partial remedy, some of the developing countries have urged capital-exporting countries that insist on the residence principle to adopt a tax-sparing provision, which would allow a credit for tax that is forgiven under an incentive scheme as well as for the actual tax liability. The United Kingdom, France, Germany, and Japan have applied such provisions through treaties, though not by general statutes. The United States negotiated a few treaties containing tax-sparing clauses, but the Senate withheld its consent and the treaties were never ratified.

An economic argument against tax sparing that has been stressed in the United States is that an efficient worldwide allocation of capital can be achieved only if investors in capital-exporting countries face the same tax rates at home and abroad (which is called capital-export neutrality). The foreign tax credit ensures that condition with respect to branch profits and remitted profits of foreign subsidiaries so long as the source country's tax rate is no higher than the rate of the residence country. Tax sparing could result in a lower rate for such foreign source income. Retained profits of foreign subsidiaries also may be subject to a lower rate than domestic income of the parent company (called tax deferral). Both tax sparing and tax deferral have been opposed as interferences with efficiency.[24]

The efficiency argument based on capital-export neutrality, however, is seriously incomplete. It neglects the fact that the United States, like other capital-exporting countries, grants investment tax credits and accelerated depreciation only for domestic investment. Furthermore, other government policies affecting rates of return and market imperfections make highly questionable any claim that before-tax profit rates

---

24. Peggy B. Musgrave, *United States Taxation of Foreign Investment Income: Issues and Arguments* (Harvard University Law School, 1969); Mitsuo Sato and Richard M. Bird, "International Aspects of the Taxation of Corporations and Shareholders," International Monetary Fund *Staff Papers*, vol. 22 (July 1975), pp. 384–455. The Sato-Bird paper covers the general issues and the complications due to schemes for integrating corporate and individual taxes.

in various countries are an appropriate guide for efficient capital allocation worldwide. Finally, political considerations, as well as economic ones, are relevant for tax policy. The government of a capital-exporting country may wish to encourage foreign investment to aid development in the recipient countries and to strengthen political ties with them, and it may believe self-restraint in taxing foreign investment is conducive to cooperation with other capital-exporting countries.

Whether tax sparing has significant advantages for capital-importing countries is debatable. As already mentioned, it affects taxes on profits of branches of foreign corporations, but net profits from subsidiaries of multinational corporations, which are the more common mode of operation, benefit only to the extent that dividends are remitted to the parent company. Thus tax sparing may encourage dividend distributions at the expense of reinvestment in the source country.

Some important technical issues pertain to the question of where income arises. The conventional answer is that the profits of a permanent establishment have their source in the country in which it operates while profits attributable to temporary or limited economic relations with a nonresident have a foreign source. Permanent establishments clearly include units that carry on processing, distribution, and other services on a continuing basis. Activities such as mere purchasing, simple order taking, and short-term construction work were historically considered not sufficient to constitute permanent establishments giving rise to locally taxable profits. That position has been maintained by the member countries of the Organization for Economic Cooperation and Development (OECD), but lately it has been increasingly challenged by less developed countries, which favor a wider definition that would bring within their jurisdiction income from short-term construction work and from additional commercial and service activities. With contemporary means of rapid communication and transportation, the traditional concept of permanent establishment may be obsolescent, and a wider, and possibly looser, definition may become generally acceptable. Practical problems in assessing income, nevertheless, will limit the gains that developing countries can attain.

The industrial countries have entered into a network of treaties with each other to prevent international double taxation and tax avoidance and also to provide for the exchange of information between tax departments. These treaties follow in many respects a model treaty of the OECD (Model Double Taxation Convention on Income and on Capital, 1977).

A considerable number of treaties between OECD countries and developing countries have been concluded in recent years, but the coverage is as yet far from complete. Representatives of developing countries have argued that the OECD model treaty is unsuitable for agreements between their countries and capital-exporting countries because it was worked out by countries that could expect a two-way flow of investment and profits, dividends, and interest between the parties. For a long time to come, investment will move from OECD countries to developing countries and returns on the investments will flow from the latter to the former. Hence, a provision that, for example, gives priority in taxing dividend or interest income to the country of residence of the shareholder or lender is less acceptable to a developing country than to a country that expects both capital exports and imports between itself and the treaty partner.

An ad hoc international group of experts held a series of meetings under United Nations auspices over a period of years and drafted guidelines and a model convention (United Nations Model Double Taxation Convention between Developed and Developing Countries, 1980). The UN model gives more weight to the source principle than the OECD model does and places more emphasis on exchange of information. It adopts a wider concept of permanent establishment and covers the allocation of income between related entities of multinational enterprises.[25] The availability of the UN model treaty and manual will no doubt strengthen the bargaining position of developing countries.

A question that frequently arises in developing countries is whether an income tax should be withheld from interest paid to nonresident lenders. Generally, this is a poor policy because it will raise the interest rates payable by resident borrowers. While some lenders could claim foreign tax credit for the withheld tax, the marginal lenders probably are not subject to tax in their home countries on interest income from foreign sources and will refuse to lend in the country applying the withholding tax unless compensated by higher interest rates. It is advisable, however, to prevent tax avoidance by treating interest pay-

25. United Nations, Department of International Economic and Social Affairs, *Manual for the Negotiation of Bilateral Tax Treaties Between Developed and Developing Countries* (New York: UN, 1979); and *United Nations Model Double Taxation Convention Between Developed and Developing Countries* (New York: UN, 1980); Stanley S. Surrey, *United Nations Model Convention for Tax Treaties Between Developed and Developing Countries: A Description and Analysis*, Selected Monographs on Taxation 5 (Amsterdam: Harvard Law School International Tax Program and International Bureau of Fiscal Documentation, 1980). The UN *Manual* includes the text of the OECD model treaty, which was published separately, with commentaries, by the OECD under the title *Model Double Taxation Convention on Income and on Capital*, Report of the OECD Committee on Fiscal Affairs (Paris: OECD, 1977).

ments by subsidiaries to foreign parent companies like dividends or otherwise limiting the amount classified as interest.

The Cash-Flow Corporate Tax

An alternative to the corporate net income tax that has been discussed particularly in the United Kingdom is a cash-flow tax. The base would be the excess of corporations' receipts from sales of goods and services over the amount paid out to produce or acquire goods and services. No distinction would be made between current and capital items; proceeds of sales of plant and equipment and purchases of durable capital goods and inventory would be included in taxable cash flow. No deduction would be allowed for interest paid.[26]

A cash-flow tax would be simpler than a net income tax. The elimination of the distinction between current and capital transactions would obviate the need to classify doubtful items. Various accrual accounts for both receipts and expenses could be dispensed with for tax purposes. Most important, it would be unnecessary to estimate the useful life of plant and equipment and set depreciation allowances. Distortions of taxable income caused by inflation, to be discussed in the next section, would not affect the base of the cash-flow tax. Nonetheless, transfer-pricing problems would remain unchanged.

The economic character of a cash-flow tax would differ fundamentally from that of a corporate net income tax. Reinvested profits would escape the tax, but interest payments on borrowed capital would be taxed. A cash-flow tax probably would discourage investment from abroad because it would not qualify for the foreign tax credits of major capital-exporting countries. Abrupt introduction of a cash-flow tax would threaten the solvency of companies with heavy outstanding debt or leases or other commitments entered into on the assumption that depreciation allowances for fixed assets would mitigate future tax liabilities. Thus the cash-flow tax, despite its administrative simplicity, is not an attractive substitute for a conventional corporate net income tax.

Inflation and the Income Tax

Inflation increases the effective rates of a progressive individual income tax in relation to real income because the value of personal exemptions

---

26. *The Structure and Reform of Direct Taxation*, Report of a Committee Chaired by Professor J. E. Meade, Institute for Fiscal Studies (London: Allen and Unwin, 1978), pp. 228–58; J. A. Kay and M. A. King, *The British Tax System* (Oxford University Press, 1978), pp. 200–07.

and rate bracket limits is reduced as the purchasing power of money declines. It also distorts the measurement of interest income and deductions for interest payments, capital gains and losses, and business income. With inflation, a delay in discharging a tax liability reduces its real amount.

The increase in effective rates of individual income tax, sometimes called "bracket creep," has attracted much attention. With personal exemptions and rate bracket limits unchanged in money terms, tax liabilities can rise sharply as a percentage of income over a few years if inflation runs at the rates that prevailed in the majority of countries during the 1970s and early 1980s. Critics object on the grounds that the tax increase is unexpected and is obtained without legislation and that it encourages additional government spending. The number of taxpayers with whom the revenue department must deal will increase, particularly in countries where personal exemptions have been high relative to average income.

While the impact of inflation could be lessened by discretionary changes in rate brackets and exemptions, a more convenient and more certain method is to provide for automatic adjustments by reference to a price index. Indexing has been adopted in one form or another in several industrial countries, including Canada, Denmark, France, Luxembourg, the Netherlands, Sweden, and the United Kingdom, and is scheduled to go into effect in the United States in 1985. Only a few developing countries that have experienced rapid and prolonged inflation—notably Chile, Brazil, Argentina, and Israel—have instituted indexing. In most of the countries, indexing is not fully automatic but may be suspended or modified by the government.[27]

Inflation-caused distortions in the measurement of taxable income are much more difficult to counteract. They can also be responsible for inequities and undesirable economic reactions. One such distortion, related to interest receipts and payments, affects many individuals and business enterprises. It is now generally understood that when the price level rises the real value of debts that are fixed in money terms declines. If a creditor is required to include in his taxable income the full amount

27. Vito Tanzi, *Inflation and the Personal Income Tax: An International Perspective* (Cambridge University Press, 1980), pp. 23–40, 150. This book contains a good treatment of the whole subject. See also Henry Aaron, ed., *Inflation and the Income Tax* (Brookings Institution, 1976); George E. Lent, "Adjustment of Taxable Profits for Inflation," International Monetary Fund *Staff Papers*, vol. 22 (November 1975), pp. 641–79; Organization of American States, *Inflación y tributación: analisis de los efectos de la inflación y de los sistemas de ajustes empleados para corregir sus distorsiones en los paises de América Latina* (Washington, D.C.: OAS, 1978).

of interest received, his true income (on an accretion basis) will be overstated by the amount of the decline in the real value of his claim. Equally—but less frequently recognized—a debtor who is allowed to deduct the full amount of interest paid will understate his true income by the amount of the reduction of his real indebtedness. If the rate of price rise exceeds the nominal interest rate, the real interest rate will be negative, and the income tax will make it more negative. Regardless of whether the real interest rate is negative or positive, income will be incorrectly measured so long as only nominal interest receipts and payments are taken into account. Creditors will be penalized and debtors favored. Saving in the form of financial claims may be discouraged and borrowing stimulated.

It may seem that the distortions could be remedied by indexing. Money claims and debts could be written down by the amount of the increase in the price level; creditors would be allowed to deduct the adjustment and debtors would be required to add it to taxable income. A complication would be that claims and debts—particularly items such as bank accounts and overdrafts—may fluctuate widely during the year; an exact adjustment would require information on average daily figures. A more fundamental question is what should be done about dividends and rents and the assets to which they are related; these income payments resemble interest in some respects but differ significantly in others. A question of equity is whether it would be fair to apply indexing to claims and debts contracted before the change in the income tax. Creditors who had successfully obtained high interest rates to compensate them for inflation and the income tax would realize windfall gains, while debtors who had counted on deducting interest payments would be disappointed and might become insolvent. Another issue is whether it would be fair to index interest-bearing claims but not currency holdings and other fixed claims that do not bear interest.

It appears that no country has instituted indexing to correct all interest receipts and payments. In some Latin American countries, Israel, and the United Kingdom, indexed loans have been issued by official and private borrowers, and creditors have not been taxed on the compensation received on account of inflation. Inflation sometimes has been cited as justification for exempting interest on savings accounts.

Inflation causes real gains realized on the sale of real estate, securities, and other capital assets to be smaller than the nominal gains and real losses to be greater than the nominal ones. Distortions will occur where capital gains are taxable and capital losses deductible, but this is a less common problem than that related to interest since the tax laws of many countries do not contain such provisions. Where capital gains are taxed, adjustments of the historical cost of assets by indexing can prevent serious distortions. Argentina, Chile, and Israel have applied indexing. Some other countries have attempted to allow for inflation by permitting the exclusion from taxable income of a fraction of gains that increases with the length of time the asset was held. This method, however, is unsatisfactory because it will make the appropriate correction of nominal gains only by accident and does nothing for losses.

One approach to correcting business profits for inflation would be to make comprehensive adjustments in the balance sheets and derive profits as the difference between adjusted net worth at the beginning and the end of the year. Chile and Brazil have applied corrections approaching that degree of comprehensiveness.[28] Attention, however, usually has been focused on depreciation allowances and, to a lesser extent, the valuation of inventories (stocks).

Depreciation allowances are a systematic means of charging against receipts the cost of machinery, equipment, and structures. Ordinarily, the allowances are designed to spread the original cost of the assets over their expected useful life. During an inflationary period normal allowances based on historical cost will understate the cost of the capital that is consumed in the production process and will thus overstate profits. This overstatement has been alleviated in a number of countries by speeding up depreciation allowances, primarily as an investment incentive but in some cases also as a corrective for inflation. Several developing countries have allowed periodic revaluations of depreciable assets to take account of inflation and have based subsequent depreciation allowances on the adjusted values rather than original cost. A few countries have provided for annual adjustments of allowances to keep pace with inflation. An issue in connection with such adjustments is whether the price index should be a general one or an index of the cost of the particular items being depreciated. A general index is preferable because the adjustment is intended to correct for inflation, that is, for the rise in the price level, rather than for changes in the relative prices of particular items. A general price index is also more readily available and easier to use. Yearly adjustments of allowances by either a general or a specific price

28. For details, see Milka Casanegra de Jantscher, "Taxing Business Profits during Inflation: The Latin American Experience," *International Tax Journal*, vol. 2 (Winter 1976), pp. 128–46.

index will not ensure that the accumulated depreciation reserve will be sufficient to cover the cost of replacing the asset when it is retired. But the purpose of the allowances is to measure costs and income, not necessarily to finance replacement of particular assets.

An alternative approach, proposed by Kaldor in another context in his well-known report on taxation in India, merits consideration as a means of simplifying depreciation accounting and obviating the need for inflation adjustments. Instead of annual depreciation allowances, tax-payers would be permitted to take a lump-sum deduction when the asset is put in service equal to the discounted value of all the allowances that normally would be allowed over its life. The lump-sum allowance would not be subject to erosion from inflation. Discounting would be essential to compensate for the advantage of the early deduction.[29] The appropriate rate of discount would be an estimate of the interest rate that would prevail in the absence of expected inflation (compare the discussion of benefit-cost analysis in chapter 3).

When inflation is in progress, the usual method of accounting for inventories will cause profits to be overstated because, in computing the cost of goods sold, it will be assumed that the items sold were those acquired earliest, when prices were lower. This overstatement can be lessened by assuming that the goods sold were those most recently acquired (last-in-first-out or LIFO rather than the conventional first-in-first-out or FIFO method). A preferable method is to adjust the value of the opening inventory by reference to the general price index used for adjusting depreciation allowances.

A delay in payment of tax after the time at which the liability accrues is always advantageous to taxpayers, and it becomes especially so during inflation because the payment is made in depreciated money. Such delays are a normal feature of the income tax. Usually they are longer in systems in which assessments are made by the tax department than where self-assessment is practiced. Further delays occur when taxpayers become delinquent in making payments, and experience shows that delinquencies usually increase during inflation. Payment lags cause fiscal problems for the state and inequities between taxpayers because of differences in the length of the lags. In conditions of rapid inflation, wage earners and

29. Nicholas Kaldor, *Indian Tax Reform: Report of a Survey* (New Delhi: Government of India, Ministry of Finance, Department of Economic Affairs, 1956). See also Alan J. Auerbach and Dale W. Jorgenson, "Inflation-Proof Depreciation of Assets," *Harvard Business Review*, vol. 58 (September–October 1980), pp. 113–18.

others who are subject to withholding will suffer discrimination compared with self-employed professional persons and business proprietors.

A combination of measures to shorten payment lags is advisable.[30] First, withholding, if not comprehensive, should be extended to cover all wages and salaries and recurrent payments of interest, dividends, rents, and royalties. Second, payments of tax on other kinds of income should be moved toward a current basis. For business income, current payment may involve a sharp break with past practices. Under the traditional British system, which is still in effect in some members of the Commonwealth, business enterprises may complete payment of their tax as late as twelve to twenty-four months after the end of their accounting year (the exact lag depending on the date at which the accounting year ends), and long lags may occur also in francophone countries. Current-payment systems require payments of estimated tax during the accounting year, with discharge of the final liability shortly after the end of the year. Transition to a current-payment system may be accomplished by gradually shortening the payment lag, by allowing one year's tax to be paid in installments over a period of years (in order to mitigate the burden of double payments when the new system is introduced), or by forgiving all or part of one year's tax. Finally, some of the administrative measures mentioned in chapter 9 are especially important for income taxes.

With the continuation of inflation at historically high rates, the steps outlined in the preceding paragraph have become urgent. More and more developing countries will also need to consider whether other adjustments in their income tax should be made in order to reduce or eliminate the effects of rising prices.

Although one-time or occasional adjustments have been made by a number of developing countries, only a few Latin American countries and Israel, which have experienced far more than average inflation, have adopted continuing adjustment provisions. Other countries no doubt have been deterred by the prospect of revenue loss and the belief that reducing taxes through the adjustments would accelerate inflation. Although that result is not axiomatic, as has often been assumed, the fear has a rational basis. Any action that lessens the response of tax yields to inflation will contribute to demand pressure provided government expenditures do not decline along with revenue, wages are not directly affected, and monetary policy is unchanged. Whether the first

30. See Carlos A. Aguirre and Teruo Hirao, "Maintaining the Level of Income Tax Collections under Inflationary Conditions," International Monetary Fund *Staff Papers*, vol. 17 (July 1970), pp. 277–325.

two conditions are likely to be met in a particular country at any time is a question that officials should examine carefully. In many countries, a significant part of government expenditures are formally linked with the price index, and in all countries many expenditures that are not so linked move up with the price level.

From the standpoint of equity, it is not clear whether action to correct some distortions, while others remain, will produce a net improvement. Inflation brings many economic distortions and inequities. Should the government give priority to the correction of some of the distortions connected with the income tax? In regard to business income, should depreciation allowances be increased without requiring enterprises that are debtors—perhaps having bought their depreciable property with borrowed funds—to reduce their deductions for interest payment?

The answer to these and similar questions may well be that at some point, if inflation continues at a fast rate, adjustments of the income tax will become essential to prevent the running down of the capital stock, insolvencies, and wholesale noncompliance. Choosing the best solution requires careful study of conditions in each country contemplating such adjustments.

The Taxation of Wealth

Wealth has appeal as a supplementary measure of ability to pay. A person with, say, income of $20,000 and wealth of $200,000 is clearly better off than one with income of $20,000 and no wealth other than his earning capacity. The former can receive income without exerting himself, and he can, if he wishes, consume more than his current income by using up his wealth. Furthermore, he can invest in an enterprise that will employ both his wealth and his personal talents. Large holdings of wealth often carry with them prestige and political power distinct from the income they yield. Taxation of wealth itself is required to take full account of the ability attributable to it. Higher rates of income tax on returns from property— or preferential treatment of earned income—will not properly tap the additional ability to pay associated with wealth, which exists even if the current yield is low or zero. Furthermore, taxes on wealth have some economic advantages compared with income taxes.

But wealth is not a rival of income (or consumption) as the primary measure of taxpaying ability. It does not reflect the economic capacity derived from income from personal effort. Although earning power may be considered a form of human capital or wealth that can be valued by capitalizing the expected future stream, there are fundamental differences between human and nonhuman wealth. It would not be possible to include human wealth in the base of a general wealth tax.[31]

The Net Wealth Tax

A measure calculated to attain the advantages of taxing wealth is a direct tax on net worth. A comprehensive tax would apply to all forms of nonhuman wealth, with deductions allowed for debts in order to determine net worth or wealth. The considerations that support progressive rates for income taxes apply also to a wealth tax, perhaps even more strongly. General wealth taxes are imposed by a number of industrial countries (including Sweden, Norway, Denmark, Finland, the Federal Republic of Germany, the Netherlands, Luxembourg, Austria, and France) and by India, Pakistan, Sri Lanka, Colombia, and Uruguay. Most of the taxes exclude from the base household goods and works of art, and several of them also exclude jewelry and other items that are difficult to assess. In none of the countries is the revenue from the wealth tax large. Only in Uruguay, which has no individual income tax, has it exceeded 1 percent of total tax revenue in recent years.[32]

An economic advantage of a net wealth tax is that it reduces incentives to invest and to work much less than an income tax does. This is true because the wealth tax on the reward for productive activities is low—zero if all the additional income is consumed. Holders of idle wealth will pay almost as much tax as active investors. A wealth tax can make an especially powerful contribution to the objective of reduced economic inequality as wealth is more concentrated than income.

There are, however, practical difficulties in discovering and valuing wealth. It is almost impossible to obtain information on bearer securities, currency, gold, and assets held abroad. The valuation of items such as real estate, livestock, and closely held business enterprises is difficult. The omission from taxable wealth of furnishings, art objects, and jewelry increases the advantages of holding such items as compared with productive

---

31. Goode, *Individual Income Tax*, p. 21; and Goode, "The Economic Definition of Income," pp. 12–13.

32. In Uruguay, the net individual wealth tax produced 3.2 percent, 2.4 percent, and 3.7 percent of total tax revenue in 1978, 1979, and 1980, respectively. Derived from International Monetary Fund, *Government Finance Statistics Yearbook*, vol. 6 (1982), pp. 743–44.

investments. A net wealth tax, although attractive in principle, must be judged impractical in most developing countries.[33]

The Urban Property Tax

An urban property tax is a form of selective wealth tax. While the ownership of urban land and buildings cannot be regarded as an indicator of ability to pay in the same sense as total net wealth, the visibility and immobility of such property make it a convenient tax handle. An urban property tax will diminish the appeal of a form of investment that is often thought to absorb resources that would contribute more to growth if devoted to industry and trade. It is justifiable in part as a charge for benefits that property owners receive from urban services and a contribution to meeting social costs created by the concentration of population in cities. The tax is especially suitable for use by local governments.

Urban property taxes are moderately significant in some British-influenced countries, but in general they are not important in other developing countries. One reason urban property taxes are not used more widely is the absence of Western-style titles of ownership and their registration in many cities. The political power of property owners, who include leading political figures and senior government officials in not a few cases, may be a greater obstacle. The minor role of property taxes in local government finance in France has counted against their acceptance in the French-influenced countries.

Property taxes may be imposed on capital value or annual rental value. They may apply to sites, buildings, or both. For many properties a tax on capital value and a tax on annual rental value will be very similar, provided the rates are set to yield the same total revenue, since capital values reflect capitalized rentals. For vacant land and unoccupied buildings, however, there will be no liability under a strict rental-value tax whereas a capital-value tax will impose a liability related to potential future gains. In this respect, the latter is superior because it places a carrying charge on properties held for speculative purposes and is less discouraging to improvements. Valuation presents problems but is technically feasible at reasonable cost using standardized appraisals based on construction costs and sales records. Legal and administrative difficulties may arise with

33. For a good compact treatment, see Noboru Tanabe, "The Taxation of Net Wealth," International Monetary Fund *Staff Papers*, vol. 14 (March 1967), pp. 124–68. A more recent work, which gives details on the European wealth taxes and examines proposals for a wealth tax in the United Kingdom, is C. T. Sandford, J. R. M. Willis, and D. J. Ironside, *An Annual Wealth Tax* (London: Heinemann, 1975). Both studies contain useful bibliographies.

respect to the taxability of certain buildings outside city boundaries, including cases of urban sprawl, beach or country houses of urban residents, and resort properties.

Despite many recommendations by foreign advisers, particularly American and British experts, little progress has been made in the establishment and improvement of urban property taxes in developing countries.[34] Although it would be unrealistic to expect rapid change in the near future, fiscal pressures and the mounting costs of public services in growing cities may make this revenue source more acceptable in the future.

Agricultural Land Taxes

Taxes on agricultural land are an ancient revenue source that formerly produced a large fraction of tax revenue in the Indian subcontinent, China, Japan, the Middle East, and other countries. For the past half century or longer, their relative contribution has decreased with changes in economic structure and the development of other taxes, and their absolute yield probably has fallen in real terms in some countries. Interest in the subject, nevertheless, continues on the part of both public finance specialists and writers on development economics.[35]

Two strands of thought that appear in the recent discussions give the subject more prominence than the current fiscal role of agricultural land taxes would warrant. One is the thesis that agriculture must be taxed heavily to transfer resources from that technologically backward sector to more progressive sectors in order to foster growth and development. Supporters of this thesis point to the large size of the agricultural sector in countries at early stages of development and often assert that disguised unemployment in rural areas is great, that farmers do not need much capital, and that they are unresponsive to price incentives. Although there has been a reaction against these views, they still influence government policies. They manifest themselves, however, in export taxes, procurement policies of state marketing boards, and the allocation of expenditures, rather than in strengthening of taxes on agricultural land. These measures will be discussed in chapters 7 and 10.

The second strand is the belief that land taxes can induce more active

34. George E. Lent reports that property taxes are unimportant in the Caribbean Community despite the British tradition and the existence of cadastral surveys for many of the islands; "Property Taxes in the Caribbean Community," *Bulletin for International Fiscal Documentation*, vol. 36 (October 1982), pp. 439–44.

35. This section draws on the excellent book by Richard M. Bird, *Taxing Agricultural Land in Developing Countries* (Harvard University Press, 1974), which includes an extensive bibliography.

use of agricultural land and the breakup of large holdings. This possibility has received special attention in Latin America, where in several countries land ownership is highly concentrated. Proposals to carry out this nonfiscal function often call for progressive taxes on individual or family holdings and sometimes for overt discrimination against land that is not cultivated or that produces less than its full potential output.

In most countries, taxes on agricultural land either are nonexistent or have been too low to yield much revenue or to have much economic effect. In most of Sub-Saharan Africa, land farmed by Africans is not subject to significant taxation, partly because much of it belongs to tribes or the state or at least is not held with European-style titles. In other developing countries, much land is either exempt or illegally omitted from the tax rolls, and for property on the rolls, nominal rates and assessed values are low.

Some essential technical and administrative features of a successful tax can be mentioned here only briefly. First, a fiscal cadastre is needed. This is a record of the location, size, and ownership or occupancy of each tract of land; it may also include information on soil types and usage and value. Often the first step in preparing a cadastre is aerial mapping. Elaborate cadastres are expensive and may take many years to complete, but simplified versions are possible.

Second, land must be valued by reference to its annual rental value or its capital value. Official valuations usually are based on a more or less detailed classification of land and estimated yields under normal conditions with average intensity of cultivation. Valuations may be based on declarations of owners, subject to revision or sanction for understatement. It has been proposed that owners' valuations be made public and that the owners be compelled to sell the land to anyone for the declared value plus a small premium. Such a provision, however, would be subject to abuse and probably would be perceived as unfair. The proposal has not been accepted anywhere. The most feasible approach seems to be through official valuations on the basis of a simple classification, with regular updating to allow for movements of the prices of the principal agricultural commodities.

Third, the legal question of whether the tax applies to the land itself (in rem) or to the owner (in personam) has to be resolved. In most countries, the taxes are regarded as in rem levies. This means that parcels are assessed as units, without regard to the owner's total wealth or income, and that payment can be enforced by seizure of the land if necessary, even if the owner cannot be found. In several Latin American countries, in personam taxes are preferred, and actions to collect them must be directed against owners. Although the in personam approach may appear to be more clearly related to ability to pay and to the objective of reducing the concentration of land ownership, an in rem tax is much easier to administer and is preferred by most experts.

Fourth, the tax rate and rate structure have to be selected. For an in rem tax, only a proportional rate is appropriate, possibly with an exemption for small tracts. Progressive rates may be used in an in personam tax, and they are included in some Latin American taxes and in proposals for other areas. However, for a tax on the gross value of one kind of wealth, progressivity gains little support from the ability-to-pay principle, and progressive rates may be avoided by artificial divisions of ownership among family members.

The specialized literature and the recommendations of expert advisers and commissions have concentrated too much on technical issues and too little on the political obstacles to successful land taxation. It is unlikely that a government can attain through taxation objectives with respect to land ownership and utilization that it cannot achieve directly. Large landowners will resist confiscatory taxation as stubbornly and successfully as they will oppose outright expropriation. In some countries, land taxes are regarded as a legacy of colonial oppression.

Against the administrative and political difficulties may be balanced the economic merits and revenue potential of taxes on agricultural land. The argument that a tax will force better land use has been overstated, but it is true that the tax will make speculative and prestige holdings more costly. The marginal tax on extra yields obtained by better cultivation will be zero. Often overlooked, however, is the possibility that investment in drainage, terracing, green manuring, and other improvements may be discouraged because assessed values will be increased.

A simple agricultural land tax, designed to produce revenue rather than to advance nonfiscal objectives, has a place in many developing countries. It is well to recognize, however, that where a cadastre does not exist a considerable investment of money and time will be required before the tax can be effective.

Estate, Inheritance, and Gift Taxes

Taxes on wealth transfers, like land taxes, have a long history. They may take the form of an estate tax, applying to the total net wealth of the deceased; an inheritance tax, applying to the amounts received by heirs; or a gift tax, applying to transfers between living persons. These taxes have been endorsed even by conservatives, as wholesomely corrective to wealth concentration and relatively innocuous in economic effects. The taxes are levied in many countries, but usually liberal exemptions and avoidance possibilities cause their yield to be trivial. They may be regarded as an instrument of social policy rather than an ordinary revenue measure.

Summary

Although a properly designed and well-administered individual income tax has great advantages, its successful use as a major revenue source depends on conditions that are not satisfied in many countries at early or intermediate stages of development. A global or unitary tax is superior to a schedular or mixed system; however, a changeover to a global tax may entail revenue losses unless the country thoroughly revises tax rates and strengthens administration.

In many developing countries, the beginning rate of the individual income tax is too low to cover administrative costs, whereas the top rate is unrealistically high. Personal exemptions appropriately may be greater in relation to average income than in developed countries in order to limit the number of taxpayers. Where the extended family prevails, it is prudent to set a limit on the number of exemptions allowed a taxpayer. *Forfaits* or other methods that determine income by indirect or external indicators are expedient where adequate accounting records are lacking.

African personal taxes, applying mainly to persons outside the reach of the regular income tax, have been reasonably successful in tapping ability to pay. These taxes appear to be well adapted for local use outside large cities.

Corporation or company income taxes are convenient sources of revenue. They supplement the individual income tax by reaching retained profits and dividends on nonregistered shares and shares owned by nonresidents. Wide rate graduation for these taxes is inappropriate. The elasticity of yield of profits taxes and the broad progressivity of their impact on investors are advantageous.

Most economists have held that a general tax on net profits will not be shifted through price increases in the short run, but that in the long run it may affect the allocation of investment between sectors and relative prices.

Statistical studies of short-run shifting in industrial countries and India have yielded contradictory findings. In an open economy, forward shifting of a profits tax is checked by the competition of imports and the high elasticity of demand for exports, and the volume of investment may be curtailed more severely than it would be in a closed economy.

Many industrial countries and some developing countries have provisions for partial or complete integration of corporation and individual income taxes. Full application of these to nonresident shareholders probably is infeasible. Countries that have partial integration may wish to continue it, but for other countries the adoption of integration is not a high-priority reform.

Assessment of the income of branches and subsidies of foreign corporations is complicated by the difficulty of verifying transfer prices for transactions between affiliates. International double taxation may occur because countries adopt different bases for tax jurisdiction. The problem is mitigated by foreign tax credits and treaties, but controversial issues remain.

Inflation pushes individuals into higher income tax brackets and distorts the measurement of income. The latter effect is more serious and more difficult to correct. During inflation it is especially important to shorten lags in payment of taxes.

A tax on net wealth has appeal as a supplement to income taxation. It is applied in a few developing countries but yields little revenue and must be judged impractical in most countries. Selective wealth taxes on urban property are moderately significant in some British-influenced countries but have not been widely accepted in developing countries, despite the recommendations of foreign advisers.

Agricultural land taxes have been advocated to raise revenue, transfer resources from agriculture to other sectors, induce more active use of land, and break up large land holdings. Administrative and political obstacles have limited their effectiveness. A simple tax, designed for revenue rather than nonfiscal purposes, has a place in many developing countries.

Taxes on wealth transferred at death or by gift yield little revenue. They should be regarded as instruments of social policy rather than ordinary revenue measures.

CHAPTER SIX

Taxation of Consumption

CONSUMPTION, like income, is a broad measure of ability to pay taxes. It is the principal base for indirect taxes, and India and Sri Lanka have experimented with direct taxes on consumption. This chapter examines the merits of the consumption tax base. It discusses briefly the practicality of a direct tax on consumption, and then turns to less novel and fiscally more significant measures—excise taxes and import duties and broad sales taxes, which apply mainly to consumption goods. Consumption taxes in centrally planned economies and the treatment of producers goods in indirect taxes are also considered.

Consumption as a Tax Base

Consumption is a less comprehensive tax base than income because it excludes the part of the accretion to economic power that a person chooses to save and add to wealth. For that reason income has been widely preferred as the primary indicator of ability to pay. However, dissenters have argued that the exclusion of savings is an advantage of a consumption tax and that an income tax is less fair because it results in the double taxation of saving. This is attributed to the application of the income tax both to the receipt of income and to the return on any savings out of the income.[1] Despite its endorsement by a number of distinguished economists, this argument is unconvincing. Saving is an individual decision about the use of income that does not diminish the saver's capacity to bear taxation. Saving itself does not attract tax. What an income tax does strike is the

1. See Joseph A. Pechman, ed., *What Should Be Taxed: Income or Expenditure?* (Brookings Institution, 1980), especially Richard Goode, "The Superiority of the Income Tax," pp. 49–73, and David F. Bradford, "The Case for a Personal Consumption Tax," pp. 75–113; Richard Goode, *The Individual Income Tax*, rev. ed. (Brookings Institution, 1976), pp. 12–36. These references contain extensive citations of other literature.

additional economic resources that a saver gains by lending or investing. In this respect, the return on savings is treated exactly like wages or any other accretion to one's command over economic resources.

A more subtle version of the double-taxation argument is that a consumption tax is fairer than an income tax because the first treats persons equally regardless of when they choose to consume, whereas the second favors those who consume early. The suggested criterion of fairness is that the present value of one's tax liabilities should be independent of the timing of consumption. This is so under a proportional consumption tax, provided that interest accrues on all savings at the same rate at which future tax liabilities are discounted. Under an income tax, the present value of tax liabilities will be greater the larger is the fraction of early income that is saved for later consumption.[2] But to conclude that this difference demonstrates the superiority of a consumption tax is only another way of stating a preference for the consumption base. Anyone who prefers an income tax equally well may point to the larger cumulative amount and greater present value of income resulting from saving and interest receipts as a justification for additional taxation.

A more weighty argument in favor of consumption taxation is an economic one, namely, that it encourages saving, which is especially desirable in developing countries. Under a consumption tax, the net return that can be obtained on income that is saved and invested is higher (in relation to the amount of immediate consumption forgone) than it is under an income tax. With comparable tax rates, the difference is due solely to the fact that postponement of consumption also postpones payment of a consumption tax but does not postpone payment of an income tax. An example may clarify the point. With a consumption tax of 100 percent, a person who receives one hundred dollars of income either can consume fifty dollars immediately and pay fifty dollars of tax or can save one hundred dollars and pay no tax. If he saves the one hundred dollars and places it in a bank deposit bearing 8 percent interest, he can increase his

---

2. Let r be the interest rate/discount rate, ty a proportional income tax rate, and tc a proportional consumption tax rate. If all income is immediately consumed, the present value of tax on each dollar of income will be ty under the income tax and tc under the consumption tax. If a fraction s of income is saved and consumed one year later, the present value of liability under the consumption tax will be unchanged:

$$tc(1 - s) + tc[s(1 + r)][1/(1 + r)] = tc - tcs + tcs = tc.$$

Under the income tax, the present value of liability associated with each dollar of income, of which s is saved and consumed one year later, will be:

$$ty + ty[s(1 + r)][1/(1 + r)] = ty + tys = ty(1 + s).$$

consumption by four dollars a year, which is 8 percent of the amount of immediate consumption forgone by saving. With a 50 percent income tax, the maximum amount that can be consumed or saved is fifty dollars. If the fifty dollars is saved and deposited, the before-tax return is four dollars and the after-tax return is two dollars, which is only 4 percent of the immediate net consumption forgone. The difference of two dollars in return is the net benefit to the saver from deferring payment of the consumption tax.

An increase in the net return may stimulate saving, but by how much, if any, is uncertain. As explained in chapter 4, the substitution effect and the income effect are opposing influences. An increased rate of return makes saving more attractive in comparison with immediate consumption, but it also reduces the amount that has to be saved to make a future purchase or to provide a retirement income. It has not been possible by empirical research to determine which influence is dominant. The impact of taxation on saving will be discussed further in chapter 10.

With tax rates set to yield equal revenue and similar degrees of progressivity or regressivity, income and consumption taxes presumably would have about the same effects on work effort and other productive activities. While nominal rates of consumption taxation would have to be somewhat higher to produce the same amount of revenue, the exemption of savings would offset the difference on the average.

The most important difference in practice between taxing consumption and taxing income is that nearly all consumption taxes have been indirect taxes that do not have the graduated rates that are characteristic of direct taxes on income. This means that, while consumption taxes have not been well adapted to the objective of reducing inequalities of income and wealth, they probably have had less adverse effects on incentives to produce than progressive taxes would have. The feasibility of applying a direct, progressive tax to consumption will be examined in the next section.

The Comprehensive Expenditure Tax

For a long time most of those who would have preferred to tax consumption rather than income shared the common judgment that a direct tax on personal consumption was impracticable. Accounting systems are designed to measure income, not consumption, and the assessment and collection methods, including withholding at the source, that are used for an income tax did not appear suitable for a consumption tax. This conclusion was challenged in the 1950s by Kaldor in an influential book and in reports for India and Sri Lanka that persuaded their governments to institute expenditure taxes (as comprehensive direct consumption taxes are usually called). Both countries twice tried an expenditure tax (limited to upper income groups) and discontinued it because the administration was excessively difficult and the yield paltry.

Despite the disappointing experiences of India and Sri Lanka, interest in an expenditure tax increased during the 1970s and in developed countries there was a tendency to revise the earlier unfavorable evaluation of its feasibility.[3] The tax under consideration would be assessed on the basis of individual returns and would feature personal exemptions and graduated rate schedules similar to those for income taxes.

Recent proposals contemplate that consumption expenditures would be assessed by reference to major cash flows rather than by the aggregation of consumption outlays or from the accounting identity, consumption equals income minus increase in net worth. Taxpayers would be required to report all cash receipts from employment, business, investment transactions, and borrowing and would be allowed to deduct cash payments for business and professional costs and for the acquisition of assets (including any increase in bank balances and debt repayment). The difference would be consumption. Certain exclusions and personal deductions would be allowed.

This bare outline omits several complications. The prevalence of accrual accounting and various credit transactions would make it undesirable to rely exclusively on cash flows in measuring consumption. Some smoothing, averaging, or imputation provisions would be needed for residences and consumer durables. The problems of distinguishing the consumption elements of employee fringe benefits and entertainment and travel expenditures from legitimate costs of earning income would be the same as under the income tax. An important conceptual question is whether expenditures for education and medical care should be classified as consumption or as

3. Nicholas Kaldor, *An Expenditure Tax* (London: Allen and Unwin, 1955); *Indian Tax Reform: Report of a Survey* (New Delhi: Government of India, Ministry of Finance, 1956); *Suggestions for a Comprehensive Reform of Direct Taxation*, Sessional Paper 4—1960 (Colombo: Government of Sri Lanka, Publications Bureau, 1960); William D. Andrews, "A Consumption-Type or Cash Flow Personal Income Tax," *Harvard Law Review*, vol. 87 (April 1974), pp. 1113–88; U.S. Department of the Treasury, *Blueprints for Basic Tax Reform* (Washington, D.C.: Government Printing Office, 1977); Sven-Olof Lodin, *Progressive Expenditure Tax—An Alternative?* Report of the Government Commission on Taxation (Stockholm: LiberForlag, 1978); Institute for Fiscal Studies, *The Structure and Reform of Direct Taxation*, Report of a Committee Chaired by Professor J. E. Meade (London: Allen and Unwin, 1978).

outlays to acquire or maintain human capital. Opinions differ on whether gifts and bequests should be considered consumption by the donor.

Although other countries would no doubt make different decisions on many points, it is instructive to note that the expenditure taxes of both India and Sri Lanka were less than comprehensive. In India, the following items were not taxable: expenditures out of an entertainment allowance granted by an employer; most insurance premiums; purchases of books, works of art, and expensive products of cottage industries; expenditures for the maintenance of livestock; expenditures for a public purpose or of a religious or charitable nature; gifts, donations, or settlements; most taxes; legal expenses; election expenses; marriage expenses; medical expenses; expenditures for education outside India. Sri Lanka exempted many of these items and also expenditures for bullion, precious stones, and jewelry and funeral expenses.

It is doubtful whether an expenditure tax could be successfully assessed without requiring taxpayers to submit balance sheets that would constitute a framework for verification of the completeness and consistency of cash flow reports. For a large number of persons whose income consists exclusively or mainly of salaries and wages subject to withholding, an expenditure tax would be far more difficult to administer than an income tax. For others, balance sheets would be useful even in assessing an income tax but usually have been required only for business income. Their absence would be more serious for an expenditure tax. The omission of any receipt or the overstatement of an investment or debt reduction would cause an equivalent understatement of consumption expenditures. In connection with capital transactions the errors would be far larger than they are under an income tax for which only taxable gains or losses related to the items would be affected. A person who concealed liquid resources held at the time an expenditure tax was introduced might be able to evade the tax later by drawing down the resources. Balances held abroad could be particularly troublesome.[4]

An expenditure tax would be difficult to apply on a wide scale even in countries with the strongest tax administrations. For developing countries, the experience of India and Sri Lanka offers no grounds for optimism about its feasibility, even if confined to a small minority. In 1977, when proposing repeal of the expenditure tax—after a second trial—the minister of finance of Sri Lanka characterized it as "unworkable and impractical in

4. In addition to the items cited in the preceding footnotes, see Michael J. Graetz, "Expenditure Tax Design," in Pechman, *What Should Be Taxed: Income or Expenditure?* pp. 161–295.

an economy like that of Sri Lanka."[5] That judgment applies more emphatically in the many developing countries with weaker tax administrations and less sophisticated financial institutions than exist in Sri Lanka.

Import Duties and Excises

Selective taxes on imports and domestically produced goods and sales taxes, rather than a comprehensive expenditure tax, are the practical means of taxing consumption. Taxes on international trade and transactions, which are mainly import duties, are the largest revenue source in the majority of less developed countries (see table 4-2). Excises are also significant. Originally they were defined as specific taxes on domestic production of enumerated goods. In some countries, excises now apply equally to imported and domestically produced goods, with either specific or ad valorem rates. Although the taxes come partly out of the income of importers and producers, they fall mainly on consumers.[6]

Import duties are an outstanding example of the use of a tax handle. The convenience of taxing goods when they pass through ports or over land borders has long been recognized and exploited. In the course of development, however, revenue from import duties tends to grow less rapidly than national income. Domestic production of goods subject to high duties increases and the composition of imports tends to shift toward semifinished goods and capital goods, which usually are subject to low import duties or which enter free of duty under a general tariff or special incentive legislation.

Although some excises have a long history, many of them appeared as complements or substitutes for import duties. Developing countries have adopted excises on cigarettes and other tobacco products, alcoholic beverages, and petroleum products to prevent the loss of revenue as these goods came to be produced locally. Taxes on them are the major source of excise revenue in most countries. Other commodities that are taxed in many countries include sugar, salt, soft drinks, matches, cosmetics, jewelry,

5. Ronnie de Mel, *Budget Speech, 1978* (Colombo: Government of Sri Lanka, Office of Minister of Finance and Planning, November 15, 1977), p. 52.

6. For more detailed treatments, including references to other literature, see John F. Due, *Indirect Taxation in Developing Economies: The Role and Structure of Customs Duties, Excises, and Sales Taxes* (Johns Hopkins University Press, 1970); Sijbren Cnossen, *Excise Systems: A Global Study of the Selective Taxation of Goods and Services* (Johns Hopkins University Press, 1977). See also David Greenway, "Trade Taxes as a Source of Government Revenue: An International Comparison," *Scottish Journal of Political Economy*, vol. 27 (June 1980), pp. 175–82.

radios, and phonographs. Some countries tax many other consumer goods, some producer goods, and also certain services. Especially extensive excise systems are found in India, Pakistan, Bangladesh, Egypt, and certain countries in the Caribbean and Central America. In a number of countries in the Middle East, Africa, Asia, and Latin America, fiscal monopolies for tobacco, alcohol, matches, sugar, and salt perform essentially the same function as excise taxation.

Although they do not conform nicely to ability to pay, import duties and excises are attractive to governments because they are far easier to administer than direct taxes on income or consumption. Because they are collected from importers or producers, the number of persons with whom the revenue administration must deal is much smaller than for comprehensive taxes on income or consumption. Some of the goods that are subject to excises commonly are produced by only one or a few enterprises. Physical controls are established in customs houses and bonded warehouses from which goods are released only on payment of duties. There is much less need for accounts, audits, and other sophisticated administrative and compliance procedures than there is in the operation of more complex taxes. In practice, selective taxes on luxury consumption items may be more effective in reaching high-income groups than poorly enforced direct taxes on income or consumption are.

Import duties and excises have additional functions that could not be performed by general taxes. They can serve regulatory or sumptuary purposes by discouraging the consumption of certain items that are believed to have undesirable effects on health or public order or merely to represent a low priority use of resources. Taxes on motor fuels allocate a portion of road construction and maintenance costs to users. Protection of domestic producers against foreign competition is a unique function of import duties.

The protective or regulatory and sumptuary purposes conflict with the revenue function. The most complete protection is afforded by a duty so high that imports are prevented. The excises that are most successful in discouraging the consumption of the items on which they are imposed will yield little or no revenue. There is a good deal of confusion about protection and some cant about sumptuary taxes. The minister of finance can always say that cigarettes and beer are not necessities and are harmful if used to excess, while counting on the continued consumption of the products to yield revenue to meet the budget target.

For bringing in revenue, the ideal objects of selective taxation are those with low price elasticity and high income elasticity of demand. Low price elasticity means that the volume of consumption will not be much affected by taxation and that, if required, more revenue can be obtained by raising the tax rate. High income elasticity in the static sense means that the tax will tend to be progressive with respect to income. In a dynamic sense, high income elasticity will result in revenue growth over time as the economy progresses. It is not easy to find commodities that satisfy both these desiderata. Some of the items with low price elasticities are basic necessities such as salt, which also have low income elasticities.

Attention has to be given to the risks of evasion through smuggling or illicit production. Smuggling is easiest for goods of high value in relation to bulk, such as watches and jewelry, but may occur for a wide range of items where borders are long and lightly policed. In these conditions it may be advisable to hold tax rates close to those in neighboring countries that might be a source of smuggling. Illicit production is a problem mainly in the case of beer, toddy, and distilled spirits. The difficulty of checking it has caused some countries to refrain from taxing certain popular beverages with low alcoholic content that compete with commercial products at the margin and no doubt has caused taxes on the latter to be held down.

Import duties and excises appeal to governments not only because of their familiarity and administrative simplicity, but also because they are hidden from consumers. Furthermore, the traditional taxes that account for the bulk of the revenue from selective indirect taxes in most countries probably do not have significant adverse effects on work incentives. Governments that wish to attract people from the subsistence sector to the market economy, however, should be cautious about taxes on incentive goods such as bicycles, radios, kerosene, textiles, and sheet metal roofing material, which may lose their effectiveness as inducements to earn money income if prices become too high.

Formerly all excises and many import duties were fixed at specific money amounts per unit or in relation to weight or volume. Such specific taxes are administratively simple, but they have disadvantages. One of these is the lack of distinction between simple and luxury versions of goods such as cigarettes, cigars, beverages, textiles, and cosmetics. Ad valorem rates will make taxes on these items less regressive—or perhaps progressive—in relation to income. More important, in times of inflation ad valorem rates will prevent the erosion of the real tax rates and will obviate the need for frequent changes in nominal rates.

Increasingly import duties have come to be ad valorem taxes or to be stated in alternative terms, as a specific amount but not less than a certain percentage of value. A few countries, mainly those that have experienced extreme inflation, have transformed all or nearly all their excises into ad valorem taxes. Other governments have hesitated to accept recommendations from experts to convert specific excises to ad valorem taxes. One reason appears to be reluctance to publicize the very high ad valorem equivalents of specific taxes on alcoholic beverages and tobacco products. Another reason may be a belief that it would be socially undesirable to allow low-grade alcoholic beverages to be sold at low prices.

On balance, the conversion of most import duties and excises to ad valorem rates seems advisable. The administrative problems, however, should not be underestimated. The verification of ad valorem taxes requires the scrutiny of import documents and sales records, for which officers need training going beyond that which is traditional for excise officers and many customs officers. During a transitional period, while the customs and excise staffs are receiving training and administrative procedures are being improved, governments may wish to consider enacting legislation that provides for the periodic adjustment of specific tax rates by reference to a general price index, in order to counteract the effect of inflation. Even if the adjustments were made no more frequently than once a year, indexing would simplify decisionmaking and lessen the political onus of raising nominal tax rates.

While both import duties and excises can produce revenue and serve sumptuary or regulatory functions, import duties also protect domestic producers from foreign competition. Decisions would be clarified and policies might be improved if governments would reserve import duties for protection and assign the other functions to excises that would apply equally to imports and domestically produced goods. For many items, the change would be a formal one initially, because there would be no domestic production. The excises on imported goods could be collected at points of entry by customs officials.

A clear distinction between excises and import duties, nevertheless, would have the important advantage of avoiding unintended protection for local production of items that are taxed for revenue or regulatory purposes. For countries that have not gone far in industrialization and that import most of the consumer goods suitable for taxation, customs duties have seemed the obvious means of taxing consumption. Especially when duty rates are high, an incentive is offered for the establishment of domestic production, even if the country enjoys no comparative advantage in the process. When the import duties are much higher on finished goods than on components or ingredients, the local production may be essentially an assembly or repackaging activity, with little value added, that contributes nothing to the acquisition of skills and improved technology. If excises apply to both imports and domestic production, the unintended inducement to establish local production is avoided. It is advisable to rely on excises even when there is no local production because it will be politically difficult to withdraw protection after domestic production begins.

The recommended policy would in no way prevent governments from offering protection to domestic producers. It would, however, cause them to do so only as the result of deliberate decisions rather than the accidental consequence of measures intended for other purposes. Since a developing country cannot reasonably expect that efficient industries can be established immediately to produce substitutes for all imports, the authorities will be well advised to give careful thought to protection policies. Such policies may try to identify and encourage the industries which offer the best prospects of efficient local operation. To that end, close consultation among the planning ministry, the finance ministry, and other departments is desirable. An alternative approach, involving less government intervention, would be to apply a uniform import duty to a wide range of goods and count on market incentives to stimulate the establishment of local production of the goods that can be produced most efficiently.

In evaluating protection, a distinction should be drawn between the nominal rate of import duty and the effective protection provided by the tariff. Effective protection is the increase in remuneration for an activity that is made possible by the tariff. For manufacturing it is the increase in the selling price of the product measured in relation to value added by manufacture that would be generated in the absence of tariffs (*not* in relation to the price that would prevail under free trade).

When value added is only a small fraction of final value, because the cost of material inputs is large, the rate of effective protection may be much higher than the nominal duty rate on the finished product. An import duty on the material inputs will reduce the rate of effective protection, but the effective rate will remain higher than the nominal rate so long as the duty on the inputs is lower than that on the finished product. To illustrate, suppose that bulk pharmaceuticals and containers enter free of duty and account for 80 percent of the value of packaged products, while the latter are subject to an import duty of 50 percent. Then the rate of effective protection for repackaging will be 250 percent rather than the nominal duty rate of 50 percent. If the components and containers were subject to an import duty of 10 percent, the effective protection rate would be 210 percent.[7]

Although practical difficulties are encountered in measuring effective protection, the general implications are clear. Countries that follow the prevalent practice of adopting tariffs combining high rates on finished products with low or zero rates on material inputs may provide higher than intended rates of effective protection for processing, assembly, and repackaging operations.

As a means of limiting imports, taxes are much superior to quotas and licenses. In the absence of effective price controls, which rarely exist for more than a brief time, prices paid by consumers will be similar under both systems. However, the state obtains revenue from taxes, whereas with quantitative controls the difference between domestic prices and import costs accrues to importers and distributors.

The taxation of imports, by curtailing the volume of imports, reduces the demand for foreign exchange and tends to make the foreign-exchange value of the local currency greater than it would otherwise be. This is true over the medium term even if the exchange rate is fixed in the short run rather than set by market forces. Thus the taxation of imports makes exporting less profitable. That result can occur regardless of whether the taxes take the form of import duties or excises on goods that are not

---

7. Effective protection, or the effective tariff rate, may be defined as follows:

$$t_e = (t_n - t_c m)/VA_w,$$

where t_e is the rate of effective protection; t_n is the nominal tariff rate on the finished good; t_c is the tariff rate on imported material inputs; m is the imported material input coefficient, that is, the value of material inputs as a proportion of the value of output, both measured at world prices (which would prevail in the absence of tariffs); VA_w is value added, measured at world prices, which is the value of the product minus material inputs.

An equivalent way of defining effective protection is

$$t_e = VA_l/VA_w - 1,$$

where VA_l is local value added measured at local prices. In practice, some additional complications have to be taken into account in measuring effective protection. See Bela Balassa, "Tariff Protection in Industrial Countries: An Evaluation," *Journal of Political Economy*, vol. 73 (December 1965), pp. 573–94; W.M. Corden, "The Structure of a Tariff System and the Effective Protective Rate," *Journal of Political Economy*, vol. 74 (June 1966), pp. 221–37; and Corden, *The Theory of Protection* (Oxford: Clarendon Press, 1971). An interesting discussion of the problems encountered in calculating rates of effective protection and a comparison of nominal and effective rates for many industries in Malaysia can be found in Lutz Hoffmann and Tan Siew Ee, *Industrial Growth, Employment, and Foreign Investment in Peninsular Malaysia* (Kuala Lumpur: Oxford University Press for the Institut für Weltwirtschaft, Kiel, 1980), pp. 66–84.

locally produced. Further comments on this proposition will be made in the discussion of growth policies in chapter 10.

Selective consumption taxes have not received as much attention as their revenue yield and economic and social consequences would justify. Expert advisers and officials alike usually concentrate on sales taxes and income taxes. In many countries import duties and excises do not conform to a coherent policy of selective taxation but comprise an accumulation of measures taken over the years in response to immediate demands. Multiple taxes or surcharges sometimes apply to the same item. Tariffs often appear to be more elaborate than any easily identifiable protective or revenue objective would require. The rationalization of rates for import duties and excises and the elimination of taxes that yield little revenue and perform no other useful function would be desirable. Although sales taxes are rapidly becoming larger revenue producers in many developing countries, selective excises and import duties remain useful.

Sales Taxes

In ordinary usage, sales taxes are distinguished from excises by their broad coverage. Usually the taxes apply to all sales at one or more stages of production and distribution, except those sales that are explicitly excluded or exempt. The simplest version applies a single rate to all taxable sales; other versions include two, three, or more rates. The forms of sales tax to be considered here are the turnover tax, manufacturers and importers tax, wholesale tax, retail tax, and value-added tax.[8]

Their limited selectivity prevents sales taxes from performing the nonrevenue functions of import duties and excises. It also restricts the possibility of achieving a progressive distribution of taxation by concentrating on luxuries. However, the avoidance of differences in taxation where no positive case for discrimination exists may be regarded as an advantage. Opportunistic or accidental differences in taxation of commodities impose special burdens on consumers with a taste for the heavily

---

8. Terminology is not fully standardized. The term turnover tax is often construed more broadly than it is here and is applied to all kinds of sales tax. Official names of sales taxes are varied; in particular, many taxes here classified as sales taxes are officially known as production taxes. The turnover taxes of centrally planned economies differ greatly from those covered in this section; they are discussed in a later section in this chapter. Cnossen, *Excise Systems*, gives useful summary information on sales taxes. Due, *Indirect Taxation in Developing Economies*, critically reviews the different forms of sales tax.

taxed goods and may also penalize those who have a comparative advantage in producing them.

Generally, sales taxes are administratively more demanding than excises because the revenue department must deal with more enterprises and because more accounting and financial information is required to verify compliance. They are, however, much simpler than income taxes or expenditure taxes. Sales taxes have been introduced in many developing countries to meet persistent revenue demands; they have become more productive because changes in economic structure have increased the tax base, especially in the newly industrializing countries. General sales, turnover, or value-added taxes are in effect in twelve of fifteen semi-industrial countries and produce almost one-fifth of central government revenue in those countries.[9]

The Turnover Tax

The simplest and oldest form of broad sales tax is the turnover tax. It applies, usually at a single low rate, to sales at all stages of production. Known as the *alcabala* in Spain, it was used in that country from the fourteenth to the twentieth century and was exported to the colonies. After discontinuing the turnover tax for a time, Spain revived it in the 1960s. In Europe the turnover tax was used after World War I by Germany, France, Italy, Belgium, the Netherlands, and Austria but has been superseded by the value-added tax. Among developing countries, turnover taxes have been applied in the Philippines, Sri Lanka, Indonesia, Korea, Mexico, Chile, Peru, Argentina, Chad, the Central African Republic, Burundi, Equatorial Guinea, and other countries but have been replaced in most of these countries by other forms of sales tax.

A virtue of the turnover tax is its simplicity. All that is required to check on a single-rate turnover tax is figures on total sales and any exempt sales. The need to collect the tax from a large number of enterprises partly offsets this administrative advantage. The low nominal rate of turnover taxes was initially an attraction, though rates tended to rise later.

A serious disadvantage of the turnover tax is the cumulative taxation that occurs as goods move through successive stages of production and distribution. For example, the turnover tax might apply to yarn, dye, cloth,

9. Unweighted arithmetic mean of country percentages, derived from International Monetary Fund, *Government Finance Statistics Yearbook*, vol. 6 (1982). The semi-industrial countries are those listed in note 6, chapter 1, except Romania, whose tax system differs from those of market-oriented economies. Brazil, Egypt, and Singapore do not have central government sales taxes, but in Brazil value-added taxes are an important source of provincial revenue.

and garments at different stages of manufacture and to wholesale and retail sales of the garments. Such cumulative or repetitive taxation has come to be known as cascading. Because different numbers of stages are characteristic of various goods, the total tax will differ according to technological and commercial practices having no proper bearing on tax policy. The products of vertically integrated enterprises, which combine several stages of production and distribution in one firm, will be subject to a lower total tax than those of other enterprises, and this will give a tax incentive to vertical integration.

Officials of developing countries sometimes look with equanimity on tax-induced integration because they believe that enterprises in their countries tend to be too small to be efficient. Although it is true that economies of scale often can be achieved by large enterprises when the market is big enough, these gains are not necessarily associated with vertical integration. The capricious process of tax cascading is a poor way of encouraging any desirable increases in the size of enterprises.

Other disadvantages of cascading relate to international trade. Imports of finished goods will be taxed at only one or two stages and will be subject to a smaller cumulative turnover tax than domestically manufactured goods. Nearly all countries try to exempt their exports from indirect taxes in order to enable exporters to compete with other producers—and because it is generally accepted that consumption taxes should be collected at the destination of the goods rather than at the place of production. Because the cumulative amount of turnover tax on any particular item is not accurately known, it is not possible to make precise adjustments to put imports and domestic products on an equal footing and to relieve exports of turnover tax. Approximations of the amount of tax are unavoidably inexact and have occasionally been a subject of controversy between taxing countries and their trading partners.

The consensus among tax economists is that the turnover tax should be avoided. Countries not having the measure should choose another form of sales tax if excises are inadequate to their needs. Where the turnover tax is in force, plans should be made to replace it. In a few countries at an early stage of development, the change may not be urgent. The turnover tax will do less harm where there is little manufacturing and exports consist of primary products or the output of integrated enterprises than in countries with more diversified economies. It should be recognized, however, that the tax is likely to handicap the healthy growth of domestic manufacturing and nontraditional exports, especially if the rate is allowed to creep up in response to increasing revenue demands.

The Manufacturers and Importers Tax

In order to avoid cascading and to concentrate on a small number of enterprises, while obtaining broad coverage, many countries have adopted single-stage sales taxes on manufacturers and importers. In one form or another, such taxes are the prevailing kind of sales tax in developing countries. The tax strikes a growing economic sector, while the exclusion of unprocessed foods and many artisans' products—either legally or because of noncompliance—mitigates the burden on the lowest income classes.

Sales taxes on manufactures are in effect in Africa in most of the francophone countries and in Kenya, Tanzania, Uganda, Botswana, Lesotho, Swaziland, Ghana, and Mauritius. In Asia, they are found in Bangladesh, Pakistan, and the Philippines, and in the Western Hemisphere in Colombia and Guyana. In some cases domestic goods and imports are subject to separate taxes, and some of the taxes apply also to certain services. Some countries have uniform rates, usually in the 10 to 15 percent range, while others tax necessities at lower rates and luxury goods at higher rates than the standard rate. In a few countries, particularly Tanzania and Uganda, the proliferation of rates makes the sales tax resemble excises. Foodstuffs, medicines, newspapers, and certain producer goods may be exempt. Export sales usually are exempt.

The usual procedure is to require manufacturers and importers to register with the tax department. Cascading is avoided by the suspensive or ring system or by the deduction or tax credit method. The former imposes a tax on sales to nonregistered enterprises or households but usually not on sales by importers to registered manufacturers or on sales of semifinished goods by one manufacturer to another. The other method resembles that of the value-added tax. Registered enterprises must pay tax on sales to all buyers but are allowed to deduct from taxable sales purchases from registered firms or, more frequently, to take credit for tax paid on purchases from other registered firms. Several of the francophone countries follow the model of the French production tax of 1936, as modified in 1948, and limit the credit or deduction to items that become physical ingredients in the production process and do not allow relief for fuel and other consumable supplies or capital goods. Both methods can eliminate simple cascading, though the production tax results in a degree of cumulative taxation. Tax is collected earlier under the deduction or credit method than under the ring system—an advantage for the government but an inconvenience for importers and manufacturers. The deduction or credit method is more secure against evasion than the ring system and is preferable especially in countries with weak administrations.

The treatment of artisans and other small producers presents a problem. They often are illiterate and in any case maintain no records or books of account showing sales and purchases. In some countries they turn out considerable fractions of the total supply of furniture, clothing, shoes, and certain food products. Failure to tax their sales causes a revenue loss and puts taxable manufacturers at a competitive disadvantage. Nevertheless, it may be expedient to provide an exemption for sales below an amount set so as to leave outside the tax net a large number of small producers. To the extent that they use material inputs bought from registered firms, the small producers will be subject to some tax, though the amount may be small in relation to their sales. As a partial offset to exemption, Tanzania and Uganda impose taxes at above-standard rates on items that are likely to be inputs of nonregistered producers. Although this is a crude adjustment, it merits consideration in other countries. Another possibility is a form of *forfait*, according to which tax is collected on the basis of one or more external indicators such as floor space, number of employees, or use of electric power. This is similar to the *forfait* system for income tax (see chapter 5), though directed toward the approximation of sales rather than net income, and administrative responsibility for the two *forfaits* should be in the same hands.

Although not without administrative problems and deficiencies, the manufacturers and importers sales tax can be recommended to developing countries that are ready to add a broad consumption tax to their excises. It is simpler than the value-added tax and more suitable to the distributive systems of developing countries than a wholesale or retail sales tax. A single-rate sales tax, supplemented by excises on traditionally taxed products and luxuries, has decided administrative advantages over a sales tax with multiple rates.

Wholesale and Retail Taxes

A wholesale tax applies to sales to retailers. It has been recommended for developing countries by some well-known experts[10] but in practice has been used only in Portugal and a few developed countries, including the

---

10. Due, *Indirect Taxation in Developing Economies*, pp. 96–98; Carl S. Shoup and others, *The Fiscal System of Venezuela: A Report* (Johns Hopkins University Press, 1959), pp. 305–11; Richard M. Bird, *Taxation and Development: Lessons from Colombian Experience* (Harvard University Press, 1970), pp. 113–14.

United Kingdom (where it was called the purchase tax), Australia, and New Zealand. The advantage claimed for the wholesale tax is that it applies at a later stage than the manufacturers and importers tax and covers the margins of wholesalers. Wholesaling is not carried on exclusively by separate enterprises but is done also by importers and manufacturers. Hence it is necessary to register all three kinds of enterprise and collect tax on their sales to nonregistered buyers, including retailers and consumers. In developing countries, many enterprises combine wholesaling and retailing and must either be classified according to their predominant activity or be required to report separately on the two activities, which may be difficult. Whether a wholesale tax will differ significantly from a manufacturers and importers tax depends on the extent to which wholesaling is carried on by separate enterprises. The lack of interest in the wholesale tax in developing countries suggests that officials believe that the difference would not be significant or that the presence of mixed wholesale-retail enterprises would seriously complicate the tax.

The retail sales tax has the advantage of applying to the final stage of distribution to consumers and thus covers all value added in the successive stages of production and distribution and avoids cascading. The retail tax is widely used by state and local governments in the United States and formerly was in effect in Sweden, Norway, Denmark, Finland, and Iceland. It has only a limited role in developing countries, where it has been applied in some of the states of India and in Honduras, Costa Rica, and Paraguay.

The great difficulty with the retail tax in developing countries is the large number of small retailers, including tiny shops and roadside vendors and peddlers with no fixed place of business. It is impractical to collect tax from many of them. Small retailers can be exempt from the registration requirement and their purchases taxed like those of final consumers. The tax then becomes a mixed wholesale-retail tax, and the gross profit margins of the exempt small retailers escape taxation. The resulting discrimination against the modern sector presumably is more serious than under a manufacturers and importers tax levied at a comparable rate because a larger fraction of retailing than of manufacturing is carried on by small enterprises. This discrimination would run counter to the view that the modern sector should be promoted.

The Value-Added Tax

The value-added tax is the most important tax innovation of the second half of the twentieth century. Its adoption as a requirement for membership in the European Economic Community (EEC) has given it great prestige and has stimulated interest in it in other countries. It is here classified as a sales tax on consumption, which is its predominant form, though, as explained below, provisions that may appear rather technical can transform it into a kind of income tax.[11]

The tax applies to the value added at successive stages of production and distribution, that is, to sales proceeds less purchases of material inputs and certain services. Value added is equivalent to the sum of wages and salaries, interest, rent, and profits. Hence, in principle, the tax base can be determined by subtracting purchases from sales or by adding up the constituent elements. In practice, a variant of the subtraction method is ordinarily used, with taxes on purchases being credited against the potential tax on sales. A value-added tax may extend through the retail stage. In that case, it is similar to a retail sales tax on the goods and services covered, with the important difference that the value-added tax is collected at each stage rather than being concentrated at the final stage of distribution. The value-added technique can also be used in taxes extending only through the manufacturing or wholesale stage. Some differences arise in classifying taxes imposed at the manufacturing stage that employ a credit method to prevent cascading but omit other features often found in value-added taxes.

The value-added tax is in effect in nine countries of the EEC. Austria, Norway, and Sweden also have value-added taxes, and Greece, Spain, and Portugal are preparing to replace their sales taxes with value-added taxes on the EEC model. In Latin America, value-added taxes exist in Brazil (at the state level), Uruguay, Peru, Argentina, Chile, Ecuador, Mexico, Bolivia, Costa Rica, Nicaragua, and Panama. Israel introduced the tax in 1976 and Korea in 1977. In francophone Africa, value-added taxes are in effect in the Ivory Coast and Senegal. Morocco's sales tax has value-added features and applies to some but not all retailing.

The treatment of capital goods has an important bearing on the economic character of the value-added tax. In the pure consumption

---

11. See Due, *Indirect Taxation in Developing Economies*, pp. 124–36; John F. Due, "Value-Added Taxation in Developing Countries," in N. T. Wang, ed., *Taxation and Development* (Praeger, 1976), pp. 64–186; Clara K. Sullivan, *The Tax on Value Added* (Columbia University Press, 1965); George E. Lent, Milka Casanegra, and Michele Guerard, "The Value-Added Tax in Developing Countries," International Monetary Fund *Staff Papers*, vol. 20 (July 1973), pp. 318–78; Alan A. Tait, *Value Added Tax* (London: McGraw-Hill, 1972); Henry Aaron, ed., *The Value-Added Tax: Lessons from Europe* (Brookings Institution, 1981); Aaron, ed., *VAT Experiences of Some European Countries* (Deventer, Netherlands: Kluwer, 1982); and Price, Waterhouse, *Value Added Tax* (New York: Price, Waterhouse, 1979).

version of the tax, which is in force in Europe, Korea, and Mexico, the tax on purchases of capital goods as well as the taxes on material inputs and on other producers goods is currently deductible. There are also two income versions: a net income version, which spreads deductions in respect of capital goods over their economic life, and a gross income version, which allows no deductions for capital goods. These bases may be compared, respectively, with net domestic product and gross domestic product. Gross income versions are found in Brazil and Peru, while in Argentina deductions for capital goods are spread over five years. The difference in treatment of capital goods is more significant than it may appear, for reasons that will be explained in chapter 10. In this section, attention will be concentrated on the consumption version.

Some countries have a single rate of value-added tax, but the majority differentiate rates to some extent with the objective of taxing some or all necessities more lightly than nonessential goods and taxing some luxuries at high rates. Services are taxed to a much greater extent than under other forms of sales tax. The tax usually applies to imports but not to exports. A significant distinction between exemption and a zero rate should be noted. An exempt enterprise receives no deduction or tax credit for its purchases and is treated in this respect like a consumer, whereas an enterprise in a zero-rated activity receives a rebate of tax on its inputs. Exports appear to be effectively zero-rated in all countries (though there are formal differences in legislation), while certain services, nonprofit activities, and sometimes agriculture are exempted.

Among the advantages of the value-added tax are its broad coverage and relative neutrality. Goods and services are subject to the same effective rate of taxation except where a deliberate decision is made to discriminate through the rate structure or exemption. Most economists consider this degree of neutrality desirable because it minimizes differences in taxation that serve no explicit social or political purpose. Both simple cascading and cumulative taxation of producers goods that are not physically incorporated in the product are avoided. Indirect taxes on exports can be fully and exactly rebated, and imports are placed on a par with domestic products. Spreading the tax over the several stages of production and distribution is often considered an adminstrative advantage compared with collecting it all at one stage because enterprises have less incentive to evade tax. Even if the tax extends through the retail stage, the difficulty of dealing with small retailers is less serious than under a retail sales tax, since failure to collect from retailers results in evasion of the tax on their margins rather than the whole tax. Advocates of the value-added tax have stressed the possibility of using information it generates as a cross check on compliance with other taxes, particularly income taxes. In practice, however, few countries make extensive use of the possibility.

The major disadvantages of the value-added tax are the large number of firms from which tax must be collected and the paperwork involved in computing and verifying credits or deductions. It is more complex than a single-stage manufacturers and importers tax. Although the value-added tax appears to have been successful in a number of developing countries, its advantages and indeed its practicability are questionable for countries where much business is carried on by small enterprises, accounting is unreliable, and tax administration is weak.

France, Italy, and some other countries make extensive use of *forfait* systems for small enterprises. A common form of *forfait* determines taxable value added on the basis of gross sales with an allowance for tax on presumed purchases; it does not require supporting records of purchases. Even cruder methods may be used in some cases. In France in 1975, 57 percent of all value-added tax assessments were *forfait* assessments, and another 25 percent were made according to simplified methods.[12] In Italy, 70 percent of retail stores, 20 percent of artists and professionals, and 50 percent of artisans are subject to the *forfait* system. Evasion and undertaxation owing to the *forfait* system appear to be extensive in Italy. In 1977 the amount of value added reported on tax returns was 40 percent less than the national accounts figures, the shortfall ranging between zero for energy production and 68 percent for hotels and restaurants.[13] In these conditions, some of the advantages claimed for the value-added tax are to a great extent hypothetical.

Consumption Taxes in Centrally Planned Economies

In centrally planned economies, turnover taxes are a major source of revenue. These taxes, however, differ greatly from the turnover taxes of other countries. They perform the double role of regulating prices and profits and of raising revenue to finance governmental activities and transfers, and it is difficult to distinguish these functions. The turnover

---

12. France, Ministère de l'Economie et de Finances, *Statistiques et Etudes Financieres*, no. 339 (March 1977), p. 204.

13. Antonio Pedone, "Italy," in Aaron, *The Value-Added Tax*, pp. 35–36.

taxes are much more highly differentiated than the sales taxes of other countries and resemble in some respects extensive excise tax systems.

The turnover tax in the People's Republic of China, adopted in 1958 and called the consolidated industrial and commercial tax, seems to be primarily a revenue measure. It applies to the sales proceeds of state enterprises, cooperatives, and other businesses engaged in manufacturing, importing, retailing, communications, transportation, and miscellaneous services.[14] Enterprises that buy agricultural products are taxed on their purchases; wholesalers are not taxed except with respect to any purchases of agricultural products or importations. Banking, insurance, and some other activities are exempt. More than one hundred categories of taxable products and services are listed, and more than forty different tax rates are applied. A general rate of 5 percent applies to industrial products not specifically subjected to another rate; the maximum rate is 66 percent on high-grade cigarettes. Many services are taxed at 5 percent, retailing at 3 percent. In 1979 the turnover tax accounted for more than three-fourths of total tax revenue in China.

The Chinese tax includes no general provision to mitigate cascading. Indeed, an effort is made to offset the advantages that integrated firms would enjoy by imputing a constructive sale and applying a tax when processed materials, components, or capital goods produced by an enterprise are used by it in further production. A manufacturer that retails its products is subject to tax at both the manufacturing and retailing stages. Tax reductions or exemptions may be granted for activities that the authorities wish to encourage or for enterprises that are experiencing difficulties. Officials are reported to be aware of the economic objections to cascading and in 1979 to have been considering reforms, including the possible substitution of a value-added tax for the turnover tax.

The turnover taxes of the USSR and other Eastern European members of the Council for Mutual Economic Aid (Comecon) are even more highly differentiated than the Chinese tax, and their regulatory function is more emphasized.[15] Marxist economists often assert that, though the turnover

14. The information on the Chinese turnover tax is from Richard D. Pomp, Timothy A. Gelatt, and Stanley S. Surrey, "The Evolving Tax System of the People's Republic of China," *Texas International Law Review*, vol. 16 (Winter 1981), pp. 16–32.

15. The most complete treatment in English is Franklyn D. Holzman, *Soviet Taxation: The Fiscal and Monetary Problems of a Planned Economy* (Harvard University Press, 1955), but it does not cover reforms made in the 1960s. More recent references, which concentrate on countries other than the USSR, are Tamas Bacskai, "New Developments in the Taxes on Enterprises in Some Socialist Countries—The Hungarian Experience," *Public Finance/Finances Publiques*, vol. 25 (1970), pp. 212–32; Zdzislaw Fedorowicz and Miroslaw Orlowski, "Recent Changes and Proposals for Change in the Administration of the Turnover Tax in Some Socialist Countries," *Public Finance/Finances Publiques*, vol. 25 (1970), pp. 307–18; Zdenek Drabek, "Estimation and Analysis of Turnover Tax in Centrally-Planned Economies

tax is included in prices, it is not a burden on consumers but a transfer to the state of part of the surplus product created because of rising industrial productivity and the failure to pay workers the full value of their net product. Outside critics usually reject this argument, and some have asserted that not only the turnover tax but the transfers of profits from state enterprises to the budget should be regarded as taxes on consumers. This disagreement is casuistic to a degree and cannot be easily resolved because the state acts both as the owner of enterprises and as a taxing authority. In principle, it should be possible to distinguish the state's ownership share from its tax revenue by imputing a return on enterprise capital, as is done in some mixed economies, but this approach is not congenial to Marxists. Recently, there has been a tendency for writers from Comecon countries tacitly or explicitly to recognize the fiscal function of their turnover taxes.

Until about the mid-1960s, the Comecon countries tended to set producer prices by reference to average costs and to adjust consumer prices to "use value" and planning targets by highly differentiated turnover taxes. Turnover taxes included not only percentage rates applying to specified commodities but differential taxes on particular enterprises. In Hungary, there were more than 2,500 percentage rates and "several tens of thousands" of differential taxes.[16] Many socialist writers became highly critical of the system, which they considered to be too centralized and to allow too little incentive or scope for efficiency. Several Comecon countries undertook reforms in the middle to late 1960s that tended to diminish the importance of the turnover taxes and to reduce the number of rates. Greater emphasis was placed on percentage rates as distinguished from enterprise-specific differential taxes. In Hungary in 1968, collection was moved from the manufacturing to the wholesale stage, and the number of rates was reduced to 1,000 as the first step in a plan to bring the number down to 300–400. Similar, though less drastic, changes were made in Czechoslovakia but later were partially reversed. The contribution to the budget from turnover taxes declined in relation to profit transfers in the two countries but still remained substantial.

The centrally planned economies have been attracted to indirect con-

---

with Special Reference to Czechoslovakia," *Public Finance/Finances Publiques*, vol. 34 (1979), pp. 196–224; Vladimir Hacik, "Fiscal Aspects of Socialist Budgets," in Karl Haeuser, ed., *Subsidies, Tax Reliefs and Prices*, Proceedings of the Thirty-Third Congress, International Institute of Public Finance (Paris: IIPF, 1981), pp. 151–61.
    16. Bacskai, "New Developments in the Taxes on Enterprises," pp. 220–21.

sumption taxes by the same characteristics that have been recognized as advantageous by many other countries—their administrative simplicity, hidden nature, and supposed light impact on work incentives. Information on the distribution of the burden by income levels is meager. Turnover tax rates are often high on articles of wide consumption, such as clothing and processed foods, which suggests overall regressivity, but it is hazardous to draw conclusions without taking into account other factors that affect money income and household budgets. Estimates for Czechoslovakia for 1970 show effective rates of 15 percent on foodstuffs, 27 percent on footwear, 32 percent on clothing, and 66 percent on tobacco. The same source reports overall progressivity of the turnover tax, with the burden ranging from 17 percent of household income for low-income groups to 22 percent at average income levels and 29 percent for high incomes.[17] As the methodology is not described, it is impossible to say whether these figures are directly comparable with estimates for other countries.

Developing countries, regardless of whether they prefer socialism, capitalism, or mixed economies, cannot with advantage emulate the turnover taxes of the centrally planned economies. The taxes operate in a context of more detailed and more centralized planning than exists in other countries, and they have been subjected to sharp criticism even in the centrally planned economies.

The Treatment of Producers Goods in Indirect Taxes

Except for cascading turnover taxes and protective import duties, indirect taxes usually are designed to keep many or all producers goods free of tax. Three kinds of producers goods may be distinguished—raw materials and components that are physically incorporated in manufactured goods, consumable supplies and services, and durable capital goods. Although excises on petroleum products are widely used, and a good many developing countries tax cement, there are relatively few excises on any of the categories of producers goods. An exception is India, which taxes metals, plastics, coal, wood, rubber, cement, and motors. Among broad sales taxes, the value-added tax is especially suited to the exclusion of all kinds of producers goods, if desired; that is less easily accomplished under the single-stage taxes.

17. Hacik, "Fiscal Aspects of Socialist Budgets," p. 160. On the basis of the 1962 input-output table, Drabek estimated much higher effective rates for the classes of goods mentioned; see "Estimation and Analysis of Turnover Tax," p. 207.

Nearly all countries except those that impose turnover taxes exempt from sales tax goods that become physical ingredients of manufactured products. That is the only class of producers goods excluded from the tax base by the francophone African countries that follow the model of the former French production tax and some other countries.

The application of single-stage sales taxes to consumable supplies and services, such as fuel, electric energy, and transportation, results in a degree of cascading but far less than under a turnover tax. Inefficiencies and inequities are most likely to result in respect to taxable services such as repairs, accounting, and computer operations, owing to the inducement that importers and manufacturers are given to save tax by performing the services for themselves.

The treatment of durable capital equipment and construction materials presents more difficult issues. The exemption of these goods is consistent with the objective of taxing consumption and with a policy of encouraging investment to promote growth. The taxation of durable capital goods will make mechanization and other capital-intensive production methods less profitable than they would otherwise be. Many economists have argued that any resulting changes in production methods are distortions that impair efficiency. The opinion that capital goods should not be taxed is prevalent in developing countries, as well as industrial countries and centrally planned economies. Recently, however, the appropriateness of that policy for developing countries has been increasingly challenged. Dissenters point to a chronic problem that many countries face in offering employment to a growing labor force and argue that labor-intensive production methods should be encouraged to use an abundant resource and to foster an egalitarian and self-reliant style of development. In many developing countries, the cost of investing in durable capital goods is artificially depressed by overvalued exchange rates, controlled interest rates, and tax incentive schemes, while wage costs are inflated by employment and payroll taxes, minimum wages, and mandatory fringe benefits. In such conditions, the application of a sales tax to capital goods may be a useful counterweight.

At present, there is no general presumption either for or against the exclusion of durable capital goods from sales taxation in developing countries. Each government should examine the question in the light of the circumstances of the country and its objectives. Further comments on tax features of alternative growth strategies appear in chapter 10.

Summary

Consumption is a measure of ability to pay taxes but a less comprehensive one than income. The argument that a consumption tax is fairer than an income tax because the latter results in double taxation of saving is unconvincing. A consumption tax may encourage saving, but that is uncertain. In practice, the greatest differences between consumption taxes and income taxes stem from the indirect character and lack of progressive rates of the former. Hence the consumption taxes are ineffective for reducing inequality but probably are less harmful than income taxes to production incentives.

A direct tax on personal consumption has been discussed and was tried unsuccessfully by India and Sri Lanka. The measure is too complex for developing countries.

Import duties and the major excises are examples of the use of convenient tax handles. They are the largest sources of revenue in the majority of developing countries. They are simpler to administer than direct taxes or broad sales taxes. When high rates are applied to luxuries, import duties and excises may be more effective in reaching high-income groups than poorly enforced direct taxes. They can also serve regulatory or sumptuary purposes. The hidden character of indirect taxes appeals to many governments.

It is advisable to convert most import duties and excises to ad valorem rates to prevent their erosion by inflation. This, however, would present some administrative problems. As an interim step, specific taxes could be adjusted annually by reference to a general price index.

Ideally, import duties should be used only to protect domestic producers, and excises, applying to both imported and domestic products, should be relied on to raise revenue. That arrangement would clarify policy and avoid granting unintended protection. Effective protection rather than nominal tariff rates is the relevant variable. Taxation of imports tends to curtail them, to raise the foreign exchange value of the currency, and to make exports less remunerative.

Sales taxes are broader in coverage and hence less adaptable to nonrevenue purposes than excises. Although administratively more demanding than excises and customs duties, they have been introduced in many developing countries and are especially important in the semi-industrial countries. The turnover tax, because of its cascading (the addition of tax at each stage of production), has serious economic disadvantages outside the least developed countries and should be avoided. Single-stage manufacturers and importers sales taxes are the most frequent form in developing countries and can be recommended to governments that are ready to adopt a sales tax. Wholesale and retail sales taxes are poorly adapted to the distributive systems of developing countries.

The value-added tax is an important fiscal innovation that gains prestige from its use in the EEC. It has advantages in avoiding cascading and facilitating exact rebates of tax on exports. The alleged usefulness of the tax as a check on compliance with income taxes has seldom been exploited. Although the value-added tax has been successful in several developing countries, it is more complex than a manufacturers and importers tax, and its suitability is questionable for countries where small enterprises are important, accounting is unreliable, and administration is weak.

Turnover taxes are a major revenue source in centrally planned economies. They also perform price regulatory functions. The rates are highly differentiated, and the incidence of the taxes is hard to ascertain. Other developing countries cannot with advantage emulate the taxes.

Except in India, only a few excise taxes apply to producers goods. Most sales taxes exempt producers goods that become physical ingredients of manufactured products. They may apply to durable capital equipment and consumable supplies and services. The consumption version of the value-added tax, which is the most common form, relieves all producers goods of tax. Freeing capital goods from tax is consistent with the objective of encouraging investment to promote growth. The policy, however, can be challenged on the grounds that it is too favorable to capital-intensive production and too little conducive to employment creation. There is no strong presumption either for or against the exclusion of durable capital goods from sales taxation in developing countries.

CHAPTER SEVEN

Taxation of Exports and Natural Resources

EXPORTS and scarce natural resources offer convenient tax handles for developing countries. This chapter covers not only formal taxes on exports and natural resources but also revenue obtained through state corporations and the foreign exchange system and from royalties and payments for concessions to exploit mineral deposits and forests. Formal taxes and revenue obtained by the state as owner of natural resources often are closely related, and their economic effects are similar. The taxation of exports and natural resources are conveniently discussed together because in developing countries a large fraction of the production of minerals and forest products is exported.

Export Taxes

Export taxes in the broadest sense include customs duties, surpluses of state marketing boards and stabilization funds, and profits from multiple exchange rate systems. They are levied mostly on agricultural, forest, and mineral products of less developed countries. Few export taxes are now imposed by industrial countries.[1] As the taxation of forest and mineral products is dealt with in a separate section, attention here will be directed mainly to exports of agricultural commodities.

---

1. For general treatments and references to other literature, see Richard Goode, George E. Lent, and P. D. Ojha, "Role of Export Taxes in Developing Countries," International Monetary Fund *Staff Papers*, vol. 13 (November 1966), pp. 453–503; excerpts in Richard M. Bird and Oliver Oldman, *Readings on Taxation in Developing Countries*, 3d ed. (Johns Hopkins University Press, 1975), pp. 154–73; and Jonathan V. Levin, *The Export Economies: Their Pattern of Development in Historical Perspective* (Harvard University Press, 1960), pp. 263–81, passim.

Functions

Export taxes are especially convenient for obtaining revenue from export crops grown by small farmers who are difficult to reach by income taxes or land taxes. Where plantation agriculture prevails, other forms of taxation may be feasible, but the administrative simplicity of export taxes may still make them preferable. Governments may also choose export taxes because they expect them to yield more stable revenue than income taxes.

In addition to raising revenue, export taxes may have other functions. They hold the domestic price of export commodities below the external price and thus offer an advantage to local processing analogous to the protection against foreign competition that is provided by import duties. This function often has been served through multiple exchange rate systems. Uruguay, for example, once had an elaborate system of multiple rates that was intended to encourage local processing by setting successively more depreciated exchange rates for greasy wool, washed wool, wool tops, and textiles and for hides, frozen beef, and canned meat. The system gave the processors a greater return in local currency for value added to the favored items than was received for other exports that sold for equal amounts in foreign markets. For commodities that are both consumed at home and exported, export taxes keep down prices for domestic consumers. Examples are coffee in Brazil and rice in Thailand.[2] A regulatory function may be served by designing export taxes to penalize low-grade or substandard exports. This is a consequence of specific duties, though they may be selected primarily because they are simpler than ad valorem duties.

Another important function, associated particularly with marketing boards and stabilization funds but also served by formal export duties, is economic stabilization. This function will be discussed in chapter 11.

Until the nineteenth century, export taxes were used by many European countries to raise revenue and to encourage domestic manufacturing. In England, for example, duties were imposed on exports of wool and hides in 1275, and by 1660 duties had been extended to more than 200 articles. Most export duties were eliminated in Europe during the nineteenth century, but a few were continued to foster domestic processing. The

2. Owing to the heavy taxation of rice exports by Thailand and the important place of rice in household budgets, the impact on the cost of living has had important economic effects on both the agricultural and nonagricultural sectors. See Edward Van Roy, "The Pursuit of Growth and Stability through Taxation of Agricultural Exports: Thailand's Experience," *Public Finance/Finances Publiques*, vol. 23 (1968), pp. 294–313.

United States never levied export duties; they were prohibited by the Constitution at the insistence of southern states that produced agricultural staples for export.

After their decline in Europe, export duties were continued in colonies in Asia and Africa to raise revenue and to favor exports to the mother country and shipping in national-flag carriers. The latter functions were served by discriminatory rates or rebates. In Latin America, export duties were used primarily to raise revenue. During World War II and immediately afterward marketing boards were established in a number of countries in Africa and Asia. They became especially important in Ghana, Nigeria, Uganda, Burma, and Thailand. Marketing boards had monopolies of exports of several commodities, including cotton, groundnuts (peanuts), cocoa, palm kernels and palm oil, and rice. The boards were intended primarily to facilitate marketing, stabilize prices, and standardize and improve exports, but for some time they realized substantial surpluses. In francophone countries of Africa stabilization funds performed essentially the same functions as the marketing boards of English-speaking countries, though with different institutional arrangements. Regardless of whether the surpluses of the marketing boards and stabilization funds were turned over to state budgets, they have been used to a great extent to finance governmental (or similar) projects.

Current Applications

At present, export taxes apply in various countries to the major tropical agricultural products including coffee, tea, cacao (cocoa), sugar, bananas, rice, groundnuts, vegetable oils, rubber, jute, and sisal and to logs, hides, tin, copper, bauxite, and other commodities. Table 7-1 shows the percentage of central government revenue obtained from export duties in 1973–79 in thirty-one developing countries for which the statistics are readily available. The countries included are those that obtained 5 percent or more of total revenue from export duties. Generally, only formal export taxes are included. The table also reveals the extreme fluctuations in the export duty share of revenue in several countries. These fluctuations are associated with the introduction and termination of duties and changes in duty rates— sometimes in connection with currency devaluations—and fluctuations in the price and volume of exports of taxable commodities. In the case of Guyana, the big bulge in export duty revenue in 1974–76 was due to the introduction and subsequent elimination of a sugar duty when the sugar price rose sharply before declining in 1977. Fluctuations of coffee prices

Table 7-1. *Export Duties as a Percentage of Total Revenue of Central Government, Selected Developing Countries, 1973–79*

Country	1973	1974	1975	1976	1977	1978	1979	Average[a]
Ghana	23	26	35	22	24	21	48	28
El Salvador	19	19	20	30	39	24	33	26
Zaire	38	40	22	21	19	8	26	25
Rwanda	20	17	16	32	36	18	...	23
Sri Lanka	11	16	10	9	12	39	35	19
Burundi	16	10	6	28	30	...	...	18
Swaziland	3	20	34	23	10	...	...	18
Ivory Coast	19	18	16	17[b]	...	...	...	18
Malaysia	13	20	12	16	18	17	19	16
Guatemala	7	8	10	12	26	24	19	15
Grenada	...	13	16	14	14	...	...	14
Guyana	2	30	46	16	4	1	1	14
Solomon Islands	...	...	10	11	16	18	...	14
Sierra Leone	...	10	8	10	18	16	10	12
Ethiopia	10	9	6	12	22	...	...	12
Mauritius	9	11	18	12	11	11	10	12
Bolivia	18	16	11	9	7	6	10	11
Dominican Republic	8	13	22	11	13	6	10	11
Ecuador	15	18	10	9	6	9	7	11
Colombia	8	6	8	9	11	10	16	10
Gambia	7	9	14	10	7	7	...	9
Costa Rica	1	10	12	10	11	8	9	9
Cameroon	...	...	12	14	10	4	2	8
Mali	...	...	5	8	12	...	...	8
Tanzania	4	7	6	4	16	9	7	8
Peru	1	c	2	6	12	16	16	7
Chad	7	7	7	8	...	...	...	7
Pakistan	13	15	8	4	c	1	1	6
Argentina	10	5	5	12	4	2	1	6
Gabon	8	7	2	2	...	...	...	5
Philippines	5	9	9	3	3	2	2	5

Source: Except for the Ivory Coast, derived from International Monetary Fund, *Government Finance Statistics Yearbook*, vol. 5 (1981); for the Ivory Coast, *Ivory Coast: The Challenge of Success*, A World Bank Country Economic Report (Johns Hopkins University Press for the World Bank, 1978), pp. 360–61. Ellipses indicate data are not available.
a. Arithmetic mean of annual percentage; computed from unrounded numbers.
b. Estimate.
c. Less than 0.5 percent.

for Rwanda and El Salvador and of cacao prices for Ghana were important influences on export duty revenue of those countries. Although comparable and comprehensive statistics are not available, it seems highly probable that, in the aggregate, export tax yields in recent years have been considerably smaller in relation to budgets and export values than at times in the past.

Detailed study is necessary to ascertain the total of export taxation, in

Table 7-2. *Rates of Implicit Taxation of Selected Export Crops
in Some African Countries, 1971–75 and 1976–80*[a]

Crop and country	1971–75[b]	1976–80[b]
Cocoa		
Cameroon	63	55
Ghana	53	60
Ivory Coast	44	62
Togo	50	75
Coffee		
Cameroon	28[c]	40[c]
Ivory Coast	32	64
Kenya	6	. . .
Tanzania	20	41
Togo	58	77
Cotton		
Cameroon	. . .	21
Ivory Coast	21	−5[d]
Mali	45	56
Senegal	35	. . .
Sudan	22	40
Togo	38	21
Upper Volta	. . .	21
Groundnuts		
Malawi	30	41
Mali	43	57
Senegal	52	66
Sudan	15	33
Zambia	30	29
Tea		
Kenya	11	. . .
Tobacco		
Malawi	58	72
Zambia	−9[d]	12

Source: World Bank, *Accelerated Development in Sub-Saharan Africa: An Agenda for Action* (Washington, D.C.: World Bank, 1981), p. 56. Ellipses indicate data are not available.

a. The rates are the complements of the "nominal protection coefficient," which is defined as "the price paid to the producer divided by the amount he would have received had he sold his crops at the world price minus transport, marketing, and processing costs."

b. The number of observations in the subperiods differs among countries.

c. Arabica.

d. Negative tax or subsidy.

the extended definition, on particular commodities. Table 7-2, which is adapted from statistics given in a World Bank report on Sub-Saharan Africa, sheds some light on the subject: it shows the rates of implicit taxation of selected export crops in several countries in the area. The implicit tax is the difference between the price paid to the producer and the amount he would have received had he been paid the world price minus transportation, marketing, and processing costs. It is made up of taxes in the formal sense—mainly but not exclusively export duties—and the margins of marketing and stabilization agencies. The implicit tax is here related to the world price minus transportation, marketing, and processing costs. The implicit taxes on the crops may be underestimated since no allowance is made for the possibility that costs are inflated because of the absence of competition or the possibility that sales proceeds are depressed because of overvaluation of the African currencies. (The countries covered in the table do not have multiple exchange rates for exports.) Cocoa was subject to especially heavy implicit taxation in the four countries covered in the table. Cacao prices in New York and London fluctuated widely from year to year and in 1976–80 averaged about three times the 1971–75 level.[3] Rates of implicit taxation of the other commodities differed greatly among the countries.

Incidence and Effects

Legal liability for formal export duties is on exporters—for agricultural commodities usually an independent dealer or state marketing agency and for minerals frequently the enterprise that extracts and concentrates them. The actual incidence is determined by economic conditions. The tax could fall on foreign consumers, export shippers, or domestic producers or could be shared by all of them. As explained in chapter 4, the economic forces determining tax incidence can be looked at under the headings of elasticity of demand and elasticity of supply. Low elasticity of demand and high elasticity of supply are conducive to shifting to consumers, whereas the opposite conditions cause a tax to be absorbed by producers.

In most cases, the elasticity of demand for a primary product exported by any one country that produces a small fraction of world output is very high at prices above or below those prevailing in the major external markets. This is true regardless of the elasticity of demand of total world consumption because the outputs of different countries are close substitutes. Substitution is especially easy for primary products that are graded on the basis of physical characteristics and sold in competitive markets. An attempt to raise the price to cover an export tax will cause foreign buyers to turn to other sources of supply.

3. International Monetary Fund, *International Financial Statistics*, yearbook, 1981, p. 79.

Exceptions can occur. For example, although Thailand produces only a small part of the world output of rice, it is an important exporter. Only about 5 percent of total world rice production normally enters into international trade, and Thailand's exports usually account for one-fifth to one-fourth of the traded volume. The rice market is subject to extensive government intervention, including quotas, subsidies, and government-to-government trading. In these circumstances, it has been estimated that the price elasticity of foreign demand for Thai rice is about − 4 and that as much as one-half of Thailand's export tax falls on foreign consumers. If international trade in rice were liberalized, the elasticity of foreign demand for Thai rice would greatly increase, and the possibility of shifting part of the export tax to foreigners would sharply diminish.[4]

When the taxing country produces a large part of world output of the commodity or other producing countries impose similar taxes, conditions are more favorable to shifting an export tax to consumers. But forward shifting is still limited by the possibility that a price rise will stimulate production elsewhere and by the elasticity of world demand. Demand may be elastic at higher prices partly because of the possibility of substituting other products for the taxed commodity—synthetic fibers for wool and cotton, synthetic rubber for natural rubber, one vegetable oil for another, beet sugar and corn sweeteners for cane sugar, paper bags or bulk shipping for jute bags, aluminum for copper, and so on. Both supply from other countries and demand are more elastic in the long run than in the short run.

It may be concluded that foreign consumers usually will bear only a small part of export taxes because of their access to untaxed sources of supply and substitute products. With rare exceptions, a country that imposes an export tax should regard it as primarily a tax on its own producers and traders.

The division of the burden of export taxation among domestic producers and traders depends to a great extent on their ability and willingness to move from the taxed field to other activities, which in turn are related to the alternative opportunities open to them. Those whose earnings from the taxed commodity were previously much greater than in their next-best opportunity will have to absorb a larger share of the tax than those who could have earned almost as much in another activity and who would withdraw their services if faced with an income cut. Owners of land planted

4. George S. Tolley, Vinod Thomas, and Chung Ming Wong, *Agricultural Price Policies and the Developing Countries* (Johns Hopkins University Press for the World Bank, 1982), chaps. 4 and 8.

to tree crops or of mines cannot immediately withdraw their capital and may continue production—bearing the export tax—so long as the price, net of tax, covers marginal variable costs, although new investment or even normal maintenance of the existing trees or mine may not be carried out. In contrast, landowners and peasant cultivators in regions well suited to several annual crops may largely escape an export tax on one crop by converting to other crops. Although traders may own some specialized collection and storage facilities, in most cases they probably gain their income mainly from trading skills and capital, or political connections, that are adaptable to other uses and hence will not be much affected by an export tax. However, where weak competition among middlemen has previously resulted in abnormal profits, an export tax may capture some of that income.

These comments assume more awareness of economic opportunities and more sensitivity to incentives than was postulated in many past discussions of export taxation or is visualized by some contemporary officials. The comments imply that export taxes ordinarily will cause a reduction in the volume of production and exports. An opposing view is that the taxes will not have much effect on production by peasant farmers because they are not well informed about alternative opportunities and are slow to respond to price incentives.

Occasionally it is asserted that export duties or marketing board policies that hold down the prices received by farmers will actually stimulate production because peasants have a "target income mentality," which makes them satisfied with a small cash income and disinclined to exert themselves to earn more. If that attitude were controlling, production would tend to move inversely with price because a smaller amount would have to be sold to reach the target income when the price was high than when it was low. (The condition may be characterized as a backward-bending supply curve.) Although there are some convincing reports of target income behavior among people who have had only limited contact with a money economy, it appears that the mentality, if ever widely prevalent, has become exceptional. The great increase in the production of cash crops in tropical Africa during the twentieth century, for example, could not be accounted for if the population's income aspirations were low and inflexible. Probably the production of cash crops, including those subject to export taxes, is much more affected by prices than the production of subsistence crops, though the influence of taxes and prices on marginal movements between household consumption or barter and market sales should not be overlooked.[5]

Informed observers and many statistical studies have reported positive price elasticities of production of agricultural commodities in countries of Asia, Africa, and Latin America. In the short run, as expected, elasticity is most noticeable for annual crops, but even some tree crops have been found to respond to prices in the short run through changes in the completeness of the harvest. In the long run, elasticity tends to be greater than in the short run. For annual crops, this is presumably because of the time needed for farmers to react and obtain required inputs. For most tree crops, the time needed for plants to reach commercial production is about five to nine years.

The statistical studies differ in technique and in the numerical value of estimated elasticities. Supply response has been measured both by area planted and by volume of production or marketings. The price variable usually is a relative measure in which the price of the commodity being studied is related to the general price level, the prices of other crops, or the prices of agricultural inputs. Expected prices at the time of harvest are relevant for planting decisions, but they are not directly observable and researchers have had to assume that farmers project future prices by reference to current prices or some average of past prices.

Among crops that have been subject to export taxes, positive short-run price elasticities of supply have been reported for rice in Thailand; groundnuts in Sudan and Nigeria; cotton in Pakistan, India, Egypt, and Uganda; jute in India and Bangladesh; sisal in Tanzania; tobacco in Nigeria and Malawi; cocoa in Ghana, Nigeria, Cameroon, Brazil, and Venezuela; coffee in Uganda, Kenya, Brazil, other Latin American countries, and Jamaica; rubber in Malaysia and Thailand; palm oil and palm kernels in Nigeria; and wool in Uruguay. Positive long-run elasticities, usually greater than the short-run values, were reported also for most of these items and for cocoa in the Ivory Coast, Ecuador, and the Dominican Republic; for coffee in Colombia; and for wool in Argentina.[6]

---

5. Judicious comments on the motivation of African farmers can be found in John C. de Wilde, *Experiences with Agricultural Development in Tropical Africa*, vol. 1 (Johns Hopkins University Press for the International Bank for Reconstruction and Development, 1967), pp. 53–70. See also Gerald K. Helleiner, *Peasant Agriculture, Government, and Economic Growth in Nigeria* (Irwin, 1966), chap. 3.

6. Hossein Askari and John Thomas Cummings, *Agricultural Supply Responses—A Survey of Econometric Evidence* (Praeger, 1976) and by the same authors, "Estimating Agricultural Supply Response with the Nerlove Model: A Survey," *International Economic Review*, vol. 18 (June 1977), pp. 257–92.

Some qualifications should be made at once. First, though the great majority of estimates show positive price elasticities, some negative values have been reported. Second, there are large differences in estimated elasticities for some items between countries, regions within countries, and time periods. These differences are no doubt due to nonprice variables that could not be adequately taken into account such as differences in social structures, tenancy systems, farm size, monetization, marketing systems, and the availability and cost of credit and material inputs. In some cases, different researchers have published results that appear to conflict.[7] Third, the numerical values of the elasticity coefficients are not impressively high in most cases. Representative short-run values are between 0.2 and 0.8; long-run values are higher but seldom above 1. (A positive price elasticity of, say, 0.2 means that the quantity supplied will increase by 0.2 percent when the price rises by 1 percent and will decrease by 0.2 percent when the price falls by 1 percent; an elasticity of 1 means that equal percentage changes in the quantity supplied will accompany small changes in price; a negative elasticity implies that a fall in price will cause an increase in the supply and a rise in price a decrease in supply.)

The available evidence suggests that an export tax on an agricultural commodity will cause the volume of production and exports to be smaller in the short run than it otherwise would have been and, if continued, will cause a still greater reduction in potential volume in the long run. The possibility cannot be completely excluded, however, that in some cases a tax will not affect production and exports or will cause them to increase.

The probable negative influence on production and export volume is a disadvantage of export taxation, but not necessarily a decisive objection to it. Three points are relevant especially to agricultural commodities. First, carefully used export taxes may discourage overexpansion during boom periods, particularly of tree crops for which plantings will yield additional production only after several years, when prices may have fallen. Second, reduction in production of the taxed commodity usually does not entail an equal loss in total production but a change in the composition of output. The net loss to the country is the decrease in the value of the social product of resources that are transferred from producing the taxed

7. For example, for cotton in Egypt the study cited in the text found a positive short-run elasticity of 0.52 for the period 1914–37, whereas another study reported an exceptionally large negative elasticity of −3.36 for 1920–40. See Askari and Cummings, *Agricultural Supply Responses*, p. 401; and Askari and Cummings, "Estimating Agricultural Supply Responses," p. 274.

commodity to other uses.[8] Third, the gain of revenue usually will be greater than the loss of export proceeds, since estimated price elasticities of supply of agricultural commodities are mostly below 1, and it may not be feasible to obtain the revenue from less harmful taxes.

A macroeconomic effect of export taxes that has received little attention is their influence on the foreign exchange rate of the local currency. By reducing exports or holding down their growth, the taxes tend to curtail the supply of foreign exchange available in the country and to increase its local currency price, that is, to cause a depreciation of the exchange rate. As is true of an opposite effect of taxes on imports, the impact on the exchange rate may not be immediately apparent, but it will tend to occur over time unless the country takes steps to restrain imports by means other than a currency depreciation. The result will be favorable to nontaxed exports—usually minor or nontraditional exports—and to industries producing import substitutes. Although these consequences may seem acceptable or desirable in themselves, they will entail a sacrifice of comparative advantage and a diminished capacity to import capital goods and to service external debt.

Forms of Taxation

Specific-rate export duties, like specific import duties and excises, are simpler than ad valorem duties but are less satisfactory in other respects. They discriminate against low-value exports—an effect that is occasionally welcomed as a stimulus to quality improvement but that usually is unintentional and undesirable. Specific duties not only fail to keep up with inflation but fail to gain additional revenue for the state during boom periods or to reduce the burden on exports when prices fall.

Graduation of duty rates in relation to the price of the export commodity gives some recognition to the presumed ability to pay of producers. It magnifies fluctuations of revenue and at the same time enhances the economic stabilizing capacity of the duties. Graduated rates usually are called sliding scales. To take a simple example, the duty might be fixed at x cents per kilogram plus y percent of the amount by which the price exceeds z cents per kilogram. More elaborate bracket or slab rates may be applied. An early example is the slab system for tea that India introduced in 1955. The duty increased from Rs 0.25 per pound at prices up to Rs 2.5

8. On welfare implications, see Tolley, Thomas, and Wong, *Agricultural Price Policies*, pp. 117–35, 163–84.

per pound, in four steps, until it reached Rs 0.75 when the price exceeded Rs 4.75. Thus the effective rate rose from 10 percent of value at the top of the first slab to almost 16 percent at the bottom of the fifth slab; within each slab the effective rate decreased slightly as the price moved from the bottom to the top of the slab. The erratic behavior of effective rates could have been avoided by stating the tax in percentages rather than in fixed money amounts.

The successful use of ad valorem duties, of course, depends on the capacity of the customs administration to value exports correctly. Where active and competitive local markets are absent, as is often the case, valuations may be based on prices quoted in external markets. A deduction can be made to convert the prices to f.o.b. (free on board) values, or the duty rate can be set to allow for the difference between delivered and f.o.b. prices. Official values or tax reference prices (*valeurs mercuriales* in French, *aforos* in Spanish) are sometimes set without a formal link to foreign quotations. Such a practice is generally undesirable, however, because failure to adjust the official prices, or their manipulation, introduces an arbitrary element into the determination of effective duty rates.

The successful use of the techniques for avoiding the explicit valuation of individual shipments depends on the correct grading and classification of exports. Grading is usually practiced for commercial reasons. Vigilance by the customs administration is necessary to prevent false documentation and deceptive sampling. That form of evasion usually is a greater threat than outright smuggling, but the latter has occurred for all kinds of exports where border controls are lax and for high-value, small-bulk items in other cases.

Operations of state marketing boards and stabilization funds differ from the application of formal export duties in significant ways. The marketing boards usually have a monopoly on the purchase and export of the designated commodity, while the stabilization funds of the francophone countries leave the trade in the hands of private firms or cooperatives but set the prices paid to local producers and the margins received by the trading firms. Revenue is never the only objective; often it is a secondary or unacknowledged purpose. Both the marketing boards and the stabilization funds were intended to realize surpluses when external prices are high and deficits when they are low. Some of them, however, have deliberately kept down prices to producers to obtain continuing surpluses. Margins are sometimes dissipated by inefficiencies or corruption.

Surpluses may be accumulated or may be used to pay for services and facilities benefiting producers, or the surpluses may finance other projects or may be transferred to the treasury. Proceeds devoted to the last two uses are clearly taxes in the broad sense; the other uses are more difficult to classify. Money transferred to the treasury is not necessarily included in the budget or made available for financing general government expenditures. In French-influenced systems, the treasury (*trésor*) performs a quasi-banking function for the whole public sector, and funds deposited with it are channeled to various users. The flexibility and ambiguous nature of surpluses or marketing agencies may make them politically more attractive than outright taxes.

When surplus funds are omitted from the budget, the principle of budgetary comprehensiveness is violated and normal controls and accountability may be absent. Budgeting would be more efficient if formal taxation were substituted for continuing surpluses or at least if surpluses were turned over to the treasury. Such proposals, however, are likely to be opposed by the marketing boards or stabilization funds and in some cases by political leaders who like the existing arrangements.

Multiple exchange rates, which were fashionable in the late 1940s and the 1950s, are now used much less frequently. At the end of 1980, the principal cases of taxation through discriminatory exchange rates for particular export commodities were coffee, cocoa, and wild animal hides in Brazil; coffee, gems, and pearls in Colombia; and cocoa in Ghana.[9] The decline in use of multiple exchange rates reflects the persistent efforts of the International Monetary Fund, together with the unhappy experiences of several countries and the evolution of opinion among economists.

While discriminatory exchange rates for certain traditional exports affected producers in the same way as other forms of export taxation, they seldom produced revenue for the state. Usually the revenue accrued to the central bank and was distributed by it in the form of implicit subsidies to importers who acquired foreign exchange at rates less depreciated than the average. There is little to be said in favor of that system. The economic effects of a unified but overvalued exchange rate, with foreign exchange rationed among importers, are broadly similar though less discriminatory and less productive of economic inefficiencies. While the burden imposed on export producers by overvaluation of the exchange rates has sometimes been estimated, it usually has not been called a tax.

---

9. International Monetary Fund, *Annual Report on Exchange Arrangements and Exchange Restrictions, 1981.*

Conclusion and Summary

Export taxes are likely to curtail export earnings and to cause a shift of economic resources to uses that are less productive than those in which they would be employed with a neutral tax system. Sometimes excessive home consumption or inefficient local processing of the taxed commodities is encouraged. Export taxes are inherently discriminatory and are not closely related to a recognized measure of taxpaying ability.

But the taxes have some offsetting advantages. They are much simpler to administer than income taxes or land taxes on export producers. As explained in chapter 11, they can be a useful feature of stabilizing fiscal/monetary policy for a primary-producing country. Realistically, the taxes that might replace export taxes would be neither economically neutral nor nicely adjusted to ability to pay and would create inefficiencies and inequities.

In the long run, export taxes probably will diminish in fiscal importance, as they appear to have done in developing countries during the past three decades and as they did earlier in Europe. This will occur because of an increase in the output of manufactured goods, which are seldom subject to export taxes, relative to taxable primary products. The development of administrative and political integration will make internal taxes more feasible. A possible means of gradual transition to internal taxes would be to treat part of export taxes as an advance payment or minimum payment of income or land tax on large producers of export commodities.

Taxation of Natural Resources

This section deals with revenues from minerals and forests, including taxes on production, exports, and net income as well as royalties and other payments received in exchange for concessions or other arrangements permitting the exploitation of state-owned resources. For economic and political reasons, the presence of natural resources is a tax handle, and governments able to do so generally have taken advantage of the opportunity of obtaining revenue from this source.

Characteristics of Mining and Forestry

Mining has some peculiarities that bear on the consequences of various forms of taxation and that should be taken into account in formulating policy.[10] Some but not all of the characteristics are shared by forestry. Substantial initial exploration costs often are involved in discovering mineral deposits and evaluating their probable yield. This is well known for petroleum, and it is true to a lesser degree for other minerals in areas that have not been carefully surveyed. Large investments in drilling wells, sinking shafts, and constructing mills and access roads or railways and ports may be required before production can begin. High risk and uncertainty prevail at the exploration stage and continue after production is started because of unstable prices, the possibility that alternative sources of supply or substitutes will be developed, and changes in technology that will affect demand and production costs. In cases of success, large economic rents may arise. (An economic rent is any income payment in excess of that required to induce participation in the production process.)

The exhaustibility of mineral deposits means that the rate of extraction, if rationally determined, will take account of the effects of present exploitation on future availability and profits. Exhaustion has not only a physical dimension but an economic one because costs increase as lower-grade and less accessible deposits have to be used. Production today entails what may be termed a user cost, measured by the sacrifice of the discounted value of future production. A rational operator will try to plan production so as to maximize the present value of profits over the whole life of a mine; this may indicate a smaller output in some years than that which would yield the greatest current profit. Forests often are exploited like mines, with no thought of replacing the trees that are cut, but it is possible to follow a sustained use policy by replanting. An evaluation of revenue policies should recognize, in addition to risk and exhaustability, the large roles of a few multinational corporations in the production and marketing of petroleum and certain other minerals and the geographic concentration of deposits of some minerals.

Certain politically significant characteristics of mining and timber cutting have greatly influenced taxation. First, in most countries subsoil rights are legally separated from surface rights, and the state owns the mineral rights. Forests also are frequently owned by the state.

Second, mining in less developed countries typically is carried on by large foreign-owned corporations, and timber cutting sometimes is orga-

10. See Mason Gattney, ed., *Extractive Resources and Taxation* (University of Wisconsin Press, 1967); Malcolm Gillis and others, *Taxation and Mining: Nonfuel Minerals in Bolivia and Other Countries* (Ballinger, 1978); Malcolm Gillis and Ralph E. Beals, *Tax and Investment Policies for Hard Minerals: Public and Multinational Enterprises in Indonesia* (Ballinger, 1980); and Albert M. Church, *Taxation of Nonrenewable Resources* (Lexington Books/Heath, 1981), which includes an extensive bibliography.

nized similarly. When concessions are initially negotiated, prospects are uncertain and the foreign enterprises usually are in a strong bargaining position. If one or more projects are successful, profits may be large in relation to the investment, and the concession is likely to appear to be unfair to the country. This perception may be strengthened by the government's ability to exact better terms from subsequent investors, once workable deposits have been found and production has started. Sensitivities about foreigners' profiting from the exploitation of the national patrimony are especially acute.

In these situations, the original concession agreements frequently have been renegotiated and taxes and royalties raised.[11] Petroleum companies have been nationalized in many countries, and other mining companies have been expropriated in a considerable number of cases. For example, Zaire, Chile, and Peru have taken over their major copper mines, and Zambia has acquired a controlling interest in its principal copper mines. Large tin mines have been nationalized in Bolivia; iron mines in Algeria, Mauritania, Chile, Venezuela, and Peru; and bauxite-producing facilities in Guyana. State-owned mining companies are also important in Brazil, Indonesia, Mexico, Korea, and India.

The possibility of expropriation or of unfavorable changes in taxation gives rise to a political risk that operators have to try to take into account in investment and production decisions. Political risk is additional to the unavoidable economic risk and uncertainty associated with mining. Political risk deters investment in exploration and development but causes the rate of production to be accelerated once an investment has been made because rapid depletion of the resource shortens the time over which the producer is exposed. Its assessment no doubt is greatly influenced by the previous record of a country and may be affected by political rhetoric and the prevailing sentiments of investors.

A third politically significant characteristic of mining is its weak links with the remainder of the economy in many developing countries. Local expenditures for labor and materials are small, most of the output is exported, and domestic private investment in the extraction of petroleum and other minerals is small or nonexistent. The paucity of economic relations with local workers, suppliers, and investors contributes to the political isolation and vulnerability of the operators. A frequent reaction

11. Theodore H. Moran, *Multinational Corporations and the Politics of Dependence: Copper in Chile* (Princeton University Press, 1974). This book gives an enlightening account and an analysis that have implications extending far beyond Chile.

is that governments, recognizing that their revenues compose a great part of the national gain from exploitation of the natural resources, are stimulated to impose high taxes and royalties. In some cases, they also insist on minimum amounts of local processing and employment as conditions for obtaining mineral rights.

Finally, issues of intergenerational equity, future national power and prestige, and conservation enter prominently into debates on taxes and other policies affecting natural resources.

Revenue Policy

An economically rational policy for a government is analogous to that for a mine operator: to maximize the present value of all expected revenue over the life of the resource. In a sense, this is no different from the policy that could be recommended for any other field of taxation, but in carrying out the policy careful account needs to be taken of the special characteristics of mining. Risk and uncertainty make the projection of future revenues difficult, and governments may have less information at their disposal than operators have.[12] The choice of an appropriate discount rate for calculating the present value of future revenues presents the same questions as does the choice of the discount rate for benefit-cost appraisal (see chapter 3).

In carrying out its revenue policy, a government will be well advised to avoid discouraging exploration and development and to encourage using natural resources at an appropriate rate. Both unnecessary delay in the use of resources and their premature exhaustion are undesirable.

Sometimes it is argued that governments have a responsibility to postpone use of natural resources in order to preserve them for future generations. From the economic standpoint, however, successful execution of a policy of maximizing the present value of all expected future revenue would also constitute the optimum conservation policy. Properly understood, conservation means intelligent use, not hoarding, of resources. An attempt to improve the economic position of future generations by restraining the use of natural resources would involve forgoing revenue in the intervening period, which could impair the heritage of the future in the form of physical and human capital or could result in a greater burden of external debt. The force of this argument is not always appreciated; sometimes it is rejected because of skepticism about the accuracy of long-term projections and the adequacy of the discount rate as a device for equating the present and the future or because of suspicion about the use

12. Both the government and private operators are assumed to be risk-averse.

governments will make of revenues from early production. The latter consideration, of course, is weighty only if one is confident that future governments will be more prudent.

To the extent feasible, the state should aim at appropriating economic rents arising from the exploitation of natural resources. By definition, their appropriation will have no harmful economic effects. The problem, of course, is to identify the economic rents, which is not easy.

Two other policy considerations may act as constraints on revenue maximization. One is the desire that some governments manifest to stimulate local processing even at the cost of sacrificing some revenue. In formal terms, such a policy could be thought of as aiming at maximizing the present value of a weighted sum of revenue and the local expenditures of producers for wages and other purchases, with the weights depending on the importance attached to the two objectives.[13] It is doubtful whether many decisionmakers put the matter in such terms, though their thinking might be sharpened by doing so. The wisdom of giving up revenue to encourage local employment and procurement is questionable because the revenue could have been used to finance government expenditures that also would create employment opportunities.

A second constraint on revenue maximization is the possibility that the government may choose to use taxation to check negative externalities or neighborhood effects. These are harmful effects on people and the environment that are associated with the use of natural resources but that are not reflected in the usual cost calculations. Examples are soil erosion, flooding, and possible climate changes resulting from deforestation and air and water pollution caused by some mining and smelting operations. Such externalities have been receiving much attention in developed countries but so far have been given little emphasis in the majority of less developed countries.

To avoid involvement in questions of industrial organization and management, it will be assumed that state enterprises involved in exploiting natural resources are required to follow commercial principles and are subject to the same tax regimes as would apply to private operators. These assumptions, however, do not eliminate all differences between the two forms of operation, and a few remarks on the remaining differences will be made in the course of the discussion and in a brief section toward the end of the chapter.

13. Church, *Taxation of Nonrenewable Resources*, pp. 19–20.

Concessions

A government that intends to permit private operation of a state-owned mineral deposit or forest will have to be prepared to enter into an agreement extending over a period that is long in relation to the expected life of the resource or the useful life of the production facilities. Otherwise, it can hardly expect private investors to finance the development.

If there is reason to believe that the resource is rich enough to yield returns in excess of costs plus the profits that are essential to attract investments in the industry—that is, if there is reason to expect economic rent—the government may be able to exact an immediate payment for entering into the agreement. Alternatively, it may attempt to capture the economic rent through taxes or royalties after production begins. If future profits could be accurately foreseen and competition among producers prevailed, it would be theoretically possible for the government to obtain the full present value of the economic rent immediately by auctioning the production rights. The government would be relieved of the task of measuring actual economic rent, and in effect a confiscatory tax on it would be self-assessed. Although the first condition is never satisfied, uncertainty is reduced where the area has been geologically mapped or a deposit has been discovered. Under these conditions, the auction system has attractions provided active competitive bidding can be expected. The government would obtain immediate revenue; the arrangement could be advantageous to both parties if the government's discount rate were higher than the producer's. Furthermore, a producer who had made an advance payment would have an incentive to proceed promptly with development and production to recoup the investment.

There would be disadvantages to such a procedure, however. Bidding may not be genuinely competitive. Even with several participants in an auction and no collusion among them, bids may be held down because of economic and political risks. Under the arrangement, the producer would assume the full burden of both kinds of risk. The requirement that payment be made in advance would limit the number of bidders and would give an advantage to companies in a strong financial position, which are not necessarily the ones that would be the most efficient producers. The government might be exposed to political criticism later if a company that had obtained a concession were making large profits and paying little taxes, regardless of whether the profits represented partly or wholly the recovery of the earlier payment for the concession.

Producers who foresaw such a situation might fear that it would result in expropriation or some less drastic modification of the concession and adjust their bids accordingly or refrain from participation.

On balance, it appears that some initial payment for a concession is appropriate where conditions are favorable enough to allow such a requirement but that the payment should not be the principal means for the state to capture the economic rent from the resource. By announcing in advance other taxes and royalties that will be in effect during the production period, the government will reduce the amount that producers will be willing to pay initially for the concession and will spread its revenues over a longer period of time. The initial payment, nevertheless, will exert some pressure in favor of early production and may be a useful substitute or supplement for explicit provisions on that point in the concession agreement.

Another form of payment for a concession is to require the company to give the government an equity in the project or a share in profits. Such arrangements, of course, do not have the same effects as an advance payment, but they can provide an extra degree of flexibility, and they seem to be politically attractive.

Taxes and Royalties

Royalties, production or severance taxes, and export duties are instruments for obtaining government revenue that is related to the rate of production or shipments. Royalties usually are attached to production from state-owned resources, while severance taxes apply to privately owned mines or forests; economically, they are similar. Export duties can have the same effect when all of the output is sent abroad.

These charges reduce the effective prices received by producers and hence make submarginal some projects that otherwise would be profitable and cause production from other projects to be smaller than it otherwise would be. They discourage the development and use of ores or timber that is expensive to work because of low grade or distant location. They also tend to retard the physical depletion of the resources. This may occur because the use of some resources is postponed until prices rise enough to make production profitable despite the tax or royalty. A more subtle explanation is that, even with constant prices, the discounted value of a future fiscal charge is less than its current amount and is smaller in relation to production costs, which can be expected to increase over time as lower-grade resources are used.

As compared with the initial sale of concessions, royalties and taxes that are related to production have the advantage for producers of making the state share some of the risks and uncertainties. If production is interrupted because of unfavorable markets or costs, the payments stop. Political risk is also lessened because producers will suffer smaller losses if their properties are expropriated without adequate compensation.

Royalties and taxes on production or exports are simpler to administer than income taxes or profit-sharing arrangements. Specific royalties and taxes are easier to apply than ad valorem ones, which require the verification of prices. For commodities that are quoted on international markets, verifying prices is straightforward; the only necessary adjustment is to subtract transportation costs. For other commodities, independent price quotations are not available. Ores and concentrates are often shipped to foreign affiliates of the company that does the mining or cutting, and it may be hard to check the transfer prices. Bauxite, for example, has no established world price, and royalties have usually been based on the price of aluminum ingots.

Specific duties or royalties become more burdensome when prices fall and less burdensome when prices rise unless some kind of sliding scale is applied. If the product extracted from low-grade ores or timber sells for less than that obtained from higher-grade resources, a specific tax will discriminate against the lower-grade resources. For these reasons, specific taxes or royalties are inferior to ad valorem charges.

Taxes or other payments related to net profits are another means of obtaining revenue from natural resources. They may consist of the regular corporation income tax, special or supplementary taxes on net income, profit-sharing payments, or dividends from state enterprises. By the early 1960s, income taxes had superseded royalties and other production taxes as the principal source of state revenue from mining.[14]

A properly designed and administered tax on net profits will not discourage the use of installed productive capacity, and, provided the rate is expected to remain constant, it will not affect the timing of production over the life of the resource. If the tax rate is expected to rise or decline in the future, there will be an incentive either to accelerate or to postpone production. Income taxation is more compatible with high levels of production and the use of low-grade resources than equal-yield severance taxes or royalties are. Income taxation also goes further than the other

14. Gillis and others, *Taxation and Mining*, p. 122. Chapter 5 of this book contains a summary of mining taxes in a number of developing countries.

measures in sharing risk and uncertainty between the state and producers. All this is true because a tax on net income does not apply to any part of output for which production costs equal or exceed the proceeds and because, with a constant rate, the tax reduces in equal proportions the present values of current and future returns.

An income tax, however, will discourage some exploration and development. Taxable net income will include not only economic rent but returns that are necessary to attract investment. A point to emphasize is that prospective profits from a new project or expansion of an existing project have a different significance than actual profits from a project that is already operating. An investor will undertake a new project only if the expected after-tax profits are attractive when evaluated either as (1) a rate of return at least equal to that obtainable from safe investments plus an allowance for economic and political risk and uncertainty or (2) a present value greater than the cost of the project, with expected returns discounted at the investor's required rate of return. Once an investment has been made, a rationally managed enterprise will make the best of the situation and will continue operations so long as losses are avoided. (In the short run, with installed capacity given, profits consist mainly of what economists call quasi rents.)

The economic effects of taxing profits from natural resources are similar to the effects of taxing profits from other sources; however, allowance should be made for the special characteristics of natural resource industries. The high profits that are often realized include compensation for the assumption of the above-average risk and uncertainty associated with the industries, as well as economic rent. A regular income tax will strike both components. The timing of production is especially sensitive to any expected changes in the tax rate.

The assessment of an income tax involves some administrative problems. One of these is the verification of the accuracy of transfer prices. For minerals and some forest products, this is less difficult than for many lines of manufacturing because of the availability of price quotations for homogeneous commodities on foreign markets. Of course, it will be necessary to check the physical characteristics of the products to make sure that they correspond to those quoted and to make appropriate adjustments for any differences. Since mining and forestry enterprises often are affiliates of multinational corporations, it is also important to examine critically deductions for services and supplies provided by parent companies and for payments under construction and shipping contracts with affiliated companies. To simplify assessment, some countries have calculated profits on the basis of estimated standard costs and prices per ton or other physical unit. Unless carefully designed and frequently changed, however, such methods alter the economic character of the tax. There is a risk, furthermore, that the so-called income taxes assessed in that way may not qualify for foreign tax credit in the United States and the United Kingdom.[15]

In an effort to capture economic rent from North Sea oil production, the British government introduced in the Oil Taxation Act 1975 a petroleum revenue tax as a supplement to a production tax and regular corporation income tax. The petroleum revenue tax, a complex measure that will not be fully described here, incorporates some features of a cash-flow corporation income tax (see chapter 5). It applies to gross receipts less both current and capital expenditures incurred in finding and producing oil. Interest payments are not deductible, but as compensation the deduction for capital expenditures is increased by an "uplift" factor. The petroleum revenue tax is assessed separately on operations in each field. It has been repeatedly amended but remains the major element in U.K. taxation of North Sea oil production.[16]

Garnaut and Clunies Ross have advanced an ingenious proposal for a tax on economic rent from mineral production that resembles in significant respects the British petroleum revenue tax. The principal features of the proposal, which they call a resource rent tax, are as follows: (1) all capital outlays, including exploration costs, would be immediately deductible in calculating assessable income; (2) no deductions would be allowed for interest payments or any costs of acquiring a concession, lease, or title to a natural resource subject to the special tax; (3) assessable receipts would include proceeds from the sale of output and any amounts realized from the sale of equipment or other property or the transfer of production rights; (4) all losses (that is, any excess of operating costs plus capital outlays over assessable receipts) would be carried forward for an unlimited period and

15. The U.S. foreign tax credit is available not only for income taxes (including excess profits taxes) in the strict sense but also for taxes in lieu of generally imposed income taxes provided they, in fact, operate as substitutes for and not additions to such an income tax (Internal Revenue Code, sec. 903; Temporary Regulations, sec. 4.903–1(b)).

16. See David Ross, "North Sea Oil," *British Tax Review*, no. 2 (1976), pp. 99–109; J. A. Kay and M. A. King, *The British Tax System* (Oxford University Press, 1978), pp. 205–07. Amendments of the 1975 act are described in various issues of the *British Tax Review*.

would be increased annually by an interest factor. In setting the interest rate, the objective would be to choose a figure equal to the prospective rate of return required to attract investment in the industry.[17]

If a resource rent tax could be successfully devised and applied, its base would indeed consist of economic rent, and the tax should not discourage development of natural resources. The essential point is that the tax would apply only after the producer had recovered its capital investment plus a normal rate of return on any deferred amortization. The adequacy of the interest rate allowed on unamortized investments would be crucial. If the rate were too low, it would delay recovery of the investment; if it were unnecessarily high, some economic rent would be excluded from the tax base. The interest rate could not be set at precisely the correct level, as the necessary return varies among investors, among projects, and over time. In practice, the rate might be linked with bond yields in international markets, with an addition that would be great or small depending on how eager the government was to attract capital. Although in operation a resource rent tax would not apply to all economic rent and to no other income, it could come much closer to doing so than an ordinary income tax does.

Under the resource rent tax, the government would defer its revenue receipts and would assume a large share of development risks and uncertainties. In this respect, the tax would differ radically from the sale of concessions. The enterprise, of course, would lose its investment if the project never yielded enough to recoup it. The intention would be to avoid adding to economic risk and uncertainty through taxation. Rapid amortization of the investment would be intended also to minimize exposure to political risk due to changes in government attitudes, but that result would not be certain for reasons to be suggested below. To limit a producer's opportunity to postpone tax payments on profitable operations by incurring exploration and development expenditures in new areas, it would probably be advisable to treat each area as a distinct tax unit, as is done under the British petroleum revenue tax.

If the tax rate were high, it would be particularly important for the revenue administration to be vigilant in checking deductible expenses to prevent siphoning off profits in the form of excessive compensation to

17. Ross Garnaut and Anthony Clunies Ross, "Uncertainty, Risk Aversion and the Taxing of Natural Resource Projects," *Economic Journal*, vol. 85 (June 1975), pp. 272–87. A similar measure was briefly discussed by William S. Vickrey and Mason Gaffney in Gaffney, *Extractive Resources and Taxation*, pp. 322, 399–402.

executives or excessive payments to contractors affiliated with the producing enterprise. Some restraint in setting the tax rate would be advisable to hold down the incentives for such evasion and to preserve the interest of the enterprise in preventing wasteful expenditures.

It seems unlikely that governments would choose the resource rent tax as the exclusive means of obtaining revenue from natural resources. They usually have urgent need for revenue and would be unwilling to postpone receipts to the extent that might occur under the resource rent tax. Failure to collect any tax before exploration and development expenditures were fully amortized might expose a government to criticism and make it difficult to resist demands for modification of the system. When operations were carried on by branches of corporations that are subject to taxation on their worldwide income by their home countries—as would be true, for example, of U.S. and U.K. companies—the failure of the source country to tax profits currently would be offset by higher liabilities to the home country since no foreign tax credit would be available.

Although caution is always advisable in adopting any novel and complex tax measure, the resource rent tax proposal merits further study and consideration by governments. Papua New Guinea recently enacted a version of the tax, and its experience may provide additional evidence on the desirability of the measure.[18]

Corporate and Geographic Concentration

As previously mentioned, only a small number of corporations and a few countries account for large fractions of the world production or marketing of certain minerals. Bauxite, copper, tin, and diamonds are examples.[19] In such cases, tactical considerations may influence tax legislation and the reaction to it.

If the main countries in which the deposits are located act in formal or informal concert to impose severance taxes, export duties, royalty payments, or profit taxes at comparable levels, individual countries will have less reason to fear that development and production will be diverted to other countries, and that may relax a constraint that otherwise would tend to hold down the rates. For example, when Jamaica sharply raised taxes

18. On Papua New Guinea, see Craig Emerson, "Mining Enclaves and Taxation," *World Development*, vol. 10 (July 1982), pp. 561–71. For skeptical comments on the resource rent tax and other measures to capture excess profits, see Gillis and Beals, *Tax and Investment Policies for Hard Minerals*, pp. 155–62.

19. Details are given by Phillip Crowson, *Non-Fuel Minerals Data Base* (London: Royal Institute of International Affairs, 1980).

and royalties on bauxite in 1974, other producing countries that were members of the International Bauxite Association (except Australia) followed its lead, and prices rose. The situation in Jamaica, however, proved to be unstable, with disputes between the government and producing companies and no expansion of the industry's capacity after 1974. The taxes were ultimately reduced, and the companies were partly nationalized.

In concentrated industries, the mining companies can bring pressure on a country by threatening to divert production and new development to other places.

It is hard to generalize about such conditions except to note that the positions of both the government and the companies frequently are less strong than they may appear. When demand is slack, individual governments may be tempted to trim their taxes and royalties to gain a larger share of total production; the companies may moderate their resistance to tax increases when demand is strong. If prices are levered up, competition from new producing areas and substitutes may be encouraged, as mentioned earlier in connection with export taxation. In addition to the other forms of substitution, recycled secondary minerals are an important and growing source of competition for primary production of some metals.

State Ownership and Production Sharing

Nationalization or retention or acquisition of a state equity in mining companies is an alternative to income taxation. Examples of minority equity participation include the ownership of 20 percent of a copper company by the government of Papua New Guinea, 49 percent of a bauxite project by the government of Guinea, and 9.5 percent of a nickel project by the government of the Dominican Republic.[20] The economic effects of income taxation and equity ownership acquired without payment are similar, but the choice of the latter may indicate an inclination on the part of the government to exert more influence on operating and investment decisions. An equity of x percent is not equivalent to an x percent tax on profits, since part of profits may be reinvested or used to repay debt and the definition of profits for tax purposes may differ from that used as a basis for dividend distributions.

Where exploitation is carried out by an enterprise wholly owned by the state, the government necessarily assumes the economic risk, and political risk disappears as an identifiable factor. Initial capital will have to be provided by government borrowing and additional capital from further

20. John E. Tilton, *The Future of Nonfuel Minerals* (Brookings Institution, 1977), p. 51.

borrowing, for which the government will have to take responsibility although it may not be the legal debtor, and from retained profits. State enterprises may face difficulties in attracting capable managers and offering them appropriate incentives and in gaining access to markets. They will not have to pay for concessions but may be subject to production or export taxes and to regular income tax. As the enterprises can be required to transfer surplus profits to the treasury in the form of dividends or ad hoc payments, a measure such as the resource rent tax is not likely to be considered necessary. Experience in several countries shows, however, that governments often have difficulty in extracting profits from state enterprises. The profits may never be realized because of inefficient operations or they may be invested in expansion or activities related only loosely, if at all, to the exploitation of natural resources. Delays in payment of ordinary taxes are not uncommon.

In the oil industry, production-sharing contracts, which have replaced traditional concessions and taxation in many countries, are a form of state participation, but they differ in economic character from equity participation or profit sharing. The typical production-sharing contract provides that the state retains ownership of the oil field and the oil company bears the exploration, development, and production costs. As compensation, the company receives a share of production, known as "cost oil," which varies between agreements and fields. The remaining production—"profit oil"—is shared between the government and the company, sometimes according to progressive rates that increase the government's share as output rises. Production-sharing contracts seem to have been motivated more by political considerations and a desire to exert control over oil production and marketing than by revenue considerations. The contracts are likely to produce less revenue than traditional taxes and royalties. The net proceeds of oil sales by the state petroleum company may suffer because of inefficiency and lack of established marketing arrangements. The value of cost oil is not, in fact, a measure of production cost; rather, it is a share in the physical volume of production. Hence, high-cost production may be discouraged except in fields covered by especially liberal contracts. At the margin in all fields, gross returns to the company from additional production are reduced by the state's share, which, despite its designation as profit oil, does not represent profit in an economic sense.[21]

21. This paragraph is based on an unpublished paper by A. M. Abdel-Rahman of the International Monetary Fund staff, "Taxation of Oil Production: From Concessionary Agreements to Production-Sharing Contracts," presented at an international seminar on taxation and development in Paris, September–October 1982.

Conclusion and Summary

Taxation of natural resources should take account of the economic and political characteristics of mining and forestry and should attempt to balance current revenue needs against future needs. Probably the best arrangement is a combination of measures including the sale of concessions or leases, royalties or taxes related to production or exports, and taxes on profits. Consideration might be given to some version of the resource rent tax as an addition to a regular income tax. Since taxes based on production or exports are economically inferior to taxes on profits but are easier to assess, the relative emphasis on the two forms of taxation should depend to a considerable extent on the capability of the tax department. An alternative to a resource rent tax could take the form of a negotiated profit-sharing clause in concessions. Such clauses would allow maximum flexibility to adapt the payment to differing circumstances but would have disadvantages. Governments would be involved in sometimes unequal bargaining with multinational enterprises, and profit-sharing payments would be ineligible for the credits allowed for foreign income taxes by the headquarters countries of some companies.

CHAPTER EIGHT

Borrowing

STRONG DEMANDS for expenditures, coupled with political and economic obstacles to taxation, have impelled governments to obtain financing by borrowing and money creation and have caused less developed countries to seek foreign aid. This chapter examines the opportunities for government borrowing at home and abroad and the consequences of these forms of financing. It is concerned exclusively with borrowing from sources other than the central bank and domestic commercial banks. Borrowing from the latter institutions is discussed in chapter 9 on financing by money creation. This chapter is divided into sections on domestic borrowing and foreign borrowing because the two forms of finance have different characteristics. Borrowing from the International Monetary Fund, which is a special form of external financing, will be discussed in chapter 11.

Domestic Borrowing

The fundamental purpose of borrowing at home is to displace spending by households and enterprises and thus to give the government command over real resources. Sovereign governments do not have to borrow to obtain money; they can acquire it from the central bank or, in archaic fashion, by printing notes. If there is no need to restrain nongovernmental spending because idle productive capacity exists, money creation is preferable to borrowing. Although government borrowing may affect consumption, usually its main impact will fall on investments of the other sectors.

Economic Characteristics

Lending is ordinarily voluntary, and interest is paid to induce it. The voluntary nature of lending and the fact that it does not reduce the wealth of the lenders but merely changes its form mean that lending ordinarily is less effective in displacing nongovernmental spending than an equal amount of taxation. This proposition has been denied in recent years by adherents to an extreme version of a rationalistic theory of the behavior of lenders and others. According to that view, which has been traced back (though with questionable justification) to the writings of Ricardo early in the nineteenth century, borrowing and taxation will have the same effect because people will perceive that borrowing will entail future taxation to service and repay the debt and will immediately adjust their behavior accordingly. On its face, the theory seems implausible. It implies that people can predict the future tax system, economic conditions, and their own position and are more concerned with long-term planning, extending beyond their life span, than common observation suggests. Political leaders certainly do not behave as if they believed that citizens consider borrowing and taxation equivalent.[1] Domestic borrowing, in fact, is seldom repaid but is reduced in relative and real amounts by growth and inflation and may be virtually eliminated by the latter.

With an orderly financial market, in normal conditions, the interest rate paid by the government would vary directly with the liquidity of the debt instrument, being lower for short-term than for long-term debt. Although holders of long-term bonds could sell their securities to obtain cash when needed, they would be subject to the risk of loss of principal if interest rates had risen after they acquired the bonds. This risk is greater for long-term bonds than for short-term securities because the market prices of the former fluctuate more in response to changes of interest rates. The lesser liquidity and higher yields of long-term bonds make them more effective than short-term borrowing in displacing household and enterprise spending.

The kind of financial market assumed in the preceding paragraph exists in only a few countries, including by no means all those that are commonly classified as developed. Although some less developed countries have fairly

---

1. Robert J. Barro, "Are Government Bonds Net Wealth?" *Journal of Political Economy*, vol. 82 (November–December 1974), pp. 1095–1117; comments by Martin Feldstein and James M. Buchanan and reply by Barro, *Journal of Political Economy*, vol. 84 (April 1976), pp. 331–49. See also James M. Buchanan, *Public Principles of Public Debt* (Irwin, 1958), pp. 114–22. Buchanan quotes a passage by Ricardo that appears to be a strong statement of the equivalence of borrowing and taxation; yet a few paragraphs later Ricardo writes of the possibility that people will be deluded by borrowing and will behave differently than they would with financing by taxation. See David Ricardo, *Principles of Political Economy and Taxation* (London: Dent, 1943), pp. 160–64. For a critical discussion of the alleged equivalence of borrowing and taxation, see James Tobin, *Asset Accumulation and Economic Activity: Reflections on Contemporary Macroeconomic Theory* (University of Chicago Press, 1980), pp. 31, 49–72.

active and sophisticated financial institutions, conditions in most of the world severely limit opportunities for buying and selling government securities and hence make them more illiquid than they would be if more active financial markets existed.

Compulsory lending is occasionally used. As a forced diversion of spending power, it resembles taxation. Compulsory lending is intended to avoid or minimize some of the adverse effects of taxation on production incentives and to avoid political objections to additional taxation. Several countries have had limited experience with general compulsory lending schemes, usually linked with income taxation but with exports in Peru and agricultural production in Nepal. General schemes, applying to persons coming within some wide classification such as income tax payers, may be distinguished from social security systems and more narrowly defined schemes in which compulsory lending is involved but sometimes only as an incidental element. In the latter category are advance deposit requirements to obtain import licenses or foreign exchange and regulations that make insurance companies and certain other organizations captive lenders. As a hybrid of ordinary borrowing and taxation, compulsory lending has some of the disadvantages of both. If the lenders and the government take seriously the obligation to repay, compulsory lending is less effective than taxation in checking the spending of the lenders, and repayment may come at a time that is inconvenient for the government. If the lenders are skeptical about repayment, the presumed advantages as compared with taxation are weak or nonexistent.[2]

Occasions for Borrowing

Domestic borrowing is most often an act of expediency by a government that would prefer to finance by taxation but finds it inconvenient to do so. Temporary borrowing may be required because of seasonal fluctuations of expenditures or receipts or because of errors in budget estimates. Borrowing may be advisable to meet an emergency that otherwise would require a sharp increase in taxation.

A more positive case for borrowing derives from the traditional view that it is appropriate for financing investment outlays as distinguished from consumption expenditures. As mentioned in chapter 2, this opinion seems to be based on a misleading analogy with enterprise finance. Governments should be guided by macroeconomic considerations and

---

2. A. R. Prest, "Compulsory Lending Schemes," International Monetary Fund *Staff Papers*, vol. 16 (March 1969), pp. 27–51. Prest comments on the experience of nineteen countries.

should not assume that borrowing to cover investment outlays is always preferable to other means of finance.

A better argument can be made for a related but different maxim: avoid borrowing to pay for government consumption expenditures. Domestic borrowing is a use of national saving, which thus becomes unavailable for enterprise investment or house construction. Total saving and investment may be reduced when consumption is financed by borrowing, whereas borrowing to finance government investment will at most change the composition of capital formation. The inference is that failure to restrict borrowing to the finance of investment will retard economic growth. A weakness of the argument is that not all outlays classified as investment actually contribute to growth, while some expenditures usually classified as government consumption promote growth.

Scope

Opportunities for government borrowing at home from nonbank lenders are severely limited in most developing countries. Several factors account for this. Personal saving may be smaller in relation to income than in the developed countries. More important, the habits and preferences of savers in the less developed countries dispose them to put their savings in land, closely held businesses, gold, or foreign balances. Few persons are accustomed to buying securities of any kind, and savers may be especially skeptical of government securities. Time is required to establish the institutions and practices that make possible wide voluntary purchases of government securities, and external economies may be an important advantage in big financial markets. In the absence of an active market, government bonds, as already noted, are less liquid than they would be if the market existed and should yield higher rates of interest. In some developing countries, particularly in Latin America, a long history of inflation has erected a virtually insuperable obstacle to the sale of long-term bonds to individuals. Recently, the spread of inflation to other countries, together with wide fluctuations in nominal interest rates, has damaged the market for government bonds in the small number of countries in which it previously flourished.

Despite such difficulties, several developing countries have obtained substantial amounts of financing by borrowing at home from nonbank lenders. Information on all the countries for which the statistics are readily available has been assembled in table 8-1, which shows data on outstanding central government debt, domestic debt, and nonbank holdings of domestic debt. Nonbank holders are all holders except the central bank or other monetary authority and so-called deposit money banks, which consist of commercial banks and other institutions whose liabilities are primarily in the form of deposits payable on demand or transferable by check. Hence certain financial institutions that are commonly called banks are here classified as nonbank holders.

The statistics are not fully comparable across countries because of differences in the definition of central government. Where feasible, the debt statistics relate to the consolidated central government, which includes all government departments and social security institutions or funds and other bodies that are instruments of the central government. However, for many countries, identified by a footnote to table 8-1, the debt statistics are for the "budgetary central government" and do not reflect a consolidation of budgetary accounts with social security and other accounts. As social security funds and the other accounts often are holders of government debt, the figures for those countries for which budgetary central government data are reported may give an exaggerated impression of the amount that has been borrowed from nonbank lenders outside the public sector.

The table shows that, on the average, central government debt is smaller in relation to gross domestic product (GDP) in the developing countries than in the industrial countries. The statistics confirm the expectation that the domestic debt is a smaller fraction of total debt—and foreign debt a greater fraction—in the developing countries and that a smaller fraction of the domestic debt is in the hands of nonbank holders. There are, however, wide differences among countries. Among the industrial countries, the debt of the United Kingdom is unusually large and a major part of it is held by resident investors other than banks. In seven of the developing countries, the ratio of domestic nonbank holdings to GDP is higher than the median ratio for the industrial countries. The figures are strikingly high for Israel and Singapore, exceeding those for any of the industrial countries except the United Kingdom. Other developing countries with relatively high ratios of domestic nonbank holdings to GDP are South Africa, Malaysia, Sri Lanka, Guyana, and Zambia.[3] These seven countries are a diverse group, though it may be noted that the financial systems of all of them have been subject to British influence. None of them is among the least developed countries, and some of them have sophisticated financial institutions.

---

3. Zambia is the only one of these countries for which the ratios may be overstated because of the absence of consolidated central government statistics.

Table 8-1. *Central Government Debt and Gross Domestic Product,*
Selected Industrial and Developing Countries, Late 1970s[a]

Country	Total debt as % of GDP	Domestic debt as % of total debt	Nonbank holdings as % of domestic debt[b]	Domestic nonbank holdings as % of GDP
Industrial countries				
Canada	26.8	94.2	60.7	15.3
Finland	9.4	41.1	85.3	3.3
Germany, F.R.	14.7	92.8	35.3	4.8
Ireland	70.4	73.1	71.6	36.8
Japan[c]	34.5	99.1	48.0	16.4
Netherlands[c]	27.2	100.0	59.6	16.2
New Zealand[c]	59.1	65.5	65.5	25.4
Norway	42.2	67.8	22.0	6.3
Sweden	32.7	79.9	41.1	10.7
United Kingdom	176.7	90.3	79.5	126.8
United States	30.8	82.2	53.8	13.6
Median	32.7	82.2	59.6	15.3
Developing countries				
Argentina[c]	9.5	74.4	34.8	2.5
Bahamas	23.8	83.3	48.2	9.6
Botswana[c]	15.2	14.0	23.4	0.5
Costa Rica[c]	108.0	59.9	11.1	7.2
Cyprus	25.7	64.2	13.9	2.3
El Salvador[c]	9.3	27.9	76.3	2.0
Ethiopia	20.9	50.2	0.5	5.2
Fiji[c]	24.5	66.6	61.0	10.0
Gambia	47.6	32.5	35.8	5.5
Greece	28.3	96.0	17.2	4.7
Guatemala[c]	12.1	73.4	26.0	2.3
Guyana	143.9	53.6	21.2	16.4
Indonesia	27.0	5.8	...	...
Israel	169.2	56.4	83.4	79.5
Jordan[c]	53.0	43.4	26.0	6.0
Kenya[c]	29.1	53.9	56.8	8.9
Korea	12.0	33.5	33.8	1.4
Liberia	30.9	14.3	19.5	0.9
Malawi[c]	35.2	34.0	21.9	2.6
Malaysia	46.1	77.8	67.6	24.2
Malta	18.2	54.4	38.7	3.8
Mauritius[c]	50.9	71.2	13.4	4.9
Morocco	39.7	34.9	29.1	4.0
Nepal	11.5	54.3	12.8	0.8
Oman	14.4	2.5	...	...
Pakistan[c]	61.8	44.3	19.4	5.3
Panama	38.2	24.6	36.5	3.4
Papua New Guinea[c]	26.7	32.4	...	...

Table 8-1. *(continued)*

Country	Total debt as % of GDP	Domestic debt as % of total debt	Nonbank holdings as % of domestic debt[b]	Domestic nonbank holdings as % of GDP
Paraguay[c]	7.2	19.3	—	—
Philippines[c]	16.9	43.7	31.3	2.3
Rwanda	12.1	8.2	50.0	0.5
Seychelles[c]	5.3	64.8	89.2	3.1
Sierra Leone[c]	39.3	47.7	19.6	3.7
Singapore	69.6	92.8	84.6	54.6
South Africa	40.0	96.5	77.4	29.9
Sri Lanka	68.8	58.3	53.1	21.3
Thailand	22.6	86.7	6.7	1.3
Trinidad and Tobago	14.2	41.5	...	...
Tunisia	39.1	30.2	1.9	0.2
Uruguay	13.1	34.2	7.7	0.3
Venezuela	15.2	12.7	57.5	1.1
Zaire	57.3	54.2	—	—
Zambia[c]	92.5	69.7	23.9	15.4
Median	26.7	47.7	29.6	3.8

Source: Derived from International Monetary Fund, *Government Finance Statistics Yearbook,* vol. 5 (1981), and *International Financial Statistics* (January 1982).

a. Consolidated central government, except where indicated by note c. Debt at end of year: for most countries 1979 or 1978 or a fiscal year ended in that period; in some cases 1977 or a fiscal year ended in 1977; and in a few cases a fiscal year ended in the first half of 1980. Where GDP statistics were not available for the fiscal year, the figure for the calendar year nearest to the fiscal year, or an average of the figures for two calendar years, was used. Ellipses indicate data are not available. Dashes indicate amounts less than 0.1.

b. Nonbank holders are all domestic holders other than the monetary authorities and deposit money banks.

c. Budgetary central government; central government institutions not fully consolidated.

Aside from social security funds, captive lenders probably account for much of the nonbank domestic debt of the great majority of developing countries. These include insurance companies and pension and provident funds. Provident funds normally are financed by contributions of employers and employees, with government contributing only as an employer. Benefits usually are paid in a lump sum when a person leaves the employment of a participating enterprise. Provident funds ordinarily are subject to government regulation and may be required to invest in government securities. They have been a leading source of nonbank financing of central governments in certain Commonwealth countries, including Malaysia, Ghana, Kenya, and Tanzania. (Social security funds resemble provident funds in certain respects but are financed by taxes and may receive a contribution from general government revenue. They are prevalent in Latin America and are found also in some francophone African countries but appear to be an important source of central government financing in only a few developing countries.) Various public and quasi-public bodies and court-appointed trustees also may be required to invest in government securities.[4]

In some cases outstanding debt has been built up over a long period. The amount of financing obtained from domestic borrowing in any one year usually is small in comparison to tax revenue.

Governments that wish to increase their capacity to borrow from nonbank lenders will have to overcome their reluctance to pay realistic interest rates. Interest rates offered on domestic debt often are much lower than the rates paid on nonofficial loans from abroad and frequently are lower than the rate of inflation. Savers can hardly be relied on to lend voluntarily if they expect prices to rise at a rate greater than the interest rate on government securities.

Because inflation is expected to continue in most countries and there is great uncertainty about its future rate, indexed bonds may be attractive to savers and advantageous to governments. If the principal amount of the securities were adjusted annually by reference to a broad price index and interest were computed on the adjusted principal, the interest rate would no longer need to include an allowance for inflation and could be much lower than on conventional loans.

Several countries have had some success with indexed bonds. Their use in Israel may help explain the exceptionally high domestic nonbank debt ratio of that country, despite a history of inflation. The majority of governments, however, have not issued indexed bonds, either because the idea has not been systematically considered or because it has been judged to be undesirable. One objection is that, by resorting to indexing, the government signals that it foresees continuing inflation and thus undermines confidence. This argument may have had some merit in the past, but after the recent experience of inflation it carries little weight. Indeed, indexing might better be interpreted as a sign of a government's confidence that inflation will not get out of hand. Probably the points that have counted most heavily against indexed bonds are the reluctance of governments to assume the uncertain and perhaps sizable commitments that would be involved and the belief that deficits can be financed by some combination of borrowing from captive lenders, foreign loans, and money creation.

---

4. This paragraph draws on an unpublished paper by Daudi T. S. Ballali, "Nonbank Financing of Budget Deficits in Developing Countries," Fiscal Affairs Department, International Monetary Fund, December 27, 1979.

Other techniques that have been used to stimulate sales of government securities include issuing treasury bills in the hope of attracting short-term investments of temporarily surplus funds of enterprises, offering small savers' certificates through post offices, incorporating lottery provisions, and exempting interest on the securities from income tax. Tax exemption, though fairly widely practiced, can be criticized as inequitable and probably inefficient. It is inefficient if the marginal investors in government securities are subject to lower tax rates than other buyers. In that case, the loss of tax revenue will exceed the saving of interest payments. Although the use of suitable techniques, together with the payment of adequate interest rates, can attract lending by the nonbank sector, a long time will have to pass before a wide market for government securities can be established in many of the developing countries.

In a good many countries, a significant, though irregular, form of government borrowing has been the floating debt. This consists mainly of overdue bills owed to suppliers. Sometimes salary payments are delayed, but most governments regard that expedient as unfair and politically risky. The accumulation of overdue bills is evidence of poor financial management. If it continues or recurs frequently, suppliers will increase their prices to allow for possible delay in receiving payment. To prevent the problems associated with the floating debt, ministries of finance need to develop reliable current information on commitments and cash balances, to make careful forecasts of cash flows during the year, and to exercise control over the rate at which departments may make purchases.

Borrowing Abroad

Borrowing abroad differs from borrowing at home in that it gives the borrowing country command over more goods than it is currently producing. Hence external borrowing allows the government to finance itself without displacing household and enterprise spending. But the payment of interest on an external debt and the repayment of the principal require a transfer of resources abroad rather than merely a reallocation of purchasing power among residents. Interest on an external debt can be paid only if the government borrows further or receives grants, or if the residents of the country use (for consumption and domestic investment) less output than they produce. And the total foreign debt can be reduced only by the two latter means or by repudiation. Clearly, the considerations that are relevant to decisions to incur or repay external debt are not the same as those that pertain to domestic debt.[5] This section deals with government borrowing abroad from both private and official lenders. Many of the points to be discussed are applicable also to enterprise borrowing, which should be a subject of concern to governments and which may need to be regulated.

Debt Servicing Capacity

Whether a government should borrow abroad is essentially a benefit-cost question: an immediate gain in resources should be balanced against the future real cost of debt service and possible debt repayment. Ideally, a decision to borrow should be made deliberately, after careful appraisal of benefits and costs.[6] In practice, much borrowing is unplanned and is undertaken in response to offers from plausible salesmen or bankers or because of emergencies, miscalculations, or weak policies, with little or no systematic comparison of benefits and costs.

In a book published in 1964, Avramovic and colleagues at the World Bank approached external borrowing in terms of a country's debt servicing capacity.[7] That approach does not conflict with the benefit-cost view, but it tends to take the benefits for granted and to concentrate on the cost factors. The approach is essentially a gap analysis, dealing with the use of external borrowing to supplement domestic resources to attain a target growth rate. Although the Avramovic analysis may be overly elaborate and somewhat mechanistic, it provides a useful framework for the examination of external borrowing.

Assuming that countries borrow only to help finance well-conceived development programs, Avramovic and his coauthors visualize three stages in the external debt cycle. In stage one, the country's saving is below the desired level of investment. It borrows abroad to finance part of its investment and also to service the external debt. The burden of servicing the debt is continuously deferred, and the debt increases rapidly. In stage two, saving has grown enough to finance all domestic investment; however,

5. Buchanan denies that there is a conceptual difference between internal and external borrowing, arguing that both forms of financing cause residents to give up the future yield on an amount of capital equivalent to the borrowing. See *Public Principles of Public Debt*, pp. 73–84.

6. For a review of theoretical treatments of the subject, see Donogh C. McDonald, "Debt Capacity and Developing Country Borrowing: A Survey of the Literature," International Monetary Fund *Staff Papers*, vol. 29 (December 1982), pp. 603–46.

7. Dragoslav Avramovic and others, *Economic Growth and External Debt* (Johns Hopkins University Press for the World Bank, 1964).

the country continues to borrow abroad to cover service costs of the debt. The external debt grows but at a slower rate than in stage one; at the end of stage two it reaches a maximum. In stage three, the country stops borrowing abroad to cover interest payments and begins to reduce the external debt. A very poor country may take a long time to move through stages one and two, and if the return on the capital obtained by foreign borrowing is low relative to the interest rate, it may never reach stage three.

The capacity of a country to service external debt may be analyzed in terms of the short-run or liquidity aspects and the long-run or productivity aspects. Debt servicing difficulties in the short run are one element in the precariousness of the balance of payments of developing countries. Avramovic and his coauthors identify the variables related to liquidity as the following.

1. Fluctuating variables
   a. Exports
   b. Capital flows not related to the borrowing
   c. Emergency and inflation-induced imports
2. Offsetting variables
   a. Foreign exchange reserves
   b. Compensatory financing from the International Monetary Fund or other sources
   c. Compressible (nonessential) imports
3. Rigid variables
   a. Minimum tolerable level of imports
   b. Debt service—interest
   c. Debt service—amortization

This outline is only suggestive. The fluctuating variables can be influenced to a greater or lesser degree by government action, and the distinction between compressible imports and the minimum tolerable level of imports must be to some extent adjustable in the light of circumstances.

In the long run, the capacity of a country to service external debt depends on the growth of output and of exports and imports. On the assumption that all external borrowing is used to finance development projects, the Avramovic study portrays the possible behavior of the debt and debt service through the three stylized stages on the basis of a simple model incorporating stable values of the incremental capital-output ratio, marginal saving rate, export and import coefficients, and the interest rate and maturity of the debt. This exercise demonstrates that with plausible assumed values for the variables it is possible for countries to benefit from external borrowing and to reach the stage at which the external debt can be reduced without undue strain. Because of the simplified nature of the model, it should be used circumspectly.

Comments on the external debt of a particular country usually concentrate on the liquidity aspects and the default risk. The most widely used quantitative indicator is the debt service ratio, which is the ratio of debt service (interest and amortization) to the value of exports of goods and services. This is at best an incomplete measure; it includes only three of the nine variables listed above. Debt service ratios differ considerably among countries and do not reliably distinguish those that have experienced severe difficulties from those that have not. Changes in the ratio may be more significant than the absolute level, but they require interpretation. A rapid increase may be a danger signal, or it may indicate only that the country is moving from a low to a higher, but still sustainable, debt level. As a suggestive indicator of the debt burden in the medium-term future or the long run, the ratio of the debt to GNP or of debt service to GNP may be superior to the ratio of debt service to exports because over time sizable changes in the shares of both exports and imports in GNP can occur. None of the ratios alone can adequately measure the external debt burden or correctly predict debt difficulties, but they have the appeal of simplicity and apparent objectivity and will continue to be used.

The servicing of a government debt presents a budget problem. Regardless of any special difficulty associated with making payments in foreign currency, the government must first provide the local currency equivalent of any net service payments, that is, of any excess of interest and amortization over new borrowing. That requires a surplus of tax revenue over local expenditures. The difficulty of achieving it may cause consternation when the net inflow from borrowing is interrupted.

In addition to the budget problem, there is also a transfer problem in regard to an external debt. Even if national income increases as a result of the wise use of external loans and the budget provides sufficient revenue to cover the service payments, the transfer problem will exist. That is so for two reasons. First, taxes ordinarily do not reduce domestic spending by the full amount of the revenue obtained. Second, a reduction in domestic spending may not improve the balance of payments by an equivalent amount by curtailing imports and freeing production for export. To improve the balance of payments on goods and services enough to cover the debt service, it may be necessary to hold domestic activity below the level that could be maintained if the payments did not have to be made or

Table 8-2. *External Public Debt of Eighty-Seven Non-Oil Developing Countries, 1972–81*[a]

Money values in billions of U.S. dollars

Item	1972	1973	1974	1975	1976	1977	1978	1979	1980	1981[b]
Amount outstanding										
Current value	61	73	92	111	135	168	210	238	266	301
Deflated value[c]	61	55	50	61	69	75	89	86	80	92
Percent of GNP	15	14	14	16	17	19	20	19	18	19
Debt service										
Current value	7	9	10	13	14	20	30	39	42	49
Deflated value[c]	7	7	6	7	7	9	13	14	13	15
Percent of exports of goods and services	12	11	10	11	11	12	16	16	14	15

Source: Bahram Nowzad, Richard C. Williams, and others, *External Indebtedness of Developing Countries*, Occasional Paper 3 (Washington, D.C.: International Monetary Fund, 1981), revised and supplemented by unpublished statistics supplied by the staff of the IMF.

a. Medium-term and long-term debt to nonresidents and repayable in foreign currency owed or guaranteed by national governments, political subdivisions or agencies, and autonomous public bodies. Transactions with the International Monetary Fund excluded. Outstanding debt (disbursed only) at end of year.

b. Preliminary.

c. Deflated by index of export unit values.

to devalue the currency and to suffer a worsening of the terms of trade.[8] The transfer problem will be aggravated if creditor countries impose tariffs or other impediments to imports from debtor countries and will be ameliorated if such restraints are relaxed.

Recent Trends in External Debt

The medium-term and long-term external public debt of non-oil developing countries increased rapidly in the 1970s and early 1980s (table 8-2). Even when corrected for inflation, the increase was substantial. The economies of the debtor countries were growing, and the external public debt of the non-oil developing countries as a group appears to have leveled off in relation to GNP in 1977–81. Debt service payments increased in relation to exports after 1976, owing to higher interest rates and shorter maturities associated with an increase in the proportion of debt owed to private creditors as distinguished from debt to governments and international institutions. Among developing countries, the debt service ratio was

8. J. E. Meade, *The Theory of International Economic Policy*, vol. 1: *The Balance of Payments* (Oxford University Press, 1951), pp. 88–93, distinguishes a "transfer problem" from a "transfer burden." The former occurs when the transfer can be accomplished by deflationary budget measures without a change in the terms of trade; a transfer burden exists when the transfer can be brought about only by a worsening of the debtor's terms of trade.

much lower for the low-income countries than for the major exporters of manufactures and the middle-income countries because of the predominance of official credit in the debt of the low-income countries.[9] By 1982 several countries faced serious external debt problems.

The effect of inflation on the debt position merits further comment. During the 1970s, developing countries like other debtors benefited from the failure of interest rates fully to reflect inflation. Over the period 1972–79, the average interest rate on the debt commitments of all developing countries was only about one-half the average increase in the unit values of exports of non-oil developing countries. This tended to hold down the ratios of debt service and to reduce the real value of the debt, though new borrowing more than offset that influence.

During the 1970s, however, an increasing fraction of new external loans carried variable (floating) interest rates. Rates on these loans usually are adjusted periodically and are linked to the London Inter-Bank Offer Rate (LIBOR), which is the rate paid by large commercial banks to attract deposits. Interest rates on such loans fluctuate with credit conditions and tend to move with the rate of inflation. In general, inflation does not cause borrowing countries to gain at the expense of creditors holding the variable rate loans.

With variable rates, the significance of interest payments changes, since they include an element to compensate lenders for the reduction of the real value of the outstanding principal. In effect, the speed of amortization of the debt is increased. The speed-up of amortization is greater the longer the maturity of the debt and the more rapid the inflation (assuming that nominal interest rates fully reflect the inflation). A consequence of this process is that indicators such as the ratio of interest payments to exports or to GNP and of debt service to these variables are biased upward. Furthermore, the more rapid effective amortization of the debt increases the frequency with which countries may need to refinance or roll over maturing debt.

A country that gets into balance-of-payments difficulties is likely to ask

---

9. See the following publications of the International Monetary Fund: Bahram Nowzad, Richard C. Williams, and others, *External Indebtedness of Developing Countries*, Occasional Paper 3, 1981; and *World Economic Outlook*, Occasional Paper 9, 1982. See also World Bank, *World Debt Tables 1981*; Organization for Economic Cooperation and Development, *External Debt of Developing Countries* (Paris: OECD, 1981). Caution should be exercised in using external debt statistics, which may include undisbursed debt and private nonguaranteed debt. Debt with an original maturity of less than one year is usually excluded. The country coverage of debt statistics has changed over time, and there are minor differences in the classification of countries by the World Bank and the IMF.

its creditors for debt relief,[10] even though the difficulties were not necessarily caused by the debt. Often they may be caused by excessively
expansionary monetary or fiscal policies, inflation, mismanagement, and
political uncertainty; in other cases, crop failures, increases in import
prices, decreases in export prices, or recession in the industrial countries
are the main cause.

Since 1956, when representatives of a number of European countries
met in Paris to renegotiate Argentina's debts owed to them or guaranteed
by them, a framework has evolved for multilateral renegotiation in certain
circumstances of debts to governments or to private lenders with government guarantee. Most of the meetings occur in Paris, and the creditor
group is called the Paris Club. Renegotiations also have been carried out
under the auspices of aid consortia. Although the renegotiations have been
conducted on a case-by-case basis, creditors have tended to follow a
common approach. The Paris Club has insisted that a debt renegotiation
not be used as an occasion for extending development aid. Generally, debt
relief has been provided in the context of a program intended to improve
the balance of payments. From 1956 to mid-1981, there were fifty-three
multilateral renegotiations of government direct or guaranteed loans to
nineteen debtor countries.[11] A rapid increase in the frequency of renegotiations followed, and in early 1983 multilateral debt reschedulings had been
arranged or were under negotiation for twenty countries.[12]

The renegotiations typically take the form of consolidating arrears of
debt service and of stretching out the maturity period of the restructured
debt. Interest rates have been set bilaterally. In principle, payments due on
previously rescheduled debts have been excluded from renegotiation, but
there have been occasional departures from that rule. Debts to commercial
banks are not renegotiated through the Paris Club but are rescheduled
when necessary after discussions with committees of bankers.

In 1980 a set of guidelines for multilateral debt renegotiation was
adopted by the Trade and Development Board of the United Nations
Conference on Trade and Development.[13] They specified that renegotia-

10. The following paragraphs are based largely on Nowzad, Williams, and others, *External Indebtedness of Developing Countries*, pp. 17–29. See also Goran Ohlin, "Debts, Development and Default,"
in G. K. Helleiner, ed., *A World Divided: The Less Developed Countries in the International Economy*
(Cambridge University Press, 1976), pp. 207–23.

11. OECD, *External Debt of Developing Countries*, pp. 25–26.

12. International Monetary Fund, *World Economic Outlook*, Occasional Paper 21, 1983, pp.
67–68.

13. UNCTAD, Resolution 222, XXI, implementing Resolution 165, S-IX.

tions were to be initiated only at the request of the debtor country; were to improve the development prospects of the debtor, taking account of its social and economic priorities and its internationally agreed development objectives; and were to aim at strengthening the debtor's balance of payments and its capacity to service debt. In acute cases, the debtor country should present a program designed for that purpose. The creditor countries assented to the resolution, specifying that within the United Nations system, debt and debt renegotiation were the responsibility of the IMF and the World Bank.

In 1982–83 Mexico, Argentina, and Brazil were unable to meet heavy debt service commitments. Following a rapid expansion of their external debts and increases in real interest rates, their balance of payments had deteriorated, partly as a result of a world recession. The three countries modified the terms of their debts, after conversations with major creditors, and sought financial assistance from the IMF.

Summary

Borrowing from domestic nonbank lenders should be distinguished from borrowing from the central bank and deposit money banks, which is likely to result in money creation. Like taxation, domestic borrowing displaces enterprise and household spending, and usually its main impact is on investment.

Opportunities for government borrowing at home are limited in most developing countries by low saving and the preference for assets other than government securities. Captive lenders, especially insurance companies and pension and provident funds, often are the principal nonbank lenders. The scope for borrowing can be extended by paying realistic interest rates (with indexing for inflation if necessary) and by using a variety of instruments and outlets.

Borrowing abroad gives a country command over more goods and services than it is currently producing but entails a future real cost and transfer problem. Whether such borrowing should be undertaken is essentially a benefit-cost question that can be analyzed by reference to the value of the debt-financed expenditures and the country's debt service capacity. In practice, however, much borrowing is unplanned and is prompted by attractive offers of credit or by emergencies, miscalculations, or weak fiscal policies.

The external public debt of non-oil developing countries increased rapidly in the 1970s and early 1980s, even when corrected for inflation. Debt service payments rose in relation to GNP and exports, owing to high interest rates and short maturities associated with an increased proportion of debt owed to private creditors rather than official lenders. The worldwide recession of the early 1980s and the deterioration of the terms of trade of primary producers exacerbated the problems of heavily indebted developing countries. A number of countries had to seek debt relief.

CHAPTER NINE

Financing by Money Creation

A GOVERNMENT finances its expenditures by money creation when it causes them to be covered by additional currency or bank deposits that are transferable and generally acceptable in domestic transactions. This form of finance neither reduces the amount of money held by residents, as taxation and domestic nonbank borrowing do, nor provides the government the means of paying for additional imports, as borrowing abroad does. This chapter discusses the consequences of financing by money creation in developing countries and the scope for it.

Nature and Effects

Money creation and borrowing are distinct in principle but may be confused because in contemporary conditions the most important kind of money creation takes the legal form of borrowing from the central bank. Although there may be exceptions, government net borrowing from the central bank generally does not displace other lending but results in an addition to deposits and currency. The balance sheet of the central bank initially shows equal increases in assets in the form of claims on government and in liabilities in the form of government deposits and currency. As the government makes payments to contractors and employees, there is an increase in deposits and currency in the hands of enterprises and households.

Government borrowing from domestic commercial banks (also called deposit money banks) may or may not entail a net addition to the money stock. If the banks have no excess reserves (are fully loaned up), according to prudential or legal standards, and no concurrent steps are taken to supplement their reserves, no additional money is created by government borrowing. In that situation, government borrowing displaces loans to the banks' regular customers, and it resembles borrowing from nonbank domestic lenders. If, however, the commercial banks have excess reserves or if the central bank provides additional reserves by rediscounting some of their claims against others, by extending loans to them, or by purchasing securities, they can lend to the government without contracting their credit to their regular customers, and a net addition to the money stock occurs.[1] Probably government borrowing from commercial banks usually results in money creation, but whether it will do so at a particular time and place is a question of fact that has to be answered on the basis of existing conditions. This chapter is concerned with borrowing from commercial banks only insofar as it results in the creation of additional money.

No elaborate demonstration is needed to show that government spending financed by net money creation results in an increase in aggregate spending. The process does not diminish the expenditures of enterprises and households, and the government spending is added to the total. The initial increase in aggregate spending will stimulate further increases in expenditures for goods and services and perhaps also the acquisition of additional financial claims by those who receive the additional money as it is paid out and passes from hand to hand.

The increase in aggregate spending will result in some combination of additional output, higher prices, and larger imports in relation to exports. When idle productive capacity exists, increased spending may stimulate additional output up to the point at which capacity is fully used. While unemployed and underemployed people are numerous in many less developed countries and manufacturing plants frequently operate below their rated capacity, unused productive capacity is much smaller in most cases than may be supposed. Usually the unemployed lack needed skills, many idle plants cannot efficiently produce the goods that consumers want to buy, and other plants must import more materials and fuel to raise their output.

Inflation and balance-of-payments deficits are the most usual results of financing government expenditures by money creation. Since balance-of-payments deficits are constrained by the availability of foreign exchange reserves and external credit (which are not increased), inflation will be the main effect when money creation is large and continuing. As will be explained in the next section, there is room for a relatively small amount of noninflationary money creation as the economy grows.

1. In the conditions mentioned, the increase in money stock nevertheless may be smaller than the bank net lending to government because other lending declines owing to higher interest rates or the application of stricter credit standards by banks.

Demands for public spending generated by the policies and aspirations of governments, the pressures exerted by interest groups, and unforeseen emergencies—together with the difficulties of taxation, borrowing at home, and borrowing abroad—have caused many governments to resort to money creation. Although this method of financing may have become more prevalent in recent years, hard-pressed governments have resorted to it at least since Rome discovered that coins could be clipped or debased. As Keynes wrote in 1922, the creation of money "has been and is a government's ultimate reserve." Although until recently almost universally considered dangerous and wrong except in great emergencies, financing by money creation has occurred so frequently that, according to Keynes, it has been a principal cause of inflation's being "*continuous*, if we consider long periods, ever since money was first devised in the sixth century B.C."[2] The rule of responsible government finance did not prevent inflation any more than moral precepts prevented sin.

During the past few decades, attitudes toward inflationary finance in developing countries have become more permissive. In the 1950s and 1960s a structuralist school, influential especially in Latin America, argued that inflation is unavoidable in developing countries. Some comments on structuralism appear in chapter 11. Economists who reject structuralism may nevertheless regard financing by money creation and inflation as a second-best method of resource mobilization that will enable governments to carry out development programs.

Although economic discussions usually imply that money creation is a deliberately chosen means of finance, probably it is more often the result of misjudgment, weakness, or fecklessness than of careful calculation. Financing by money creation appeals to a weak government. Unlike taxation, no administrative machinery is required and no administrative cost is incurred. The process is impersonal and at first usually unnoticed. Adverse incentive effects are not apparent.[3]

In the remainder of this chapter, attention will be given to the scope for noninflationary financing by money creation and the potentiality and limits of inflationary finance. The effects of inflation on government revenues and expenditures will be examined, and measures to protect tax revenues during inflation will be enumerated. Some comments will also be made on the consequences of inflation.

2. *The Collected Writings of John Maynard Keynes*, vol. 4: *A Tract on Monetary Reform* (London: Macmillan for the Royal Economic Society, 1971), pp. 8–9, 10.

3. Ibid., *Tract on Monetary Reform*, p. 37; Carl S. Shoup, *Public Finance* (Aldine, 1969), pp. 457–61.

Noninflationary Finance by Money Creation

A growing economy will require more money to facilitate its transactions and to serve as a liquid asset. The counterpart of the increased money stock may include lending to the government by the central bank and the commercial banks. If the increase in the money stock—and the counterpart in the form of loans and investments of the banking system—does not exceed the quantity that enterprises and households desire to hold at stable prices, money creation to finance the government will not be inflationary.

The relations can be clarified by reference to a consolidated, and condensed, balance sheet of the banking system, comprising the central bank and the commercial banks (deposit money banks).

Assets	Liabilities
Foreign assets (net claims on nonresidents)	Money
	Currency and coins
Domestic credit	Deposits
Claims on enterprises	Other deposits (quasi money)
Claims on households	
Claims on government (net)	Other liabilities
Other domestic assets (buildings, etc.)	Capital

Since the totals of assets and liabilities (plus capital) must always be equal, any bank net lending to government must be accompanied by an equivalent reduction in another asset—claims on nonresidents or on resident enterprises and households—or by an increase in liabilities—usually monetary liabilities in the form of currency and deposits. For convenience, foreign assets are shown net of the banking system's liabilities to nonresidents, and claims on government are net of government deposits. With minor variations in terminology and details, the International Monetary Fund publishes such consolidated balance sheets for the banking systems of a large number of countries in the monetary survey section of its monthly *International Financial Statistics*.

How much the banking system can lend to the government and other borrowers without causing inflation depends on how much money people are willing to hold at stable prices. That question has prompted a great deal of theorizing and quantitative analysis. Early versions of the quantity theory of money asserted that normally people wish to hold money balances equal to a constant fraction of their income. If other items in the consolidated balance sheet remain constant, that assertion implies that bank credit and money can increase at the same rate as real income without causing inflation. This version of behavior is now regarded as a special case, but it is a useful first approximation if no other information is available.

According to a more sophisticated formulation, the quantity of money that people wish to hold depends on income, wealth, the rate of return on other assets, and institutional factors, including the degree of monetization of the economy and payments practices. Also allowance has to be made for the current price level and any expected change in it.[4]

In condensed form this relation may be written algebraically as follows:

$$M/P = b(Y, P^*, W, r, F),$$

where M is money, P is the current price level, Y is real income, P^* is the expected rate of change in the price level, W is wealth, r is the rate of return on financial assets other than money, and F stands for other relevant factors mentioned above. The value M/P—often called real cash balances— is expected to vary positively with Y and W and negatively with P^* and r. In the special case in which P^* is zero (implying that no change in the price level is expected) and W, r, and F are unchanged, M/P varies only with Y.

Recently considerable effort has been devoted to studying the relationship between M/P and Y—real money balances and real income—in developing countries. Attempts have been made to isolate the relationship by statistically holding constant the estimated influence of certain other variables and assuming that wealth, the degree of monetization, and payments practices change so slowly that they can safely be ignored in an analysis intended to cover no more than a few years. It has been hypothesized that money holdings are a luxury and hence will display an income elasticity above 1. Although findings differ, many statistical studies report elasticities between 1 and 2 (with respect to real per capita income), and some support can be adduced for a figure of the order of 1.5.[5]

4. Milton Friedman, "The Quantity Theory of Money—A Restatement," in Friedman, ed., *Studies in the Quantity Theory of Money* (University of Chicago Press, 1956), pp. 3–21; Ralph C. Bryant, *Money and Monetary Policy in Interdependent Nations* (Brookings Institution, 1980), pp. 53–57, and the references there cited.

5. Morris Perlman found an income elasticity of 1.4 for 47 countries (developed and developing) in 1952–61. See his "International Differences in Liquid Assets Portfolios" in David Meiselman, ed., *Varieties of Monetary Experience* (University of Chicago Press, 1970), pp. 299–332. Lubin K. Doe, in a study of twelve developing countries in 1960–77, reports elasticities (real per capita GDP in relation to real per capita money holdings) ranging between 0.6 for Thailand and 3.1 for the Ivory Coast; the median figure is 1.5 ("Demand for Money in Some Developing Countries," *Indian Journal of Economics*, vol. 63 (May 1982), pp. 91–114). These estimates are not directly comparable because of differences in the definition of income; Perlman's estimates are from a cross section, with two observations for each country (with some exceptions), whereas Doe's figures are time-series estimates for each country.

To see the relevance of the income elasticity of the demand for money for the question of the scope for noninflationary financing by money creation, it is necessary to combine the elasticity estimate with the ratio of money to income in a base period. This ratio differs among countries. In the majority of developing countries, the ratio of money (narrowly defined as currency plus demand deposits) to gross domestic product falls in the range 0.10 to 0.20. Combined with an income elasticity of 1.5, this implies that per capita money holdings will grow by an amount equal to 0.15 to 0.30 of an increase in per capita income. If, for example, real GDP per capita increases by 4 percent, real money holdings will increase by an amount equal to 0.6 percent to 1.2 percent of per capita GDP. In the absence of changes in any of the other relevant variables, the banking system can extend credit up to that amount without causing inflation. The ratio of money holdings to GDP tends to be somewhat higher in developed countries than in developing countries, but the income elasticity of the demand for money may be lower.

These figures illustrate a method of analysis and give an impression of possible orders of magnitude. A careful and detailed study would be needed to establish the basis for an estimate for a particular country. It appears, nevertheless, that in conditions that may be reasonably representative of those existing in developing countries, the amount of money that can be created annually without causing inflation—or adding to it—is only a small fraction of GDP. Furthermore, the government is not the only claimant for the credit counterpart of money creation. As the balance sheet of the banking system shows, the total has to be allocated among credit to domestic enterprises and households and net foreign assets as well as credit to government. In a growing economy, additional provision should normally be made for the nongovernmental uses. If the government attempts to appropriate the entire margin for noninflationary credit expansion, production and international trade will be handicapped or total credit expansion will exceed the noninflationary amount.

Inflationary Finance

When financing of government expenditures by money creation exceeds the noninflationary limit, total spending in the country becomes greater than production valued at stable prices. As already explained, prices rise and the balance of payments tends to go into deficit. The noninflationary limit of money creation is not rigidly fixed, and there may be some delay in reactions. Especially if prices have been stable in the recent past, people may temporarily add to their money holdings, and many transactions may take place at the old prices for a time. The experience of inflation in most countries during the past decade, however, probably has made people sensitive to rising prices and has shortened the lags in adjustments.

The use of newly created money gives the government command over real resources, while the price rise reduces the purchasing power of each monetary unit. Broadly viewed, the holders of money involuntarily give up the equivalent of the real resources obtained by the government. Economists often call the process the imposition of an inflation tax and the resources so transferred the real revenue from the tax, though in a strict sense no tax is imposed.

If inflation had no effect on real income or the amount of money that people wish to hold in relation to income, prices would rise in proportion to the ratio of the actual money stock to the noninflationary stock. For example, if the noninflationary limit to money creation were a 6 percent increase in the money stock and the actual increase were 16.6 percent, the price level would rise by 10 percent ($116.6/106 = 1.1$). If all the new money were used by the government, it would obtain real resources equal to 15.1 percent of the initial money stock ($16.6/1.1 = 15.1$). To take another example, if government spending financed by money creation were equal to 112 percent of the initial stock and the noninflationary limit were 6 percent, prices would double and the government would gain real resources equivalent to 56 percent of the initial money stock. These figures, of course, reflect the assumption that, within the range under consideration, the ratio of money holdings to nominal income, hence the velocity of circulation of money, is constant.

Money holdings, however, will not remain constant in relation to income as inflation proceeds. Before long people will come to expect that prices will continue to rise and will adjust their behavior accordingly. In particular, they will recognize that they are suffering losses of purchasing power by holding money and will reduce their cash balances in relation to their income and wealth. In terms of the equation given earlier, P^* will no longer be zero but will be positive and will exert a negative influence on M/P, causing it to be smaller for any given values of the other variables. That is another way of saying that the velocity of circulation of money will increase. These adjustments will tend to accelerate the inflation and induce further adjustments that will perpetuate it.

The beginning of inflation does not immediately cause a flight from money. The use of money is a great convenience, and, as Keynes observed during the hyperinflations in several European countries after World War I, people will bear a cost before giving it up. Those who have studied cases of extreme inflation agree that, even after people come to understand what is occurring, they will continue to hold and use money. The function of money as a store of liquid wealth weakens first and may virtually disappear if rapid inflation persists. The use of money in current transactions continues in the face of prolonged and rapid inflation, though the velocity of circulation may become very high. Barter comes to be practiced, even in industrial countries, and foreign currency and other media of exchange (such as cigarettes) are used. Toward the end of a hyperinflation, domestic money is used only for small transactions or where creditors cannot prevent extinction of their claims by payment in depreciating money. Government claims are likely to be discharged in domestic money after its use becomes exceptional for other purposes.

The decline in the ratio of money to income reduces the real gain that the government can obtain from inflationary finance. To evaluate quantitatively the potential yield of financing by money creation, it would be necessary to know—or to guess—how people's expectations about inflation are formed and how these influence their money holdings. Expectations are not directly observable but may be inferred from behavior. In econometric studies, it has been assumed that people project into the future the price increases of the current period and the recent past. The value of P^* has been measured as an average of these rates (usually weighted exponentially so that the most recent period has the greatest influence on the estimate). Many studies have passed quickly over difficulties due to unstable expectations and adjustment lags and have estimated the sensitivity of money holdings to expected inflation (M/P to P^*) on the assumption that inflation has been maintained at a steady rate long enough to condition expectations and for actual money holdings to be equated with desired holdings at that inflation rate. For simplicity, the studies usually have assumed that inflation has no effect on real income, wealth, or other variables that affect the demand for money and the inflation that will result from a given amount of money creation.[6]

6. Most writers follow the approach developed by Phillip Cagan in "The Monetary Dynamics of Hyperinflation," in Friedman, *Studies in the Quantity Theory of Money*, pp. 23–117. See also Robert A. Mundell, "Growth, Stability and Inflationary Finance," *Journal of Political Economy*, vol. 73 (April 1965), pp. 97–109; Milton Friedman, "Government Revenue from Inflation," *Journal of Political Economy*, vol. 79 (July/August 1971), pp. 846–56; Vito Tanzi, "Inflation, Real Tax Revenue, and the Case for Inflationary Finance: Theory with an Application to Argentina," International Monetary Fund *Staff Papers*, vol. 25 (September 1978), pp. 417–51; and George M. von Furstenberg, "Inflation, Taxes, and Welfare in LDCs," *Public Finance/Finances Publiques*, vol. 35 (1980), pp. 183–212.

Even with such simplifying assumptions, estimates of the sensitivity of real money holdings to expected inflation differ widely. Most of the estimates indicate that in developing countries the amount of real resources obtainable from money creation increases up to steady-state inflation rates somewhere between 33 percent and 200 percent a year and declines at higher inflation rates. The size of these transfers in relation to income would depend on the ratio of money holdings to income in the absence of inflation. For a country in which that ratio is 15 percent at zero inflation, the maximum yield would range from about 2 percent to 11 percent of GDP.[7] The width of the ranges suggests the uncertainty that surrounds the subject and the difficulty of using the analysis for policy purposes. Critics have argued that the figures greatly overstate the maximum potential yield of inflationary finance (and the range of values) but have not settled on other estimates.[8]

A sudden and unexpected burst of inflation will be especially effective in diverting resources from money holders. Time is required for people to appreciate what is occurring and to adjust their money holdings. Hence the existence for a short time of inflation rates higher than those that would yield the maximum amount if steadily maintained does not necessarily indicate that the government would have gained more real resources from a smaller amount of money creation. It is also possible that the gains from continued but irregular inflation over a period of years will exceed those obtainable from a steady inflation rate equal to the average rate.[9]

In the preceding paragraphs, it has been implicitly assumed that the government obtains the proceeds of all money creation. In the usual banking system, however, central bank lending to the government creates high-powered money (currency and deposits at the central bank), which serves as a reserve for commercial banks and allows them to expand their loans to enterprises. The banks and their customers will share in the real yield of inflation unless steps are taken to prevent this by raising reserve requirements against commercial bank deposits, requiring the

7. See Tanzi, "Inflation, Real Tax Revenue, and Inflationary Finance," p. 433, for illustrative calculations on a range of assumptions.

8. The maximum-yield inflation rates mentioned in the text, like those usually discussed in the literature, assume no growth in income. This is assumed on the grounds that the real growth rate would be small relative to the inflation rate, which is true of hyperinflations but not necessarily of other cases. More serious is the question of the validity of the estimates of the sensitivity of desired money holdings to inflation. Friedman believes that the usual estimates are much too low; see "Government Revenue from Inflation," pp. 850–53.

9. Harry G. Johnson, "A Note on the Dishonest Government and the Inflation Tax," *Journal of Monetary Economics*, vol. 3 (July 1977), pp. 375–77.

banks to buy government securities, or other measures. The potential leakage to the banks and their customers will be greater the larger the proportion of the money stock consisting of commercial bank deposits as distinguished from currency.[10]

The Impact of Inflation on the Budget

Inflation also affects tax revenue and government expenditures. These effects must be taken into account in evaluating the possible net fiscal contribution of financing by money creation.

In regard to tax revenue, two important factors are the elasticity of tax liabilities with respect to nominal income (that is, income in current prices) and the length of time between tax accrual and tax payment, or the collection lag.[11] Inflation will reduce the real value of liabilities for specific taxes and all other taxes with an elasticity below 1. On the assumption that real income is not affected, inflation will have little if any impact on the real value of liabilities for broad sales taxes, the short-run elasticity of which is approximately 1. It will increase the real value of liabilities for taxes such as progressive income and profits taxes with elasticities above 1. Elasticities with respect to nominal income may differ from those with respect to real income. For example, an ad valorem excise tax on a luxury commodity may have a high elasticity in relation to changes in real income but an elasticity of approximately 1 in relation to changes in the price level and in nominal income. Delays in adjusting exchange rates often reduce the elasticity of import duties with respect to both nominal income and real income.

If tax liabilities are not indexed, the real value of tax collections will be reduced because of the collection lag. At any given inflation rate, the longer the lag, the greater the reduction in the real value of collections; and with any given lag, the faster the inflation, the greater the reduction. For example, if prices are rising by 1 percent a month, a three-month delay in tax collection will reduce the real value of the payment by about 3 percent,

10. John V. Deaver estimates that in Chile, where prices increased in all but three years of the period 1929–55, the amount of real resources captured by inflation was equivalent to 3.4 percent of national income, of which 28 percent accrued to the government and 72 percent to banks and their borrowers; the government's share was equal to 6.0 percent of its other revenue. See "The Chilean Inflation and the Demand for Money," in Meiselman, *Varieties of Monetary Experience*, pp. 47–48.

11. Vito Tanzi, "Inflation, Lags in Collection, and the Real Value of Tax Revenue," International Monetary Fund *Staff Papers*, vol. 24 (March 1977), pp. 154–67; Tanzi, "Inflation, Real Tax Revenue, and Inflationary Finance," pp. 423–30.

a six-month delay, by almost 6 percent. With inflation at 5 percent a month, the loss of real value will be 13.6 percent with a three-month collection lag and 25.4 percent with a six-month lag. The characterization of a collection lag as long or short is rather arbitrary. In the context of inflation, perhaps a lag of more than three months may be considered long.

Following Tanzi, we may distinguish six cases of various elasticities and collection lags:[12]

	Long lag	Short lag
Elasticity below 1	A	B
Elasticity equal to 1	C	D
Elasticity above 1	E	F

Particular taxes may be classified according to this scheme, and tax systems by reference to the weighted average of the component taxes. Case A is the most unfavorable for the real value of tax revenue, case F, the most favorable. In case D, inflation may have little effect on real tax revenue. Generally, specific excises and customs duties fall under case B; ad valorem excises and sales taxes under D; the withheld part of income taxes under D or F; and the nonwithheld part under E. The behavior of ad valorem import duties depends on whether the exchange rate is promptly adjusted for domestic inflation. These duties usually will fall under B or D, depending on the promptness of adjustment of the exchange rate. Some countries, however, allow long delays in payment of excises, customs duties, and sales taxes, which will mean that these taxes will fall under A or C. Taxes on agricultural land and urban property are likely to be examples of case A. Tanzi considers cases A and C most typical of developing countries; however, the possibility that their tax systems as a whole will fall under B or D should not be excluded.

The impact of inflation on revenues, given the elasticities and collection lags, will be greater the higher the tax ratio. Thus a country that has a productive tax system may suffer a greater loss of real revenue than another that has used its taxable capacity less fully.

Tanzi concluded that in Argentina in 1969–72, when wholesale prices rose by 36 percent a year, the government's loss of real tax revenue because of the collection lag exceeded the real resources that it obtained from central bank financing. In the next four years, the gain from central bank financing exceeded the loss of tax revenue, but the inflation rate reached almost 150 percent a year.[13]

12. Tanzi, "Inflation, Real Tax Revenue, and Inflationary Finance," p. 424.
13. Ibid., pp. 442, 449–50.

In practice, the tax system and the way it is applied will change during a period of inflation, and these changes may overwhelm the automatic responses just described. New taxes may be added or old ones dropped, tax rates may be raised or lowered, delayed tax payments may be indexed, enforcement may become more or less stringent, and compliance may worsen. It seems safe to predict that tax collections will suffer from a deterioration of compliance. Taxpayers will have a strong inducement to delay payments unless they are indexed and, even with indexing, may choose to delay as a means of alleviating a squeeze on their liquidity. Enforcement also may deteriorate if, as often occurs, revenue officers suffer a decline in real compensation that causes them to devote less time to their duties and to be more susceptible to bribes.

The nature of changes in tax legislation has varied among countries undergoing inflation. Changes that will counteract some of the adverse effects of inflation on revenue are frequently made. On the other hand, legislation that will lessen the elasticity of income and profits taxes by changing exemptions, rate schedules, and the profit measure is not uncommon. Countries with long histories of inflation usually devise methods of limiting its effects on real tax revenue, whereas countries without such experience often are slow to do so.

For expenditures, the automatic response to inflation is less important than discretionary adjustments, at least in the short run. Salaries and wages, a major component of expenditures, usually lag prices in the early stages of inflation and later are subject to irregular adjustments, with periods of declining real compensation followed by large corrective increases. Governments cannot control the prices they pay for most other goods and services in the same way, but within limits they can alter the real volume of purchases. Countries experiencing continued rapid inflation are virtually compelled to adjust their nominal expenditures to allow for rising prices. Subsidies to state-owned enterprises often have to be increased because their selling prices lag behind costs.

Aghevli and Khan have advanced the hypothesis that government expenditures are adjusted more quickly to inflation than taxes are, with the result that the budget deficit is enlarged. If, as is likely, the additional deficit is financed by more money creation, inflation will be further increased and the process will become self-perpetuating. Their findings from an econometric study covering Brazil, Colombia, the Dominican Republic, and Thailand over the years 1961–74 (1964–74 for Brazil) are consistent with their hypothesis. They asserted that "in developing countries, fiscal policy tends to be automatically destabilizing, the principal built-in destabilizer being the various revenue lags. . . ."[14] The use of the word "automatically" may be misleading, as Aghevli and Khan did not try to distinguish automatic responses from discretionary changes. Indeed, this points to a weakness of their approach. Although it may be possible to predict automatic responses of tax revenue and certain expenditures from a simple econometric model, discretionary actions cannot be predicted in that way.

Testing the Aghevli-Khan hypothesis for a sample of twenty-four developing countries, Heller concluded that the net impact of inflation on the budget deficit is not generally predictable. His study, like that of Aghevli and Khan, examined the actual behavior of expenditures and revenues, without regard to whether changes were due to automatic responses or discretionary actions. Heller found that expenditures did adjust more rapidly than revenue in more than half of the countries in the sample, but the opposite was true in a sizable minority of countries. Furthermore, his results indicate that as the inflation rate accelerates expenditures tend to adjust more quickly than revenues, but once the inflation rate stabilizes at a new high level the difference in speed of adjustment tends to disappear, with both expenditure and revenues settling at lower real levels than in the low-inflation period. Heller reports that expenditures for salaries and wages and for government investment tend to adjust less quickly than other expenditures for goods and services. At high inflation rates, he found that sales tax revenue adjusts more quickly than income tax revenue.[15]

Considerable uncertainty thus surrounds the question of how inflation affects the budget. It is possible that a developing country will find its tax revenues declining relative to expenditures during a period of inflation, enlarging the deficit, inducing more money creation, and thus perpetuating the inflation. Under these conditions, a policy of deliberate inflation to mobilize resources would require a continually accelerating inflation rate up to the point of maximum yield and thereafter would become self-defeating. But some countries appear to have avoided these hazards, either because of the automatic or quasi-automatic responses of their fiscal systems or by discretionary adjustments.

14. Bijan B. Aghevli and Mohsin S. Khan, "Government Deficits and the Inflationary Process in Developing Countries," International Monetary Fund *Staff Papers*, vol. 25 (September 1978), pp. 383–416; quotation from p. 411.

15. Peter S. Heller, "Impact of Inflation on Fiscal Policy in Developing Countries," International Monetary Fund *Staff Papers*, vol. 27 (December 1980), pp. 712–48.

The Protection of Tax Revenues during Inflation

A number of measures to protect the real value of tax revenues from inflation are technically feasible; some of them have already been mentioned, and others are easily understood. The principal measures are the following:

1. Convert all specific taxes to ad valorem rates or adjust them frequently in proportion to the increase of a broad price index.

2. Promptly adjust the exchange rate used for valuing taxable imports and exports to reflect the declining purchasing power of the local currency.

3. Shorten the lag between accrual and payment of indirect taxes as much as feasible. In an inflationary period, most enterprises should be required to remit excise taxes, customs duties, and sales taxes within no more than one month after the taxable transaction.

4. For income taxes, adopt the administrative measures mentioned in chapter 5, particularly the extension of tax withholding to all periodic income payments and current payments of estimated taxes on other forms of income. Withholding agents should be required to remit withheld amounts promptly.

5. For overdue taxes, either (a) index the tax amount and apply conventional interest and penalty rates to the adjusted liability, or (b) apply an interest rate (and/or penalty) reflecting the depreciation of the currency. It would be wrong to do both, for overcorrection would result.

6. Strengthen administrative efforts to ensure compliance and to prevent delay in tax payments. Vigorous enforcement will be needed to overcome the temptations that taxpayers face to delay payments and risk insolvency by accumulating large indexed tax debts.

Although a program containing these measures would be technically feasible, it may be unrealistic to expect it to be applied. Inflation is often a sign of government weaknesses or indecision, and continued inflation is a symptom of social and political conflict. These conditions are not conducive to decisive action on taxation.

The Consequences of Inflation

Beyond its fiscal impact, inflation has far-reaching consequences. Even if everyone correctly anticipated inflation, it would cause inconvenience

226

Government Finance in Developing Countries

and additional transaction costs that would be associated with a reduction of money balances. It would also cause inefficiences in production and distribution related to the premium on holding real assets rather than money claims. These are the only real social costs recognized by some econometric models, which assume that the actual and expected inflation rates are identical and that real income is not affected.[16]

In reality, of course, people's ability to foresee inflation and to protect themselves against it differs greatly. Except perhaps in countries in which inflation has been going on at a rapid rate for a long time, there are many medium-term and long-term contracts that are fixed in money terms. Unanticipated inflation causes the real value of contractual receipts and payments to diverge from the expected value and brings about an arbitrary redistribution of income and wealth between creditors and debtors. It also distorts relative tax burdens. These effects are now widely recognized, and arrangements to mitigate them have been adopted in some countries. Nowhere, however, have the arrangements become so complete and effective that the redistributive effects of inflation are confined to a transfer of real purchasing power from money holders to the government and other recipients of the credit that is the counterpart of money creation.

There is no conclusive evidence that inflation either speeds or retards economic growth. Examples can be cited of rapid growth or of stagnation combined with inflation or with price stability. This, of course, does not prove that inflation has no effect on growth. Growth is the result of many factors, which in the aggregate may outweigh any influence that inflation exerts on the process.

It has been asserted that inflation promotes development by redistributing income from workers and peasants to capitalist entrepreneurs, thereby fostering saving and investment. Although such shifts of income may occur, especially in the early stages of inflation, they do not continue if inflation is prolonged. Wages come to be increased more frequently and at certain periods may advance more rapidly than prices. If agricultural prices do not keep pace with other prices, farmers resort to subsistence production and barter or migrate to cities. Holders of real estate, foreign currency, and speculative inventories often gain more than the owners and managers of productive enterprises.

Inflation, especially erratic inflation, distorts economic calculations and

---

16. Martin J. Bailey, "The Welfare Cost of Inflationary Finance," *Journal of Political Economy*, vol. 64 (April 1956), pp. 93–110. Bailey recognizes that inflations are not deliberately planned and fully anticipated and that disruptions and redistributions occur.

makes planning more difficult. This effect must be very harmful at high inflation rates. The loss of real income may not be accurately measured by available statistics, because price and output statistics may be unreliable in such conditions.

In the past, inflation must have retarded the development of financial intermediaries such as savings banks, building societies, and life insurance companies that collect and lend the savings of persons who have neither the knowledge nor the opportunity to make direct investments efficiently. Although this adverse effect is still present, it has become less serious in countries that have permitted the intermediaries to adopt indexing or flexible interest rates that compensate for inflation.

Perhaps the most harmful economic consequences of inflation actually are attributable to the bad policies that commonly accompany it. Governments frequently impose price controls in an effort to repress inflation or lessen the hardships that rising prices impose on consumers. Food prices and rents are especially likely to be regulated, and sometimes the controls are much more extensive. Although such controls may be tolerably effective for short periods and in special circumstances, they usually result in shortages, black markets, and inefficient production and distribution. Often urban transportation fares and public utility rates are held down, and public enterprises suffer losses, subsidies from the budget are needed, and service deteriorates.

The consequences of inflation for international trade and payments usually impose economic costs. Most theoretical and econometric treatments implicitly assume either a closed economy or a flexible exchange rate moving in step with the price level, but in fact there are no closed economies and the majority of developing countries maintain fixed exchange rates subject to periodic adjustments. Because of inertia and a desire to avoid price increases for imports and exports, governments usually do not move the exchange rate in proportion to inflation. Imports rise while exports fall, and quantitative restrictions on imports and foreign exchange controls must be instituted or tightened to contain the balance-of-payments deficit. For imports, shortages and black markets may become even more prevalent than for price-controlled domestic goods. The lack of imported materials, fuel, and spare parts may prevent factories, transportation systems, and farms from operating at capacity. Export production will be severely handicapped.

A few countries, including Chile in the 1960s and Brazil and Colombia in the 1970s, adopted crawling-peg systems, with frequent small devaluations of the currency to alleviate the effects of inflation on production and trade and thus reduce pressure on direct controls. Although a great improvement over the situation in which the exchange rate is allowed to become more and more overvalued in the course of inflation, the crawling peg does not eliminate distortions, and it can cause disruptive inflows and outflows of financial capital.

The social and political consequences of inflation, though hard to trace, may be more important in the long run than its direct economic effects. Viewing the European scene after World War I, Keynes conceded that inflation had the socially useful result of checking the growth of idle wealth by acting as "a weighty counterpoise against the cumulative results of compound interest and the inheritance of fortunes."[17] This conjecture was more relevant for the mature capitalistic economies of Europe of the early twentieth century than for the less developed countries today. In many of the latter, the rich hold their fortunes largely in land, buildings, gold, and foreign balances, which cannot be expropriated by inflation.

In the less developed countries that favor mixed economies, the need is to foster saving and the accumulation of financial claims, not to frustrate them. Inflation contradicts the prudential virtues of capitalism. It nourishes the attitude that looks to lottery tickets rather than savings accounts as the means of bettering oneself.

For a time, inflation may perform the political function of avoiding a direct confrontation between interest groups that press demands beyond the economy's capacity to meet. By public spending and increases in money income, the government can seem to satisfy the conflicting demands and thus avert strife and possible violence. Later people will realize that their gains were illusory, and the feeling of having been cheated may heighten bitterness and intensify strains on the political system. But it is also possible that the disappointing experience will prepare the way for more realistic policies.[18]

Summary

Financing by money creation now takes the form of borrowing from the central bank or from deposit money banks under conditions in which

17. Keynes, *Tract on Monetary Reform*, p. 9.

18. See Albert O. Hirschman's discussion of inflation in Chile in his *Journeys toward Progress: Studies of Economic Policy-Making in Latin America* (New York: Twentieth Century Fund, 1963), pp. 161–223, especially pp. 220–23.

other lending is not displaced. It results in an increase in aggregate spending and causes inflation unless the additional spending can be matched by increased output or imports. Any increase in imports brought about in this way necessarily is temporary. Although unemployed people and underused manufacturing plants exist in many developing countries, usually they cannot be quickly drawn into production.

In a growing economy there is scope for a noninflationary increase in the money stock and hence an opportunity to finance some expenditures by creating money without causing inflation. The amount, however, is small relative to GDP, and its counterpart in the form of loans and investments of the banking system should be divided among credit to the government, credit to other sectors, and foreign exchange reserves.

By using more than the noninflationary amount of money creation, a government causes a rise in the price level and obtains real resources from money holders. Sometimes this is a deliberate policy; often it is unplanned. To protect themselves, people will reduce their money holdings in relation to income. The amount obtainable by inflation depends on the initial stock of money, the sensitivity of money balances to inflation, and the impact of inflation on production. Econometric studies have estimated the maximum amount obtainable on the basis of restrictive assumptions.

Inflation affects the government budget. Real tax revenue will be reduced if the elasticity of liabilities with respect to nominal income is low or the collection lag is long. Tax compliance and administration usually deteriorate. Expenditures for salaries and wages may increase less rapidly than the price level for a time but later will have to be raised by ad hoc adjustments or indexing. Inflation, once started, may become self-perpetuating if revenues decline relative to expenditures and the increase in the budget deficit is covered by money creation. This hazard, however, seems to have been avoided by a number of countries that have experienced inflation.

Technical measures can be taken to protect tax revenue against inflation. The weakness and indecision of the government and the conflicts that usually accompany inflation, however, may prevent their adoption.

There is no conclusive evidence that inflation either speeds or retards economic growth. While some of the transfers of income and wealth that it brings about may be favorable to growth, inflation distorts calculations, retards financial intermediation, and induces the adoption of government policies that harm economic efficiency. The political consequences are ambiguous.

CHAPTER TEN

Government Finance Policies to Assist Growth and Development

THIS CHAPTER and the next two consider the use of fiscal instruments to advance the objectives of growth and development, economic stability, and equitable distribution. These three chapters are intended to bring together and supplement the analyses of the various fiscal instruments in preceding chapters.

Growth and Development as Objectives

Growth and development are closely related, but distinguishable, objectives. Growth may be defined as an increase in measured output or income, either in the aggregate or per person. The usual measures are gross domestic product (GDP) or gross national product (GNP) at market prices and, less frequently used, net domestic product or net national product. When stated in constant prices, these statistics are fairly reliable indicators of growth over periods of a few years. They are less reliable when a growth rate is derived for a long period of time, during which production and consumption patterns have changed greatly. For the latter purpose, a special weakness is that no one set of weights for the components of the price index is suitable for the entire period.

Development is a vaguer word. Writers and speakers attach different meanings to it. Usually the word implies growth plus changes in the economic structure toward more modern methods and less reliance on primary production. Development may also be thought of as including social and political modernization. Lately, there has been a tendency to extend its meaning to include more equitable distribution of income and wealth, but in this book that is regarded as a separate objective and is treated in chapter 12.

Table 10-1. *Annual Growth of Gross National Product per Person, 1950–80*[a]

In constant prices, as percentages

Group	1950–60	1960–70	1970–80
Low-income countries	0.6	1.8	2.4
Middle-income countries	2.5	3.5	3.1
Capital-surplus oil exporters	. . .	7.3	1.3[b]
Developed countries	3.1	3.9	2.4[c]

Source: World Bank, *World Development Report 1980* (Oxford University Press, 1980), pp. 34, 99, and *World Development Report 1982*, p. 21.

a. Excludes centrally planned economies before 1970; coverage and country classification differ somewhat between periods.

b. High-income oil exporters—Kuwait, Libya, Saudi Arabia, and the United Arab Emirates.

c. Industrial market economies.

It is now generally agreed that governments should take responsibility for speeding up growth and promoting economic development. In less developed countries, the desire for growth is not merely for the satisfaction of material wants. In the words of one writer, "It arises from a desire to assume fully human status by taking part in an industrial civilization, participation in which alone enables a nation or an individual to compel others to treat it as an equal."[1]

By historical standards and in comparison with the expectations of experts, the growth record of both the less developed and more developed countries was remarkably good in the aggregate from about 1950 until the early 1970s. After the mid-1970s growth rates became slower and more erratic. Some statistics on growth rates are given in table 10-1.[2] The rates differed widely among countries in the groups shown in the table.

Growth Strategies

Theories of economic growth and development are linked with strategies for advancing them. These strategies, in turn, have implications for government finance policies and the suitability of available fiscal instruments. With some oversimplification, three broad strategies may be identified—the neoclassical, industrialization with a dualistic economy, and general growth. The latter two strategies could be implemented by

1. Ernest Geller, quoted in Rockefeller Foundation, *Modernization, Economic Development, and Cultural Values* (New York: Rockefeller Foundation, 1979), p. 4.

2. See also David Morawetz, *Twenty-Five Years of Economic Development, 1950 to 1975* (Washington, D.C.: World Bank, 1977).

reliance on market forces or by central planning. The neoclassical strategy is exclusively market oriented and has no place for central planning. Outside Eastern Europe, detailed central planning has been attempted by only a few countries, notably the People's Republic of China, Cuba, and North Korea.

In practice, the distinctions between strategies and implementation methods are less rigid than the ensuing discussion may imply. The industrialization and general growth strategies draw on some of the theories underlying the neoclassical model. A strategy that relies predominantly on market forces may nevertheless have room for macroeconomic planning, and central planning cannot safely ignore market incentives.

A neoclassical strategy would be based on the conviction that a government can best foster growth by performing a narrow range of functions and avoiding interference with market forces. The functions would be the traditional ones of maintaining law and order, protecting property rights, and ensuring national defense. Monetary policy would be directed toward a stable or secularly declining price level. Government financing by money creation would be constrained by that policy. The exchange rate would be flexible, and international trade and capital movements would be free, with no differences in the taxation of domestic goods and imports and exports. Production patterns would reflect the country's international comparative advantages. Interest rates would be set by market forces, and aggregate saving would be determined by individual decisions as influenced by interest rates, without government interference. Adherents to a neoclassical strategy would not necessarily reject progressive taxation, though they would emphasize that it would tend to retard growth. Generally they would favor consumption taxes over income taxes on the grounds that the latter cause inefficiencies owing to the double taxation of saving. The growth rate would emerge as the resultant of individual decisions, particularly those affecting investment in material and human capital, technical change, and participation in the labor force.

Although supporters can be found for each of the elements of a neoclassical strategy—and some of them have powerful appeal—the whole set may appear to be a caricature rather than an acceptable strategy. No government of a less developed country follows it in pure form, and only Hong Kong and a few small tax-haven countries accept a version approaching that.

The remainder of the chapter, therefore, will deal with the two other strategies. The industrialization strategy stresses the expansion of manufacturing production in the urban sector and accepts a dualistic economy in which agriculture and the rural sector continue with traditional methods and low productivity of labor. The general growth strategy aims at increased productivity and development in all major sectors.[3]

Industrialization with Dualism

Industrialization often has been regarded as synonymous with development. Indeed, a frequent practice—not avoided in this book—is to call the more developed countries the industrial countries.

The appeal of industrialization as a strategy for growth and development is strong. Except for a few oil producers, the high-income countries generally have large manufacturing sectors. The beginning of rapid growth of income in Western Europe appears to have been associated with the Industrial Revolution, though modern scholarship calls attention to the preceding agricultural improvements and tends to play down the characteristics of abruptness and pervasiveness that the word revolution conveys. In more recent times, the examples of the Soviet Union and Japan seem to offer striking confirmation of the belief that government-supported industrialization can rapidly transform a country and enhance its power and prestige. Industrialization has been considered essential to provide employment opportunities for growing populations.

When a large number of colonies and protectorates attained independence after World War II, many of their political and intellectual leaders associated industrialization with moving from a subordinate and dependent status to a position of independence and equality. They tended to look down on agriculture and to feel that government policies supporting agriculture, although they were advised by some experts, would keep their countries in a subordinate position. Many intellectuals were influenced by the Marxist view that sees peasants as a reactionary element and assigns the principal role in change to the urban proletariat and their leaders.

Persons holding these views were receptive to economic and social theories that stressed differences in behavior and growth potential between the modern industrial sector and the traditional sector of agriculture, handicrafts, and small trade. The strategy of industrialization with dualism

---

3. An alternative name for the third strategy is balanced growth, but that term has been used in different senses and is likely to cause misunderstanding.

was intended to bring about development by concentrating on policies to foster growth in the modern sector, which would coexist with the traditional sector. From the traditional sector, labor and capital would be gradually transferred to more productive uses in the modern sector.

As the result of the disappointing experience of many countries, the evolution of the technical literature of economic development, and changes in the policies of the World Bank and other lending and aid-giving organizations, support for the dualistic strategy diminished greatly during the 1970s. Nevertheless, the underlying ideas are still influential, and government policies include elements of the strategy.

Economic assumptions favoring industrialization and seeming to justify neglect of agriculture and handicrafts included the following: (1) agriculture and handicrafts are subject to diminishing returns, whereas manufacturing can achieve important economies of large-scale production; (2) the supply of agricultural commodities is inelastic with respect to price and may even be negative; hence higher prices for farmers are ineffective and possibly harmful; (3) saving rates are low in the agricultural sector, whereas savings from industrial profits are high; (4) little capital is required for agriculture (some econometric models assumed that no capital is used and attributed agricultural output entirely to labor and land); and (5) physical capital formation in infrastructure and manufacturing plants is the critical factor in raising industrial output.

It was widely believed that a great amount of surplus labor was present in the agricultural sector of less developed countries, in the sense that the same output could be produced with fewer workers, without adding capital or changing cultivation methods. Hence labor could be transferred from agriculture to industry without reducing agricultural production or raising wages. An influential article by Lewis was published in 1954 under the title, "Economic Development with Unlimited Supplies of Labour."[4]

Most supporters of the strategy of industrialization with dualism argued that the quickest and most reliable approach was through import substitution, that is, the production at home of manufactured goods that previously had been imported. They held that it could be encouraged by protective tariffs, quantitative restrictions on imports, and foreign exchange controls.

Advocates of the strategy tended to favor economic planning, and some

---

4. W. Arthur Lewis, "Economic Development with Unlimited Supplies of Labour," *Manchester School of Economic and Social Studies*, vol. 22 (May 1954), pp. 139–91. Lewis asserted that in many countries an unlimited supply of labor is available at the subsistence wage and that the marginal productivity of labor is "negligible, zero, or even negative" in the traditional sector.

of them were sympathetic to detailed centralized planning. The latter, however, was generally considered infeasible in the less developed countries. Its absence left open a role for the fiscal system as a means of influencing the economy along desired lines.

Implications for government finance of the strategy of industrialization with dualism can be derived partly by deduction and partly by observation. They may be briefly summarized as follows:

1. Heavy government spending is required for infrastructure, particularly for transportation and communication facilities and electric power generation and distribution. Government investment in industrial enterprises may be needed.

2. Large increases in taxation to mobilize resources are essential.

3. A major factor in judging a government's economic performance is the size of its saving (defined as the excess of revenues over current expenditures).

4. Agriculture should be taxed to capture a surplus for financing the infrastructure required for industrialization and possibly for direct investment in industry. The taxes will not have serious adverse effects on agricultural production and in some cases may stimulate production.

5. Taxes on imports have useful protective functions and can raise revenue.

6. Taxes on exports of primary products are a convenient way of obtaining revenue from agriculture and mining.

7. Special tax incentives for industrial investment and new enterprises are desirable in countries that favor a mixture of private and public enterprises.

These principles were followed to varying degrees. Government expenditures and tax revenue in developing countries have increased substantially in absolute amounts and in relation to GDP. Expenditures for infrastructure have grown but so have expenditures for general administration, defense, consumer subsidies, and other purposes, with the result that the proportion of additional tax revenue devoted to infrastructure and the government saving ratio have been lower than contemplated in many of the writings on development. In most countries, agriculture has not been subject to especially heavy explicit taxation, but in a considerable number of cases it has been the object of implicit taxation in the form of unfavorable official procurement prices and exchange rates. Import and export taxes have been used for the expected purposes and have added to the taxation of the nonindustrial sectors.

After the sharp oil price increases in 1973–74 and the slowdown of growth in the mid-1970s, dissatisfaction and unsolved problems were increasingly evident in less developed countries. A vehement complaint was that growth and accompanying changes in economic structure had not solved the problem of poverty. Absolute poverty persisted and the number of poor people increased. Inequalities of income between regions and persons remained great and appeared to have increased in countries such as Pakistan, Brazil, and Nigeria. Food deficits occurred in many countries, including some that formerly had been net exporters of food. The number of jobs created by industrialization was disappointingly small, and open (recorded) unemployment remained high. Social and economic problems associated with the rapid growth of cities were visible, with millions of people living in crowded and squalid conditions, usually in settlements on the outskirts. Deficits of public enterprises, covered by bank credit or subsidies from the budget, and subsidies for foods and other consumer goods absorbed large proportions of the resources at the disposal of the public sector in many countries. The potentialities of import substitution were exhausted in many cases, especially in small countries; production costs were high, sometimes resulting in negative value added (appraised at international prices). At the same time, a few countries pursuing policies favorable to international trade and foreign investment— for example, Korea, Taiwan, and Singapore—achieved exceptionally high growth rates, and these and other newly industrializing countries success-fully penetrated world markets.

The dissatisfaction was partly a matter of perception—an example of the tendency of people to be most discontented when their conditions are improving but at a rate that they find disappointing. But it also reflected a growing realization that some of the key economic assumptions and policies of the strategy of industrialization with dualism were mistaken.

The economic character of agriculture in the developing countries had been seriously misunderstood. Observers who alleged that there was much disguised unemployment often made the elementary mistake of failing to take account of the seasonal nature of farm work. More careful study indicated that the amount of labor that could be withdrawn from agricul-ture without adversely affecting output was small—negligible in many cases—unless techniques were changed. The price elasticity of agricultural production was found to be generally positive. Farmers proved to be willing to apply profitable innovations. The so-called green revolution, which brought striking increases in the production of cereals, demonstrated this, as did the acceptance of improved varieties of cotton and potatoes.

The introduction of new techniques and new seeds, it was found, could be facilitated by schooling and extension services and by the revision of tenure arrangements, marketing practices, and taxes that reduce profits from innovation. Saving and investment in agriculture had been underestimated because of omission or undervaluation of the work of farmers in improving their land, buildings, and livestock.[5]

In growth models and in development plans of the 1950s and 1960s, the contribution of physical capital formation was greatly overstated in relation to other influences. The Harrod-Domar model, which attracted much attention because of its simplicity and elegance, attributed growth solely to capital formation and equated the growth rate to the ratio of the saving rate to the incremental capital-output ratio. This model, inspired by the authors' study of the unemployment problems of mature capitalistic economies, assumed that skilled and unskilled labor, management, and other production prerequisites would always be available.[6] Much more elaborate growth models, incorporating input-output analysis and mathematical programming techniques, were sometimes used. Usually, however, these models also made physical capital formation the critical constraint. They gave inadequate attention to technological change and neglected human capital formation and institutional factors.[7]

The preference for physical capital formation, combined with the prestige of modern, large-scale installations, often resulted in excessively capital-intensive technology. This tendency was strengthened in many countries by overvalued exchange rates, subsidized credit, and tax systems that exempted capital goods from sales taxes and customs duties and granted special incentives for investment. All of this contributed to the disappointing record of job creation in industry.

The emphasis on government saving as a performance criterion, together with the identification of investment with physical capital

5. Theodore W. Schultz contributed much to the understanding of agriculture and of growth in both rich and poor countries. See especially his *Transforming Traditional Agriculture* (Yale University Press, 1964) and *Investing in People: The Economics of Population Quality* (University of California Press, 1981). See also World Bank, *World Development Report 1982* (Oxford University Press, 1982), pp. 3–6.

6. R. F. Harrod, *Towards a Dynamic Economics: Some Recent Developments of Economic Theory and Their Application to Policy* (London: Macmillan, 1948); Evsey D. Domar, "Capital Expansion, Rate of Growth, and Employment," *Econometrica*, vol. 14 (April 1946), pp. 137–47, reprinted in Domar, *Essays in the Theory of Economic Growth* (Oxford University Press, 1957). Most textbooks on economic development describe the Harrod-Domar model and other growth models. Domar recognized that his model could give "the misleading impression" that capital accumulation "is the primary and sole cause and condition of growth" and explicitly rejected that opinion (*Essays*, pp. 11–12).

7. For comments with special reference to the use of the models in India, see John W. Mellor, *The New Economics of Growth: A Strategy for India and the Developing World* (Cornell University Press for the Twentieth Century Fund, 1976), chap. 11.

formation, led to the neglect of recurrent costs and of human capital formation through education, improved nutrition, and better health. Expenditures for these items are commonly classified as government consumption, which often was criticized en bloc by visiting experts and starved for funds by budget makers.

Overurbanization, with its accompanying social problems and economic costs, was encouraged by policies that held down the prices of agricultural products, especially foodstuffs, while pushing up the cost of inputs. Similarly, policies that provided better public services and amenities in cities than in rural areas attracted migrants to cities but often could not accommodate the influx.[8]

Exports were handicapped by exchange rates that were overvalued and maintained only by quantitative restrictions on trade and payments. If not overvalued in that sense, exchange rates often set a higher value on the local currency than would have prevailed with a tax system that did less to limit the demand for imports.

This mixture of policies perpetuated and accentuated inequalities in personal income and wealth. Taxation, government expenditures, pricing, credit policy—indeed, the acceptance of a dualistic economy—were biased against the rural population, which on the average had lower income than the urban sector. Poverty and the continuance, or memory, of high death rates in rural areas seem to work toward high birth rates and rapid population growth, which add to the difficulty of raising living standards.

General Growth and Development

The complexity of the growth and development process is now better appreciated. It requires not only increases in the stock of physical capital but changes in the organization of production and distribution, the adoption of new attitudes and habits, the acquisition of knowledge and skills, and other innovations. No one pattern can serve equally well the needs and aspirations of all developing countries.

Both agriculture and industry need to be encouraged. Especially in the poorest countries, improvements in agriculture are essential for bettering

8. Michael Lipton, *Why Poor People Stay Poor: A Study of Urban Bias in World Development* (Harvard University Press, 1976). On the political aspects of policies that discriminate against agriculture and the rural population, see Robert H. Bates, *Markets and States in Tropical Africa: The Political Basis of Agricultural Policies* (University of California Press, 1981).

the life of the masses. In middle-income countries more productive agriculture can enhance growth and strengthen the balance of payments. It can assist industrial growth by creating demand for industrial inputs to agriculture and for consumption goods and by supplying raw materials. The experience of the newly industrializing countries shows that rapid growth of manufacturing is possible outside the established centers of Europe, North America, and Japan.

Outward-looking policies are more conducive than import substitution to the establishment and expansion of efficient manufacturing, job creation, and consumer welfare. Although these policies do not preclude protection of domestic industry, they require moderation in its use and emphasize the encouragement of exports. Fostering import substitution through high duties and restrictions on imports results in high prices, which are burdensome to consumers, and relieves producers of pressure to keep costs down. For many products, the home market of most developing countries is too small to permit domestic producers to take full advantage of economies of scale and specialization. The manufacture of import substitutes tends to be more capital intensive than the production of exports and thus is biased against job creation.[9] High protection increases the cost of inputs for agriculture and other primary production.

The opportunity to pursue outward-looking policies depends, of course, on access to foreign markets, particularly those of the high-income countries, on reasonable terms. Despite some concern about the threat of increased protection during the 1970s, the non-oil developing countries were able to expand their exports in that decade at almost the same rate as in the more buoyant markets of the 1960s (export value in U.S. dollars deflated by an index of the unit value of imports). Their share of world exports rose slightly during the 1970s despite the sharp increase in the share of oil exporters. Exports of manufactures grew more rapidly than exports of primary products.[10]

A strategy of general development should pay attention to the creation of employment opportunities. This may involve offering explicit tax

9. See Ian Little, Tibor Scitovsky, and Maurice Scott, *Industry and Trade in Some Developing Countries: A Comparative Study* (Oxford University Press for the Organization for Economic Cooperation and Development, 1970); Bela Balassa, *Policy Reform in Developing Countries* (Pergamon, 1977), pp. 1–29; and Balassa, *The Process of Industrial Development and Alternative Development Strategies*, Essays in International Finance 141 (Princeton University, International Finance Section, 1980).

10. Statistics on total exports and the unit value of imports from International Monetary Fund, *International Financial Statistics: Supplement on Trade Statistics*, Supplement Series 4 (Washington, D.C.: IMF, 1982), pp. vii, 2–3; data on exports of manufactures and primary products from World Bank, *World Development Report 1981*, p. 23.

incentives for employment of labor, removing tax provisions that retard employment, and correcting distorted exchange rates and interest rates.

The simple criterion of government saving as conventionally measured—or the more sophisticated criterion of total national saving—is inappropriate for judging fiscal policy to support general growth. In its place, one can hardly suggest anything more definite than that policies should aim at bringing about a reallocation of resources from uses that contribute little to growth and development to uses that contribute more.

Alternatively, it would be possible to define investment more broadly and to measure government saving as total revenue minus noninvestment expenditures. (Saving would then equal investment, more broadly defined, minus the budget deficit.) Following a recommendation by Schultz, investment or capital formation would include all uses of resources that add to future income, comprising additions to the stocks of machines and structures, land improvement, and increases in knowledge and skills. Government expenditures for schooling and higher education, health, research, and economic information would be classified as investment.[11] Although this proposal rightly identifies a variety of growth-promoting expenditures, an attempt to introduce such an extended definition of saving and investment would be likely to cause confusion, at least during a lengthy transition period, because it would conflict with long-established usage.

Government Expenditures

Earlier chapters have touched on features of government expenditures that are relevant for a strategy of general growth. The traditional, narrow functions of the state are essential for maintaining an environment in which growth and development can proceed. Sometimes better pay and better quality personnel—payments for more efficiency and less corruption—may facilitate growth. There are credible reports of enterprises, especially middle-sized ones, being victimized by onerous and inept controls and procedures imposed by incompetent or venal civil servants. These conditions, at best, add to business costs; at worst, they forestall innovation and growth.

The contribution of government expenditures for increasing the productive capacity of human beings and adding to knowledge should be recognized, and these functions should be adequately financed within the limitations of resources. Expenditures for education are the most important of these programs. Averaging the findings of twenty-two studies, Psacha-

11. Theodore W. Schultz, *Investment in Human Capital* (Free Press, 1971), pp. 4–8.

ropoulos reports that annual social rates of return on public education in less developed countries were 27 percent for primary education, 16 percent for secondary education, and 13 percent for higher education.[12] To serve better the purpose of growth, schooling and higher education should be less academic and elitist than they are in many developing countries.

Other growth-promoting expenditure programs include those for health, agricultural extension services, and research. Health expenditures should concentrate on sanitation, public health, and preventive measures, making maximum use of semiskilled and paramedical personnel rather than hospitals and expensive treatments like those provided in high-income countries. For all except a few developing countries, research should be directed not toward original contributions to knowledge but to the adaptation of the findings of foreign scientists and technicians to local conditions.

A general growth strategy calls for substantial government expenditures for physical infrastructure, especially in the least developed countries, though these items would not be given as high a priority as in the strategy of industrialization with dualism. They include the familar outlays for roads, bridges, ports, railways, and internal airlines; storage facilities; telephone, telegraph, and radio communications; electricity systems; irrigation; water supply and sewerage; school buildings; and health centers and hospitals. There is little risk that this class of expenditure will be underemphasized. The big problem is to choose among numerous possibilties. Choice can be aided by benefit-cost analysis, although uncertainties and imponderables will remain.

There is a danger that the recurrent costs of infrastructure projects will be inadequately considered or will be underestimated. These include operating costs—for salaries and wages, fuel, supplies, and so forth—and maintenance costs—for routine servicing of machinery, repairs, and spare parts. Casual observation and official reports have revealed that in a great many cases facilities have operated below capacity or only intermittently because of lack of funds to cover recurrent costs. Although in principle recurrent costs are taken into account in benefit-cost analysis, systematic analyses may be undertaken only for certain major projects and estimates are subject to error.

Heller has made estimates of recurrent costs as a proportion of investment expenditures for several classes of project. The coefficients vary

12. George Psacharopoulos, "Returns to Education: An Updated International Comparison," *Comparative Education*, vol. 17 (1981), p. 329.

greatly, being low for forestry and trunk roads, for example, and high for health centers, hospitals, agricultural colleges, and polytechnics.[13] More studies of this subject are needed. The coefficients derived from general studies should not be mechanically applied to particular projects, but they can serve as useful checks on the estimates that ministries should be required to present to the planning and budget offices. The coefficients may be useful also in estimating recurrent costs of groups of small projects for which detailed individual estimates are not feasible. Planning and budget officials should be on guard against the tendency of operating agencies to underestimate recurrent costs at the planning stage.

An encouraging example of systematic consideration of recurrent costs is provided by the Club du Sahel, a group sponsored by the Organization for Economic Cooperation and Development, which brings together representatives of the governments of Cape Verde, Chad, the Gambia, Mali, Mauritania, Niger, Senegal, and Upper Volta, and of aid-donor countries. Studies have been made by officials and consultants,[14] and a symposium on recurrent costs of development projects in the Sahel countries was held in Ouagadougou, Upper Volta, in January 1982. It is especially appropriate that the subject be examined jointly by aid donors and recipient countries, because the preference of donor countries for restricting their aid to investment outlays has contributed to the underfunding of recurrent costs.

As part of a general growth strategy, the urban bias of government expenditure allocation, which exists in the majority of developing countries, should be corrected for reasons of equity and productive efficiency. Allocating more expenditures to rural areas would also lessen incentives for migration to overcrowded cities.[15]

13. Peter S. Heller, "Public Investment in LDCs with Recurrent Cost Constraint: The Kenyan Case," *Quarterly Journal of Economics*, vol. 88 (May 1974), pp. 251–77, and "The Underfinancing of Recurrent Development Costs," *Finance and Development*, vol. 16 (March 1979), pp. 38–41.

14. Comité Permanent Inter-Etats de Lutte contre la Sécheresse dans le Sahel/Club du Sahel Working Group on Recurrent Costs, *Recurrent Costs of Development Programmes in the Countries of the Sahel: Analysis and Recommendations* (Ouagadougou, Upper Volta, and Paris: Club du Sahel, 1980). See also Clive Gray and André Martens, "The Political Economy of the 'Recurrent Cost Problem' in the West African Sahel," *World Development*, vol. 11 (February 1983), pp. 101–17.

15. Econometric studies confirm that people move for economic gain from poorer to wealthier areas; however, the studies do not include as a gain a measure of public service expenditures or utilization of services. It is unclear whether greater expenditures for rural education would stimulate or retard migration. On the one hand, migrants to cities are better educated than those who stay in rural areas. On the other hand, there are some indications that the availability of superior educational opportunities in cities is an attraction to migrants. See Lorene Y. L. Yap, "The Attraction of Cities: A Review of the Migration Literature," *Journal of Development Economics*, vol. 4 (September 1977), pp. 239–64; Michael P. Todaro, "Internal Migration in Developing Countries: A Survey," in Richard A. Easterlin, ed., *Population and*

Three types of public works that are especially important in rural areas are road construction, irrigation and water supply projects, and storage facilities. Many rural areas need three kinds of roads—simple roads or paths for farmers to go from their villages to the fields, roads linking villages to district markets, and roads between district markets and other centers.[16] Expenditures for schooling can reduce the high rates of illiteracy in rural areas that are an obstacle to innovation and political participation. The World Bank's *World Development Report 1980* summarized research studies confirming the contribution of primary education to farmers' productivity in developing countries as follows: in ten cases in which complementary inputs in the form of improved seeds, irrigation, transportation to markets, and so on were available, farmers with four years of primary education produced on the average 13 percent more than those with no schooling; in seven cases in which complementary inputs were not available, those with primary schooling produced 8 percent more than farmers with no schooling.[17] Expenditures to improve sanitation and to control parasitic and vector-borne diseases can improve labor productivity and open more land to cultivation.

Taxation

Important points to consider in formulating tax policies suitable for a strategy of general growth may be summarized as follows:

1. An adequate and growing amount of revenue is essential to finance the heavy responsibilities that governments must assume.

2. Taxes should not unduly limit the capacity and willingness to work.

3. The tax system should avoid unnecessary reductions in household and enterprise saving.

4. Special incentives should be provided for industrial production.

5. A bias against labor-intensive production should be avoided, and, if feasible, tax incentives for employment creation should be offered.

6. Tax obstacles to nontraditional exports should be minimized, and special incentives for them should be considered.

7. In taxing commodities, unintended and excessive protection to domestic production should be avoided.

Economic Change in Developing Countries, Universities–National Bureau Report 30 (University of Chicago Press, 1980), pp. 361–402.

16. Michael P. Todaro with Jerry Stilkind, *City Bias and Rural Neglect: The Dilemma of Urban Development* (New York: Population Council, 1981), pp. 36–46.

17. Unweighted averages: World Bank, *World Development Report 1980*, p. 48.

8. Explicit and implicit taxes on exports of primary products may be used but in moderation, mainly as a substitute for other taxes and as a means of economic stabilization.

An additional point, important although commonplace and not especially related to the general growth strategy, is that taxes should be designed with an eye to the administrative and compliance capacities of the country. All of these points have been discussed in preceding chapters. Some of them apply also to a dualistic strategy. Here the intention is to bring them together in the context of balanced growth and to develop more fully points 3, 4, 5, and 6.

A tax system whose yield increases as rapidly as national income, or more rapidly, it will be recalled, is termed a buoyant system. Buoyancy can be attained by introducing and increasing new taxes that become feasible and productive as the economy develops and by emphasizing elastic taxes, the yield of which increases automatically in response to economic growth.

The net impact of taxation on the amount of work done is unclear because the income effect and the price or substitution effect press in different directions. Theoretical and econometric treatments elaborated for developed countries, however, give too little weight to an aspect that is significant especially for low-income countries at early stages of development—the possible influence of taxation on the capacity to work. Working capacity may be impaired by heavy taxation of essential consumption, particularly food. Heavy explicit taxes on food are exceptional; subsidized food prices for urban consumers are more common. But implicit taxation of agriculture can cut the food consumption of the rural population, and controlled prices may curtail production of food for urban consumption. Adverse effects on the amount and character of work done can arise in low-income countries from heavy taxation of marketed farm products, especially export commodities, and of incentive goods such as bicycles, radios, kerosene, sheet metal roofing material, and textiles. Steeply progressive income taxes, though evaded by many, may hit employees of government and large enterprises and may discourage extra work or the assumption of demanding and well-remunerated duties. The possible negative effects on mobility, however, are mitigated by the attractions of untaxed perquisites and nonpecuniary advantages often associated with high-paid jobs.

TAXATION AND SAVING. The impact of taxation on household saving has received much attention. It has been asserted that saving can be promoted by (1) taxing consumption rather than income; (2) avoiding progressive taxation; (3) refraining from heavy taxation of profits; and (4) selective tax incentives for saving.[18]

The argument that taxation of consumption rather than income or wealth is favorable to saving is plausible but, as stated in chapter 6, is not theoretically conclusive. Empirical studies have not resolved the question of how tax-caused differences in the net rate of return will influence saving.

The contention that progressive taxes are especially harmful to saving rests on the belief that saving ratios rise with income. Family budget studies—mostly for developed countries but including some for less developed countries—confirm the supposition. This evidence, however, is insufficient to establish the conclusion about taxation. The relevant variable is not the average saving rate in successive income classes, as derived from the budget studies, but the marginal saving rate, that is, the proportion of an increase or decrease of income that will be reflected in savings. The observation that average savings in relation to average income rise over income classes is not necessarily inconsistent with the existence of an approximately constant marginal saving ratio. (A linear saving curve that intersects the zero saving axis at an income level above zero will have that characteristic.) Virtually all the family budget studies cover only a single year, and it is now recognized that they exaggerate differences between saving behavior at high and low normal income levels. This is true because family consumption expenditures tend to be more stable than income, with the consequence that in any one year upper income classes include a disproportionate number of families with temporarily high incomes and temporarily high saving ratios whereas the lower income classes include more families with temporarily depressed incomes and savings.

If profit recipients are especially high savers, as some economic theorists have assumed, moderation or avoidance of tax progressivity will favor saving because these persons usually have above-average income, but selective measures that lower taxes on profits will be more favorable because they do not extend to other recipients of large incomes, such as landowners, who are assumed to save little. The meager evidence available is consistent with the hypothesis that saving from profits is relatively great.

18. For a fuller discussion, see Richard Goode, "Taxation of Savings and Consumption in Underdeveloped Countries," *National Tax Journal*, vol. 14 (December 1961), pp. 305–21, reprinted in Richard M. Bird and Oliver Oldman, eds., *Readings on Taxation in Developing Countries*, 3d ed. (Johns Hopkins University Press, 1975), pp. 273–93.

Two cross-section studies of national aggregates have estimated that saving out of employment income is much lower than out of other income, including profits.[19] A time-series study of Korea over the period 1956–72 found that the saving ratio was significantly lower for urban labor income than for rural income and urban property income (but not significantly different for the latter two income shares).[20] A study of family budget data for one region in Indonesia found that the marginal propensity to save was much higher for nonfarm entrepreneurs (traders and craftsmen and other business owners) than for farmers, government employees, and other wage earners.[21] These findings, however, should be viewed cautiously because of the poor quality and probable incompleteness of most of the data. Except for the Indonesian study, the estimates do not allow for differences in the size distribution of the income shares. None of the estimates cited takes account of age and miscellaneous variables that may influence household saving rates, and the role of corporate saving is not explicitly treated.

Selective measures to promote saving include deductions from taxable income for specified forms of saving and exemption from income tax of interest on bank accounts and eligible bonds and of dividends on certain shares. These provisions may influence the allocation of savings and investment and may be justifiable for that purpose, but probably they do not have much effect on total saving. Usually it is possible to qualify for the benefits by diverting current savings or accumulated wealth from other uses. In principle, it would be possible to limit the benefits to net additional saving, but to do so would involve the administrative difficulties similar to those that make the expenditure tax impracticable for developing countries.

The tax system can affect enterprise saving by influencing the amount of profits retained by corporations rather than distributed as dividends. As explained in chapter 5, the so-called classical system, providing for separate taxation of corporations and shareholders, is more conducive to corporate

19. H. S. Houthakker, "On Some Determinants of Saving in Developed and Under-Developed Countries," in E. A. G. Robinson, ed., *Problems in Economic Development*, Proceedings of a Conference held by the International Economic Association (London: Macmillan, 1965), pp. 212–24; Jeffrey G. Williamson, "Personal Saving in Developing Nations: An Intertemporal Cross-Section from Asia," *Economic Record*, vol. 44 (June 1968), pp. 194–209.

20. Byung-Nak Song, "Empirical Research on Consumption Behavior: Evidence from Rich and Poor LDCs," *Economic Development and Cultural Change*, vol. 29 (April 1981), p. 606.

21. Allen C. Kelley and Jeffrey G. Williamson, "Household Saving Behavior in the Developing Economies: The Indonesian Case," *Economic Development and Cultural Change*, vol. 16 (April 1968), p. 391.

saving than systems that partially integrate corporate and shareholder taxes, but critics argue that the savings tend to be inefficiently allocated.

The government's deficit is a form of negative saving. In many countries it is large relative to the positive components of saving, and a reduction in the size of the deficit might well influence net national saving more than any feasible alteration of tax provisions to encourage household and enterprise saving. Government policies affecting international capital outflow and inflow—exchange rates and exchange restrictions, interest rates, inflation, and actions or statements influencing confidence in the security of persons and property—also may be important determinants of the amount of savings available for local use.

TAX INCENTIVES FOR INVESTMENT. Tax incentives for industrial and mineral production usually take the form of special provisions favoring investment. Presumably the incentives are directed toward investment rather than production itself because capital is considered especially scarce and is regarded as a strategic factor closely associated with entrepreneurship. They include accelerated depreciation and tax credits for eligible investments and tax holidays for new enterprises. Frequently they apply to hotels and other tourist facilities, as well as manufacturing and mining. The provisions are intended to encourage the favored activities by increasing the after-tax rate of return on investment. They apply primarily to income and profits taxes, but temporary or permanent exemption from import duties or excises on machinery, equipment, and materials is often granted. The incentives may be intended primarily to encourage foreign-owned enterprises, but generally they are offered also to domestic enterprises.[22] In some cases (Ghana, for example), local participation in the ownership is required for an enterprise to qualify, and in a few cases (Mexico, for example), majority or complete ownership by residents is required.

A survey by the U.S. Department of Commerce found that, in 1977, 22 percent of the affiliates of U.S. companies operating in developing countries received tax concessions and 14 percent received tariff concessions. About

22. See Dan Usher, "The Economics of Tax Incentives to Encourage Investment in Less Developed Countries," *Journal of Development Economics*, vol. 4 (June 1977), pp. 120–48; George E. Lent, "Tax Incentives for Investment in Developing Countries," International Monetary Fund *Staff Papers*, vol. 14 (July 1967), pp. 249–321; Jack Heller and Kenneth M. Kauffman, *Tax Incentives for Industry in Less Developed Countries* (Harvard University Law School, 1963); David Lim, "Taxation Policies," in John Cody, Helen Hughes, and David Wall, eds., *Policies for Industrial Progress in Developing Countries* (Oxford University Press for the World Bank, 1980), pp. 169–88.

one-fourth of the affiliates enjoying these concessions reported that they were available only to foreign-owned companies. Incentives were most frequently granted for manufacturing, much less frequently for mining, and still less frequently for trade and finance. Tax concessions were only a little less prevalent in developed countries in 1977 (reported by 19 percent of affiliates of U.S. companies), but tariff concessions were much less usual than in developing countries (probably because protective tariffs were less important in the developed countries). Among developing countries, incentives—including subsidies and other measures, as well as tax and tariff concessions—were most extensively granted by Korea, Israel, Taiwan, and Brazil, but none of these countries granted incentives to as large a proportion of its U.S. affiliates as did Ireland.[23]

Special tax and tariff incentives reduce or eliminate taxes that otherwise would apply. Another way of favoring investment would be to refrain from imposing high taxes on profits or cost items, which would lessen or eliminate the need for special incentive provisions. Both approaches offer the removal or avoidance of tax disincentives, rather than positive inducements to investment. Special incentives, however, may influence the allocation of investment and, in some circumstances, can cause the preferred activities to be carried further than they would be with a zero tax rate.

Accelerated depreciation allows investment outlays to be written off against taxable income at a faster-than-normal rate. It can reduce risk and increase the present value of after-tax profits. A tax credit is set off directly against tax liability and can reduce the net cost of an investment outlay. These provisions are effective only to the extent that the eligible firms have enough taxable income or potential tax liability to allow their use, immediately or through a carry-forward of deductions, net operating losses, or tax credits. A tax holiday (sometimes called pioneer industry status) relieves a new enterprise of income tax for a period that is commonly set at five to ten years but that may be shorter or longer. The more profitable the company, the greater the benefit. None of these three provisions can turn an unprofitable enterprise into a profitable one. Exemptions from import duties or excises can do so because—given the tax system—they reduce the cost of the equipment or materials to which they apply, without regard to the profitability of the enterprise.

23. U.S. Department of Commerce, International Trade Administration, Office of International Investment, Investment Policy Division, *The Use of Investment Incentives and Performance Requirements by Foreign Governments* (Government Printing Office, 1981).

The possible benefits to the country offering tax incentives to investment are not always clearly specified. They may include (1) noneconomic gains from industrialization; (2) creation of jobs for persons who otherwise would be unemployed or would earn lower wages; (3) transfer of technology and training, with benefits to other enterprises; and (4) increases in revenue from taxes to which the incentive provisions do not apply or from taxes payable after the initial reduction has ended.

The possible costs of the special incentives are (1) a sacrifice of revenue; (2) uneconomic increases in wage rates that may occur if the favored enterprises, either voluntarily or because of government or union pressures, pay wages above the marginal product of the workers employed; (3) administrative complications; and (4) political discord generated by favors to foreign-owned enterprises.

It may seem that tax incentives could be evaluated by a formal benefit-cost analysis similar to that for government expenditures. A monetary value could be assigned to job creation, and the present value of this expected gain plus expected increases in future tax revenue could be compared with the present value of expected revenue sacrifices. Other possible benefits and costs, however, could hardly be given monetary values, and the analysis at best would be incomplete.

Even the effects on revenue and employment are difficult to evaluate because of uncertainty about the response to the incentives. Advocates of the provisions often assume that they involve no sacrifice of revenue because in their absence the activities that benefit would not occur. But that may be incorrect. Some of the beneficiaries might have gone ahead without the special incentives, or others might have invested in similar undertakings. To that extent, the incentives are redundant and the revenue sacrifice is wasted. Critics may make an opposite error by calculating hypothetical amounts of forgone revenue that could never have been realized because the regular taxes are prohibitively high.

For a particular project, it is not legitimate to set the present value of the net tax savings of the eligible enterprise against the number of jobs created in order to arrive at an estimate of the government's cost per job. To the extent that the incentive is redundant, it produces no gain in employment; to the extent that it is not redundant, it has no revenue cost. For the program as a whole, a calculation could be made if the degree of redundancy could be accurately estimated. That is virtually impossible since there is no generally accepted econometric formulation of the investment function and most countries lack the statistical data that would be needed for estimating proposed versions of the function. Survey data on the attitudes of investors are of questionable value because of the respondents' self-interest in exaggerating the need for the provisions.

Tax specialists tend to be skeptical of the effectiveness of special tax incentives, stressing the importance of nontax factors such as the size of the market, the availability of raw materials and competent workers, the quality of infrastructure, the nature of regulations governing profit remittances abroad, and the attitude of the government toward investors. They have hesitated, however, to argue that the incentives are completely redundant. Governments have not been deterred from adopting such provisions, and they are in effect in many developing and developed countries.

Governments are attracted to special tax incentives because it is simpler to adopt them than to try to change the other factors that influence investment. They tend to prefer special incentives to lower tax rates, which would also improve the return on investments, because they believe that the sacrifice of revenue from taxes on existing activities would be wasted and because they do not allow for redundancy in the special incentives or optimistically estimate it to be small. Selectivity among lines of activity may be an additional attraction of special incentives, and possibly the opportunity of rewarding political supporters is considered an advantage.

The appropriate degree of selectivity in incentive schemes is a major issue. Practices differ greatly. At one extreme, accelerated depreciation allowances or investment credits may be granted automatically to a wide range of investments. At the other extreme, tax rates or tax holidays may be negotiated on a case-by-case basis and embodied in enterprise agreements or concessions. Tax holidays, which are the most frequent form of incentive, may be available to new enterprises in fields specified by statute or regulation or may be subject to approval by a minister or committee guided by detailed or only very general criteria. Selectivity has the appeal of seeming to exert the maximum influence in desired directions with minimum redundancy. But in practice it is hard to be intelligently selective. If elaborate conditions are laid down in the statute or regulations, the system may be so cumbersome and difficult to understand that it will be ineffective. A minister or committee that is given wide discretion is likely to lack the technical and business expertise to make the best choices. A discretionary system is subject to corruption and to charges of corruption or favoritism even when none is present.

There are several differences between tax holidays and accelerated depreciation or tax credits that should be taken into account if a choice is to be made between the approaches. (Many countries use both.) Tax holidays for new firms are more dramatic, though they are no longer novel. They are especially valuable to highly profitable firms that expect to attain a high rate of production and sales within a short time. These may include subsidiaries of multinational corporations that carry on assembly operations or work such as clothing manufacturing for foreign markets. The fact that the most profitable firms benefit most suggests a high rate of redundancy for tax holidays, but that inference may be incorrect. It may be necessary to surmount a threshold of indifference or inertia to attract a new firm. Export-oriented firms that are not tied to local raw materials, moreover, usually are free to choose among several locations and will come to a country only if they expect their after-tax profits to be greater there than in the next most profitable location.

Tax holidays may be unfair and inefficient if the expansion of an existing firm would produce most of the benefits for the country that a new firm would bring. The identification of a genuinely new firm requires the exercise of administrative judgment since existing firms may be reorganized to take advantage of a tax holiday, and firms may attempt to prolong their tax exemption at the end of the holiday period by artificially changing their identity.

Accelerated depreciation and tax credits typically are less selective than tax holidays. This makes them easier to administer but less effective in influencing the structure of industry. These provisions may encourage more capital-intensive activities than are optimal for most developing countries. The increasing prevalence of such provisions in industrial countries has weakened their capacity to attract investment to less developed countries.

An extreme form of accelerated depreciation is to allow a full writeoff of capital outlays in the year in which they are made, which is often called expensing (because outlays for depreciable capital are treated like current expenses). If the company has enough income to absorb the full deduction, and the income tax is levied at a proportional rate, expensing is equivalent to tax exemption for the return on an equity investment. This can be demonstrated by a simple example. Assume that the tax rate is 40 percent and the rate of return that a company must expect to induce it to invest is 15 percent. Then a tax-exempt investment of $1,000 would be acceptable if it were expected to yield $150 a year. With expensing, the net cost of a similar taxable investment would be $600 ($1,000 less $400 of tax saving), and the after-tax return of $90 would equal 15 percent of the net investment.[24] For a debt-financed investment, the tax could be negative, when allowance is made for expensing and the deduction of interest payments. Expensing is more generous than is commonly appreciated in its treatment of additional investments by established firms but no more helpful than a short tax holiday for a new firm that lacks sufficient income to absorb the full deduction immediately.

The benefits of incentives that lower income taxes on foreign-owned enterprises, or a simple rate reduction, may be partly or wholly canceled by higher tax liabilities in the capital-exporting country in which the company's head office is situated (see chapter 5). This is true of branches or subsidiaries that remit their profits to the parent company if the latter is resident in a country that taxes income on a worldwide basis, as do the United States, the United Kingdom, and some other capital-exporting countries. For special tax incentives, the effect may be prevented by tax-sparing arrangements that are granted on a bilateral basis by many capital-exporting countries (not including the United States). For both special incentives and general rate reductions, the cancellation of benefits can be avoided by reinvestment of the profits of a subsidiary in the developing country or sometimes by remitting the profits to a base company in a low-tax country for reinvestment elsewhere.

Much of the impetus to tax incentive schemes arises from the fear of governments that failure to match the benefits offered by neighboring countries will cause new firms and additional investments to be located in the other countries. Any comparison between countries should take account of both special incentives and the normal tax system. Although worries about comparative generosity are sometimes exaggerated, they have a real basis, particularly in regard to export industries. It could well be advantageous for capital-importing countries to work out formal or informal regional understandings limiting competition in the granting of tax incentives. Members of customs unions have recognized the desirability of harmonizing tax incentives, but other countries have not moved in that direction.

TAXATION AND EMPLOYMENT. Ironically, special tax incentives for investment, which are supported as a means of creating jobs, have often

24. E. Cary Brown, "Business-Income Taxation and Investment Incentives," in *Income, Employment, and Public Policy: Essays in Honor of Alvin H. Hansen* (Norton, 1948), pp. 309–10, reprinted in Richard A. Musgrave and Carl S. Shoup, eds., *Readings in the Economics of Taxation* (1959), pp. 525–37; Carl S. Shoup, *Public Finance* (Aldine, 1969), pp. 301–02.

added to the bias against labor-intensive production that exists in many developing countries. Special tax incentives for employment have been suggested as a more direct attack, and some have been put into effect.[25] The best form of incentive would encourage the employment of unskilled workers, of whom there is a surplus in most developing countries, accompanied by a shortage of skilled workers, technicians, and managers. One approach would be to give tax credits to firms that employ low-paid workers. To limit budgetary costs, it is usually suggested that tax credits be restricted to increases in employment. Another possibility would be to try to shape investment incentives to favor machinery and equipment that operate in combination with large numbers of unskilled or semiskilled workers. Larger depreciation allowances or other tax benefits could be given for multiple-shift operations.

The efficacy of measures that reduce labor costs usually by only moderate amounts has been challenged. Skeptics point out that wages of unskilled workers are much lower in developing countries than in industrial countries and question whether a tax incentive designed to reduce the cost of unskilled labor will attract foreign-owned enterprises. The possibility of encouraging more labor-intensive production methods by both foreign-owned and local enterprises has been disputed by some who assert that labor-capital ratios are determined by the example of industrial countries and technological factors. The available evidence is inconsistent with an extreme version of that argument. Econometric and engineering studies indicate that there is room for different degrees of labor intensity in many lines of production. Except in continuous-process industries, labor intensity can be increased by multiple-shift operations. Even where highly automated processes have great cost advantages, more or less labor-intensive methods for ancillary services such as handling materials and packaging are practical. Decisions about these questions may be influenced by tax incentives. But the extent of the response to changes in the relative costs of labor and capital is uncertain.[26]

25. International Labor Office, *Fiscal Measures for Employment Promotion in Developing Countries* (Geneva: ILO, 1972); Charles E. McLure, Jr., "Colombian Tax Incentives," and "The Design of Regional Tax Incentives for Colombia," in Malcom Gillis, ed., *Fiscal Reform for Colombia*, Final Report and Staff Papers of the Colombian Commission on Tax Reform (Harvard University Law School, 1971), pp. 530–56; McLure, "Administrative Considerations in the Design of Regional Tax Incentives," *National Tax Journal*, vol. 33 (June 1980), pp. 177–88; and Richard M. Bird, "Taxation and Employment in Developing Countries," *Finanzarchiv*, vol. 40 (1982), pp. 211–39.

26. David Morawetz, "Elasticities of Substitution in Industry: What Do We Learn from Econometric Estimates?" *World Development*, vol. 4 (January 1976), pp. 11–15; Lawrence J. White, "The Evidence on Appropriate Factor Proportions for Manufacturing in Less Developed Countries: A Survey," *Economic Development and Cultural Change*, vol. 27 (October 1978), pp. 27–59.

Tax incentives for employment would involve technical difficulties. Any provision related to numbers of employees should adjust for part-time workers and possibly for levels of skill and pay. If the incentive were related to increases in employment, a suitable base period from which to measure the increase would have to be selected, and safeguards would be needed to prevent firms' qualifying by hiring workers and then dropping them after a short time. That might be done by building up and drawing down inventories or by altering the proportions of direct and indirect labor. For example, a firm could shift between direct manufacturing and purchase of components for assembly or between direct processing of raw materials and purchase of semifinished goods. Another problem would be to prevent an entrepreneur from qualifying for a tax credit by winding up a company and setting up a new one without increasing employment.

Because of technical problems and budgetary costs, special tax incentives for employment appear less promising than policies to reduce biases against labor-intensive production.

A question that is likely to become significant in an increasing number of developing countries is whether payroll taxes to finance social security should be avoided or minimized because they adversely affect employment by increasing labor costs and encouraging the substitution of capital for labor. Many economists would dispute this, arguing that the taxes are borne by workers and have little or no effect on employers' costs. That would be so in a competitive and efficient market, and evidence that it is so in reality has been provided for industrial countries.[27] The narrow coverage of the taxes in most developing countries may facilitate shifting to workers owing to the feasibility of substituting capital for labor selectively. The incidence of payroll taxes in developing countries has not been systematically studied.

Another basis for disputing the claim that payroll taxes favor the use of capital rather than labor is that any increase in labor costs that may be caused by the taxes will raise the cost of capital goods more or less equally because wages are a major component of the cost of producing capital goods. This argument, however, has little force in developing countries, which import a large part of their capital goods at prices that will not be affected by their payroll taxes.

The inclusion of machinery and other capital goods in the base of indirect taxes would increase their relative prices and would diminish the advantage of capital-intensive production methods. That action would be

27. John A. Brittain, *The Payroll Tax for Social Security* (Brookings Institution, 1972).

anomalous in countries that offer extensive tax incentives for investment but could be rationalized where the incentives are selectively awarded.

In addition to influencing the choice of methods for producing particular goods, the tax system possibly could promote employment by favoring the consumption of goods produced by labor-intensive methods. There has been little conscious effort to pursue such a policy, though India, Pakistan, and some other countries have imposed lower taxes on the products of cottage industries than on factory-made goods. It is not clear how far tax discrimination on the basis of labor intensiveness is feasible and consistent with policies regarding income distribution. Items such as footwear and textiles on the average have a greater direct labor content than consumer durables and also form a larger fraction of the consumption of the poor than of the rich. But there are variations around the average, and for clothing and some other goods the items bought by low-income consumers may be less labor-intensive than those preferred by high-income consumers. Probably the most important source of differentiation is attributable to legal provisions dictated largely by administrative expediency and to evasion, which cause sales taxes and excises to fall lightly on artisans' production, sales of small retailers, and services, in which labor contributes a large fraction of value added.

EXPORTS AND IMPORTS. Protection of domestic production by means of import duties or other measures handicaps exports. The cost of material inputs may be increased, and scarce productive factors are attracted to protected industries, which may increase their cost for export producers. The limitation of imports tends to keep up the foreign exchange value of the domestic currency and to reduce the domestic currency proceeds of exports whose prices are set on external markets.

Specialists in international trade and development have given much attention to possible ways of mitigating the handicaps. A helpful general approach is to moderate the degree of protection and emphasize comparative advantage in production. Unintended protection resulting from import taxes motivated by revenue needs can be avoided by substituting excises or sales taxes for the import taxes (see chapter 6). These measures alone, however, are likely to be considered insufficient.

Manufacturing can be promoted by subsidizing exports as well as by taxing imports. By combining taxes on imports of manufactures with subsidies for exports of manufactures, the industrial sector as a whole would be favored compared with agriculture and other sectors. The taxes would finance the subsidies, at least in part.

A thorny set of technical and political issues would have to be resolved to select a coherent schedule of tax and subsidy rates and to win acceptance for them. Overt subsidies to exports will arouse more local opposition than the subsidies to import substitutes provided by import duties. Other countries may retaliate by imposing countervailing duties on their imports of the subsidized goods. The General Agreement on Tariffs and Trade (GATT) requires that signatory countries notify the secretariat of export subsidies and discuss them with other countries that may be harmed; the other countries have the right to offset the subsidies by countervailing duties when established industries are injured (Articles XVI and VI). Developing countries, however, enjoy a large measure of freedom to use export subsidies, though those that participate in the GATT undertake not to use them in ways that cause serious injury to another signatory country.[28] U.S. law calls for the automatic application of countervailing duties to goods that have received export subsidies.

Cash export subsidies have not been widely used, probably because of their obvious budgetary cost and worries about controlling it. Subsidies through the exchange system have been more frequent. Although this form of subsidy can give rise to inefficiencies similar to those involved in import-substitution strategies, in practice export promotion schemes generally have tended to reduce or eliminate biases against exports rather than to create biases in favor of exports.[29]

It is accepted international practice to allow exporters rebates of import duties on goods that are reexported in the same form in which they were imported or after processing. Developing countries that have not done so can benefit by establishing simple and reliable systems for prompt rebates. Exemption or rebate of other indirect taxes on export products is also acceptable. This practice is consistent with the view that the taxes generally enter into prices and are taxes on consumption that should apply where the consumers live, that is, in the country of final destination. Exports are nearly always relieved of taxes that would apply to other goods at the final stage of production or sale, but there may be no rebate for taxes at earlier stages or for other taxes that affect production costs. The possibility of making accurate rebates for taxes at all stages of production and, if desired,

28. General Agreement on Tariffs and Trade, *The Tokyo Round of Multilateral Trade Negotiations* (Geneva: GATT, 1979), pp. 129–31, 167–68.

29. Jagdish Bhagwati, *Anatomy and Consequences of Exchange Control Regimes*, vol. 11: *Foreign Trade Regimes and Economic Development* (Ballinger for the National Bureau of Economic Research, 1978), pp. 46–47, 210–11. Bhagwati draws on detailed studies of eleven developing countries included in a National Bureau of Economic Research project.

for taxes on purchased supplies, energy, and the like is an advantage of the value-added tax over other forms of sales tax, especially the turnover tax.

Under GATT rules, rebates of direct taxes related to exports are considered subsidies, and rebates or exemptions for income and profits taxes and payroll taxes have been so classified. In practice, income tax exemptions seem to have excited less opposition than overt subsidies or preferential exchange rates; as with other subsidies, developing countries have broad scope for tax exemptions. Income tax exemptions or rebates are subject to abuse because for firms producing for both export and domestic consumption there is no demonstrably correct way of allocating profits between exports and other sales.

Summary

The objectives of growth and development have social and political as well as economic aspects. Three strategies to advance the objectives are the neoclassical, industrialization with a dualistic economy, and general growth. Each has implications for government finance.

The neoclassical strategy would rely on market forces with a small government sector. It lacks appeal to governments of less developed countries, which prefer a more active role.

Industrialization with dualism calls for an active government following policies to promote a modern industrial sector, which would coexist with a traditional sector of agriculture, handicrafts, and small trade. Implications for government finance include heavy government spending for infrastructure, high taxation, emphasis on government saving as a performance indicator, taxation of agriculture, taxation of imports and agricultural and mineral exports, and special tax incentives for investment.

The strategy of industrialization with dualism had a wide following in the 1950s and 1960s, and it continues to attract support. By the mid-1970s, however, growth was slowing and dissatisfaction and unsolved problems became evident in regard to inequalities, persistent poverty, food deficits, unemployment, overurbanization, and other matters. The key economic assumptions and fiscal policies were increasingly questioned.

A general growth strategy attempts to encourage both agriculture and industry and is more outward-looking. It recognizes that many kinds of government expenditure can contribute to growth and development. Particular attention is given to the recurrent costs of capital projects and spending that will augment labor productivity. In the tax field, the goal is to obtain adequate amounts of revenue from widely applied taxes without unnecessarily reducing work effort or saving. Special incentives for industrial production are considered appropriate, but biases against agriculture and labor-intensive production should be avoided. Tax obstacles to nontraditional exports should be minimized, excessive and unintended protection through import taxes should be avoided, and export taxes on primary products should be used cautiously.

The impact of taxation on household saving is uncertain. Special tax measures may influence the form in which savings are held more than their total amount. The classical system of corporate taxation is more favorable to enterprise saving than the partially integrated system. The budget deficit—a form of negative saving—has a direct and often great impact on national saving.

Special tax incentives for investment include tax holidays, accelerated depreciation, tax credits, and exemption from indirect taxes on capital goods and materials. These are intended to lower tax deterrents and to influence the allocation of investment. Significant issues concern the degree of selectivity, the measurement of benefits and costs, and competition between countries.

Special tax incentives to promote employment appear less promising than policies that would reduce biases against labor-intensive production that often are present in tax, credit, and foreign exchange systems.

Stimulation of exports by subsidies financed by taxes on imports, as has been proposed, would involve technical and political issues and possible retaliation by other countries. Provision for complete rebate of indirect taxes on export products is internationally acceptable and should be introduced where it is lacking.

CHAPTER ELEVEN

Fiscal Policies for Stabilization

STABILIZATION policies are intended to lessen undesirable variations of economic activity, excessive balance-of-payments deficits or surpluses, and fluctuations in the price level. Shortfalls of activity are regarded as more undesirable than temporary excesses, though the latter may arouse worries about a subsequent collapse. An excessive balance-of-payments deficit is a current account deficit that cannot be financed on acceptable terms by borrowing abroad or foreign aid. Such a deficit poses more urgent problems than an excessive current account surplus, which results in more accumulation of claims on foreigners than is consistent with growth, stability, and distributional objectives. In the past, both declines and increases in the price level were causes of concern, but in recent decades inflation has predominated and its control has preempted the attention of policymakers.

This chapter examines the usefulness of fiscal policies for stabilization in developing countries and contrasts their position with that of industrial countries. The content of typical stabilization programs is analyzed. A separate section is devoted to the special stabilization problems of oil-exporting countries.

Policies to Lessen Cyclical Instability

Cyclical or short-run instability of activity may be caused by (1) variations in enterprise and household investment; (2) changes in the volume of exports because of fluctuations in external demand; (3) changes in the terms of international trade; (4) natural conditions, including weather, pests, and plant and animal diseases; (5) errors in the conduct of fiscal or monetary policies; and (6) political uncertainty or disturbances.

For industrial countries, variations of domestic investment and of exports have been emphasized in economic literature as the sources of instability of output and employment. It has been recognized that the other causes may operate also, but usually they have been considered less important.

In less developed primary-producing countries, variations in harvests due to natural conditions and changes in the terms of international trade caused by unequal movements of export and import prices are especially significant sources of instability. Political disturbances associated particularly with the transfer of power by coups and with strife between political, racial, or tribal rivals have taken place in many developing countries with unsettling influences on economic activity and international capital flows.

Weaknesses and mistakes of governments in the management of fiscal and monetary matters have aggravated instability orginating from other sources and frequently have been the initial causes of cyclical fluctuations. Although no group of countries has been spared these problems, the most extreme cases of government-caused instability have occurred in less developed countries.

Oversimplifying a little, one may contrast the positions of industrial countries and primary-producing countries by saying that cyclical fluctuations of output in the former result from changes in the intensity of use of productive capacity in response to variations in volatile elements of demand, whereas fluctuations in real income in primary-producing countries occur without visible changes in the intensity of productive effort. For industrial countries, fluctuations in domestic investment and exports result in changes in the unemployment rate of workers and the capacity utilization rate for manufacturing plants. For a primary-producing country, a crop failure or a deterioration in the terms of international trade causes a loss of real income even though everyone works as hard and continuously as in a good year. Actually, some variations in employment and capacity utilization rates are likely to occur also in the primary-producing country, but the contrast with conditions in industrial countries is valid.

In the past, the price level was expected to move in the same direction as output in industrial countries, rising when output approached its full potential and falling when surplus productive capacity appeared. There was no similar presumption for primary-producing countries. A crop failure was associated with high prices and a big harvest with low prices. Recently, the link between fluctuations of output and the price level has become loose in industrial countries. Prices of industrial products are more flexible upward than downward, and slack periods are expected to be associated with a lower rate of inflation rather than a falling price level.

Semi-industrial countries fall between the industrial and primary-producing types, being subject to both sets of influences. Some of the countries have experienced wide fluctuations in reported rates of utilization of manufacturing capacity, which may be attributable partly to the marginal character of much of the capacity created in conditions of protectionism and inflation.

The contrast between industrial and primary-producing countries suggests that the scope for stabilizing policies and their content will differ. In industrial countries, a broadly Keynesian interpretation came to be widely accepted in the years following World War II. It held that fluctuations in activity could be reduced by stabilizing aggregate demand. Fiscal measures could compensate for autonomous fluctuations in domestic investment demand and in demand for exports and thus would prevent the secondary or induced effects that otherwise would occur. The application of the fiscal instruments in that way was aptly called compensatory fiscal policy. Variations in government expenditures and dependable responses of household consumption to changes in tax revenue were central to the policy. Expenditure increases and tax reductions were prescribed when a downturn in activity began, and opposite fiscal actions were called for when aggregate demand threatened to become excessive and to result in rising prices, and a balance-of-payments deficit. The tax changes could be either discretionary or automatic responses to changing activity. Expenditure adjustments depended mainly on discretionary actions, with some element of automaticity in the response of transfer payments to economic conditions.

Most of the early discussion of fiscal policy in the United States implicitly assumed a closed economy or gave little attention to the international aspects of fluctuations and compensatory policy. However, the implications for the balance of payments were recognized by specialists in international finance.

The monetary assumptions of writers on fiscal policy usually were unstated or vague. In general, monetary policy was assumed to be "accommodating," that is, to allow changes in money and credit to occur so as to avoid interference with the fiscal effects.

Fiscal and other policies broadly consistent with the analysis and prescriptions outlined in the preceding paragraphs contributed to a record of rapid economic growth, low unemployment, and low or moderate inflation in the industrial countries from the late 1940s to the early 1970s. Developing countries benefited from strong markets in the prosperous industrial countries. But recently confidence in the analysis and policies has been weakened. Experience has shown that inflation appears earlier and is more resistant to control than had been foreseen. Balance-of-payments disequilibria have proved troublesome. Greater recognition is now given to monetary phenomena and policy. A reaction against large government budgets and heavy taxation has set in. However, no new consensus has yet emerged.

Keynesian-inspired compensatory fiscal policies were never applicable to less developed primary-producing countries because the origin and nature of the fluctuations experienced by these countries differed from those of industrial countries. The balance-of-payments aspects of stabilization had to be recognized as the strategic factor for the primary-producing countries.

A primary-producing country that suffers a crop failure clearly cannot compensate for that loss of real income by immediately producing more of other goods and services. Neither can a loss of purchasing power due to a decline in the prices of exports relative to the prices of imports be offset in the short run by stimulating domestic activity.

If a country that experiences such misfortunes has no foreign exchange reserves and no capacity to borrow abroad or obtain additional aid, it will have no alternative to austerity. It will have to avoid a balance-of-payments deficit by cutting imports. To do so in an orderly way, the government should follow fiscal policies that will accentuate the decline of incomes. Thus tax increases and expenditure cuts will be needed, rather than the tax reductions and expenditure increases prescribed by the doctrine of compensatory fiscal policy. Usually quantitative restrictions on imports will be instituted or intensified, but contractionary fiscal measures will be advisable to strengthen them and make them less inefficient.

Nearly all countries have some access to credit from abroad, but the terms may be onerous and the amount too small to obviate disruptive reductions of imports. The appropriate strategy for a primary-producing country is to try to cope with crop failures and cyclical declines in the terms of trade by measures that will allow imports to be stabilized or, if necessary, temporarily increased. To that end, foreign exchange reserves should be built up, and external debts reduced, during good times so that reserves and borrowing can be used in bad times. Drawings on the International Monetary Fund (IMF) and repurchases may be elements in the management of reserves and external debt.

A supporting fiscal policy could combine variable revenues from export taxes with stable government expenditures. When export earnings were large, because of high prices or a good crop, part of the proceeds would be captured by export taxes; the budget deficit would be reduced and possibly replaced by a surplus. The absorption of part of the income of exporters would curtail their expenditures for both imports and home goods and as a secondary effect would also reduce the expenditures of others. A surplus in the current account of the balance-of-payments would be realized, allowing the accumulation of foreign exchange reserves or debt repayment, but its domestic inflationary impact would be neutralized or reduced by the fiscal measures. When export earnings were small, owing to low prices or crop failure, export tax revenue would be reduced, and a budget deficit would be incurred. The balance-of-payments deficit would be financed by drawing down reserves or borrowing.

From the economic standpoint, it is not essential that the variations in tax revenues be obtained from export taxes. Changes in other taxes could serve the same purpose. However, it would be simpler and would be likely to be seen as more equitable to rely primarily on export taxes. Successful use of export taxes would mitigate the boom and bust conditions that have characterized the production of some export commodities. It would discourage investment in excessive capacity during boom periods and encourage good cultivation, grading, and marketing practices during bad times. Over a period of years, the production of the taxed commodities probably would be curtailed because of the blunting of incentives offered by high prices in good times. Revenues from import duties, domestic consumption taxes, and income taxes would tend to fluctuate in the same direction as export tax revenues because of the pervasive influence of export earnings on the economies of less developed primary-producing countries.

The variations in export tax revenues theoretically could be obtained by discretionary imposition and removal of taxes and changes in tax rates. But that would require prompt recognition of fluctuations in export earnings and immediate legislative action. The frequent changes would inevitably place heavy demands on the government's attention and its political capital. Adjustments of export taxes to changing prices could be obtained much better by the use of sliding scales of rates that would automatically impose or increase duties as prices rose and reduce or remove them as prices fell. These automatic adjustments could not take account of variations in the volume of exports, although some automatic response of revenues would occur from export duties if they were a permanent part of the tax system and from other taxes.

The fiscal policy just outlined would differ from a policy of attempting to stabilize the income of export producers by collecting taxes when export prices are high and paying subsidies when prices are low. That policy, if executed as intended, either through the budget or by an autonomous marketing board or stabilization fund, would on average neither tax nor subsidize export producers. The fiscal policy suggested here would tax export producers on average because the taxes collected during good times would not be balanced by subsidies in bad times. Conceivably the fiscal policy could be combined with a tax-and-subsidy scheme, though doing so would strain the judgment and political strength of the government.

The success of the stabilizing fiscal policy would require the government to resist the temptation to increase spending as much as revenues rose during good times. That would be difficult but might be feasible pursuant to a coherent policy, especially if additional revenues were appropriated to the reduction of foreign debt or debt to the central bank.

To summarize, a successful stabilization policy for a less developed primary-producing country spreads the use of export earnings more evenly over time and avoids the disruption of domestic activity that would otherwise be necessary. In contrast, a successful compensatory fiscal policy for a more developed industrial country raises the average level of activity and real income by offsetting the effects on aggregate demand of fluctuations in investment and industrial exports.[1]

A great difficulty for a primary-producing country that attempts to follow the policy that has been sketched in the preceding pages is to foresee the duration and extent of favorable and unfavorable movements of export prices and earnings. Past records may be a basis for forecasting variations due to weather conditions, but history is not a guide to the future of export prices. The most that can be learned is that for many commodities prices tend to be dominated by market conditions in developed countries, and these in the past have corresponded to business cycles of variable amplitude and duration.

As a guide for fiscal policy in a less developed primary-producing country, Mansfield has proposed a "norm" for a stabilizing budget policy.[2] It would require projection of long-term trends but not forecasts of year-

---

1. The contrast between stabilizing fiscal policies for industrial and for primary-producing countries was analyzed in a paper presented at the third Rehovoth Conference in 1965. See Richard Goode, "Impact of Fiscal Measures," in David Krivine, ed., *Fiscal and Monetary Problems in Developing States* (Praeger, 1967), pp. 238–52.

2. Charles Y. Mansfield, "A Norm for a Stabilizing Budget Policy in Less Developed Export Economies," *Journal of Development Studies*, vol. 16 (July 1980), pp. 401–11.

to-year changes. The norm could be used also to appraise past policy, classifying it as expansionary or contractionary by distinguishing between active and passive components of the budget. It would resemble the full-employment budget concept that has been used in the United States and the cyclically neutral budget concept of the German Council of Economic Experts.[3]

Mansfield's norm is based on the hypothesis that economic activity and tax revenues of what he calls less developed export economies are closely correlated with the value of exports. This does not imply that a major part of revenues comes from export taxes but only that the tax base as a whole fluctuates with exports. The budget is considered neutral in its impact on total demand if actual tax revenues equal their trend value and government expenditures bear a stable, normal relationship to the trend value of revenues. The resulting neutral budget balance may be either a deficit or surplus, depending on financing possibilities and other structural characteristics of the economy.

A neutral revenue trend and "allowable" government expenditures are estimated in relation to the trend value of exports as follows:

$$R_T = f(X_T)$$
$$G_A = (G_B/R_B)(R_T),$$

where R_T is the trend value of government revenues, X_T is the trend value of exports, G_A is allowable expenditures, and G_B and R_B are government expenditures and revenues, respectively, in a base period that is considered normal and reasonably stable. The implicit budget deficit is then defined as $R_T - G_A$. Fiscal policy is regarded as neutral if the actual deficit equals the implicit deficit and as expansionary or contractionary if it exceeds or falls below the implicit deficit. The budget is classified as stabilizing if it is contractionary in years when exports are above their trend value and expansionary when exports are below trend. (Another way of looking at the budget would be to regard any deficit as expansionary and any surplus as contractionary and to classify fiscal policy as more or less than "normally" expansionary or contractionary by comparing the actual deficit or surplus to the implicit deficit.)

Applying these ideas to a small sample of eight countries (Honduras,

3. On the full-employment budget surplus (deficit) concept, see Alan S. Blinder and Robert M. Solow, "Analytical Foundations of Fiscal Policy," in Blinder and others, *Economics of Public Finance* (Brookings Institution, 1974), pp. 11–36; on the cyclically neutral budget, Thomas F. Dernburg, "Fiscal Analysis in the Federal Republic of Germany: The Cyclically Neutral Budget," International Monetary Fund *Staff Papers*, vol. 22 (November 1975), pp. 825–57.

Jamaica, Ghana, Sierra Leone, Peru, Guyana, Paraguay, and Malaysia), Mansfield found that revenues were highly correlated with the current value of exports and exerted a stabilizing influence. Expenditures, however, tended to exceed the allowable level, particularly in boom years. The total budget impact was judged clearly stabilizing in somewhat less than half of the observations (one observation for each country for each year over periods ranging from fourteen to twenty-five years), clearly destabilizing in about one-fourth of the observations, and intermediate in the remaining observations.

The concept of the stabilizing budget norm may be an aid in analyzing and planning fiscal policy for the kind of country for which it is intended. Further study of it would be worthwhile. Users, however, cannot avoid the problem of distinguishing between temporary fluctuations above or below a stable trend and a change in the trend. If, for example, exports are below the estimated trend, is this only a temporary aberration, the beginning of a long period of slower growth, or the first phase of a declining trend? Independent analysis mixed with guesswork is needed to answer that question. Furthermore, it is doubtful whether strong political support could be mustered for application of the norm in a symmetrical way. The norm might well have more appeal as a justification of a budget deficit in poor years than as an indication of the need for holding down or eliminating the deficit in good years. The full-employment budget surplus concept seems to have been used in that way in the United States and, partly for that reason, to have lost standing.

A weakness of the preceding exposition, and of many other discussions of fiscal policy, is the failure to specify the means of financing budget deficits or disposing of surpluses and to analyze their consequences. The stabilizing function of fiscal policy is clearest, and strongest, when these financial transactions have no countervailing effect on spending by households and enterprises. Generally, this will be so if deficits are covered by borrowing from the central bank or drawing down balances with it and surpluses are used to repay debt to the central bank or build up deposits there. In certain conditions, the impact of financial transactions with commercial banks will be substantially the same (see chapter 9). Also, borrowing abroad and repayment of debt to foreign lenders will have no immediate impact on spending by residents. In many developing countries, marginal changes in the budget deficit associated with cyclical fluctuations will be financed in one of the ways mentioned.

In some developing countries, however, fluctuations in the budget deficit will be associated with debt transactions with domestic nonbank lenders. In these cases, government borrowing is likely to displace some expenditures of enterprises and households, with the result that the expansionary effect of an increase in the budget deficit will be reduced. And repayment of debt held by the nonbank lenders will tend to stimulate spending and to lessen the contractionary impact of a reduction of the budget deficit or a surplus. It is possible, moreover, that government securities differ enough in liquidity so that transactions in various issues affect spending to different degrees. A possible way of taking account of such effects would be to prepare a financing table with weights attached to the items according to their estimated or presumed impact on nongovernmental spending. Although the weights probably could be no more than rough approximations, the exercise might yield some useful insights.

The Relationship between Fiscal and Monetary Policies

If budget deficits are financed entirely by transactions with the central bank or nonresidents and budget surpluses are disposed of in a similar way, they will result in equal increases or decreases in the sum of currency and deposits at the central bank. The mechanics are simple. A deficit so financed involves the government's paying out more in checks and currency than it takes in. The recipients will hold part of their receipts in deposits at commercial banks and part in currency. The commercial banks will build up their deposits at the central bank by an amount equal to the initial increase in deposits of their customers. For a budget surplus, the flows will move in the opposite direction.

Currency and deposits at the central bank are reserve money and are sometimes called high-powered money. They can satisfy the legal or customary requirements of the commercial banks for reserves against their deposit liabilities, and they are high powered because they can support a multiple expansion of loans and deposits of the banking system. The maximum extent of the expansion is indicated by the money multiplier, which depends on the fraction of any increase in the money stock that people choose to hold in currency and the reserve ratio of the commercial banks.[4] Generally, the currency component of money tends to be high in

---

4. The money multiplier is $1/(b + c - bc)$, where b is the reserve ratio of commercial banks and c is the ratio of the public's currency holdings to total money. This definition can be adjusted to take account of nonmonetary deposits and any difference in reserve requirements for different classes of deposits. The multiplier is explained in many treatises and textbooks. For an especially clear and full exposition, see Richard S. Thorn, *Introduction to Money and Banking* (Harper and Row, 1976), pp. 92–95.

developing countries, which limits the scope for the expansion of deposits. Legal reserve ratios differ among countries; sometimes especially high marginal ratios are applied to increases in deposits for the purpose of limiting monetary expansion.

The increase or decrease of reserve money that accompanies a budget deficit or surplus may be regarded as part of an expansionary or contractionary fiscal policy. Some economists take a different view, arguing that the changes in reserve money are part of monetary policy. The difference in approaches has led to some quibbling and confusion in debates about the relative effectiveness of fiscal and monetary policies.

Whatever the situation may be in a few developed countries, ministries of finance and central banks of less developed countries do not have a wide range of choice in financing budget deficits or in influencing the quantity of reserve money that is created or destroyed. If marginal changes in the budget balance are reflected largely in transactions with the central bank or nonresidents, there is little point in trying to distinguish the fiscal actions that bring about the changes in the budget balance from the actions that cause the corresponding changes in reserve money.

In less developed countries, changes in reserve money are dominated by transactions with the government and the balance of payments. There is virtually no possibility of affecting reserve money by open market operations because of the absence of financial markets. Rediscounting of commercial bank assets and direct lending by the central bank occur in some developing countries but generally are not systematically employed as instruments of monetary policy.

Up to a point, the secondary effects of the operation of the money multiplier may be a welcome addition to the primary impact of an expansionary or contractionary fiscal policy. If, however, the money multiplier is high, the secondary effects may be considered excessive. They can be moderated by varying legal reserve requirements against commercial bank deposits. Another attack is through direct controls on bank lending. Advance deposit requirements for imports and other modifications of foreign exchange controls have also been used to influence the availability of bank credit. Moreover, with a fixed exchange rate, or a rate that is adjusted only occasionally, the secondary expansionary or contractionary effects of fiscal policy on aggregate demand and the money stock are partly dissipated through the balance of payments, except in the unlikely event that rigid exchange or import controls are successfully maintained.

In very few developing countries is it either technically or politically feasible for the ministry of finance and the central bank to carry out independent policies. Ordinarily the best hope for stability is offered by giving the government responsibility for the general direction of policy and relying on the central bank for collaboration in the execution and appraisal of policies.

The Susceptibility of Developing Countries to Inflation

Inflation has become a worldwide problem. For a long time, severe and prolonged inflation was confined mainly to Latin America, particularly Argentina, Chile, Uruguay, and Brazil. In the 1950s and 1960s rates of price increase in Asia, Africa, and the Middle East were only moderately greater than in the industrial countries. After the oil price increase in 1973, the rate of price increase rose sharply in all areas and has remained high by historical standards. The developing countries of the Western Hemisphere have continued to experience the fastest average rate of price increase, with the regional average being pushed up not only by the chronically inflationary countries but also by Peru, Colombia, Mexico, Jamaica, and other countries. The regional averages are shown in table 11-1.

Inflation has multiple causes. The fiscal system is invariably an important contributor. As brought out in earlier chapters, ambitious government spending programs, ineffective budgeting and expenditure controls, weak tax systems, and limited opportunities for borrowing from nonbank domestic lenders have often led to deficits financed by money creation in excess of the noninflationary limit. In some cases inflation induced in that way may become self-perpetuating as the deficit grows because tax revenues lag behind expenditures (see chapter 10). It is also possible that an initial price rise touched off by some nonfiscal cause will start a series of growing budget deficits, each financed mainly by money creation. The majority of developing countries benefit less than most industrial countries do from an automatic stabilizer in the form of the built-in flexibility of yield of the tax system. In the developing countries built-in flexibility usually is lower in relation to money income because the tax ratio is lower and the principal taxes are less elastic.

Nonfiscal causes of inflation in developing countries have included at times increases in the prices of imports and exports originating abroad, bank lending to enterprises, and wage increases. There appear to have

Table 11-1. *Increases in Consumer Prices, 1951–80*[a]

Compound annual rates, in percent

Group	1951–60	1960–66	1966–72	1972–80
Industrial countries	2.0	2.6	3.7	10.3
Oil-exporting countries	3.2[b]	1.5	3.7	13.7
Non-oil developing countries				
Africa	3.0	4.1	5.1	15.7
Asia	3.8	6.1	5.8	11.1
Europe	2.9	10.9	5.8	26.0
Middle East	2.9	4.8	3.6	24.8
Western Hemisphere	12.7[c]	25.0	16.1	62.5

Source: Derived from International Monetary Fund, *International Financial Statistics*, yearbook 1981, pp. 64–65.
a. Computed from weighted indexes. Country coverage varies between periods.
b. 1953–60.
c. 1952–60.

been few cases, however, of severe or prolonged inflation that were not associated with fiscal deficits financed by excessive money creation.

Attempting to isolate the strategic factor in inflation, a distinguished economist asserted, "Inflation is always and everywhere a monetary phenomenon."[5] A monetarist school prescribes for developed and developing countries alike the remedy of monetary restraint. No doubt it is true that inflation cannot go far unless the stock of money increases faster than the real volume of production. But that observation does not tell much about what governments can and should do to prevent inflation. In developing countries, the most effective course is to regulate money creation and aggregate demand by operating the public finances so as to hold down the trend rate of growth in government debt to the central bank and to try to make cyclical adjustments in government borrowing from the central bank and foreign lenders so as partly to offset swings in the balance of payments.

A structuralist school, which not surprisingly originated in Latin America, has dissented from the opinion that inflation can be successfully controlled by fiscal and monetary policies. According to the school, inflation is caused by structural characteristics of the economies of less developed countries and can be extirpated only by changing the structures. Characteristics that are emphasized are resource immobility, market segmentation, and bottlenecks that impede the equilibration of demand and supply of strategic items. Preeminent significance usually is attached

5. Milton Friedman, "Inflation: Causes and Consequences," in Friedman, *Dollars and Deficits: Living with America's Economic Problems* (Prentice-Hall, 1968), p. 39.

to the alleged inelasticity of supply of food owing to the backward nature of agriculture. Combined with inelastic demand for food, the result is held to be shortages and rising food prices that provoke wage increases in the urban sector and further price increases. A recent writer gives a more extensive list of the "main bottlenecks," including "the supply of food products; the availability of foreign exchange; the rigidity in the tax and expenditure structure of the government; the inability to raise enough internal saving; and the supply of various intermediate inputs" including "fuels, fertilizers, transport facilities, and credit availability."[6] Structuralists argue that the elimination of inflation requires a long-term program, including measures such as changes in land tenure, direct state intervention to remove bottlenecks, promotion of import substitution, and fiscal reform.

If formulated very broadly, the structuralist interpretation loses its sharpness as a challenge to the orthodox fiscal/monetary approach to stabilization. The critical issues are whether inflation can occur without excess demand and whether controlling aggregate demand can check it without imposing intolerable hardships. Deficiencies in the tax and government expenditure systems, inability to mobilize internal savings, and resource shortages can be fitted into almost any explanation of the problems of less developed countries. The existence of these characteristics helps account for the susceptibility of the countries to inflation but does not justify the conclusion that fiscal and monetary policies are ineffective.

The structuralist hypothesis has not been well supported. Little convincing evidence has been presented for the existence of the special bottlenecks in food production and their inflationary consequences. The weight of the evidence, rather, is that agricultural production is responsive to price incentives and that farmers will accept new and improved seeds and cultivation methods when they are available and profitable. Domestic food production can be supplemented by imports, which, of course, have to be paid for by exports. Countries to which the structuralist arguments allegedly apply may be able to stimulate exports of nonfood agricultural commodities and manufactured products by removing obstacles in the form of an overvalued exchange rate and burdensome taxation. Admit-

---

6. Alejandro Foxley, "Stabilization Policies and Their Effects on Employment and Income Distribution: A Latin American Perspective," in William R. Cline and Sidney Weintraub, eds., *Economic Stabilization in Developing Countries* (Brookings Institution, 1981), pp. 191–225; quotation from p. 193. See also comments by Arnold C. Harberger, ibid., pp. 227–29; Werner Baer and Isaac Kerstenetsky, eds., *Inflation and Growth in Latin America* (Irwin, 1964), especially Dudley Seers, "Inflation and Growth: The Heart of the Controversy," pp. 89–103, and W. Arthur Lewis, "Concluding Remarks," pp. 21–33; Susan M. Wachter, *Latin American Inflation: The Structuralist-Monetarist Debate* (Lexington Books/ Heath, 1976).

tedly, some of them, which have established highly protected and inefficient import substitute industries, would face both economic and political difficulties in rationalizing production, increasing exports, and strengthening import capacity.

To criticize structuralist arguments is not to deny that structural characteristics of an economy and its recent history may influence the extent to which aggregate demand has to be compressed to stop inflation and the speed with which it can be controlled. The resistance of wages and industrial prices to downward pressure, cost-push forces, and inflationary expectations growing out of experience are obstacles to stabilization. They are not peculiar to less developed countries but exist also in industrialized countries. Their presence has caused many governments to consider the cost of quickly eliminating inflation by tight fiscal/monetary policies excessive in terms of lost output and social disruption and has induced them either to adopt gradualism or to tolerate continuing inflation. It is true, furthermore, that a simple fiscal/monetary explanation of inflation is superficial. A more penetrating analysis must find reasons to account for chronic fiscal deficits and the failure of inflation-prone countries to strengthen their fiscal systems. These conditions are a manifestation of lack of consensus about the division of the social product and inability to aggregate and reconcile conflicting interests. Their root causes must be sought in the complex of historical and cultural factors that have made it so difficult for most of the countries that are especially inflation prone to establish and maintain orderly democratic political regimes.

Stabilization Programs

Many developing countries have found it necessary to adopt stabilization programs to correct unsustainable balance-of-payments deficits, severe and prolonged inflation, and distortions of production. The immediate pressure to act often comes from the balance of payments. Despite direct controls on imports and foreign exchange allocations, the external deficit will have become increasingly difficult to finance, often resulting in payments arrears and threatened or actual defaults on external debts. Curtailment of imports will disrupt production, result in shortages, and provoke discontent. These problems cannot be resolved without dealing also with inflation and some of the other distortions.

A stabilization program is a more or less comprehensive set of measures intended to rectify the difficulties over a period of no more than a few years. Often the programs are worked out in collaboration with the IMF and receive its financial support. The IMF cannot impose a stabilization program on a member country, but its policy of "conditionality" means that a country can gain access to its financial resources only with an acceptable stabilization program. More important in many cases than the financing obtained from the IMF is its endorsement of the program, which commercial banks and other lenders may make a prerequisite of further financial support.

The main features of a typical stabilization program include the liberalization of international trade and payments, usually accompanied by a devaluation of the exchange rate or the adoption of a flexible rate; internal price adjustments to correct distortions; monetary and credit restraint; reduction of the fiscal deficit; the settlement of arrears of foreign payments; and the limitation of short-term and medium-term foreign borrowing. The program is expected to affect both real output (the supply side) and the level and composition of demand.

All the measures are likely to be controversial and politically sensitive. The price adjustments may be especially so. They usually include increases in the controlled prices of public utility services, which often are supplied by state enterprises, and may include also price increases occasioned by the reduction or elimination of subsidies for foods, petroleum products, and other items. Not surprisingly, a government may find it paradoxical to attack inflation by raising prices and may fear that beneficiaries of the subsidies will object and possibly launch demonstrations or violence. Corrective price increases, nevertheless, may be necessary to reduce the losses of state enterprises and the fiscal deficit and to encourage economical use of previously underpriced items.

The IMF extends its endorsement and financial support of a stabilization program through approval of a standby arrangement or an extended arrangement under which the member country may borrow in installments provided it satisfies certain "performance criteria." The arrangement may cover a period of one to three years. The usual practice is for the responsible minister or other representative to set out the country's program in a letter of intent. The letter usually covers a wide range of intended actions, which will have been discussed in detail with the IMF staff and described and analyzed in a report to the Executive Board. However, only a few items will be chosen as performance criteria. These are supposed to be limited to the minimum number "necessary to evaluate implementation of the program with a view to ensuring the achievement of its objectives."[7] Normally only macroeconomic variables and actions necessary to carry out specific provisions of the IMF's articles of agreements are performance criteria.[8] Failure to observe a performance criterion will interrupt a member's ability to borrow and will precipitate consultations that ordinarily will lead to a modification of the arrangement or a new arrangement.

Preference is given to macroeconomic variables as performance criteria to avoid the IMF's being unnecessarily involved in the details of politically sensitive matters. The discussions with the member country and the letter of intent, nevertheless, cover the details of the program, including microeconomic questions relating to matters such as pricing policy, taxation, and government expenditures. Almost invariably a broad monetary aggregate is the principal macroeconomic performance criterion. Usually it takes the form of a ceiling on expansion of domestic credit by the banking system, and often there is a subceiling on credit to the government. Much less frequently, a ceiling on the budget deficit will be included as a performance criterion.

The emphasis on a credit ceiling as a performance criterion is consistent with the view that monetary phenomena exert important influences, but it does not imply that monetary policy is given priority over fiscal policy. In fact, the principal actions required in most cases to ensure observance of the credit ceiling are fiscal measures that make possible the limitation of bank lending to the government. An overall credit ceiling or a subceiling on credit to the government is preferred to performance criteria of a specifically fiscal nature for both policy and technical reasons. The government may limit its use of bank credit by any combination of higher taxes, increased nontax revenues, expenditure reductions, or borrowing from nonbank sources.[9] Technically, a credit ceiling has the advantage that in most countries statistics on bank credit become available more promptly than fiscal statistics, which is important for programs monitored each quarter as is the usual practice of the IMF.

7. International Monetary Fund, Executive Board Decision 6056-(79/38), March 2, 1979, included in International Monetary Fund, *Annual Report of the Executive Board for the Financial Year Ended April 30, 1979*, pp. 136–38.

8. Joseph Gold, *Conditionality*, International Monetary Fund Pamphlet 31 (Washington, D.C.: IMF, 1979); Manuel Guitian, *Fund Conditionality: Evolution of Principles and Practices*, International Monetary Fund Pamphlet 38 (Washington, D.C.: IMF, 1982).

9. W. A. Beveridge and Margaret R. Kelly, "Fiscal Content of Financial Programs Supported by Stand-By Arrangements in the Upper Credit Tranches, 1969–78," International Monetary Fund *Staff Papers*, vol. 27 (June 1980), pp. 205–49.

Most IMF stabilization programs have concerned developing countries. This is only partly explained by the fact that a large majority of members are developing countries. The industrial countries and some of the large semi-industrial countries have preferred to avoid recourse to the IMF because an application has come to be seen as an admission that serious problems exist and because acceptance of conditionality is politically distasteful. These countries, moreover, have better access to credit from foreign commercial banks. In the decade 1973–82, the United Kingdom and Italy were the only industrial countries that entered into IMF arrangements requiring a high degree of conditionality. In that period, nine semi-industrial countries—Argentina, Egypt, Korea, Mexico, the Philippines, Romania, South Africa, Turkey, and Yugoslavia—entered into such arrangements; Brazil did so in early 1983.[10]

IMF conditionality has been the subject of extensive controversy that can be only summarily noted here.[11] First, IMF policies have been criticized for failing to distinguish between balance-of-payments deficits attributable to external causes and those brought on by poor policies. In reply it has been pointed out that internal causes are usually contributory factors and that, regardless of origin, a country must adjust in some way to eliminate an unsustainable balance-of-payments deficit. This does not necessarily require equilibrium in the current account of the balance of payments, rather the limitation of the current account deficit to an amount that can be covered by the inflow of capital from abroad in the form of equity, long-term debt, and normal trade credits or by foreign aid.

Second, IMF programs are said to be too harsh because they call for quick elimination of the balance-of-payments deficit. But a prolonged period of adjustment is possible only if sufficient external financing is available, and the IMF's resources are limited and are intended for

---

10. The arrangements are standby or extended arrangements covering upper credit tranches, that is, allowing a member access to IMF credit above 25 percent of its quota (excluding the use of certain low-conditionality facilities). IMF credit consists of drawings other than the member's reserve tranche, normally 25 percent of quota. For data on IMF transactions through 1981, see *International Financial Statistics: Supplement on Fund Accounts*, Supplement Series 3 (Washington, D.C.: IMF, 1982). All programs are reported in issues of the *IMF Survey*.

11. See Tony Killick, ed., *Adjustment and Financing in the Developing World: The Role of the International Monetary Fund* (Washington, D.C.: IMF in association with the Overseas Development Institute, 1982); also, Sidney Dell, *On Being Grandmotherly: The Evolution of IMF Conditionality*, Essays in International Finance 144 (Princeton University, International Finance Section, 1981); in the same series, Bahram Nowzad, *The IMF and Its Critics*, no. 146, December 1981; and Corrado Pirzio-Biroli, "Making Sense of the IMF Conditionality Debate," *Journal of World Trade Law*, vol. 17 (March–April 1983), pp. 115–53.

temporary use. Even if ample finance were available, the advantages of prolonging the adjustment period should be balanced against the cost of accumulating external debt. Standby arrangements (or extended arrangements) actually allow the adjustment to be spread over a longer time and to be more orderly than would otherwise be possible.

Third, the programs have been held to be too monetarist and to take too little account of structural problems. It is true that the monetary approach to the balance of payments has been prominent at the IMF, but as already noted stabilization programs usually rely primarily on fiscal actions. Possibly more allowance could be made for structural differences among countries that affect the real cost of stabilization, but it is unlikely that member countries would wish the IMF to prescribe sweeping structural reforms as a condition for its support.

Fourth, stabilization programs allegedly have taken too little account of growth and development objectives and have sometimes worked against them. Admittedly, the relation between inflation and growth is ambiguous, though countries suffering from inflation frequently take palliative actions that are harmful to growth and development. The correction of distortions attributable to the palliatives, the liberalization of foreign trade, and the adoption of a realistic exchange rate are essential to efficiency and growth. The resolution of a balance-of-payments crisis may allow a quick revival of activity. However, some high-cost industries previously operating behind protective barriers may have to be cut back or eliminated.

Fifth, it has been charged that stabilization programs often increase inequality of income by reducing real wages and increasing prices of necessities. The programs do affect income distribution and relative prices, and inevitably they result in the disappointment of expectations because to be successful they must restrict income and consumption claims that previously exceeded the capacity of the economy to meet. A common course of events is for a populist regime to raise wages and consumption to levels that can be maintained only by using up inventories, running down the capital stock, and piling up external debt. When these practices are ended the former beneficiaries will suffer. Statistics on real wages, however, may exaggerate the reduction because they fail to allow for shortages and black markets before the adoption of the program and sometimes because the base period reflects a real wage level that existed only briefly. Urban wage earners, in any case, usually have higher incomes than workers in the rural sector, who are likely to gain from the adjustments. In controlling aggregate demand, governments have some scope in the choice of measures that will be most consistent with their preferences in regard to income distribution.[12]

The record of stabilization programs is mixed. Generally, they have been more successful in improving the balance of payments than in checking inflation. Effects on growth and income distribution are harder to isolate.

The political aspects of stabilization problems and policies are critically significant and are more complex than the economic literature recognizes. The difficulties that make necessary a stabilization program may be brought on, or adjustment to external shocks delayed, because of the short time horizons of political leaders. Frequently, new regimes, desiring to demonstrate a contrast with their predecessors, embark on practices intended to produce immediate results with little consideration of future costs. When large balance-of-payments deficits appear and inflation accelerates, the government is likely to be reluctant to acknowledge that its promises have been unrealistic and to disappoint expectations that it has aroused. Corrective action may be postponed until drastic measures are required. In developing countries that have neither effective parliaments nor provisions for orderly changes of government, the possibility exists that a stringent stabilization program will provoke street demonstrations, rioting, and overthrow of the regime. Yet rapidly rising prices and shortages are also unpopular and can arouse strong opposition to a government.

Up to a point it may seem convenient for a government to divert attention by blaming the country's difficulties on external forces, inciting a confrontation with the IMF and foreign bankers, and saying that the stabilization program is being imposed by those institutions. Within limits, it may be useful for the IMF to be held responsible for necessary but unpopular measures. But this is risky for the government, which appears weak and unable to defend national interests. It is undesirable for the international community because other countries may be deterred from approaching the IMF at an early stage when their problems could be dealt with by a less drastic program than will be required if action is postponed.

---

12. Omotunde Johnson and Joanne Salop, "Distributional Aspects of Stabilization Programs in Developing Countries," International Monetary Fund *Staff Papers*, vol. 27 (March 1980), pp. 1–23; Carlos F. Diaz-Alejandro, "Southern Cone Stabilization Plans" and comment by Ronald McKinnon in Cline and Weintraub, *Economic Stabilization in Developing Countries*, pp. 119–46.

In guidelines on conditionality adopted in 1979, the Executive Board of the IMF recognized the political sensitivity of the subject and implicitly noted criticisms of IMF operations in the following careful language: "In helping members to devise adjustment programs [the term that has largely replaced "stabilization programs" in IMF usage], the Fund will pay due regard to the domestic social and political objectives, the economic priorities, and the circumstances of members, including the causes of their balance-of-payments problems." Although this restatement doubtless has influenced operations, stabilization programs continue to rely heavily on management of aggregate demand by the use of fiscal/monetary instruments.

Special Problems of Oil-Exporting Countries

The oil-exporting countries face some special stabilization problems. In the 1970s, these countries provided a dramatic example of a rapid increase in exports resulting from enclave activity by multinational corporations or state enterprises exploiting a natural resource. A significant institutional feature of the major oil-exporting countries is that a large fraction of the value of oil exports consists of state revenue, production costs being relatively small. The state revenue is initially sterilized in the form of state-owned foreign assets that are not matched by income and asset accumulation in the nongovernmental sector.

Under these conditions, the impact of fiscal policy on liquidity and income is best measured by the domestic budget balance rather than the overall budget balance.[13] The domestic budget balance is the difference between domestic expenditures and domestic revenues of government; the overall balance is the algebraic sum of the domestic balance and the foreign budget balance, defined as the difference between government expenditures abroad and revenues from abroad. Oil revenues are classified as revenues from abroad on the assumption that, if they had not been collected by the state, either they would have accrued as profits of nonresidents or the oil price would have been lower. In short, the collection of oil revenues has no direct effect on the income of residents. Government expenditures abroad consist of direct imports, payments for construction and service contracts with nonresident enterprises, and the like. Conceptually, they

13. See David R. Morgan, "Fiscal Policy in Oil Exporting Countries, 1972–78," International Monetary Fund *Staff Papers*, vol. 26 (March 1979), pp. 55–86.

should also include government purchases of imported items supplied by resident enterprises, but it may not be feasible to obtain statistics on these.

Fiscal operations may be expansionary despite an overall budget surplus, reflecting a deficit in the domestic budget balance that is exceeded by a surplus in the foreign budget balance. On the assumption that the government does not borrow from residents, the deficit in the domestic budget will be financed by reduction of deposits with the central bank or conversion of foreign assets into local currency. Money and quasi money (demand deposits and certain nonmonetary liabilities of commercial banks) will increase by the full amount of the domestic budget deficit. Thus the excess of local expenditures will add to domestic income, while the growth of money and quasi money will expand liquidity. The demand for imports will be stimulated, and the inflationary impact will be partly offset by a reduction in the balance-of-payments surplus. Because imports and home goods are not perfect substitutes, spending on home goods also will be stimulated and prices will tend to rise. The analysis would be similar for a country with an overall budget deficit, though the existence of inflation would seem less strange.

After the 1973–74 increase in oil prices, most of the oil-exporting countries greatly increased government expenditures and followed highly expansionary policies. The result was inflation and a rapid reduction in balance-of-payments surpluses. By 1978, the current account balance-of-payments surplus of the major oil-exporting countries as a group had almost disappeared. In the late 1970s, the growth of government expenditures was curtailed, and the inflation rate declined. Following another big increase in oil prices in 1979–80, government spending was again accelerated, but in most oil-exporting countries the shift toward expansionary policies was much less pronounced than in the period after 1973–74. After 1979–80, world demand for oil declined and oil prices softened because of conservation, the substitution of other energy sources for oil, and sluggish or declining activity in industrial countries. By 1982, the large current account surplus in the combined balance of payments of the oil-exporting countries had disappeared.[14] Mexico, Nigeria, Venezuela, and some other oil exporters that had rapidly increased government spending encountered severe financial difficulties.

A country with a strong export position resulting from enclave produc-

14. International Monetary Fund, *World Economic Outlook*, Occasional Paper 9 (Washington, D.C.: IMF, 1982), pp. 45–50, 126–27; and Occasional Paper 12 (Washington, D.C.:IMF, 1983), pp. 46–55, 187–88.

tion suffers less from inflation than other countries do. Indeed, rising prices of home-produced goods are one way in which the benefits percolate through the community. If, however, the authorities do not recognize what is occurring, the price rise may become excessive and may cause an initial balance-of-payments surplus to be eroded at too rapid a rate. Furthermore, the increase in the domestic price and wage level will be an obstacle to modernization through the development of domestic financial intermediaries, the establishment of import substitute industries, and the diversification of exports. Another hazard, revealed by the recent experience of oil exporters, is that rapid growth of government expenditures will entail much waste and will result in a momentum that will be hard to check when the balance of payments weakens.

Summary

Stabilizing fiscal policies in industrial countries have aimed especially at compensating for fluctuations in enterprise investment demand by variations in taxation and government expenditures. The considerable success of these policies from the late 1940s to the early 1970s benefited developing countries by offering them strong markets for exports.

Cyclical fluctuations in less developed countries originate mainly in the balance of payments and political disturbances. These cannot be compensated by stimulating and retarding aggregate demand through fiscal actions. A stabilizing fiscal policy for a less developed primary-producing country can aim at spreading the use of export earnings more evenly over time and thus avoiding disruption of domestic activity. It may rely especially on flexible export taxes, relatively stable government expenditures, and careful management of foreign debt and international reserves. A possible norm for a stabilizing budget policy would set "allowable" government expenditures by reference to a neutral revenue trend and would let actual revenues fluctuate with current exports, thus producing variable budget deficits.

In devising fiscal policies, account should be taken of monetary conditions. Often budget deficits or surpluses in developing countries are accompanied by transactions with the central bank and increases or decreases in reserve money, leading to multiple changes in total bank credit. Central banks cannot realistically be expected to pursue independent policies.

Inflation is a worldwide problem, to which less developed countries tend to be especially susceptible. It is invariably associated with excess money creation, which most often is the counterpart of central bank financing of a government deficit. Hence, strengthening the fiscal system is the most effective way to lessen the inflationary bias evident in many countries. Structuralist arguments that inflation cannot be controlled by fiscal and monetary means are unpersuasive. Nevertheless, they call attention to differences in the real cost of controlling inflation and suggest the need to seek historical, cultural, and political explanations for the persistence of inflation in certain areas, particularly parts of Latin America.

Many developing countries have found it necessary to adopt stabilization programs to correct balance-of-payments deficits, severe and prolonged inflation, and other distortions. Frequently these programs are established with the technical and financial support of the IMF. IMF conditionality in relation to the programs raises controversial issues. Although performance criteria typically take the form of ceilings on domestic bank credit, their observance usually depends primarily on fiscal actions to control the budget deficit. The political aspects of stabilization are sensitive and complex.

Oil-exporting countries encounter special stabilization problems related to the economic character of the petroleum sector. It is largely an enclave generating export income with only limited transactions with the domestic economy. Fiscal policy in the oil-exporting countries should be appraised by reference to the domestic budget balance rather than the overall balance. After the 1973–74 increase in oil prices, large domestic expenditures financed by foreign receipts had an inflationary impact and contributed to the rapid reduction of the balance-of-payments surpluses of the oil exporters. Although an expansionary policy was appropriate, care was needed to prevent excessive and wasteful expenditures and to limit the rise of domestic prices and wages.

CHAPTER TWELVE

Equitable Distribution and the Fiscal System

EQUITABLE has the dual meaning of equal and fair. Emphasis may be placed on equality—or less inequality—in the distribution of income, wealth, or consumption. Or the concern may be with the fairness or legitimacy of economic differences in relation to effort, social contribution, need, or status. The equality interpretation has dominated the economic literature, probably because in principle it is subject to numerical measurement, despite conceptual and statistical difficulties. The other interpretation seems to be influential with political leaders and a wider public. The recent increased attention to poverty may offer an opportunity for bringing the two approaches closer together.

The objective of equitable distribution of the economic product is endorsed by most governments, though its precise meaning is seldom specified. The same forces that promulgate the objective of growth and development impel at least nominal acceptance of the distribution objective. In examining the possible contribution of taxation and government expenditures to equitable distribution, this chapter deals with a major set of instruments, but it does not attempt to evaluate measures such as wage and price regulation, land reform, and nationalization of enterprises or to appraise the effects of changes in the political system.

Interpretations of the Objective

The identification of equity with equality leads to concentration of attention on the relative shares of income, wealth, or consumption accruing to persons or families arrayed in classes such as quintiles, deciles, or percentiles. The distribution often is shown graphically by a Lorenz curve, which plots the cumulative percentage of income (or the other economic variable) against the cumulative percentage of number of units and shows the departure from a diagonal line of complete equality. The departure from equality can be summarized numerically in the Gini index. Other measures of inequality are also employed.[1] According to the equality interpretation, government policies should be directed toward the reduction of differences in relative shares and measures can be evaluated by their contribution to the changes.

Another approach concentrates on poverty, viewed as either absolute or relative deprivation. Long a subject of concern among social reformers and others, the problem received more attention in the 1970s as it became apparent that the number of poor people was increasing and doubts were raised about whether the poor were benefiting from the growth of total income in the developing countries. The provision of basic necessities for the poor is easier to understand than the more abstract goal of lessening inequality of income shares throughout the distribution and seems less threatening to those above the average. The concern with poverty recently has taken the form of a "basic needs approach" to development, which would give first priority to providing everyone certain minimum quantities of food, clothing, shelter, clean water, and sanitation. Although frequently described as absolute or physiological necessities, the basic needs should be seen as rising to some extent as average consumption rises in a particular country and in the world.[2]

A third aspect of equitable distribution, which has attracted support in some developing countries, is reduction of the income and wealth of the rich. Big landowners, foreigners, and members of racial minorities have been the main targets. Actions tend to be episodic and opportunistic rather than part of a continuing formal program.

The three interpretations of the objective of equitable distribution are not completely inconsistent. Clearly, improving the position of the poor or worsening that of the rich reduces to some extent inequalities of relative shares. But the different interpretations suggest that different measures should be emphasized and different standards used to judge their success or failure.

1. Richard Szal and Sherman Robinson, "Measuring Income Inequality," in Charles R. Frank, Jr., and Richard C. Webb, eds., *Income Distribution and Growth in the Less-Developed Countries* (Brookings Institution, 1977), pp. 491–520; William Loehr and John P. Powelson, *The Economics of Development and Distribution* (Harcourt Brace Jovanovich, 1981), pp. 97–126.

2. Paul Streeten and others, *First Things First: Meeting Basic Human Needs in Developing Countries* (Oxford University Press for the World Bank, 1981).

Fiscal Instruments and Distribution

Regardless of which interpretation of equitable distribution is emphasized, fiscal measures are best suited to an incrementalist strategy for
advancing toward the objective. They are not the best instruments for a
sudden redistribution, but over time they can help move the distribution
of income, wealth, and consumption in the desired direction and can be
used to help meet the needs of the poor.

Budget Strategies

Three budget strategies can be visualized in relation to equitable
distribution: (1) an ability-to-pay budget, in which expenditures would be
determined mainly by nondistributional considerations and revenue would
be obtained to the extent feasible from progressive taxes; (2) a redistributive
budget, which would add to normal government expenditures equalizing
expenditures in the form of transfer payments and free services, with
revenue provided by progressive taxes; and (3) a basic needs budget, which
would add to the ability-to-pay approach expenditures designed specifically to meet more fully the basic needs of the poor and to increase their
earning capacity.

The ability-to-pay approach is concerned only secondarily with distribution. Its impact will be weak unless the budget is large in relation to
national income, the tax system is highly progressive, and expenditures
turn out to be favorable to the poor. Theoretically, a redistributive budget
could go far in equalizing relative shares, benefiting the poor, and taxing
the rich, since the size of the budget could be increased to advance the
objectives. Although basic needs is an elastic term, the share of income
received by the lowest one or two quintiles in many developing countries
is so small that well-directed government expenditures could significantly
improve their standard of living without enormously increasing the size of
the budget.

Actual budget policies usually cannot be unambiguously classified as
representing one of the approaches. A nondoctrinaire ability-to-pay approach seems to have been the preference of progressive governments in
many developed and developing countries. Scholars, however, have often
tried to judge policies by strict redistributive standards and have been
disappointed by the results. The basic needs idea has only recently begun
to attract attention, and it is not yet clear how much influence it will exert.

Taxation

The possibility of developing countries' applying markedly progressive tax systems is constrained by administrative and economic factors, as well as political opposition. The conditions recited in chapter 5 limit the role of the individual income tax. When high graduated rates of income tax can be applied, their effect may be attenuated by the outflow of financial capital and by increases in before-tax income that are induced by actual or threatened emigration of persons with large earning capacity. The incidence of the corporation income tax is a subject of dispute. The part of the tax that is collected at the expense of nonresident shareholders and foreign governments (because of the foreign tax credit)—which is considerable in those developing countries that make the heaviest use of the tax—has no effect on income distribution within the taxing country. Excises and customs duties on goods for which the demand is income elastic are progressive but are likely to be only mildly so if substantial amounts of revenue are sought from that source. An agricultural land tax can contribute to progressivity, but the administrative requirements are considerable, and the political obstacles may be especially great where its potential appears most promising because land ownership is highly concentrated. In a few situations, export duties or betterment taxes can add to progressivity.

Because of the difficulty of applying progressive direct taxes and the prevalence of consumption taxes, the tax systems of developing countries are often thought to be regressive. Over the past thirty years, there have been many efforts to confirm or refute this belief by quantitative studies. Surprisingly, the majority of them have concluded that the tax system of the country being studied was to some degree progressive. De Wulf surveyed forty-four studies covering twenty-two developing countries. Twelve of them, because of limited coverage or approach, did not provide a basis for evaluating progressivity. Of the remaining thirty-two studies, twenty-two indicated some progressivity, although it was often uneven and frequently did not extend to the highest income or expenditure brackets. Countries for which such results were reported include Brazil, Colombia, Guatemala, Jamaica, Panama, Peru, Lebanon, Pakistan, and Tanzania (urban population). Eight studies (mainly for Latin American countries) suggested "some wandering proportionality," while two studies (for Greece and the Philippines) found a regressive pattern.[3]

3. Luc De Wulf, "Fiscal Incidence Studies in Developing Countries: Survey and Critique," *International Monetary Fund Staff Papers*, vol. 22 (March 1975), pp. 70, 111–14. The article contains an extensive bibliography.

These findings should be viewed cautiously, as De Wulf emphasizes.[4] There are at least four serious problems with quantitative studies of tax incidence: (1) the poor quality or absence of statistics on income distribution; (2) the uncertainty as to whether statistics on income, expenditures, and taxes for one year—when available—are representative of long-run conditions and the experience of people over their life cycle; (3) unsettled questions in the theory of tax incidence; and (4) the neglect of the influence of taxation on the before-tax distribution of income. These problems, except for the first, are equally great for studies of more developed countries and of less developed countries.

The findings can best be interpreted as estimates of "differential incidence," that is, the difference between the actual tax system and a hypothetical proportional system yielding the same amount of revenue. The absolute incidence of the tax system cannot be ascertained because it is impossible to visualize how the economy would operate and income would be distributed if there were no taxes. Even a moderate change in the amount of taxation must entail a change in government expenditures or in nontax financing, which will affect economic activity and may alter income distribution.[5]

The studies do not describe observed facts about the amount of taxes borne, directly and indirectly, by individuals or groups. At best, they are careful and systematic summaries in numerical form of the authors' hypotheses concerning tax incidence. Some of the better studies alert users to the unsettled theoretical issues and show how alternative assumptions about the incidence of particular taxes would affect the results. The statistical exercises can be enlightening and useful, but their nature and limitations should be understood.

Even if the problems mentioned are put to one side, a finding that a tax system is progressive does not necessarily mean that it has much influence on income distribution. Table 12-1 has been constructed to illustrate the point. It shows a hypothetical distribution of income among three broad groups in a developing country with a high degree of inequality, which is fairly representative of such countries for which estimates have been compiled.[6] Two sets of effective tax rates were applied to the before-tax

4. See also Richard M. Bird and Luc De Wulf, "Taxation and Income Distribution in Latin America: A Critical Review of Empirical Studies," International Monetary Fund *Staff Papers*, vol. 20 (November 1973), pp. 639–82.

5. Richard A. Musgrave, *The Theory of Public Finance: A Study in Public Economy* (McGraw-Hill, 1959), pp. 212–13.

6. Montek S. Ahluwalia, "Income Inequality: Some Dimensions of the Problem," in Hollis Chenery and others, *Redistribution with Growth* (Oxford University Press for the World Bank and the Institute of Development Studies, University of Sussex, 1974), pp. 8–9.

Table 12-1. *Hypothetical Distribution of Income and Effective Tax Rates for Households by Income Level in a Developing Country with High Inequality*[a]

Percent

Item	Lowest 40%	Middle 40%	Top 20%	Total
Share of income before taxes	10.0	25.0	65.0	100.0
Effective tax rate				
System A	7.6	8.9	17.7	14.5
System B	3.8	8.9	24.6	18.6
Share of income after taxes				
System A	10.9	26.6	62.6	100.0
System B	11.8	28.0	60.2	100.0

a. For explanation, see text.

distribution. System A was derived from McLure's careful study of the incidence of taxes in Colombia in 1970.[7] The effective rates cover all taxes, including coffee export duties, and are based on the assumption that the corporation income tax and retained earnings of corporations should be attributed to Colombian shareholders. Colombia's income distribution is highly unequal—not very different from the hypothetical one—and its tax system is generally regarded as unusually progressive for a developing country. Nevertheless, the distribution of income after taxes does not differ much from the distribution before taxes.

System B illustrates the impact of a more progressive system incorporating (1) lighter taxes than in system A on households with the lowest incomes and (2) heavier taxes on the top quintile, while taxes on the middle-income group are the same as in system A and total tax revenue is greater. The effective tax rate for the lowest-income group is half that in system A, which would require a quite different structure of indirect taxes. The effective rate of the top income group was obtained by substituting for the estimated effective rate of Colombian individual income tax the estimate by Pechman and Okner of the effective rate of individual income taxes (federal, state, and local) on families in the highest quintile in the United States in 1966.[8] The differences in shares of income after taxes under the two systems reflect both the much more progressive effective tax

7. Charles E. McLure, Jr., "The Incidence of Colombian Taxes: 1970," *Economic Development and Cultural Change*, vol. 24 (October 1975), pp. 155–83. The effective rates are those for McLure's assumption a. The rates shown in table 12-1 were derived from distributions obtained by logarithmic interpolation.

8. Joseph A. Pechman and Benjamin A. Okner, *Who Bears the Tax Burden?* (Brookings Institution, 1974), pp. 53, 56, 61. The effective rate is for incidence variant 1c, the most progressive.

rates of system B and its greater revenue yield. Even with system B, the distribution of after-tax income would be highly unequal, much more unequal than in the most egalitarian developing countries or in industrial countries for which information is available. In the Republic of Korea, for example, the shares of disposable income of the two lowest quintiles and the top quintile in 1976 have been estimated at 17 percent and 45 percent, respectively. In eleven industrial countries, the average shares of these groups were 19 percent and 40 percent, respectively, according to estimates for various years in the late 1960s and the 1970s.[9]

The income tax included in system B no doubt goes well beyond what could realistically be expected in the great majority of developing countries. No allowances are made for political opposition, inadequate administration, evasion, or changes in the distribution of income before taxes. Steep rates of income tax would be imposed on families whose income is high relative to the average in their own country but low in comparison with that of more developed countries. For example, the top quintile in Colombia in 1970 began at a household income equivalent to approximately $1,040, whereas in the United States in 1966 the top quintile began at an adjusted family income of more than $15,600.[10]

Expenditures

A government that is concerned about equitable distribution should look not only to taxation but also to its expenditures. But the conceptual problems of allocating expenditures for goods and services are even greater than those relating to tax incidence. Theories comparable to those built up for tax incidence over centuries do not exist for expenditure allocation. As explained in chapter 3, the analysis at present has to be limited to some plausible statements and a numerical display of the implications of allocating expenditures on the basis of money flows or the presumed intentions of government. A more fundamental allocation of benefits as distinguished from costs and a full analysis of the impact on prices and income payments are not yet feasible.

Transfer payments, abstractly viewed, are the neatest means of improving the distribution of income and consumption through the budget. Their allocation to recipients is clear; hence the issue of distinguishing between

9. Unweighted arithmetic means of country statistics, derived from World Bank, *World Development Report 1982* (Oxford University Press, 1982), pp. 159, 171.

10. Amounts in U.S. dollars. For other illustrative calculations, see Arnold C. Harberger, "Fiscal Policy and Income Redistribution," in Frank and Webb, *Income Distribution and Growth in Less-Developed Countries*, pp. 264–74.

costs and benefits does not arise. Transfer payments, however, are a much smaller fraction of government expenditures in developing countries than in industrial countries. The difference is accounted for mainly by the smaller scale of social security and welfare expenditures in the developing countries.

In many developing countries, the analogue of transfer payments for welfare purposes is consumer subsidies provided by pricing foods, petroleum products, public utility services, and certain other items below production cost or below world market prices. These subsidies often are rationalized as a protection for the poor, but they are seldom restricted to the poor. Usually they benefit the urban population much more than the rural population, whose average income is lower. They encourage wasteful consumption and misuse. Food subsidies made possible by imports or price controls on domestic production have been harmful to agricultural prosperity. Governments frequently have had to cut back subsidies when adopting stabilization programs.

Sri Lanka's experience with food subsidies is interesting and ambiguous. Food rationing was instituted during World War II and continued after the war. A rice ration was provided partly free and partly at a subsidized price. Wheat flour was subsidized throughout the 1970s and sugar after 1973. The program covered rural as well as urban areas. In the early 1970s, the ration was estimated to provide about 20 percent of the total caloric intake of the poorest families and to be equivalent to about 14 percent of their income. Although it is hard to isolate the effect of the food policies, they apparently contributed to the good performance of Sri Lanka in certain social indicators, including life expectancy and infant mortality, which was much superior to that of other countries with similar per capita income. Nonetheless, the food subsidies absorbed a large part of the budget and seem to have discouraged domestic cereal production.

Unlike most other developing countries, Sri Lanka instituted an income criterion for its rice subsidy in 1972, when income tax payers and their dependents (about 10 percent of the population) were made ineligible for the free ration. In 1978 a new government, faced by balance-of-payments and budget problems, restricted the free rice ration and the subsidized sugar ration to families in the lower half of the income distribution. In 1979 a food stamp and kerosene stamp program was substituted for the ration system with the income restriction on eligibility retained. Although several foods were covered and unused stamps could be converted into savings deposits, most of the stamps were used to purchase rice. Income declarations were subject to check by local officials, but in 1981 an official report stated that there were reasons to believe that as many as one-third of the beneficiaries were ineligible because their incomes exceeded prescribed limits.[11]

Government expenditures for goods and services can contribute to equitable distribution by supplementing current real consumption and by improving earning capacity. The latter function is the more attractive because its effects are more lasting and because it can increase the social product instead of merely redistributing income. It is also more acceptable to those who interpret equity in terms of fairness or equality of opportunity rather than equality of results.

Expenditures for education appear to be a promising means of promoting more equitable distribution. The positive correlation between earnings and educational attainment is well established.[12] The extension of free or subsidized schooling to persons who otherwise would not be educated because they are members of poor families can be expected to increase their lifetime earning power. In effect, the beneficiaries would be endowed with human capital. Although the differential between the earnings of the educated and uneducated might be narrowed, the resulting impairment of the relative positions of the previously educated would be likely to be resisted less strongly than other forms of redistribution of income and wealth. Equity interpreted as fairness or equality of opportunity would be enhanced, and equity in the sense of reduced inequality of economic position might also be served, though that is less clear because the most gifted persons would be best able to take advantage of educational opportunities and would earn more than others.[13]

This picture, however, is too rosy. Government expenditures for education, though substantial, are skewed toward secondary and higher education in many developing countries while primary education is still not available to all. Rural areas are less well provided than urban areas with schools, and the quality usually is poorer. Although the percentage of children between the ages of six and eleven who were in school in

11. Paul Isenman, "Basic Needs: The Case of Sri Lanka," *World Development*, vol. 8 (March 1980), pp. 237–58; Ministry of Plan Implementation, Food and Nutrition Policy Planning Division, *Evaluation Report of the Food Stamp Scheme* (Colombo: Government of Sri Lanka, Ministry of Plan Implementation, 1981), pp. 35–36, 41, passim.

12. For a convenient summary of research findings, see George Psacharopoulos, "Returns to Education: An Updated International Comparison," *Comparative Education*, vol. 17 (1981), pp. 321–41.

13. On the scanty available evidence, see Loehr and Powelson, *Economics of Development and Distribution*, pp. 228–33.

developing countries increased from 47 percent to 62 percent between 1960 and 1975, the absolute number not enrolled grew by 11 million. Enrollment in higher education, which is far more costly than primary education, increased more rapidly. In 1975, 32 percent of total educational expenditures were for higher education, which enrolled only 3 percent of all students. Unit costs in higher education in 1970–73 were twenty-four times unit costs in primary schools in developing countries, whereas in OECD countries the ratio was 3.4:1.[14]

Access to primary and especially secondary schools by the poor often is limited by fees, while no fees are charged the more privileged persons who attend universities. For example, in Kenya the annual fees for secondary schools are approximately equal to the per capita national income, whereas university students pay no fees and receive allowances to cover their living costs.[15] Other costs, particularly the forgone earnings of pupils, are more burdensome to poor families than to the more prosperous. Frequently school certificates or diplomas are used as a screening or rationing device for jobs in government or public enterprises without close attention to the actual requirements of the work. And pay for the jobs may be kept at artificially high levels in the face of urban unemployment. Such considerations led one writer to conclude that "the educational systems of most developing nations act to increase rather than to decrease . . . income inequalities."[16]

Regardless of whether the judgment just quoted is correct, it seems clear that steps could be taken to make educational expenditures serve better the basic needs of the majority without diluting their contribution to growth. In many countries, higher priority should be given to the extension of primary education and the improvement of rural schools. Primary and secondary schooling should be less formalistic and literary than it is in many developing countries but need not be vocational. In a period of rapid technological and social change, general education is likely to be more useful than vocational training, which often is poor in quality, narrow in content, and subject to obsolescence. The spread of education may indirectly advance equitable distribution by making people

14. World Bank, *Education Sector Policy Paper*, 3d ed. (Washington, D.C.: World Bank, 1980), pp. 70, 102–06, 122–23.

15. Loehr and Powelson, *Economics of Development and Distribution*, p. 234.

16. Michael P. Todaro, *Economic Development in the Third World*, 2d ed. (Longman, 1977), p. 312. Chapter 11 of Todaro's book contains a good discussion of the economics of education, taking a somewhat more skeptical view than is presented here. Psacharopoulos, "Returns to Education," pp. 331–32, criticizes the arguments that question the productivity of education.

readier to take advantage of other public services and by broadening political participation.

Ideally, a large part of the cost of higher education should be covered by fees, with loans available to students who are unable to pay. Nearly all university graduates receive higher income than the average taxpayer. Financing by fees along with loans, however, appears to depart too far from established practices to be politically acceptable and would involve administrative problems. An alternative that may be more acceptable is to extend the system in effect in some countries that requires graduates to spend some years working in rural areas or performing national service at a low rate of remuneration.

Government expenditures for health services and sanitation are an essential component of a basic needs budget. Their influence on relative income shares above the poverty level is unclear but presumably is somewhat equalizing because the earning capacity of the near-poor and low-middle income groups is improved. Health conditions are worse in rural areas than in urban areas as indicated by crude death rates, infant mortality, and the prevalence of intestinal parasitic and vector-borne diseases. The rural areas usually are poorly served by health and sanitation programs. Government expenditures for health tend to be devoted disproportionately to hospitals in urban areas and to medical education, which together consume as much as two-thirds of the health budget in many developing countries. A basic needs budget would give higher priority to simple and accessible health centers staffed by mid-level health workers. Subsidies and educational programs to encourage construction of simple privies and village wells and installation of pumps are cost-effective means of reducing chronic and debilitating intestinal parasitic diseases, which impair the productivity of the poor, and preventing acute diarrheal illnesses, typhoid, and cholera. Programs to combat vector-borne tropical diseases including malaria, sleeping sickness, Chagas' disease, schistosomiasis (bilharzia), and onchocerciasis (river blindness) are more expensive but can also improve productivity in poor areas.[17]

Labor-intensive rural public works can serve the dual function of immediately supplementing the income of those employed and of creating assets that will yield future returns in the form of measured income and amenities. These might include local roads and paths, drainage, small-scale irrigation works, wells, privies, and some buildings. To be successful,

17. This paragraph draws on World Bank, *Health Sector Policy Paper*, 2d ed. (Washington, D.C.: World Bank, 1980).

a program would require careful planning and execution. So far as feasible, the work should be timed to occur during the agricultural slack season. Some outside financing from national tax revenue or foreign aid would be required. Political skill and determination would be needed to ensure that the projects were not selected and designed to benefit mainly the rural elite.[18]

Although public works proposals of this kind have been discussed for a long time, they have won little acceptance. The projects would be less dramatic than large-scale projects, and the technical, financial, and political requirements would be considerable. Sometimes it is alleged that labor-intensive construction methods are more costly than capital-intensive methods even for projects of the kind suggested. For example, in Kenya, a study by consultants concluded that a highly capital-intensive method of building rural roads would be cheaper than a highly labor-intensive method, even assuming a shadow wage well below the prevailing wage. However, a review by an International Labor Office mission pointed out that mixed methods could be less costly than either the most capital-intensive or most labor-intensive method.[19] Further research on the subject would be desirable.

Government expenditures for family planning programs, though small in amount, can appreciably influence average income per capita and income distribution. A reduction in fertility will be partly offset by a decline in the death rate but can be expected to reduce the rate of population growth. In time, the smaller labor supply, combined with stocks of physical capital and land as large or larger than otherwise would have existed, may result in a smaller aggregate national income but a larger per capita income (because the marginal product of labor is above zero but below the average product). On certain assumptions— a very low marginal product of unskilled labor and favorable effects on investment in physical and human capital—aggregate national income could be increased. A number of studies have reported impressively high benefit-cost ratios for expenditures that reduce birth rates, without allowance for effects on income distribution. The reduction in births owing to both the information and service components of programs to

18. John P. Lewis, "Designing the Public Works Mode of Anti-Poverty Policy," in Frank and Webb, *Income Distribution and Growth in Less-Developed Countries*, pp. 337–78.

19. *Employment, Incomes and Equality: a Strategy for Increasing Productive Employment in Kenya*, Report of an Inter-Agency Team Organized by the International Labor Office (Geneva: ILO, 1972), pp. 385–90. For references to other studies of road building, see Loehr and Powelson, *Economics of Development and Distribution*, p. 184.

promote contraception and sterilization will be greater in middle- and low-income groups (but perhaps not the lowest) than in high-income groups. The tendency for poor families to have more children than other families will be lessened, income per family member will be increased, and inequality will be reduced.[20]

There have been fewer statistical studies of the distribution of benefits of government expenditures than of tax incidence. The studies that have been made usually distribute the costs of government programs among the users or intended beneficiaries. Thus they omit the more interesting and significant questions of how current and future incomes are affected. For example, the benefits of educational expenditures would be equated with current costs and attributed to families with children in school, without regard to any influence on the current earnings of teachers or the future earnings of different groups. Typically, about one-third of government expenditures of developing countries are for general administration and defense, which cannot be assigned to individuals and which usually are arbitrarily allocated on a per capita basis or in proportion to income.

Most of the studies surveyed by De Wulf indicated that benefits of government expenditures were regressively distributed, that is, that the benefits declined as a percentage of income over successively higher income classes. The results were heavily influenced by the assumption made about general expenditures, but a generally regressive pattern appeared for Brazil, Colombia, and Puerto Rico, even when the benefits of these expenditures were allocated in proportion to income. Five studies that gave separate estimates for items other than general expenditures agreed in showing a regressive pattern for Brazil, Colombia, Panama, and Puerto Rico (two studies).[21]

Estimates such as these, which attempt to attribute to households the benefits of all government expenditures, considered together, are even more precarious than estimates for particular programs. As it is impossible to visualize a contemporary society wholly without government expenditures, there is no meaningful zero-expenditure base against which the estimates can be set. A similar problem in regard to taxes has been circumvented by the differential-incidence concept, but it is hard to

20. See Bryan L. Boulier, "Population Policy and Income Distribution," in Frank and Webb, *Income Distribution and Growth in Less-Developed Countries*, pp. 159–213.
21. De Wulf, "Fiscal Incidence Studies in Developing Countries," pp. 90–92, 118–19.

describe a neutral set of expenditures analagous to the hypothetical proportional tax system underlying differential tax incidence.

Net Budget Incidence

Combining estimates of the distribution of taxes and benefits from government expenditures, several studies have obtained estimates of net fiscal incidence or net budget incidence. The pattern that emerges is a net excess of benefits over taxes that is sizable in relation to income in low brackets, declines over middle brackets, and disappears in upper brackets, to be replaced by a net excess of taxes. This has been reported for Argentina, Brazil, Colombia, Guatemala, Panama, Puerto Rico, and West Malaysia.[22] These findings, clearly, are subject to all the weaknesses of their two major components. Also, they may be misleading because the total amount of benefits allocated is larger than the amount of taxes, the difference being made up by nontax revenues, borrowing, or money creation.

In summary, it seems that statistical studies of tax incidence, though subject to reservations, are useful for stating succinctly judgments about the distributional impact of the tax system, whereas the problems relating to estimates of expenditure benefits and net budget incidence are so serious that their meaning is highly questionable. At present, qualitative statements, supplemented by partial data on the utilization of government services, appear to be more informative than statistical estimates of the benefits from expenditures or net budget incidence.

The Tradeoff between Equity and Growth

An opinion long held by most economists is that every gain in equality of distribution is obtained at the cost of less growth. The principal reason that has been adduced is that progressive taxation will curtail saving and capital formation. A second argument is that progressive taxes adversely affect incentives to work and invest. Also, redistributional expenditures, whether for transfer payments or for goods and services, may compound the bad effects on incentives to work because they weaken the link between individual earnings and consumption. The inference often drawn is that in the long run everyone, including the poor, will be worse off if redistribution is attempted.

22. Ibid., pp. 92–95, 120–21.

In chapter 10, reasons were advanced for thinking that the argument about saving and capital formation may be less weighty than it appears. In summary, marginal saving rates may not rise with income as much as assumed, if at all; household savings may be held in forms that do not finance investment in the country where the savers reside; and government saving or dissaving may be large enough to overwhelm any differences in the impact of alternative taxes on household saving. To these points may be added two recurrent themes of this book—the importance of additions to the stock of human capital, which are not included in customary definitions of saving and investment; and the possible contribution to growth, especially in developing countries, of productive consumption, which enhances working capacity.

An interesting study by Cline illustrates how a reduction of saving caused by a redistributive policy might affect growth and the position of the poor in Argentina, Brazil, Venezuela, and Mexico. He assumed that income in these countries would be redistributed to the extent required to establish the degree of inequality prevailing in the United Kingdom, which would involve big changes. He then estimated the impact on saving, using assumptions favorable to the thesis that it would be reduced. This was done by fitting nonlinear consumption/saving functions. For Venezuela, however, the best fit was for a linear function, indicating that redistribution would not affect saving. Next, on the basis of a simple Harrod-Domar model, which attributes growth entirely to saving/investment, Cline estimated the effect on growth. He found that, on the assumptions adopted, growth rates would be reduced by large fractions in Argentina, Brazil, and Mexico. Nevertheless, for many years the absolute income of the poorest 70 percent of the population would remain higher than it would have been without redistribution—for thirty-four years in Argentina, fifty-six years in Brazil, and forty-nine years in Mexico.[23]

As Cline recognized, his assumptions produced a highly simplified set of economic relationships and abstracted from the practical difficulties of redistributing income by fiscal measures. He appears to be justified in asserting that his calculations yielded a high estimate of the harm to growth operating through saving. On the other hand, they did not take account of

---

23. William R. Cline, *Potential Effects of Income Redistribution on Economic Growth: Latin American Cases* (Praeger, 1972), pp. 136–52. In a later publication, Cline reviewed a number of other simulation studies and concluded that they indicate that "redistribution of income would have a largely neutral effect on economic growth." See his "Distribution and Development: A Survey of Literature," *Journal of Development Economics*, vol. 1 (February 1975), pp. 378–87, 394–95.

possible bad effects on work incentives or good effects on human productivity.

There is some statistical evidence casting doubt on the existence of a tradeoff between the satisfaction of basic needs and economic growth. In a study of the experience of a large number of developing countries in 1960–73, Hicks found that literacy and primary school enrollment in 1960 were positively related to the growth of per capita GNP in 1960–73 and were statistically significant in equations explaining growth that also included imports and investment. The increase in literacy in 1960–73 was also positively related to growth in the same period and statistically significant; however, the increase in school enrollment was negatively related to growth but not statistically significant when combined with other variables. Growth was also positively related to life expectancy in 1960. The interpretation of the findings, however, is subject to the usual uncertainty in distinguishing cause from effect and to statistical problems. The separate influence of the basic needs variables cannot be clearly identified because they were positively related to each other and to the economic variables; furthermore, all these variables were positively related to per capita income in 1960, and the growth rate in 1960–73 was positively related to per capita income at the beginning of the period.[24]

An evaluation of the tradeoff between equitable distribution and growth can be formalized by adopting a weighted measure of growth. It may not be generally appreciated that GNP or GDP growth rates reflect the weights implied by the existing distribution of income. This is true in two senses. First, a dollar, a peso, or a rupee of income is counted the same regardless of who receives it. Second, the prices of the product reflect the demand and cost structures generated by the existing distribution. If the poorest 40 percent of families receive only 10 percent of total income, what happens to them will have little influence on the GNP or GDP growth rate. One alternative weighting would assign equal social value to a 1 percent change in the income of each member of society, making the weights for each percentile equal because they include equal numbers of people (or households). Thus on the basis of the hypothetical distribution shown in table 12–1, a 1 percent increase in income of the poorest 40 percent of households would be given twice the weight of a 1 percent increase for the top 20 percent, although the absolute amount of the latter would be six and one-half times as great. Another alternative would be to adopt "poverty

24. Norman L. Hicks, "Growth vs. Basic Needs: Is There a Trade-Off?" *World Development*, vol. 7 (November/December 1979), pp. 985–94.

weights," giving still greater emphasis to what happens to the poor. The rationale of the alternative weights is that they are better indicators of welfare than the market weights implied by GNP statistics.

In general, a comparison of the alternative index and the GNP growth rate will show how well a country has succeeded in reconciling equality with growth. According to Ahluwalia and Chenery, such a comparison shows that, for various periods in the 1950s and 1960s, growth measured by the alternative weights was lower than the GNP growth rate in Panama, Brazil, Mexico, and Venezuela; the alternative measures exceeded the GNP growth rate in Colombia, El Salvador, Sri Lanka, and Taiwan; and the two indexes were about the same in Korea, the Philippines, Yugoslavia, Peru, and India. If the weighting approach is accepted, it may be concluded that the widely used GNP growth rate overstates the performance of the first group of countries, understates that of the second group, and is about right for the third group. Furthermore, while the average GNP growth rate of Panama, Brazil, Mexico, and Venezuela exceeded that of Colombia, El Salvador, Sri Lanka, and Taiwan (7.3 percent compared with 6.0 percent), the alternative index giving equal weights to each quintile is greater for the second group of countries (7.4 percent compared with 6.0 percent).[25] Although growth and distribution in the thirteen countries no doubt were influenced by their fiscal systems, the statistics relate to income before taxes and exclude real income in the form of government services. Hence, they do not reflect the impact of net budget incidence.

Summary

Equitable distribution may be interpreted as greater equality of relative income shares, alleviation of poverty, or a reduction in the income and wealth of the rich. Fiscal instruments can serve the objective, however interpreted, but are not well suited for bringing about big changes quickly.

Because of constraints on the use of progressive taxation, the tax systems of developing countries are commonly believed to be regressive. The majority of statistical studies of tax incidence, however, have reported some degree of progressivity. These findings should be viewed cautiously because of unsettled theoretical questions and statistical weaknesses. Even

25. Montek S. Ahluwalia and Hollis Chenery, "The Economic Framework," in Chenery and others, *Redistribution with Growth*, pp. 41–42. The poverty weights applied by the authors were 0.6 for the lowest 40 percent of income recipients, 0.3 for the middle 40 percent, and 0.1 for the top 20 percent.

if the difficulties are overlooked, the impact on relative disposable income shares of the existing tax systems or of systems including heavier progressive income taxes is unlikely to be impressive. Although the relative position of the poor may be improved, their absolute consumption cannot be increased by progressive taxation alone.

A government that is concerned about equitable distribution should consider whether its expenditures can be shaped to further the objective. Transfer payments for that purpose are not well adapted to the conditions of developing countries. Consumer subsidies are common but are inefficient. Certain expenditures for goods and services can supplement private consumption and can improve the earning capacity of beneficiaries. Educational expenditures appear to be especially promising in the latter respect but often fail to realize their potential. Other forms of government spending that can help satisfy basic needs and improve distribution are expenditures for health services and sanitation, labor-intensive rural public works, and family planning.

Statistical studies of the allocation of benefits of government expenditures are subject to even greater conceptual difficulties than studies of tax incidence. The available studies distribute costs among presumed immediate beneficiaries but do not measure the more significant effects on current and future earnings. Their usefulness and that of estimates of net budget incidence are questionable.

Gains in equality of distribution may have a cost in less growth because of adverse effects on saving and incentives. The terms of the tradeoff—and indeed its existence—are uncertain. Emphasis on the satisfaction of basic needs appears to be less threatening to growth than a radical redistribution of income would be. It should be recognized that growth rates of GNP or GDP are implicitly weighted by existing unequal income shares. Alternative more egalitarian weights would give a different perspective.

CHAPTER THIRTEEN

Making Policies Effective and Efficient

BOTH the literature of public finance and economic development and the deliberations of ministers and officials are, in general, preoccupied with the elaboration of policies and little concerned with how they can be carried out effectively and efficiently. A policy may be distinguished from a declaration of intention to respond to a need unsupported by action. Such declarations—which often appear in presidential and ministerial speeches, medium-term plans, and legislative acts—are part of symbolic politics. They have their uses but are not policies properly speaking. A policy is a decision plus action to carry it out. It is effective to the degree to which the intentions are realized, and it is efficient if effectiveness is attained at reasonable cost in scarce resources or sacrifice of other objectives. Performance of the traditional functions of the state and fulfillment of the four major economic objectives—growth and development, stability, equitable distribution, and national independence—require many policies.

In the preceding chapters, policies that employ fiscal instruments have been discussed, and judgments have been made about their probable effectiveness and efficiency. This final chapter contains a general discussion of conditions bearing on the effectiveness and efficiency of fiscal policies. The field is vast, and the points covered are treated in summary fashion without detailed examination of differences among countries. Few of the problems identified are unique to the less developed countries, but they face special difficulties in dealing with them and can less afford frustration and waste than can more developed countries.

Aspirations and Accomplishments

Throughout the world many government declarations of intentions are never carried out, because nothing is done or because the action taken is ineffective. Other intentions are partly realized but at high cost. The reasons for these failures are too varied and complex to catalog. Important factors in many cases appear to be the high expectations about the responsibilities and capacities of government, inadequate understanding of the intrinsic difficulties of accomplishing the desired results, lack of needed information, and inconsistencies of policies.

Weaknesses in the formulation and execution of policies occur in all countries but are especially noticeable in developing countries. Writing on South Asia in 1967, Myrdal characterized the countries of the region as "soft states." In his words:

> We mean that, throughout the region, national governments require extraordinarily little of their citizens. There are few obligations either to do things in the interest of the community or to avoid actions opposed to that interest. Even those obligations that do exist are enforced inadequately if at all. This low level of social discipline is one of the most fundamental differences between the South Asian countries today and Western countries at the beginning of their industrialization.[1]

Although Myrdal's comments may strike many readers as excessively Eurocentric or patronizing, probably most will agree that they refer to conditions that help account for the gaps between aspirations and accomplishments in much of the developing world and consequent frustrations. Observers from both Western industrial countries and less developed countries have asserted that in the latter countries people—including many political leaders and government officials—are motivated by a strong sense of identification with the interests of their immediate and extended families and tribal, linguistic, or regional groups and often are little concerned with wider community or national interests. Weak devotion to the ideal of disinterested public service, however, does not necessarily distinguish the less developed countries from the more developed ones. Many Western scholars find the hypothesis of self-interest as a motivation of political and

---

1. Gunnar Myrdal, *Asian Drama: An Inquiry into the Poverty of Nations*, vol. 2 (New York: Twentieth Century Fund, 1968), pp. 895–96. See also Myrdal's *The Challenge of World Poverty* (Vintage, 1971), pp. 208–52.

administrative behavior both empirically serviceable and ethically accept-able for their own countries.

The social attitudes and institutions of the least developed countries and some of the middle-income countries are basically those of preindus-trial societies as influenced by the colonial experience. Voluntary cooper-ation with the government could not be expected to flourish during the colonial period, and resistance to authority was inculcated in countries that went through a struggle for independence. The contemporary aspi-rations of political leaders and ordinary citizens have been formed by the dissemination of modern political ideas and the international demonstra-tion effect on public and private consumption desires. Programs being undertaken by governments of less developed countries, and modern fiscal measures, depend for their success on the cooperation of the public and the discipline and probity of civil servants, reinforced by only occasional application of sanctions.

Poverty is a general cause of policy ineffectiveness, especially in the least developed countries. It limits the means of carrying out government decisions just as it restricts household consumption and enterprise invest-ment. The shortage of trained persons in these countries, which is aggra-vated by emigration to richer countries, hinders the execution of all policies. High rates of illiteracy, which typically accompany poverty, complicate the application of modern forms of taxation. So also does the absence of reliable accounting on the part of enterprises. Poor postal and telephone services and underdeveloped banking systems often force taxpayers to spend much time in queues waiting to obtain information, file returns, and make payments; poor communications also delay governmental disburse-ments and the completion of accounts and reports. The lack of adequate demographic and economic statistics may deprive decisionmakers and administrators of basic information for policy formulation and evaluation.

But some governments are more successful than others in overcoming the obstacles. This is evidenced by differences in growth rates of similarly endowed countries, in the degree of economic instability, in economic inequality, and in the satisfaction of basic needs. More qualitatively, differences in effectiveness and efficiency are reflected also in the reputation of governments among informed observers, their credit standing, the extent of reported waste and corruption, and the apparent quality of public services. A number of more or less objective indicators can be used to evaluate fiscal performance. They include the size of the budget deficit in relation to expenditures and national income, the existence or absence of a unified or comprehensive budget, the informational value of the classification of expenditures and revenues, the accuracy of budget estimates, the proportion of revenue obtained from modern taxes, revenue buoyancy, the international tax comparison index, the size of tax arrears, the promptness with which government accounts are issued, and the existence or absence of audit reports and of action on them.

Policy Formulation

Fundamental to effectiveness and efficiency is the character of the policies adopted. Policy formulation includes the selection of one or more objectives and the choice of an action or actions to carry out the decision, though the means of implementation need not be specified in detail in advance. The clarity and realism of policy formulation are vital to success.

A writer on public administration has asserted that in less developed countries the character of the political process frequently causes political leaders to fail to formulate clear and enforceable policies. Administrators try to fill the gaps and in doing so engage in essentially political action. "When this happens," the writer observes, "politicians discover that the laws and rules they adopt, thinking they are policies, are not actually carried out" and often assume that the failure is due to willful obstruction. The politicians then become excessively involved in the details of administration, sacrificing a distinction between politics and administration that is useful and characteristic of highly developed systems, though never complete.[2]

Although policy formulation and administration are conceptually distinguishable activities, it is debatable whether they can be separated in practice and assigned to different persons. Indeed, the writer quoted in the preceding paragraph concedes that "the normal condition in human history has not been to separate politics and administration."[3] It is true, nevertheless, that the failure to formulate policies clearly at the outset can result in ineffectiveness or inefficiency and in the casual resolution of important questions by subordinates who are insensitive to the intentions of those who initiated the policies. Dissatisfaction with the results of poorly formulated policies may be partly responsible for the tendency in devel-

2. Fred W. Riggs, *Administration in Developing Countries: The Theory of Prismatic Society* (Houghton Mifflin, 1964), pp. 55–56.
3. Ibid., p. 54.

oping countries to give ministers and senior officials great discretionary power for carrying out certain tax and expenditure policies. The consequence, however, is loss of predictability and overburdening of these persons.

Tinbergen has emphasized the advantages of clear formulation of intention and specification of action. His theory of economic policy holds that economic variables can be classified as targets or instruments, instruments being the means of reaching targets or objectives, and that there must be an equal number of targets and instruments.[4] This theory is highly convenient for builders of econometric models (among whom Tinbergen was a distinguished pioneer) because it calls attention to the requirement of an equal number of structural equations and unknowns to ensure that the system is determinate but not overdetermined. For others it is less useful. A major weakness is the difficulty of defining targets and instruments. In regard to taxes, for example, should the target be thought of as an amount of revenue to be raised, a contribution to one of the broader economic objectives, or a means of reaching a narrower objective? Is the individual income tax an instrument, or are each of its rate brackets, exemptions, deductions, and credits the relevant instruments? With a little ingenuity it usually will be possible to satisfy the formal requirement of matching targets and instruments, but that may not significantly aid policy formulation. Nevertheless, the theory does point to the need to consider carefully whether the means are available for carrying out a decision. Specifically, it may alert decisionmakers to the risk that a policy will be ineffective or inefficient because the preferred instrument for carrying it out has been preempted for another purpose.

A sound principle in policy formulation is to economize on scarce resources. This applies first of all to the decisionmaking process itself. Because of limitations on the time and the information available to senior persons and on human intellectual capacity, an incrementalist approach has advantages over the classical model that calls for an explicit statement of objectives and a systematic comparison of a full range of alternative measures for reaching them. Incrementalism usually relies on a series of small and reversible changes in expenditure programs, taxation, and financial administration rather than on the occasional introduction of sweeping reforms. Its supporters consider satisfactory results a more realistic goal than optimal results. Although this approach lessens the cost

4. Jan Tinbergen, *On the Theory of Economic Policy* (Amsterdam: North-Holland, 1952), and Tinbergen, *Economic Policy: Principles and Design* (Amsterdam: North-Holland, 1956).

of decisionmaking and reduces the risk of big mistakes, it has a conservative bias that may inhibit needed changes.

The desirability of economy in the use of skilled civil servants will be generally acknowledged. In practice, this is frequently given too little attention when new expenditure programs or tax provisions are under consideration. For example, a government may overlook or underestimate the additional staff time required for verifying compliance with a sales tax having multiple rates and exemptions compared with a uniform tax. Also it may neglect the cost in staff time of continuing procurement practices that are more formalistic than functional and taxes that yield trivial amounts of revenue.

Much less consideration typically is given to the demands that government procurement and tax measures place on persons in other sectors. This subject has not been extensively studied. However, research in the United Kingdom indicates that the household and enterprise sectors' costs in time required to comply with the income tax and value-added tax are substantial.[5]

Another scarce resource is the willingness of taxpayers to comply. That no doubt is influenced by factors such as attitudes toward the government and evaluations of public spending and especially by assessments of the risk that evasion will be detected and penalized. To encourage compliance, therefore, audits and penalties are necessary. Auditing may be particularly important when a new tax is introduced, but not infrequently it is neglected. For example, a sales tax may be introduced without an adequate staff and procedures for audit of taxpayers' records. Initially enterprises may comply fairly well if the tax provisions have been well publicized, but they will soon learn that returns are not checked and compliance will deteriorate. It may be more costly to reestablish the habit of compliance than it would have been to inculcate and maintain it from the outset.

Policies that rely on the application of general rules or responses to economic incentives are likely to be more effective and efficient than policies that require the exercise of discretion by ministers or senior officials. An example discussed in chapter 10 is a policy for the encouragement of investment and employment. Provision for the discretionary award of tax incentives by the minister of finance or an interdepartmental committee may be made because the procedure is thought to be essential for selectivity or because too little advance thought has been given to the

---

5. Cedric T. Sandford, *Hidden Costs of Taxation* (London: Institute for Fiscal Studies, 1973); and Sandford and others, *Costs and Benefits of VAT* (London: Heinemann, 1981).

feasibility of devising provisions that can be applied routinely. The discretionary systems may prove to be slow and subject to corruption or, at the other extreme, indiscriminately generous.

When innovations are planned it is prudent to avoid overly ingenious measures or ones that may be stylish in industrial countries where real cost constraints differ from those faced by developing countries. Examples of such policies that have proved ineffective or inefficient in some less developed countries include program budget systems, premature and incompletely planned computerization of government accounts, personal expenditure taxes, capital gains taxes, and graduated property taxes.

Organization, Management, and Procedures

Perceptive students of public administration have given up the idea that there is "a body of principles and skills of administration, detached from the surrounding tissue of culture, [which] can be effectively applied without regard to spatial or temporal elements."[6] Japan's success with a management style different from Western doctrine has forced the recognition that more than one set of principles can work effectively and efficiently. Research on comparative public administration has called attention in developing countries to the lingering influence of the former colonial systems as conditioned by the indigenous culture. Technical assistance and ideas acquired by nationals in the course of study abroad also have marginal effects. Although techniques and procedures such as budget controls and specialized training methods are readily transferable, they must operate in an administrative culture that should be taken into account in evaluating organization, management, and personnel policies.[7]

A condition that visiting experts often notice in less developed countries is that a few capable senior government officials are severely overworked while their subordinates appear to be underemployed, idle much of the

6. Ralph Braibanti, "Transnational Inducement of Administrative Reform: A Survey of Scope and Critique of Issues," in John D. Montgomery and William J. Siffin, eds., *Approaches to Development: Politics, Administration and Change* (McGraw-Hill, 1966), p. 164.

7. Gabino A. Mendoza, "The Transferability of Western Management Concepts and Programs: An Asian Perspective," in Lawrence D. Stifel, James S. Coleman, and Joseph E. Black, eds., *Education and Training for Public Sector Management in Developing Countries* (New York: Rockefeller Foundation, 1977), pp. 61–62; in the same volume, Jon R. Moris, "The Transferability of Western Management Concepts and Programs, an East African Perspective," pp. 73–83; William J. Siffin, "Two Decades of Public Administration in Developing Countries," *Public Administration Review*, vol. 36 (January–February 1976), pp. 61–71; and Moses N. Kiggundu, Jan J. Jorgensen, and Taieb Hafsi, "Administrative Theory and Practice in Developing Countries: A Synthesis," *Administrative Science Quarterly*, vol. 28 (March 1983), pp. 66–84.

time, or absent from their duty stations. To the foreign experts it seems obvious that many responsibilities should be delegated to lower levels and much work decentralized, leaving the senior persons with more time for planning, policy review, and control.

The judgment usually is valid; more delegation and less centralization would improve administration in most cases. But the speed with which such changes can be introduced and the distance to which they can be carried in the near future are less than often supposed. The conditions in existence in many countries are characteristic of what has been called the "hub-and-wheel" pattern of managerial control.[8] This places at the hub an official who assumes the functions of coordination and control and passes out simple tasks along the spokes to subordinates who have little understanding or information about the unit's functions and who may be poorly trained. This pattern was adopted during the colonial period and was highly functional for retaining control in the hands of officers from the metropolitan country and employing local staff for routine work. It still has the capacity to operate in difficult circumstances. The disadvantages are inefficient employment of the talents available in all except possibly the least developed countries, weakness in innovation, and the disruption that often occurs when the occupant of the hub position changes.

Delegation, decentralization, and communication between and within organizational levels are most practical when the social and educational levels of the participants are similar and participants share common attitudes and values. These conditions are more the product of social modernization than of administrative reform. Nevertheless, the recruitment of well-educated young persons has created opportunities for senior officials to delegate more work in most developing countries. There is now scope in many countries for well-considered moves toward decentralization of financial administration. It would be desirable in a number of countries, for example, to establish more regional revenue offices and to assign to them day-to-day assessment and collection functions while allocating to the head office planning, budgeting, research, statistics, internal audit, recruitment, training, legal and administrative advice, taxpayer appeals, and field audit.[9]

8. Moris, "The Transferability of Western Management Concepts and Programs," pp. 81–82.

9. Carlos A. Aguirre, Peter S. Griffith, and Zühtü Yücelik, "Tax Policy and Administration in Sub-Saharan Africa," in International Monetary Fund, *Taxation in Sub-Saharan Africa*, Occasional Paper 8 (Washington, D.C.: IMF, 1981), pp. 38–39.

The adequacy of staffing differs greatly among countries and among positions within countries. Overstaffing has occurred in countries in which governments have attempted to make up for a scarcity of employment opportunities in the enterprise sector by creating government jobs. In several countries, the practice is to hire virtually all university graduates who do not obtain other positions. The contribution of many new recruits may be negative because their idleness and lack of promotion prospects create discontent that damages the morale of all. In the long run, the absorption of continually growing numbers of staff will be untenable, but until economic growth creates more jobs outside government or the number of graduates declines, governments are likely to hesitate to eliminate overstaffing. Shortages of specialized personnel can coexist with overstaffing in the aggregate. They are especially noticeable in the least developed countries but occur also in other countries where an expanding enterprise sector creates employment opportunities. In the latter countries, persons who acquire skills in subjects such as accounting and computer operations through training and experience in government departments find better jobs in public or private enterprises. A large fraction of technical positions in the revenue department, procurement service, and accounting office may be vacant at any one time.

The problem of excessive turnover in technical positions is, of course, related to the attractiveness of compensation. Although compensation for professional and technical positions in government service is much higher in relation to average income in most of the developing countries than in the developed countries, on average it is inferior to compensation in the modern enterprise sector. Government pay may also compare poorly with earning opportunities in foreign countries for trained persons with a good command of Arabic, English, or French. Poverty and populist sentiments deter governments from offering competitive rates of compensation; in countries where overstaffing is practiced, low compensation may be necessary to keep down total expenditures. Efficiency would be improved in many cases if staffs were smaller, better trained, and better paid, but usually it would be difficult to bring about those conditions in the short run. Public finance experts sometimes propose that tax officials, procurement officers, and government auditors be paid more than persons of comparable rank in other civil service positions. Probably that would be unacceptable in most countries; however, it may be expedient to be more liberal in classifying positions for which it is especially difficult to retain a sufficient number of qualified staff.

Systematic training is needed to develop and maintain the skills required for efficient performance in financial administration. Some countries have schools attached to the ministry of finance for training in taxation, customs duties, accounting, and management. Other countries could benefit by establishing training institutions. Supplementing their national programs, former colonies of France and the United Kingdom have access to training institutions in those countries. In addition to preentry and refresher courses in the training institutions, on-the-job training is needed to impart specific knowledge and skills and to help staff members keep abreast of changes in laws and procedures.

A general issue with respect to training can be appreciated in light of the theory of human capital. Human capital incorporates the present value of the increased productive capacity resulting from general education, technical training, and work experience. Its acquisition, like the accumulation of physical capital, entails an immediate cost, for which the investor expects to be compensated by future returns. However, human capital belongs to the individual worker, regardless of who originally paid for it, and is taken with him when he changes jobs, whereas physical capital ordinarily belongs to the organization that purchased it.

Because of the uncertainty as to whether trained staff will remain with the department, ministry of finance officials might rationally incline toward investing in office equipment and computer facilities in preference to staff training to impart easily transferable skills such as stenography, bookkeeping, and computer programming. In practice, both kinds of investment often are neglected because of the short time horizons of ministers and pressures to use available money to hire more staff.

A distinction can justifiably be drawn between general training to impart transferable skills and specialized training in the form of instruction in departmental procedures. Staff members engaged in general training might be paid at reduced rates, or such training could be scheduled after regular working hours or subsidized by the ministry of education. Admittedly, it is not always easy to distinguish between transferable general training and nontransferable specialized training. Tax officers, for example, may gain earning opportunities in the enterprise sector because of familiarity with the revenue department's audit procedures and personnel.

Procedural manuals containing guidelines and detailed instructions for the performance of routine functions are virtually essential for good financial administration. Finance ministries that do not have such manuals may be able to speed up their preparation by reviewing manuals used in other countries with similar systems or by obtaining the assistance of consultants. This approach may be followed also when manuals have to be revised or expanded to take account of changes in applicable laws.

Codes and Regulations

The absence of up-to-date codes of tax, customs, and financial management laws handicaps administration in many countries. The proliferation of legislation and decrees, including provisions that are inconsistent or obscure, creates uncertainty and can result in delays or the disregard of enactments. Good practice calls for putting general provisions in basic codes and detailed procedural matters in regulations. Codification inevitably raises many policy issues that should not be left to legal draftsmen alone; it can best be undertaken in connection with a general review of the subject covering policy and administration. Regulations can be drafted simultaneously but of course can be issued in final form only after the basic law has been worked out. A country can advantageously borrow provisions from other countries, but it should exercise great care to ensure that they are consistent with its own policies and legal system. Codes and regulations once prepared should be reproduced in adequate numbers, distributed to officials, and made available for sale to the public. Subsequent amendments should be promptly circulated in the form of supplements, and complete new editions should be issued whenever supplements become numerous or lengthy.

Corruption

Corruption hinders the execution of government policies in many countries. As here interpreted, it is the misuse of public office by performing or refraining from performing official acts in exchange for some reward other than an established fee. A definition from the Indian Penal Code, which calls attention to many ramifications of corrupt practices, provides that a person is guilty of corruption who

> being or expecting to be a public servant, accepts, or obtains, or agrees to accept, or attempts to obtain from any person, for himself or for any other person, any

gratification whatsoever, other than legal remuneration, as a motive or reward for doing or forbearing to do any official act or for showing or forbearing to show, in the exercise of his official functions, favour or disfavour to any person or for rendering or attempting to render any service or disservice to any person.[10]

Corruption is not confined to any class of country or region. It has been reported in industrial countries, notably in the United States and Japan, as well as in developing countries ranging from most to least advanced, from large to small, from those with relatively high incomes to the poorest. It is widely believed, however, that corruption is more prevalent in the majority of developing countries than in the industrial countries and that it is a more serious problem in the former.

Although corruption is frequently reported in the press of industrial countries and of some developing countries, it has received inadequate attention in technical literature. The neglect is due, as Myrdal remarks, partly to excessive diplomacy on the part of scholars and advisers from developed countries and partly to the application of models that abstract from illegal and irrational behavior.[11]

Apologists from developing countries sometimes attribute corruption to the immoral practices of foreign businessmen or ethnic minorities. Although it is undoubtedly true that there are at least two parties to every corrupt transaction, the misbehavior of foreign or local businessmen does not excuse government officials or make the problem less serious. Some scholars, taking a cynical view, have termed bribery a useful lubricant for cumbersome administrative machines.[12] For an individual wishing to expedite the clearance of goods through customs, the issuance of a visa, or some other official act, a bribe may indeed be an expedient means of oiling the administrative machinery; for the community, however, corruption aggravates, rather than alleviates, cumbersome administration.

Corruption increases the cost of government contracts for major construction projects, equipment, and routine procurement of supplies. It holds down revenue collections and requires higher tax rates on those who comply with the law. It causes delays in two ways: by provoking the

---

10. Quoted by B. Venkatappiah, "Office, Misuse of," in *International Encyclopedia of the Social Sciences*, vol. 11, David L. Sills, ed. (Macmillan and Free Press, 1968), p. 272.

11. *Asian Drama*, pp. 938–39.

12. This and other possible beneficial and harmful effects of administrative corruption are expounded by David H. Bayley, "The Effects of Corruption in a Developing Nation," *Western Political Quarterly*, vol. 19 (December 1966), pp. 719–32; and J. S. Nye, "Corruption and Political Development: A Cost-Benefit Analysis," *American Political Science Review*, vol. 61 (June 1967), pp. 417–27. See also Gerald E. Caiden and Naomi J. Caiden, "Administrative Corruption," *Public Administration Review*, vol. 37 (May–June 1977), pp. 301–09.

establishment of elaborate safeguards, including the proliferation of paperwork, and by encouraging procrastination by officers who hope to exact "speed money." The existence of corruption increases the hesitancy to delegate on the part of ministers and senior officials, who try either to check misconduct or to share in the illicit income. It may stimulate disaffection and contribute to political instability. The leaders of successful coups frequently adduce the corruption of their predecessors as a justification, but such statements have to be regarded skeptically.

Strict standards of official conduct, such as those implied by the Indian statute quoted above, are of fairly recent origin. In the past in Europe as well as in Asia, Africa, and the Americas, many payments that would now be defined as bribes to officials and politicians were customary and incurred no disapprobation. The ideal of an incorruptible civil service and judiciary, free of improper interference, seems to have become established in Western Europe in the period of limited government activities between the abandonment of mercantilism and the advent of the welfare state.[13] It is much harder to establish and maintain such standards of conduct today in developing countries where governments intervene extensively in economic affairs and where social and political integration is incomplete.

Corruption can occur because certain persons have the power to perform or not perform acts that result in economic benefits or harm to individuals or enterprises. It has been characterized as "the secret and usually illegal abuse of conferred monopoly status."[14] Some bribes are exacted for services to which the applicant is legally entitled. These differ from other payments for services, not only in their illegality but in their secrecy and the absence of alternative sources of supply. An import license or a tax clearance can be obtained only from a designated government official, who has a degree of monopoly power that is small or great depending on the ease and cost of appealing his inaction or adverse decision to higher authority. Other bribes are paid to induce an official to collude in illegal behavior such as tax evasion. The opportunity for an official to obtain bribes depends on the probability of independent review and revision of his action or inaction.

Corruption is fostered by administrative laxity and by the existence of complex tax and procurement systems and fiscal provisions that grant

13. Myrdal, *Asian Drama*, pp. 957–58. A more involved account of the virtual disappearance of the extensive corruption that formerly existed in Great Britain and the establishment of the modern civil service in that country is given by Ronald Wraith and Edgar Simpkins, *Corruption in Developing Countries* (London: Allen and Unwin, 1963).

14. Michael Beenstock, "Corruption and Development," *World Development*, vol. 7 (January 1979), p. 16.

discretionary power to ministers and officials subject to vague and general standards. Rates of pay that are too low to enable officials to maintain the standard of living that is generally considered proper for their social status are a contributory factor. An incidental cost often imposed by inflation is erosion of the real compensation of officials to a degree that causes them to succumb to the temptation to demand illegal supplements. The belief that corruption is widely practiced, especially by the rich and powerful, even when exaggerated, is conducive to misconduct by civil servants and others.

The remedies for corruption most commonly urged are the elevation of moral standards and the punishment of wrongdoers. However desirable the former may be, it is an end rather than a means available to governments. Punishment certainly has a place in a campaign against corruption, as a deterrent and as a means of satisfying a social demand for retribution. It most often takes the form of monetary penalties. Theoretical analyses of penalties have not advanced much beyond the rather trite conclusions that the probability and immediacy of application of a penalty as well as its nominal amount should be considered and that the size of the penalty should vary with the amount of the gain realizable by the illegal conduct. Experts from more developed countries, particularly Americans, have strongly advocated imprisonment for tax fraud and extreme cases of official corruption. Most developing countries have ignored or rejected such advice, possibly because of fears that the imprisonment penalty would be abused.

The best anticorruption program would emphasize preventive measures. It would provide for simplified accounting, the elimination of nonfunctional procurement specifications and procedures, and internal auditing, all designed to forestall abuses. It would include the simplification of tax laws, reduced reliance on discretionary awards of tax incentives and tariff protection, greater dependence on market incentives and less use of direct controls and allocations in both government and public enterprises, and improved salaries for civil servants.

Although the whole program is unlikely to be introduced at one time, progress can be made by adopting elements of it from time to time. The individual measures have advantages in addition to their effect on corruption and may be supported for a variety of reasons. Open campaigns against corruption are most likely to be launched when changes in political leadership occur. In many countries, the importance of action is appreciated by growing numbers of influential persons.

Technical Assistance

Governments of developing countries may be able to increase the effectiveness and efficiency of policies by drawing on foreign experts to assist in their formulation and execution. The assistance may take the form of advice or operational services.

A government may obtain the services of foreign experts by contracting with individuals or with economic or management consulting firms, legal firms, or accounting firms. Or it may apply to an international organization or a friendly foreign government. For technical assistance in public finance, the most active international organizations in recent years have been the International Monetary Fund, the Organization of American States, and the United Nations. Technical assistance on public finance matters has been provided occasionally by the Inter-American Development Bank, the Asian Development Bank, and the Colombo Plan. World Bank economic reports include sections containing analysis and recommendations on government finance; the World Bank ordinarily does not give technical assistance on the specifics of taxation and financial administration, but some of its loans provide funds to hire consultants on these subjects. Government finance experts have been supplied by the bilateral aid programs of France, the United States, the United Kingdom, the Federal Republic of Germany, Canada, the Netherlands, and some other countries.

Governments may seek assistance to resolve a specific technical problem or to overcome general fiscal difficulties manifesting themselves in excessive budget deficits or lack of finance for desired projects. They may believe that receiving technical assistance will improve their prospects for obtaining loans or grants. The identification of subjects on which assistance is most likely to be productive, the choice of source and form of assistance, and the establishment of priorities merit more careful consideration than usually is given to them. An idealized version of the process, as set out by a writer with extensive experience in advising developing countries, prescribes that "the needs and uses of technical assistance, including continuity and training, should be as carefully planned and programmed as should be capital projects."[15] Such an approach is likely to be impractical, however, because of uncertainties about needs and the availability of

15. Louis J. Walinsky, *The Planning and Execution of Economic Development: A Nontechnical Guide for Policy Makers and Administrators* (McGraw-Hill, 1963), p. 167.

assistance and about the rate of progress that can be expected in dealing with problems. Both recipient governments and providers of technical assistance should be aware that the diagnosis of difficulties often requires study to distinguish transitory or surface manifestations from underlying problems.

Some governments have arranged for professors at foreign universities or other scholars to organize missions to study their tax and budget systems and recommend reforms. Governments have contracted with private firms for specific technical services of an operational nature such as accounting, the installation of computer systems, and the auditing of tax returns of multinational enterprises or other companies with complex structures and operations. Direct contracting can be used to obtain legal advice on enterprise agreements, draft statutes, and proposed tax treaties. This procedure may appeal because it avoids any actual or apparent interference by an international organization or foreign government. It is expensive, but the return can be large relative to cost. Care in the choice of the firm is necessary, and a government may need an expert consultant to help it select experts well qualified to render the desired service.

For advice on broad questions of tax policy and budget formulation, governments generally have preferred to seek advice from individuals or international organizations rather than from other governments. Bilateral assistance on administration is less sensitive.

Assistance in the form of the secondment, or temporary assignment, of officers to administrative posts in the host government has been a prominent feature of the French bilateral program. The United Nations has provided some operational experts in financial administration. The assignment of operational experts may produce more immediate results than can be obtained by supplying advisers and may also relieve national officials of responsibility for unpopular functions such as expenditure control and tax auditing. In my opinion, however, advisory assistance is more appropriate in the public finance field because it is important that national officials assume responsibility for matters that are so closely involved with national sovereignty, and be seen to do so, and because it is desirable that they begin without delay to acquire experience in discharging the functions. An adviser, of course, may need to be involved in the details of the work and may properly exercise initiative in making suggestions. Unlike an operational expert, an adviser can be effective only by persuading another person to act.

An organization that provides technical assistance either free or at rates of charge below costs, as international organizations and government bilateral programs do, usually will have to ration its services by choosing among requests. The selection inevitably will be influenced by a variety of factors, including the interests of managers of the organization, as well as by an appraisal of the probability that helpful advice can be offered and will be carried out by the requesting government. Often a government's record in using past assistance will be known, and some requests will seem more serious than others. To conserve scarce resources, it will be reasonable to withhold approval of requests in cases where the probability of success appears remote and also in cases where the need is judged not to be urgent because the subject is unimportant or the requesting government has the capacity to deal with the problem without assistance. Field surveys to identify needs and assess the cooperativeness of the requesting government are advisable in many cases.

Advice can be provided either by short-term missions that prepare reports of findings and recommendations or by long-term field assignments. Generally, short-term missions are most suitable for advising on broad policy issues or answering narrow technical questions, whereas long-term assignments or repeated short visits by an expert or a team are more effective for assisting in the implementation of policy advice and in training.

A stylized outline of the stages of technical assistance by an international agency begins with an informal request or inquiry and may include a visit to ascertain needs; agreement with the authorities of the requesting country on the subject or subjects on which advice should be given, followed by confirmation or formalization of the request; a study mission that submits a written report; follow-up discussions of the report after a few weeks or months; provisional decisions by the requesting government on which recommendations it will accept or reject; a request from the recipient government for further assistance in implementing the recommendations that have been accepted; agreement to the further request by the organization giving the assistance and the preparation in consultation with the recipient of terms of reference and a tentative work program for long-term advisers; assignment of the advisers; support of the advisers from the headquarters of the technical assistance organization, together with occasional visits to the field by headquarters staff; periodic reports on progress and their evaluation by the technical assistance organization and the recipient government, resulting in continuation of the assistance, ordinarily with revised terms of reference, or its termination on the grounds that the work either has been completed or is judged unlikely to be productive.[16]

Success in giving technical assistance requires an unusual combination of knowledge, skills, and personal traits. Technical knowledge and skills are essential but need to be accompanied by tact, patience, persistence, persuasiveness, and adaptability to an unfamiliar environment. Prior experience in other developing countries, particularly those with similar institutions, is helpful but not indispensable.

Many technical assistance reports are ignored by the governments that receive them; less frequently they are rejected after being fully considered. The reasons are varied. There may have been no serious interest in advice, conditions may have changed, or the minister who requested the report may have left office. The request may have been misinterpreted. The recommendations may appear too radical or too concerned with nonessential refinements. The presentation may be too detailed or obscure and may seem to be addressed to other experts or to the world at large rather than to the official readers who must be convinced if the report is to influence action. Currie, an economist with long experience as an adviser in the United States and Colombia, writes of "the occupational hazard of advisers that makes one unable to resist suggesting sweeping reforms" and leaving behind a comprehensive report as a "monument." He adds:

> No academician, and I would not exclude myself, is free from this hazard, especially if he leads a mission or is responsible for a report. The good strategy of accomplishing a smaller but very worthwhile reform is lost sight of in the desire to indicate what a really thorough-going reform would look like, regardless of whether it is feasible or requested. If one thinks a broad change is desirable, it is not difficult to persuade oneself that it is also feasible.[17]

The style of a report is likely to be influenced by the prospect of publication or its absence. A published report needs to include background material, explanations, and arguments that may be redundant in a document for limited official use. But the decision to publish or not to do so has other, more significant aspects. The practice of the International Monetary Fund has been to refrain from publishing its technical assistance reports or disseminating the substance of their findings and recommendations. (A few of the reports have been published by recipient governments, and in

---

16. See the description of procedures in International Monetary Fund, *Technical Assistance Services of the International Monetary Fund*, Pamphlet Series 30 (Washington, D.C.: IMF, 1979), pp. 11–19.

17. Lauchlin Currie, *The Role of Economic Advisers in Developing Countries*, Contributions in Economics and Economic History 44 (Greenwood, 1981), p. 114.

some other cases ministers have publicly given intimations of their contents.) The IMF's practice, influenced by the importance that it attaches to the confidentiality of its relations with member countries, also reflects a belief that governments will be more willing to request advice and to consider it on its merits if publicity is avoided. The absence of publication, however, entails forgoing any opportunity of informing and influencing opinion outside official circles and also forgoing the benefit of outside criticism by professional peers.

To make good use of technical assistance, a recipient government should take account of many of the points mentioned in the discussion of the concerns of assistance givers. Especially valuable are clear, agreed terms of reference, explicit though flexible work programs, and periodic reviews of progress.

The appointment of national counterparts for foreign advisers, whether short term or long term, is essential. Ideally, the counterpart should be senior enough to facilitate access to information and to arrange meetings with officials and ministers, should be acquainted with the subject matter, and should not be so immersed in other duties that he has no time for the visitors. On important policy issues, ministers and senior officials should take time for informal conferences with visiting missions. They should expect to be ready to outline their general objectives, to authorize the collection of relevant information, and to react to tentative ideas. They cannot reasonably be expected to have systematically thought out all their specific objectives and priorities, which should be subject to elaboration and revision in light of the advice received. It is prudent to prepare staff for the arrival of outside advisers by explaining their functions in a way that will minimize the danger that they will be seen as rivals.

Governments should insist that all long-term technical assistance have a significant training component. An objective should be for national staff to learn how to do the work of the foreign expert and to supersede him. Often the counterpart, if well chosen, can succeed a visiting expert. There is a tendency for both providers and recipients of technical assistance to neglect or underemphasize the training component and to prolong assignments unduly. This has a cost in wasted resources and failure to build up the national expertise and self-reliance that are elements of development.

Governments, of course, may seek technical assistance from more than one source. Especially on major policy questions, a second opinion may be valuable. But too much shopping for assistance can result in unproductive duplication, conflicting advice, and delay of action. Even when provided without charge, technical assistance has a cost in the time and attention devoted to it by ministers and officials and in the provision of facilities for the foreign experts.

Concluding Remarks

The successful execution of fiscal policies depends not only on the quality of public administration but also on the formulation of policies that are realistically adapted to the available resources. Administrative resources, however, are not rigidly fixed; they can be increased by staff training and supplemented to a limited extent by technical assistance. Administrative capacity can be strengthened in ways mentioned in this chapter and more fully treated elsewhere. Usually, improvements can best be attained by a cumulative series of changes, many of them small in themselves. Some setbacks must be expected.

Administrative officers can benefit from contacts with those engaged in similar duties in other countries. They can learn from the experience of the others and can gain a better perspective on their own problems. In the tax field, the Inter-American Center of Tax Administrators (usually known by its Spanish acronym CIAT) has organized many useful seminars and congresses for tax and customs officers of Western Hemisphere countries. The possibility of creating similar organizations in Africa and Asia has been discussed. Less active but also useful is the International Organization of Supreme Audit Institutions (known as INTOSAI). Government agencies of the Federal Republic of Germany and France have sponsored seminars and workshops for fiscal officers, as have the United Nations and the International Monetary Fund.

More effective and efficient fiscal policies are possible. Ordinarily, they can be better achieved by making incremental improvements than by attempting comprehensive reforms. Because of the complexity of fiscal problems, competition between objectives, and conflicting interests, ideal solutions may be difficult to state and often are impossible to effect. But on a great many subjects the desirable direction of change is fairly clear. Opportunities for improvements may arise when a new minister or new government takes office, perhaps having ideas about changes or at least being receptive to proposals. Policy decisions often have to be taken to meet a specific problem or to respond to an emergency. Too frequently, opportunities are missed on these occasions because of lack of preparation, and the ad hoc actions taken are inadequately considered. Muddle rather than incremental progress results unless decisions are clearly specified and are guided by concern with broad national objectives and awareness of the costs and constraints likely to be met in acting on them.

Much depends on the quality of leadership and on external events and chance. But superior leadership and good luck cannot be ensured. The best course is to seek practical means of overcoming or compensating for some of the handicaps to policymaking and administration present in many developing countries. Prominent among these are the weakness or absence of nongovernmental organizations that can articulate and aggregate various interests. There are also few if any independent research organizations concerned with public affairs, and university studies usually are not oriented toward immediate issues in government finance. These conditions deprive the government of information and analysis that could assist the evaluation of objections and obstacles to policies under consideration and the appropriate specification of decisions. The handicaps will diminish in the course of development. In the medium term, it may be possible to hasten the process by moderate expenditures for higher education and statistical programs.

Some early benefits may be obtainable by the creation of one or more small advisory groups, located in the ministry of finance or budget office or possibly in the office of the prime minister or president, with the function of studying selected problems of government finance and preparing recommendations for the consideration of policymakers at opportune times. Only a few persons—in many countries no more than three or four— would be required to start the work. Those assigned to the unit should have a good education and some experience in government service. The assignment should be regarded as temporary, lasting no longer than a few years.

Index